D1211605

 **booksonline**

Read this book online today:

With SAP PRESS BooksOnline we offer you online access to knowledge from the leading SAP experts. Whether you use it as a beneficial supplement or as an alternative to the printed book, with SAP PRESS BooksOnline you can:

- Access your book anywhere, at any time. All you need is an Internet connection.
- Perform full text searches on your book and on the entire SAP PRESS library.
- Build your own personalized SAP library.

The SAP PRESS customer advantage:

Register this book today at *www.sap-press.com* and obtain exclusive free trial access to its online version. If you like it (and we think you will), you can choose to purchase permanent, unrestricted access to the online edition at a very special price!

Here's how to get started:

1. Visit *www.sap-press.com*.
2. Click on the link for SAP PRESS BooksOnline and login (or create an account).
3. Enter your free trial license key, shown below in the corner of the page.
4. Try out your online book with full, unrestricted access for a limited time!

Your personal free trial **license key** for this online book is:

cg7n-yesq-6ikv-b9z4

Materials Management with SAP® ERP:
Functionality and Technical Configuration

 PRESS

SAP PRESS is a joint initiative of SAP and Galileo Press. The know-how offered by SAP specialists combined with the expertise of the Galileo Press publishing house offers the reader expert books in the field. SAP PRESS features first-hand information and expert advice, and provides useful skills for professional decision-making.

SAP PRESS offers a variety of books on technical and business related topics for the SAP user. For further information, please visit our website: *www.sap-press.com*.

Akash Agrawal
Customizing Materials Management Processes in SAP ERP Operations
2010, 395 pp.
978-1-59229-280-6

Faisal Mahboob
Integration of Materials Management with Financial Accounting in SAP
2010, 429 pp.
978-1-59229-377-7

Martin Murray
SAP Warehouse Management: Functionality and Technical Configuration
2007, 504 pp.
978-1-59229-133-5

Ashish Mohapatra
Optimizing Sales and Distribution in SAP ERP
2010, 517 pp.
978-1-59229-329-2

Martin Murray

Materials Management with SAP® ERP: Functionality and Technical Configuration

Galileo Press

Bonn • Boston

Galileo Press is named after the Italian physicist, mathematician and philosopher Galileo Galilei (1564–1642). He is known as one of the founders of modern science and an advocate of our contemporary, heliocentric worldview. His words *Eppur si muove* (And yet it moves) have become legendary. The Galileo Press logo depicts Jupiter orbited by the four Galilean moons, which were discovered by Galileo in 1610.

Editor Meg Dunkerley
Copyeditor Julie McNamee
Cover Design Graham Geary
Photo Credit Getty Images/Andrew Onyemere
Layout Design Vera Brauner
Production Manager Kelly O'Callaghan
Production Editor Graham Geary
Typesetting Publishers' Design and Production Services, Inc.
Printed and bound in Canada

ISBN 978-1-59229-358-2

© 2011 by Galileo Press Inc., Boston (MA)

3rd Edition, updated and revised, 2011

Library of Congress Cataloging-in-Publication Data
Murray, Martin, 1964–
   Materials management with SAP ERP : functionality and technical configuration / Martin Murray. — 3rd ed.
      p. cm.
   Includes bibliographical references.
   ISBN-13: 978-1-59229-358-2
   ISBN-10: 1-59229-358-1
   1. Inventory control—Computer programs. 2. Business logistics—Computer programs. 3. Material accountability—Computer programs. 4. SAP ERP. I. Title.
   TS161.M85 2011
   658.7'850285—dc22
   2010039263

Contents at a Glance

Dear Reader,

If you are using or need to get up to speed on Materials Management in SAP ERP, this is your must-have resource. In this third edition of our best-selling book, Martin Murray will help you navigate these vast, sometimes overwhelming waters by offering a practical and straightforward guide to the ins and outs of Materials Management. This book focuses on everything from goods receipt and invoice verification to balance sheet valuation and the material ledger.

I welcomed the opportunity to work with Martin Murray again — it is always a pleasure to witness such dedication and expertise in SAP. I'm confident that you will find Martin's most recent book with SAP PRESS up to the same standard as his previous books: *SAP Warehouse Management Functionality and Configuration, Discover Logistics with SAP ERP, Maximize Your Warehouse Operations with SAP ERP*, and *Understanding the Logistics Information System*.

We appreciate your business, and welcome your feedback. Your comments and suggestions are the most useful tools to help us improve our books for you, the reader. We encourage you to visit our website at *www.sap-press.com* and share your feedback about this work.

Thank you for purchasing a book from SAP PRESS!

Meg Dunkerley
Editor, SAP PRESS

Galileo Press
100 Grossman Drive, Suite 205
Braintree, MA 02184

Meg.Dunkerley@galileo-press.com
www.sap-press.com

Contents

3 Master Data in Materials Management ... 65

6 Vendor Master Data 189

7 Purchasing Information Data 221

8   Batch Management Data 237

9   Material Master Record 261

11   Purchasing Overview 301

14 Quotation 361

15 Purchase Order 371

20   Inventory Management Overview 463

21 Goods Issue 489

22 Goods Receipt 505

23 Physical Inventory 521

26 Material Ledger 577

27 Classification System 589

Preface

Welcome to the third edition of *Materials Management with SAP ERP: Functionality and Technical Configuration*. The first edition was published in 2006 and was based on the SAP R/3 Release 4.7. The second edition was published in 2008 and incorporated the new functionality of ECC 6.0. Both editions of the book were favorably received and have led to this updated third edition.

This book is a comprehensive review of the Materials Management functionality in the latest version of SAP, which at the time of this writing is SAP ERP Central Component 6.0 (SAP ECC 6.0). Throughout this book, we'll refer to it simply as MM. In addition, we discuss the MM functionality that exists outside of SAP ERP and can be found in the SAP Supply Chain Management business suite, which currently is release SAP SCM 7.0.

Who Is This Book For?

The subject matter in this book is not just of interest to those who work directly with MM but also for those who work in related SAP areas, such as Warehouse Management (WM), Production Planning (PP), and Sales and Distribution (SD). The subject matter should also be of interest to those in supply chain management and to purchasing managers who want to understand more of the functionality that they have implemented and the functionality that they may be considering, such as material ledger, Service Purchasing, and Handling Unit Management.

If you are involved in WM, this book will help you understand more of the functions that occur prior to the material arriving in the warehouse and how the WM functionality interacts with the functionality in MM.

On the other hand, if you are working with SD, you will benefit from a greater understanding of the material movements relating to a sales order and how material is issued for customer sales orders.

PP staff will benefit from additional familiarity with how material is received from production and the purchasing of material for production orders.

Other staff working with SAP ERP functionality such as Quality Management (QM) and Plant Maintenance (PM) will benefit from a greater understanding of the general topics within MM.

As you can see, this book on MM has wide applicability across the SAP ERP landscape. Before going deeper into the book, you will find it useful to see how the book is organized so you can either go directly to the chapter that has the information you seek or proceed in a more linear fashion.

How This Book Is Organized

The organization of this book is structured to serve best the purposes of the various individuals that work in the MM environment, whether they are SAP configuration experts or users who have been tasked to use MM as part of their everyday work experience and want to gain more understanding of the functionality they work with each day.

Each chapter focuses on a specific MM function, exploring the different facets of the function and providing examples relating to it. The book starts examining the MM functionality; from the very basic key elements through standard MM functions such as purchasing and inventory movements to more complex functions such as material ledger and classification. Let's now get an idea of what is included in each chapter:

- **Chapter 1:** This chapter provides a brief history of SAP and the core functionality of the SAP ERP system. The chapter discusses the role of the Materials Management (MM) functionality within the Logistics function and the supply chain.

- **Chapter 2:** This chapter describes the organizational structure of the MM functionality. This structure forms the basis of the building blocks in SAP ERP and is key to understanding the makeup of MM, including the client, company, plant, storage location, and warehouse. The chapter takes you though these key elements by showing you key configurations and examples.

- **Chapter 3:** In this chapter, you can examine the master data that is found in the MM functionality. The Material Master, Vendor Master, Batch Management, serial records, and the purchasing information records are described in detail. The chapter describes how this data is created and used by showing configuration steps and examples.

- **Chapters 4 and 5:** Continuing from where Chapter 3 left off, Chapters 4 and 5 carefully examine the structure and makeup of the Material Master file. The

Material Master is used throughout the system, and this chapter describes the elements that go into each Material Master record.

▶ **Chapter 6:** This chapter is similar in structure to Chapters 4 and 5 except that it examines the Vendor Master file and the three elements that go into creating a Vendor Master record.

▶ **Chapter 7:** Chapter 7 describes the elements and functionality of the purchasing information record and how it contains data specifically for a particular material and vendor.

▶ **Chapter 8:** This chapter examines the data related to Batch Management. This includes the batch record for a material and how that batch can be selected by using the batch determination functionality.

▶ **Chapter 9:** Here we describe the transaction functionality associated with creating, changing, and deleting a material. Other key information, such as how to load Material Master records, is included.

▶ **Chapter 10:** This chapter includes descriptions of the transaction functionality associated with creating, changing, and deleting a vendor. It also examines the function of blocking a vendor and the concept of a one-time vendor.

▶ **Chapter 11:** This chapter reviews the functionality included in purchasing. This includes an overview of the purchase requisition, request for quotation (RFQ), purchase order (PO), source list, and vendor evaluation. These topics are then examined in more detail in later chapters.

▶ **Chapter 12:** This chapter focuses on the purchase requisition. It examines the creation of the purchase requisition, either entered directly or created indirectly, and how the requisition is processed.

▶ **Chapter 13:** This chapter examines the request for quotation (RFQ) function. Not all companies use RFQs, but this chapter examines how they are created, released, and sent to selected vendors.

▶ **Chapter 14:** This chapter examines the other side of the RFQ, that is, the quotation received from the vendor. The chapter explains how to enter quotations, compare competing quotations, and reject losing bids.

▶ **Chapter 15:** With this chapter, we move into the area of the PO, including the various functions associated with the PO, such as account assignment, message output, and order type. The chapter also investigates the variations such as outline purchase agreements, scheduling agreements, and contracts. The functionality of purchase release strategy is also discussed.

▶ **Chapter 16:** This chapter discusses external service management (ESM). The procurement of services is as important to companies as the procurement of materials, and this chapter reviews the ESM functionality. The Service Master record, Standard Service Catalog (SSC), and service entry are all examined in this chapter.

▶ **Chapter 17:** This is where we review the functionality of consumption-based planning. The chapter reviews the master data required and the planning process involved. The planning evaluation, using the MRP (material requirements planning) list, is also discussed.

▶ **Chapter 18:** In this chapter, we discuss the three elements of material requirements planning (MRP). This will be more familiar to those with a production planning background. The chapter reviews reorder point planning, forecast-based planning, and time-phased planning.

▶ **Chapter 19:** Now we examine the forecasting functionality in MM. This subject is reviewed here to give you an overview of the forecast models, parameters, and options that can be used in forecasting within SAP ERP.

▶ **Chapter 20:** This chapter offers you an overview of the Inventory Management functionality. It briefly examines the goods issues, goods receipts, returns, physical inventory, reservations, and stock transfers. These items are then examined in greater detail in the following chapters.

▶ **Chapter 21:** This chapter identifies the various goods issues that can be carried out within Inventory Management. The chapter describes the issues most often seen in a plant, such as issue to production and issue to scrap. The goods issue process is also examined in this chapter.

▶ **Chapter 22:** This chapter reviews the function of the goods receipt. The most common goods receipts, which are the goods receipt from a production order and the goods receipt for a PO, are examined in detail.

▶ **Chapter 23:** This chapter examines the function of the physical inventory. This process is still a staple in most companies, and this chapter reviews how the physical inventory process can be completed in SAP ERP.

▶ **Chapter 24:** This chapter describes the SAP ERP process of Invoice Verification. The chapter describes the standard three-way match as well as other invoice options in SAP ERP such as the evaluated receipt settlement or the two-way match. The chapter also reviews the function of blocking and releasing invoices.

▶ **Chapter 25:** In this chapter, we review the SAP ERP functionality of Balance Sheet Valuation. This chapter examines the LIFO (last in first out) and FIFO (first in first out) functionality as well as that of lowest value determination.

▶ **Chapter 26:** This chapter focuses on the material ledger. This may not be something that most MM consultants have been involved in, so this chapter provides a general understanding of the functionality.

- **Chapter 27:** This chapter examines the classification system. Although not part of the MM functionality, it is important to understand how classification works because it is a powerful tool that is used not only in the Material Master but also in the PO release strategy and a number of other areas. This chapter describes the elements of classification, such as the class and the characteristics, and how these are used to classify materials and other objects.

- **Chapter 28:** In this chapter, we review a subject not necessarily core to MM: the Document Management System. Documents are often linked to the Material Master record, and it is useful to understand how these documents are linked via the document information record. This chapter shows how a document record is created and how it is linked to an object.

- **Chapter 29:** This final chapter reviews the contents of the chapters covered and the lessons learned. In addition, this chapter provides some advice regarding the future direction of SAP ERP and MM.

Conclusion

Reading this book will provide you with a comprehensive review of Materials Management in SAP ERP. The topics discussed will reinforce your current knowledge and help you develop your skills in unfamiliar areas. This book should become a key reference in your current and future MM experiences.

Let's now proceed to Chapter 1, where we will introduce you to SAP and SAP ERP.

Materials Management (MM) is a core functionality of SAP ERP. The functionality within MM is the engine that drives the supply chain. In this chapter, we will describe the elements that make MM such an important part of SAP ERP and the Logistics function.

1 Materials Management Overview

In this book, we will describe the importance of the Materials Management functionality in SAP ERP (which we'll refer to as MM throughout), as it relates to the overall functionality within the SAP software and as a part of the supply chain.

MM contains many aspects of SAP functionality, including purchasing, goods receiving, material storage, consumption-based planning, and inventory. It is highly integrated with other functionalities or components such as Finance (FI), Controlling (CO), Production Planning (PP), Sales and Distribution (SD), Quality Management (QM), Plant Maintenance (PM), and Warehouse Management (WM).

This chapter examines why MM is a core functionality of SAP and of any SAP ERP implementation. You'll learn why MM can be described as the engine that drives the supply-chain functionality within SAP ERP and how MM is integrated with the other SAP components or functionalities.

1.1 Materials Management as a Part of SAP ERP

This section provides a brief overview of the history of SAP, the core SAP ERP functionality, and where MM fits into the structure.

1.1.1 SAP History

SAP was founded in 1972 and is now a market and technology leader in client/server enterprise application software. It provides comprehensive solutions for companies of all sizes and all industry sectors.

SAP is the number-one vendor of standard business-application software and the third largest software supplier in the world. SAP delivers scalable solutions that enable its customers to further advance industry best practices. The company is constantly developing new products that allow its customers to respond to dynamic market conditions and help them maintain competitive advantage.

In 1979, SAP released its mainframe product called R/2. Materials Management (then called RM) was a core module of this release. R/2 was the successor to SAP's first software release, RM/1, which was a Materials Management software suite. SAP dominated the German market, and in the 1980s, SAP developed a broader market in the rest of Europe. In 1992, SAP developed the client/server application we all know now as R/3. This allowed SAP to bring the software to the U.S. market, and within a few years, SAP became the gold standard for ERP (enterprise resource planning) software.

When businesses chose SAP as their enterprise application software, they identified the integration of the modules as a key advantage. Many other software companies used a best-of-breed approach and developed highly complex interfaces to integrate the separate software packages. Supporting and maintaining just one system rather than several systems with different hardware platforms has yielded a significant cost saving for companies.

1.1.2 Core SAP ERP Functionality

SAP was originally developed as an enterprise application-software package that was attractive to very large manufacturing companies. As the number of companies adopting SAP began to grow, a number of smaller companies in many different industries came to believe that SAP was the product that could give them a competitive advantage.

Many of these companies required just the core SAP ERP functionality. That usually comprises Materials Management (MM), Financial Accounting (FI), Sales and Distribution (SD), and Production Planning (PP). Often companies would start their implementations with this core functionality and then on the second and third phases of their implementations, they would introduce functionalities such as Controlling (CO), Warehouse Management (WM), Human Resources (HR), and so on.

In Release 4.7 Enterprise of SAP R/3, the company introduced the concept of the Enterprise Core. This included all of the R/3 4.6 functionality and some limited functional enhancements and developments to the existing 4.6 functionality. SAP announced that going forward, all legal changes and support packs, including stabilization and performance enhancements, would be applied at the Enterprise Core level.

For Release 4.7 Enterprise, several core areas were included: Finance (FI, CO), HR, Product Lifecycle Management (PP, AM [Asset Management], QM), and Supply Chain Management (WM, PP, MM).

In June of 2004, SAP introduced the successor to 4.7 Enterprise called mySAP ERP 2004, also known as the Enterprise Central Component or ECC 5.0, which is the next level of SAP R/3 evolution. This new software suite included four core functional areas: mySAP ERP Financials (FI, CO); mySAP ERP Human Capital Management (HCM); mySAP ERP Corporate Services, which includes QM and Environmental Health and Safety (EH&S); and mySAP ERP Operations (PP, WM, MM).

The latest release of core SAP, rolled out at the end of 2005, is SAP ERP 2005 or ECC 6.0. With this release, SAP announced its plan for future releases dubbed "innovation without disruption," whereby the upgrade cycles are minimized, but a number of enhancement packages will be released over the lifecycle of the product. SAP has indicated that mainstream maintenance for ECC 6.0 (SAP ERP) will continue until March 2015, and extended maintenance will expire in March 2017. The examples and screenshots in this edition are all from the ECC 6.0 release, unless otherwise stated.

As SAP develops more extensive solutions and tools for its customers, MM continues to be an important part of the foundation on which subsequent functionality is built.

1.1.3 Business Suite Functionality

In addition to the core ECC 6.0 MM, consultants should also be aware of functionality in the SAP Supply Chain Management (SAP SCM) business suite that can be implemented alongside SAP ERP. Functionality found in SAP SCM, for example, SAP Extended Warehouse Management (SAP EWM), may be implemented by your client, which will require you to understand the interaction between the functions. The current release SAP SCM 7.0, which was made available at the end of 2009.

SAP SCM 7.0 includes SAP Advanced Planning & Optimization (SAP APO), SAP Extended Warehouse Management (SAP EWM), SAP Supply Network Collaboration (SAP SNC), SAP Auto-ID Infrastructure, and SAP Transportation Management (SAP TM).

Now that we have reviewed the history of MM as part of SAP, the next section examines how MM functions as part of the Logistics function.

1.2 Materials Management as Part of Logistics

The SAP Logistics function incorporates a number of distinct areas that together follow the movement of materials from manufacturer to consumer. This section reviews the function of the MM functionality as part of logistics.

1.2.1 Definition of Logistics and Supply Chain

Logistics is the management of business operations, including the acquisition, storage, transportation, and delivery of goods along the supply chain. The supply chain is a network of retailers, distributors, transporters, storage facilities, and suppliers that participate in the sale, delivery, and production of a particular product.

1.2.2 Management of the Supply Chain

From these definitions, it is clear that MM is an integral part of the Logistics function within SAP ERP. Three flows are important when we look at MM in the supply chain. These are briefly discussed here before we investigate them in more detail:

▸ **Material flow:** The material flow describes the movement of materials from the vendor to the company and then on to the customer (and, potentially, customer returns). Today, companies are integrating with suppliers and customers, not just interfacing. Therefore, any improvements companies can provide to the visibility of their material flow will allow them to be flexible and responsive to their customers. Customers want to do business with companies who are responsive. Those companies can gain a competitive advantage and increase market share by being more flexible, quicker, and more dependable.

▸ **Information flow:** The information flow includes transmitting orders (EDI, fax, etc.) and updating the status of all deliveries. Companies that can show customers and vendors viability by using real-time information have a distinct competitive advantage over others.

▸ **Financial flow:** The financial flow includes the financial documents that are created at each material movement. If a material is valuated, then a movement, credit or debit, is made between accounts to reflect the value moving from, for example, inventory accounts and accounts payable (AP) clearing accounts.

1.2.3 SAP and Logistics

We have defined the Logistics function and the flows within the supply chain. So how does SAP help clients manage this supply chain to gain a competitive advantage?

SAP ERP software provides a company with the ability to have the correct materials at the correct location at the correct time with the correct quantity and at the most competitive cost. The competitive advantage is achieved when the company can manage the process. This involves managing the company's relationships with its vendors and customers. It also involves controlling their inventory, forecasting customer demand, and receiving timely information concerning all aspects of the supply-chain transactions.

When you break this down and look at the functionalities and components involved in the management of the supply chain, you can see that although MM is an integral part of Logistics, it is only part of the big picture.

The Logistics function in SAP ERP includes the following:

- Materials Management (MM)
- Sales and Distribution (SD)
- Quality Management (QM)
- Plant Maintenance (PM)
- Production Planning (PP)
- Project Systems (PS)
- Finance (FI)
- Warehouse Management (WM)
- Logistics Information System (LIS)

Additional functionality in the Logistics area includes Batch Management, Handling Unit Management, Variant Configuration, Engineering Change Management, and SAP Environment, Health, and Safety Management (SAP EHS Management). These can be important in the Logistics area, depending on the individual customer requirements.

Next, let's review the integration of the MM functionality with other SAP software.

1.3   MM Integration

MM is thus one of many functionalities or components that are important in the Logistics function of SAP. Looking at the supply chain, you can see where MM integrates with the other tools to create an efficient product for managing the supply chain.

The following sections further examine the supply chain flows.

1.3.1 The Material Flow of the Supply Chain

The material flow is the movement of the material from the vendor to the customer. To instigate a flow, a material must be created by either the Production Planning functionality (PP) via a materials requirements planning (MRP) system or by a sales order created in Sales and Distribution (SD). The need is created, and a purchase requirement is sent to the vendor, relating to instructions on delivery date, quantity, and price.

The vendor sends the material, and it is received and may be subject to a quality inspection in Quality Management (QM). Once approved, the material may be stored in a warehouse using Warehouse Management (WM).

The material could be required in a production order in PP or be part of a larger project defined in Project Systems (PS).

After a final material is available for the customer, it can be picked from the warehouse and shipped to the customer using the SD functionality.

From the description of this simple flow, it is easy to see that MM is highly integrated with the other SAP software.

1.3.2 The Information Flow of the Supply Chain

To more clearly understand the financial flow, work through this example that starts with an order from a customer. This order could be transmitted via electronic data interchange (EDI) to the SAP system. The information on SAP communicates whether the item is in stock, and if not, the information is sent to the MRP tool. Information is sent back to the customer giving the delivery date.

The MRP tool takes all of the information regarding the production schedules, capacity of the production facility, and the available materials involved in production to create production orders and material requests that appear as information in the Procurement system.

The information in the Procurement system creates orders with required delivery dates that are transmitted to vendors. The return information from the vendor confirms the date of delivery of the material.

The vendor can send EDI transmissions informing the company of the status of the delivery.

Upon receipt of the material, information is passed from the receiving documents to the warehousing system (WM) to store the material correctly. The information is passed to the production systems (PP) to calculate if the production order is ready to commence.

When the material is ready to ship, SAP produces information for shipping (SD) and can send that information to the customer.

At all of the touchpoints with SAP, information has been recorded and is available to be reviewed and analyzed. The more information that is shared across the total supply chain, the more cost benefits can be achieved with improvements based on the analytical data.

The Logistics Information System (LIS) and other standard reports in SAP can give the supply-chain management team invaluable insights into how their Logistics function operates.

1.3.3 The Financial Flow of the Supply Chain

The typical flow of financial information in the supply chain includes the invoices received by the company from its vendors, the payments to the vendors, the billing of the customers for the materials, and the incoming payments.

The vendor supplies material to the company and sends an invoice to be paid.

The company has choices within SAP on how to pay the vendor:

▶ Pay on receipt of the materials (two-way match)
▶ Pay on receipt of the vendor invoice (three-way match)

The Accounts Payable (AP) department carries out this function. The Invoice Verification process within the SAP system is an excellent example of the integration between the MM and the FI software.

The financial flow of the supply chain has not changed in magnitude, as did the information and material flows. However, the current SAP ERP system allows the supply chain users to analyze the financial key performance indicators (KPIs) that are part of the overall supply chain.

These KPIs can include inventory turns, days of working capital, days of inventory, days sales outstanding, and days payables outstanding. The integration of MM and the other key functionalities within the Logistics function combine to provide this important information in an accurate and timely fashion.

Developments in the financial flow of the supply chain have direct impacts on the MM functionality. The imaging of invoices is an important development that allows companies to scan the incoming invoices (either internally or using a third party) and create a workflow to speed approval. A message is sent to the purchaser, and approval time is shortened.

Companies now use Procurement cards (P-cards) to reduce costs and speed up the financial flow. Purchasing with a P-card ties purchasers into an approved vendor list and allows companies to focus on obtaining discounts and favorable rates with certain vendors. The other benefit is that the P-card reduces the invoice processing by the AP department. The individual purchases are managed by spending limits associated with each P-card user, and payment is made directly to the vendor by the P-card company. The use of P-cards is an example of how developments in the supply-chain management outside of SAP influence the integration between SAP software, in this case FI and MM.

1.4 Summary

In this chapter, you have seen that the MM functionality of SAP ERP is a core component of any SAP implementation. MM can be described as the engine that drives the supply-chain functionality within SAP. It also integrates with most other SAP software in some way. The aim of the following chapters is to focus on the functionality and configuration of MM and its complex integration with other SAP tools.

Let's move on to Chapter 2 to examine the MM organizational structure, which includes sections on client structure, company codes, plants, storage locations, warehouses, and so on.

Correctly defining the Materials Management organizational structure is the foundation for a successful SAP implementation. It is extremely important to make accurate decisions about company codes, plants, and storage locations.

2 Materials Management Organizational Structure

In any new SAP implementation, a number of decisions need to be made to ensure a successful project. Decisions regarding the client structure, company codes, plants, and warehouses are all important to the project and require knowledge of the objects to be decided upon and consensus between the customer and the project-implementation team.

2.1 Client Structure

This section will examine the client, the client landscape, and some of the general technical questions about SAP clients.

2.1.1 What Is a Client?

A company that purchases SAP software will install it on its servers, and then configured to the company's specific needs. This is called an instance. Companies can have more than one SAP instance, but the instances will exist on different SAP systems. A number of clients will be created within one SAP instance. A client is an organizational and legal entity in the SAP system. The master data is protected within the client because it cannot be accessed from outside. The master data in a client is only visible within that client and cannot be displayed or changed from another client. There will be multiple clients in an SAP system. Each of these clients can have a different objective, and each client represents a unique environment. A client has its own set of tables and user data. Objects can be either client dependent or client independent. SAP objects that are used by only one client are client dependent. Objects that are used by all of the clients in an SAP system, such as ABAP/4 programs, are client independent.

SAP delivers the software with three clients: 000, 001, and 066, which are discussed next.

Client 000

The SAP reference client contains tables with default settings but no master data. Client 000 can be copied, using the client copy function, to create the clients that will be used in the implementation. For important configuration work, you will need to log on to SAP Client 000. This client must be used to configure the Correction and Transport System (CTS). Client 000 also plays an important role in upgrade processes. Each time an SAP customer upgrades its system, client-dependent changes automatically will be upgraded into Client 001, the production preparation client, and the changes then can be copied to other clients. Neither Client 000 nor Client 001 should be removed from the system.

Client 001

This is delivered as the preparation production client and is initially identical to Client 000. After any upgrades, Client 001 will not be identical to Client 000. Customizing can be done in this client, but it cannot be used as the production client. SAP customers can choose whether or not to use this client.

Client 066

This is the client used for the SAP EarlyWatch service. This client enables SAP to remotely access the customer system. SAP provides this service to the customer to improve system performance and for system support. SAP recommends having an SAP EarlyWatch session before a customer's implementation goes live and another after the go-live date.

2.1.2   Creating the Client Landscape

After the SAP software has been installed with the three delivered clients, the technical team will need to create a number of clients that reflect the customer needs. The general client structure for an SAP implementation includes a development client, training client, quality client, and production client.

The development client is where all development work should take place. There may be more than one development client created. For example, there may be a *sandbox client* for general users to practice and test configuration. In addition there may be a *clean* or *golden* development client where the specific configuration is made and from which it is then transported to the quality client for review before moving to the production client.

The training client usually reflects the current production system and is used primarily for the training of project staff and end users. When configuration is transported to the production client, it is transported to the training client at the same time. The training client is useful for training but is not a necessity for implementation.

Other clients may be needed for SAP NetWeaver Business Warehouse (SAP NetWeaver BW) and other software, such as SAP Supply Chain Management (SAP SCM) and SAP Customer Relationship Management (SAP CRM).

To successfully manage this client environment, there should be strict procedures and security so that the integrity of the clients is maintained.

2.1.3 Defining a Client

Four aspects should be considered when defining a client:

▶ **Organization structure:** The customer should define a client as the highest organizational unit in its organizational structure. The client is the basis for the construction and configuration of other organizational units.

▶ **Business environment:** A client should be a representation of a holding company or group of companies in the physical business world.

▶ **Technical environment:** The client defines the boundary of the master data. The information can only be accessed inside the client.

▶ **Work environment:** The client is the work area that end users interact with in the system. Ninety percent of the tables in the client are client dependent.

2.1.4 Correction and Transport System (CTS)

Changes created in the development client must be moved, or transported, to the quality client for testing and then to the production client. CTS is the vehicle by which you can move objects such as programs, screens, configurations, or security settings from one client to another. CTS provides consistency between the clients by maintaining log entries. CTS provides a standardized procedure for managing and recording changes made to a client.

When you are configuring functionality in the development client that has been designated as the client to migrate from, you will find that saving the configuration will require extra steps.

On saving, there will be an ENTER CHANGE REQUEST dialog screen. This will require you to either add this configuration step to an existing Customizing request or to create a new request. If you opt to create a new request, another pop-up screen will appear that requires a short description of the change you are making and that may default the other information, such as your user ID, source client, category, and target client. If the target client is blank, ensure that you enter the correct target client for your change request.

On saving this change request, the system will display the change-request number. The system will have saved the configuration change you have made and logged that change in the change request.

The change request can be viewed by using Transaction SE01. On the initial screen, enter the change request number, or press F4 to find your request. Click on the display button, and the request will be displayed. By expanding the view, you can see the changes that have been made to the tables in the current client and that will be migrated to the target client. If you have authorization, you may also release the change request so that it can be migrated. If you do not have authorization, the change request will need to be released by a designated resource.

By using Transaction SE10, you can see all requests and repairs that are owned by a user ID.

> **Note**
>
> A change request cannot be released if it is empty, if the objects are not locked properly, or if the objects are not locked in another task or change request.

The next section will explain the functionality of company codes: creating and assigning a client.

2.2   Company Code

The company code is a familiar term in SAP, and it is important to understand the difference between a physical company and what a company is, as defined in the SAP system.

2.2.1   What Is a Company?

The U.S. Census Bureau (2002) defines a company as follows:

> *A company comprises all the establishments that operate under the ownership or control of a single organization. A company may be a business, service, or membership organization; it may consist of one or several establishments and operate*

at one or several locations. It includes all subsidiary organizations, all establishments that are majority-owned by the company or any subsidiary, and all the establishments that can be directed or managed by the company or any subsidiary.

SAP defines a company and a company code separately. SAP defines a company as the smallest organizational unit for which legal financial statements can be prepared. A company can contain one or more company codes, but they must use the same chart of accounts and the same fiscal-year breakdown.

SAP defines a company code as the smallest organizational unit for which a complete self-contained set of accounts can be drawn up. You will be able provide data for generating balance sheets and profit-loss statements. The company code will represent legally independent companies. Using more than one company code allows a customer to manage financial data for different independent companies at the same time.

For example, when a customer is deciding on its organizational structure, the customer can use one or many company codes. Thus, if a U.S. company has components of its organization in Canada and in Mexico, it may decide that it should use three company codes. The company-code currencies can be different for each component, but they would be required to use the same chart of accounts.

2.2.2 Creating a Company Code

The creation of a company and company codes is usually part of the Financials configuration, but you may need to create these on occasion.

The company field is defined in Transaction OX15 as a six-character alphanumeric string. The transaction can be found using the navigation path, IMG • ENTERPRISE STRUCTURE • DEFINITION • FINANCIAL ACCOUNTING • MAINTAIN COMPANY.

The company code can be created using Transaction OX02. The transaction can be accessed using the navigation path, IMG • ENTERPRISE STRUCTURE • DEFINITION • FINANCIAL ACCOUNTING • DEFINE, COPY, DELETE, CHECK COMPANY CODE. The company code field is defined as a four-character alphanumeric string. In Transaction OX02, it is possible to copy from an existing company code and change the name, city, and country to your company details. This transaction will update Table T001.

After creating the company code, you will need to maintain the company-code address by using Transaction OBY6, which will update the Table SADR.

2.2.3 Assigning a Company Code

After a company code has been defined, it must be assigned to a number of objects. In the IMG, a number of financial configuration steps need to be carried out. The company code can be assigned to the following:

- Credit Control Area
- Financial Management Area
- Company

The next section follows on from the SAP structure of a company to the structure, creation, and assignment of a plant.

2.3 Plants

You may not think of yourself working in a plant, but SAP uses plant to describe many different types of environment.

2.3.1 What Is a Plant?

The definition of a plant depends on its use. From a MM view, a plant can be defined as a location that holds valuated stock. A PP view defines a plant as an organizational unit that is central to planning production. A plant also can be defined as a location that contains service or maintenance facilities. The definition of a plant will vary depending on the need of the customer.

2.3.2 Prerequisites for a Plant

Before setting up a plant, certain other settings need to be defined:

- **Factory calendar:** A factory calendar identifies the workdays, public holidays, and company holidays. The SAP system is delivered with some factory calendars, but a new factory calendar can be configured based on a company's schedule. The factory calendar is defined as a two-character field, such as NO, which is the factory calendar for Norway, or Z6, which could be a customer-defined factory calendar for a six-day workweek.
- **Country key:** A country key is required to define a plant. The system is delivered with country keys, and new country codes need to be configured if they are not in the system. For example, the United States is represented by US, Switzerland represented by CH, and so on.

▸ **Region keys:** A region code is required along with the country code. The region is defined as a state or province associated with a country. For example, if the country code is defined as US for the United States, the two-character region keys will represent the individual states and U.S. protectorates such as Guam and Puerto Rico.

2.3.3   Defining a Plant

_OX10_

A four-character string defines the plant field. It can be configured using Transaction OX10. The transaction can be found using the navigation path, IMG • ENTERPRISE STRUCTURE • DEFINITION • LOGISTICS • GENERAL • DEFINE, COPY, DELETE, CHECK PLANT.

Figure 2.1 shows the program screen for entering initial plant information, and Figure 2.2 shows the screen for entering secondary information after the initial information is entered.

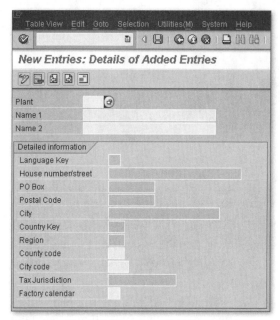

Figure 2.1   The Initial Screen for Entering a Plant

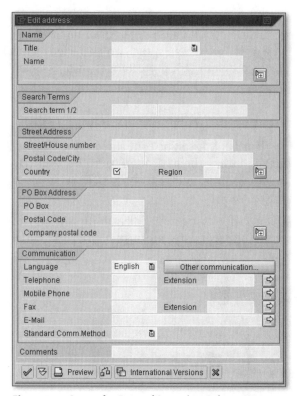

Figure 2.2   Screen for Entry of Secondary Information

2.3.4   Valuation Level

The valuation level is an important configuration step because it specifies the level at which material stocks are valuated for the whole client. There are two options for the valuation level: plant level or company code level.

The valuation level can be defined using Transaction OX14 or using the navigation path, IMG • ENTERPRISE STRUCTURE • DEFINITION • LOGISTICS – GENERAL • DEFINE VALUATION LEVEL.

There are several situations in which there should be valuation at the plant level, for example, if PP or Costing will be implemented, or if the application is using the SAP Retail system. After a valuation is determined, it should not be changed.

2.3.5   Assigning a Plant

After a valuation level has been established, it is possible to assign a plant to an existing company code. This assignment is performed so that all plant transactions can be attributed to a single legal entity; that is, a company code. This can be achieved in Transaction OX18 or by using the navigation path, IMG • Enterprise Structure • Assignment • Logistics – General • Assign Plant to Company Code.

Figure 2.3 illustrates the assignment of plants to company codes. A plant is assigned to one company code, but a company code can have more than one plant assigned to it.

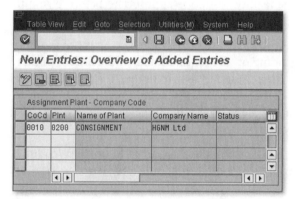

Figure 2.3   Assignment of Plants to Company Codes

This section has described the importance of the plant within the organizational structure. In the next section, the storage location functionality is explained.

2.4   Storage Locations

After discussing the plant, the next level in the physical structure defined in MM is the storage location.

2.4.1   What Is a Storage Location?

In its systems, SAP traditionally defines a storage location as a place where stock is physically kept within a plant. There will always be at least one storage location defined for one plant. It is the lowest level of location definition within the MM functionality.

When we look at a physical storage location, there are no set rules on what a storage location should look like. Some SAP customers may have a highly developed inventory-monitoring system that uniquely defines a physical location, storage bin, tank, tote, tray, drawer, cabinet, and so on, as a location that contains inventory separated from other inventory. Depending on the physical size of the materials involved, this may be as small as a 5cm square bin or as large as a whole building.

Some customers may not have sophisticated inventory systems, and you may be presented by a location with no obvious storage definitions. Materials may not be stored in individual locations and may be mixed without procedural picking or placement strategies. In this case, an assessment of the current state and proposals on how to re-engineer the storage facility would be appropriate before trying to define storage locations.

Although the storage location is the lowest location level in MM, it is not the lowest level in the SAP system. Depending on the requirements of the SAP customer, the number of materials that are stored, the number of unique locations, and the sophistication of the customer's current inventory system, there may be a need to implement the Warehouse Management (WM) functionality. This provides the opportunity to manage inventory at a bin level.

When WM is implemented in an SAP system, there is a need to tie the WM functionality to MM . This is achieved by assigning a warehouse to a storage location or number of storage locations.

2.4.2 Defining a Storage Location

A four-character string defines the storage location. It can be configured using Transaction OX09. The transaction can be found using the navigation path, IMG • Enterprise Structure • Definition • Materials Management • Maintain Storage Location.

Enter the plant number in the initial screen of Transaction OX09, as shown in Figure 2.4. This will then direct you to this screen. Press the New Entries icon and then you will be able to add the storage location number and a description. You can then highlight your new storage location and click on the addresses of storage location in the dialog structure.

Click on the New Entries icon to enter a number for the storage location address, as shown in Figure 2.5. This can be up to three characters. Once entered, you will be directed to another screen for the entry of secondary information such as address and telephone number. This screen is the same as shown in Figure 2.2.

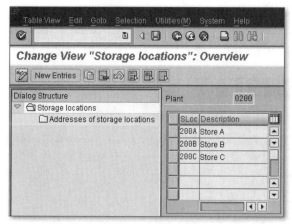

Figure 2.4 The Initial Screen of Transaction OX09

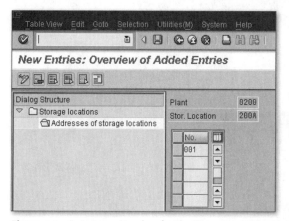

Figure 2.5 Entering a Number for the Storage Location Address

automated creation based on GR.

2.4.3   Automatic Creation of Storage Locations

It is possible to create storage locations automatically when an inward goods movement for a material is performed. The configuration needs the plant and/ or the type of movement to be defined to allow the automatic creation of storage locations. This configuration can reduce storage-location data maintenance. The automatic storage location will only be activated if the movement is for normal stock, not special stock.

This configuration can be entered using Transaction OMB3 by going to the navigation path, IMG • MATERIALS MANAGEMENT • INVENTORY MANAGEMENT AND PHYSICAL INVENTORY • GOODS RECEIPT • CREATE STORAGE LOCATION AUTOMATICALLY.

Automatic creation of storage locations can be set for each plant where this functionality is needed, as shown in Figure 2.6, or for a particular goods movement as shown in Figure 2.7.

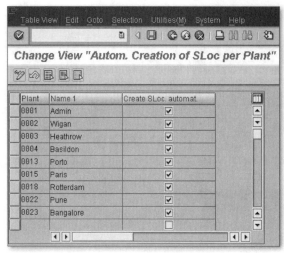

Figure 2.6 Automatic Storage-Location Creation by Plant

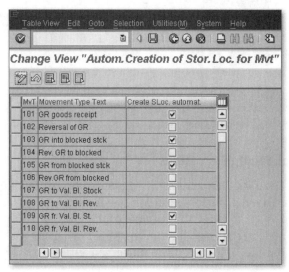

Figure 2.7 Automatic Storage-Location Creation by Movement Type

The storage location is the lowest level of the organizational structure of MM. However, in the next section, we will examine how the Warehouse Management functionality integrates with MM.

2.5 Warehouse and Storage Types

Although not part of MM functionality, it is important to understand the integration points with Warehouse Management (WM). It is important for MM users to have some knowledge of WM as many companies implement both MM and WM. The warehouse is linked to the MM functionality by assigning the warehouse to the storage location in MM; if a company has WM and MM activated, the goods movements will require knowledge of the major elements of WM.

A warehouse is a physical location that contains defined areas called storage types, which are then further divided into smaller locations called storage bins. In WM, it is possible to define stock placement and picking strategies based on material location and sequence.

To create a warehouse, you can use the following navigation path, IMG • ENTER-PRISE STRUCTURE • DEFINITION • LOGISTICS EXECUTION • DEFINE, COPY, DELETE, CHECK WAREHOUSE.

The warehouse is defined by a three-character string, as shown in Figure 2.8. Be aware that no address details are associated with a warehouse.

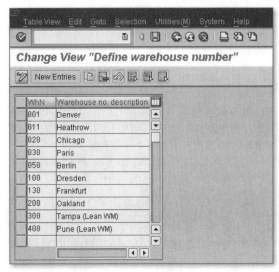

Figure 2.8 Defining the Warehouse

2.5.1 Assign a Warehouse to a Plant and Storage Location

To ensure that SAP correctly identifies the certain storage locations that are controlled by the functionality in WM, you assign a warehouse to a storage location. The navigation path for assigning a warehouse to a plant and storage location is IMG • Enterprise Structure • Assignment • Logistics Execution • Assign Warehouse Number to Plant/Storage Location. Figure 2.9 shows the display view.

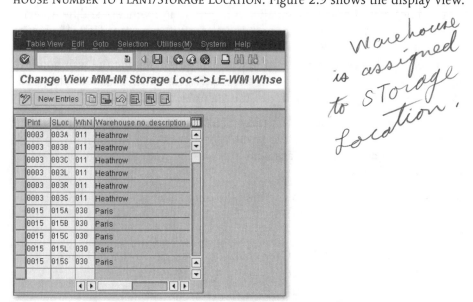

Warehouse is assigned to storage location.

Figure 2.9 Assigning a Warehouse to a Plant/Storage Location Combination

2.5.2 Storage Type

A storage type is defined as an area of the warehouse that is a subsection containing a number of storage bins. The storage type is available to the warehouse user for creating searches based on storage types. Common storage types in a warehouse include a cold room, bulk storage, and high rack area. Storage types predefined by SAP are called interim storage types. These are defined numerically from 900 to 999. The areas are used by SAP for movement postings such as goods receipt, goods issue, and posting differences.

The navigation path for creating storage types is IMG • Logistics Execution • Warehouse Management • Master Data • Define Storage Type.

Each warehouse can have any number of storage types defined as shown in Figure 2.10.

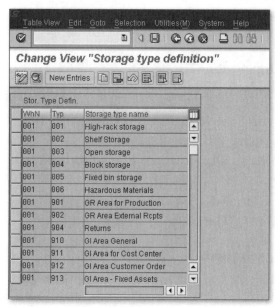

Figure 2.10 Warehouse with Storage Types Defined

2.5.3 Storage Sections and Storage Bins

A subdivision of the storage type is the storage section, which is simply a group of similar storage bins. Even if the customer does not want to define storage sections, one storage section must be defined per storage type. This is normally defined as 001 in the IMG. The navigation path to use is IMG • LOGISTICS EXECUTION • WAREHOUSE MANAGEMENT • MASTER DATA • DEFINE STORAGE SECTION.

Storage bins are the lowest level of storage available in the warehouse. Storage bins are not defined in the IMG and are not transportable. Authorized warehouse staff can quickly and frequently change these. Storage bins can be defined manually using Transaction LS01N or automatically using Transaction LS10.

Now that the structural organization of MM is defined for the physical elements, the next section goes on to explain an important logical aspect of MM: purchasing and the purchasing organization.

2.6 Purchasing Organization

The purchasing department of a company may be a single person calling vendors manually or hundreds of purchasing agents spread over the world using the latest in Internet purchasing. The purchasing organization is an important element in the procurement of materials.

2.6.1 What Is a Purchasing Organization?

The purchasing function for SAP customers can range from simple to very complex. The largest SAP customers may spend hundreds of millions of dollars in purchasing each year and have a sophisticated purchasing department that works at many different levels, from strategic global procurement to low-level vendor relationships. SAP can be defined to allow all purchasing departments to be accurately reflected.

A purchasing organization is simply defined as a group of purchasing activities associated with all or a specific part of the enterprise.

2.6.2 Types of Purchasing Organizations

Several types of purchasing organizations are used, including on the plant, company, and enterprise levels.

Purchasing at an Enterprise Level

Purchasing for an SAP customer may take place at the highest level within an organization. If a customer has a central purchasing department that coordinates purchasing for all companies within the enterprise, then the purchasing organization can be configured in that manner. The purchasing organization is defined in SAP ERP and then assigned to all companies.

Purchasing at the Company Level

If an SAP customer does not have a single enterprisewide purchasing function, it may have purchasing centralized for each company. This may be appropriate for customers with companies in various countries; in which case, an enterprise purchasing department may not be possible. In this scenario, the purchasing organization is created and assigned for each company code. Even with this scenario, a purchasing organization may cover several companies. For example, a purchasing organization for Latvia may be assigned as the purchasing organization for the companies based in the countries of Latvia, Lithuania, and Estonia.

The purchasing organization can be assigned to a company code using Transaction OX01. The transaction can be accessed using the navigation path, IMG • ENTERPRISE

Structure • Assignment • Materials Management • Assign Purchasing Organization to Company Code.

Purchasing at the Plant Level

In an enterprise that has companies with large autonomous plants; the purchasing decisions may be made at a local level. The SAP customer may decide that assigning one purchasing organization to one company is not appropriate, and it would be a better business decision to assign a purchasing organization at the plant. This scenario has an advantage when the vendors are at a local level, and few vendors supply materials or services to more than one plant.

The purchasing organization can be assigned to a plant with Transaction OX17 using the navigation path, IMG • Enterprise Structure • Assignment • Materials Management • Assign Purchasing Organization to Plant.

Reference Purchasing Org

Reference Purchasing Organization

One purchasing organization can be defined as a reference purchasing organization, which can be set up as a strategic purchasing department. In large companies, the strategic purchasing function analyzes purchasing data and works to negotiate the best prices for materials and services from global vendors. This strategic purchasing department can obtain prices and special conditions that can be used by purchasing organizations across the enterprise.

Often this reference purchasing organization is not assigned to any company code because it is a function of the whole enterprise. A purchasing organization must be assigned to this reference purchasing organization to have access to the information on the system.

To assign a purchasing organization that will reference another purchasing organization, use the navigation path, IMG • Enterprise Structure • Assignment • Materials Management • Assign Purchasing Organization to Reference Purchasing Organization.

2.6.3 Create a Purchasing Organization

The navigation path to create a purchasing organization is IMG • Enterprise Structure • Definition • Materials Management • Maintain Purchasing Organization.

Figure 2.11 shows the screen for creating a purchasing organization.

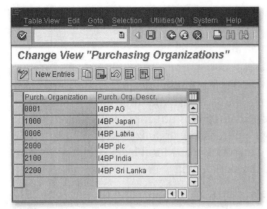

Figure 2.11 Creating a Purchasing Organization

people

2.6.4 Purchasing Groups

An SAP customer has the opportunity to define its purchasing department below the level of purchasing organization. The purchasing group can be defined as a person or group of people dealing with a certain material or group of materials purchased by the purchasing organization.

The purchasing group is defined in configuration. The navigation path is IMG • MATERIALS MANAGEMENT • PURCHASING • CREATE PURCHASING GROUPS.

The purchasing group is a three-character alphanumeric field that is entered along with a description, telephone number, and fax number. Figure 2.12 shows purchasing group details that have been created.

Figure 2.12 Creating a Purchasing Group

2.7   Business Examples — Organizational Structure

The organizational structure in the MM area enables businesses to configure the system to reflect their needs in many ways. Some implementations are very straightforward where a business will only need a single company code, a single plant, and simple storage location requirements. Other companies with an international presence might require a number of company codes with hundreds of plants, storage locations, and warehouses, with a complex purchasing structure.

2.7.1   Client Structure

The SAP client structure adopted by a business can vary based on any number of variables, including the size of the company, the scope of the SAP implementation, or international requirements.

Example

An international retailer with a presence in 12 European and Latin American countries had implemented an SAP project in Brazil as a pilot. The success of that project led to a global implementation in the other 11 countries. The production system in Brazil was based on one client, and the company decided that each of the additional implementations would have just one production client. As each implementation progressed, the one client per country assumption was questioned. Initially the implementation teams for the Netherlands and Belgium decided that a single client would be suitable for them based on a number of business requirements, including shared inventory, shared vendors, and the structure of the sales departments. The next implementation after the Netherlands was in Germany. Because the company had numerous business reporting requirements, the team wanted to have a client for its production system and a separate client for the data warehousing solution. After further consultation with external management consultants, the German implementation team decided they needed to keep their confidential HR data separate from the main production system and would therefore require a third client for SAP ERP Human Capital Management (SAP ERP HCM) processing. Subsequent European implementations used the German model of moving the SAP ERP HCM to a separate client.

2.7.2   Plants

We have found that a plant can have a number of uses in SAP, but for MM, a plant can be defined as a location that holds valuated stock, while Production Planning (PP) and Plant Maintenance (PM)can view a plant very differently.

Example

A mid-sized automotive parts business in the United Kingdom had been using a series of in-house customized systems to run its production, distribution, and maintenance facilities. The company moved its AS400-based accounting and purchasing system to a new SAP ERP system and was in the process of planning the next phase of the implementation. To achieve the biggest cost saving, the company needed to move the production, distribution, and maintenance processes to SAP ERP and decommission a number of costly servers. After the initial analysis, the company was unsure of how many plants to create. In the legacy system, the company had defined one location for three physical buildings: one for the manufacturing of parts, one maintenance facility, and a distribution center that was located a quarter mile from the maintenance and production site. The final decision was to create one plant for the manufacturing and maintenance facility because it was physically at the same location, and a separate plant for the distribution center. The decision to create a separate plant for the distribution center was made after management decided to make modifications to their business processes. Management decided to create storage locations at the manufacturing site for material that was being shipped out immediately after being produced and for material received from vendors using a just-in-time (JIT) methodology. The distribution center then became a facility whose primary function was to keep finished goods inventory, rather than having the additional responsibility of holding raw materials for manufacturing.

2.7.3 Storage Locations

MM functionality usually defines a storage location as a place where stock is physically kept within a plant. The system requires that at least one storage location be defined for one plant. Companies that implement MM can have widely different views on what constitutes a storage location, so when advising a company, you should be aware that their idea of a storage location may contradict what you may have seen in other implementations.

Example

A woodworking tools manufacturer in Texas had been using a number of disparate and heavily customized manufacturing and purchasing computer programs that ran on a number of desktops. The company recently purchased its largest vendor, saving it from bankruptcy, and ensuring that the company had no interruption of supply. However, after the purchase, the company had to move its newly purchased company from its current location due to an expiring lease. The new organization found that combining processes and inventories would not be successful without upgrading its aging legacy systems. The company decided on an SAP ERP implementation for finance, manufacturing, purchasing, and inventory.

The decision was made early on to implement one plant, and, at that time, the implementation team decided on three storage locations: one for raw materials, one for finished goods, and one for returns. When the implementation team began to review the functionality of SAP ERP compared with the customized computer programs they had been using, they found that the functionality they were using described the plant in a lot more detail than three storage locations. The customized systems used several hundred rack locations to inform staff where material could be found and where to store incoming material from vendors.

The company had been through a rationalization project and reduced its material master file by 40%. In addition, the company removed a number of unused racks to simplify the layout of the finished goods areas. Despite these improvements, the implementation team realized that the three storage locations would be too simple, and replicating the locations from the legacy system would be too complicated, resulting in more than 100 storage locations. The company performed a review of the WM functionality in SAP ERP, but ultimately decided against bringing in additional functionality. Finally the implementation team developed a plan to implement one storage location per rack, which led to 24 storage locations being used for finished goods, and 7 for raw materials.

2.7.4 Warehouse Management

Warehouse Management (WM) is not part of MM but because of the close integration, there are occasions when you need to explain to your client the WM organizational structure so the client can make an informed decision.

Example

After a chemical company based outside of Vancouver, Canada had implemented its SAP ERP system, the company found that the time to ship product from its finished goods location had risen by 10%. The implementation had not included WM because the company had decided that the MM functionality could maintain, if not improve, delivery times to its customers. The company brought in a group of warehouse specialists to analyze the problem. They found that the major delay caused by the implementation was that the forklift drivers were taking longer to find product after the implementation than before. The reason for this increased travel time was that the company had implemented a very simple storage location structure. As a result, the forklift driver had to search along a 20-meter rack, two levels high for the product. Prior to the implementation, the forklift driver was directed to a single-level area that was 5 meters long.

The company revisited the decision on WM, particularly with regards to adding storage types and bin locations. The company decided to carry out a six-month pilot WM project for an off-site location that shipped finished material to overseas customers. The pilot project found that the introduction of WM reduced the delivery time to customers, but there was an additional resource expense to process the relevant transactions in SAP ERP.

2.7.5 Purchasing Organization

The purchasing department of a company varies between companies and can be as simple as a single person dealing with all aspects of the purchasing function. In contrast, purchasing at a multinational corporation can include departments that procure materials for dozens of companies across the globe.

Example

A supermarket chain in Brazil implemented SAP ERP for its finance and purchasing processes. The purchasing processes included only those relating to non-food purchases, including services for every store, in-store fixtures, and head office functions. Prior to and immediately after the implementation, the purchasing department was comprised of 3 purchasing professionals and a department head. Having only 3 full-time purchasing staff to procure items and services for 29 stores meant that purchases were made with vendors that had been used for many years. The result was that the purchasing staff was not finding the vendor with the best price nor were they negotiating with their current vendors. The company realized that it was not benefiting from the SAP ERP implementation and that nothing had changed in the purchasing area.

To achieve a return on its investment, the company hired a dozen purchasing clerks whose jobs were to review each purchase to see if items or services could be found cheaper at the same quality. The new staff was organized regionally so that they could focus on vendors closer to the groups of stores, while the existing purchasing staff concentrated on purchases that benefited the company as a whole. The company changed the purchasing structure in SAP ERP to reflect this new organization, with four regional purchasing organizations and a single purchasing organization at the head office.

2.8 Summary

In this chapter, we have seen that knowledge of the SAP organizational structure is important to anyone working on an SAP implementation. Each company will create its own version of the SAP landscape, correction and transport, and other technical elements. It is important that you understand what these are and how your company adopts them. Understanding the principle of the Materials Management structure is important to anyone working with the SAP ERP functionality, whether as a configurator or while advising a company on the organizational structure.

The Materials Management functionality includes a number of important master data files. The Material Master and Vendor Master files are at the core of Procurement, Inventory Management, and Invoice Verification.

3 Master Data in Materials Management

A number of master data files in Materials Management require a significant amount of understanding, not only on the part of the SAP consultant but also on the part of the SAP customer. When implementing SAP, customers are generally transitioning from one or more legacy systems. A key aspect of any implementation is the conversion of data to the master data files in SAP.

A fundamental indicator of a successful implementation is the level to which the data has been correctly converted into the SAP master data files. In this chapter, we will examine the master data files that are integral to the practice of materials management.

3.1 Material Master

The Material Master is the repository of the data used for a material. The Material Master is more than a single file for each material, it is where all information on a material is entered and accessed from. It is used throughout the SAP system.

3.1.1 Material Master Overview

When customers implement SAP, they are often overwhelmed by the information contained in the Material Master file. When customers examine their existing systems, such as BPICS, JDEdwards, or Lawson, they find that their product or material files contain a fraction of the data contained in the Material Master in the SAP system.

3.1.2 Material Master Tables

The Material Master transaction allows the users to enter all of the information relevant to a particular item of material into the correct tables. The Material Master isn't just a single file but a number of tables of information that combined reflect all of the information for that material.

Many tables are updated when information is entered into the Material Master transaction. The Material Master transaction is structured so that there are entry screens for different functional information such as Purchasing, Sales, or Accounting, but there is also an organizational dimension to data entry. The material information can be entered at each level of the organization, for example, at the levels of plant, storage location, or sales organization.

3.1.3 Material Numbering

An issue that SAP customers can face when converting their item files over to the Material Master is whether to keep their legacy numbering scheme. This means they would continue entering their own material numbers. They have the option of allowing SAP to automatically assign material numbers.

Often, legacy systems have meaningful material numbering. This numbering has usually been in place for some time, and staff members are familiar with the numbering. For the simplicity of maintenance, automatic assignment of material number is the best choice. When working with your client, be aware that there are arguments to use and not to use a meaningful numbering scheme in SAP.

The material number field is defined in configuration. Use Transaction OMSL or the navigation path IMG • LOGISTICS – GENERAL • MATERIAL MASTER • BASIC SETTINGS • DEFINE OUTPUT FORMAT FOR MATERIAL NUMBERS.

Figure 3.1 shows the configuration screen for defining the output format for material numbers.

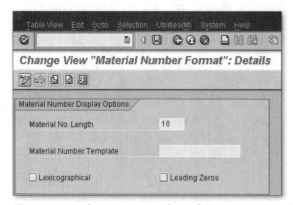

Figure 3.1 Configuration Screen for Defining Output Format

This configuration screen does not have many input fields but is extremely important when initially defining the Material Master. After your customer has decided upon the Material Master numbering scheme, you can first enter the length of the material number.

Then the customer may decide that it needs the automatically assigned material numbers in a certain format that can be defined. In this case, you can define the template and the special characters required. Figure 3.2 shows the template defined for internally assigned material numbers.

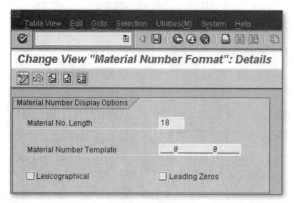

Figure 3.2 Template for Internally Assigned Material Number.

In this case, the customer requires the material numbers to appear as this example 123@45678901@23456. The only character that cannot be used in the template is the underscore because that is used to signify a non-template field.

The two other fields in the OMSL transaction have to do with how the material number is stored and how SAP determines what the number is.

The LEXICOGRAPHICAL indicator is only relevant for numeric material numbers, either internally or externally defined. In Figure 3.2, the indicator is not set, which means that the numbers are stored with leading zeros that are right-justified. For example, if a user enters the number 12345678, the number will be stored as 000000000012345678, for example, with 10 leading zeros.

If the indicator is set, then the numeric number is not right justified and not padded with zeros. The field acts more like a character string, where a leading zero becomes as valid character.

In the following example, the indicator is now set. A user entering material 12345678 would find that the material number would be stored as 12345678, with no padding. If the user then entered 0012345678, it would be stored in that way, and this would be a different material number in SAP. However, an internally assigned material number would be padded with the leading zeros, 000000000012345678. Therefore, there would be three separate material numbers.

Remember that this indicator cannot be changed after there are numeric material numbers in the system, so it must be defined before any tests are run in the system.

The other field in Transaction OMSL is the LEADING ZEROS indicator. If this indicator is set, then the material number is shown with the leading zeros. However, if the LEXICOGRAPHICAL indicator is set, then the LEADING ZEROS indicator is ignored by the system.

3.1.4 Material Number Range

When the definition of the material number has been decided upon, the configuration for the material number range can be completed.

The material number ranges can be configured in Transaction MMNR or via the navigation path IMG • LOGISTICS – GENERAL • MATERIAL MASTER • BASIC SETTINGS • MATERIAL TYPES • DEFINE NUMBER RANGES FOR MATERIAL TYPES.

The transaction allows a range of numbers to be entered and the option to make that range either external or internally assigned. Figure 3.3 shows the number ranges defined for internal and external number assignment.

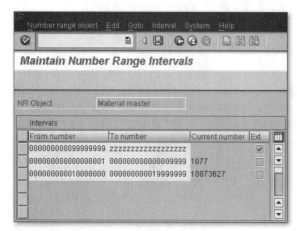

Figure 3.3 Defined Internal and External Number Ranges

3.1.5   Material Type

A material type is a definition of a group of materials with similar attributes. A material type must be assigned to each material record entered into the Material Master.

The transaction for the material type definition is OMS2. The transaction can be accessed using the navigation path, IMG • LOGISTICS – GENERAL • MATERIAL MASTER • BASIC SETTINGS • MATERIAL TYPES • DEFINE ATTRIBUTES OF MATERIAL TYPES.

The material type is configured so that fields in the Material Master are predefined for the materials assigned to that material group, as shown in Figure 3.4. For example, you can configure the price control for a material type to be Standard Price, and all materials assigned to that material type will be standard price.

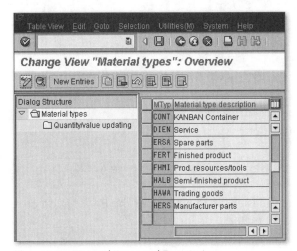

Figure 3.4   Material Types and Descriptions

After the material type has been created, the attributes can be defined. Figure 3.5 shows the attributes that can be assigned to each material type. After the material type has been defined, then the number range can be assigned.

Now we have looked at the details that go into making up the Material Master. The next section will explain the functionality of another important element in the Materials Management functionality, the Vendor Master.

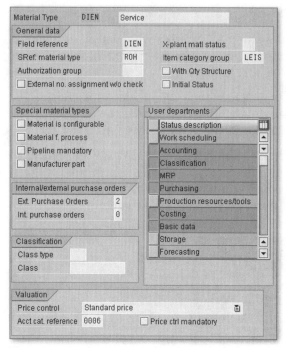

Figure 3.5 Attributes Assigned to Material Types

3.2 Vendor Master

The Vendor Master is an important master file that contains the information on a supplier required for purchasing any material or service.

3.2.1 Definition of a Vendor

We define a vendor as a person or company who supplies materials or services to the person or company requiring those materials or services. For SAP customers, every supplier that they need to convert from their legacy systems will require a Vendor Master record in SAP.

3.2.2 Vendor Master in SAP

The Vendor Master in SAP holds details about each vendor used by the customer. The Vendor Master has three distinct sections. These are discussed in some detail in the following subsections.

General Data

The general data is, as the name suggests, general information about the vendor that can be entered into the system by the group identified to create vendor records. The basic date entered at this level includes name, search terms, address, telephone, and fax. After this data is entered, further information can be added to the Vendor Master record by Accounting and Purchasing. This data can be entered using Transaction XK01.

Accounting Data

The accounting data is the financial data that is entered at the company code level. This data includes tax information, bank details, reconciliation account, payment terms, payment methods, and dunning information. The transaction used in Financial Accounting to enter this information is FK01.

Purchasing Data

The purchasing data is entered for the vendor at a purchasing organizational level. We will discuss the purchasing organization later in the book. The data entered is relevant for one purchasing organization and may be different between purchasing organizations. The data entered includes control data required in purchasing, partner functions, purchasing default fields, and Invoice Verification indicators. This data can be entered using Transaction MK01.

3.2.3 Vendor Account Groups

When you create a vendor, you must assign an account group to that vendor. Therefore, these account groups must be defined in configuration before vendor creation.

The account group is defined using the navigation path IMG • FINANCIAL ACCOUNTING • VENDOR ACCOUNTS • MASTER DATA • PREPARATIONS FOR CREATING VENDOR MASTER DATA • DEFINE ACCOUNT GROUPS WITH SCREEN LAYOUT (VENDORS).

In Figure 3.6, you can see the existing account groups. If you need to define another account group, click on the New Entries icon. The screen shown in Figure 3.7 will appear.

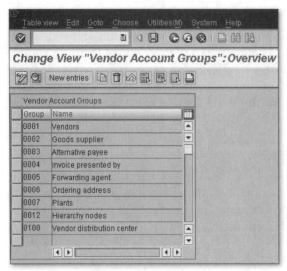

Figure 3.6 Account Group with Description

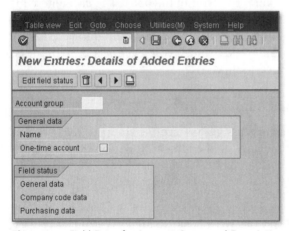

Figure 3.7 Field Entry for Account Group and Description

On this screen, you can specify whether an account group is just for one-time vendors. For vendors that you only deal with once, their data is entered into the document and not as master data. After you have entered the account group and description, you can then modify the field status as needed. This transaction allows you to configure the system to show or to not allow users to enter information into certain fields. Highlight the field status for the general, company code, or purchasing data, and then click on the EDIT FIELD STATUS icon.

Figure 3.8 shows the specific field groups that are available to configure. For the general data screen, these are the ADDRESS, COMMUNICATION, CONTROL, PAYMENT TRANSACTIONS, and CONTACT PERSON groups. Double-click on the group you want to configure.

Figure 3.8 Field Groups for the General Data Screen

This configuration screen, shown in Figure 3.9, allows you to make certain fields either a required entry or an optional entry because they all are in this figure; display only, or suppressed. This configuration becomes specific to the account group that is entered when a Vendor Master record is created.

The screen layouts can also be modified for company code using the navigation path, IMG • FINANCIAL ACCOUNTING • VENDOR ACCOUNTS • MASTER DATA • PREPARATIONS FOR CREATING VENDOR MASTER DATA • DEFINE SCREEN LAYOUT PER COMPANY CODE.

The screen layout can also be modified by the particular activity. In other words, the screen for creating a vendor can be modified to appear different from the screen for modifying a vendor. The transaction is accessed using the navigation path, IMG • FINANCIAL ACCOUNTING • VENDOR ACCOUNTS • MASTER DATA • PREPARATIONS FOR CREATING VENDOR MASTER DATA • DEFINE SCREEN LAYOUT PER ACTIVITY.

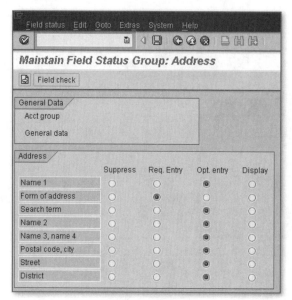

Figure 3.9 Some Fields Used to Configure Address Field Group

3.2.4 Vendor Number Range

When defining the vendor number range, it is important to remember that vendor numbers, like material numbers, can be externally or internally assigned. Many SAP customers decide to create different number ranges for each of their account groups. This requires careful consideration when defining number ranges to prevent the number ranges from overlapping.

The transaction to create vendor number ranges is XKN1, or you can use the navigation path, IMG • FINANCIAL ACCOUNTING • VENDOR ACCOUNTS • MASTER DATA • PREPARATIONS FOR CREATING VENDOR MASTER DATA • CREATE NUMBER RANGES FOR VENDOR ACCOUNTS. Figure 3.10 shows the configuration for vendor number ranges.

For this transaction, you should enter a unique number for the range, defined by a two-character field, and then the range for the numbers for your defined number range. The CURRENT NUMBER field allows you to define the current number. The EXT. field allows you to define whether the number range is externally, or user, defined.

No.	From number	To number	Current number	Ext
01	0000000001	0000099999		☑
02	0000100000	0000199999	100222	☐
03	0000200000	0000299999	200059	☐
04	0000300000	0000399999		☑
06	6000000000	6999999999	0	☐
EB	1000000000	1000009999	0	☐
XX	A	ZZZZZZZZZZ		☑

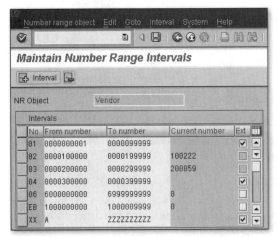

Figure 3.10 Configuration for Vendor Number Ranges

After the number range is defined, it can be assigned to a vendor account group using the navigation path, IMG • Financial Accounting • Vendor Accounts • Master Data • Preparations for Creating Vendor Master Data • Assign Number Ranges to Vendor Account Groups.

The number range can be assigned to many vendor account groups, as shown in Figure 3.11. Therefore, if your SAP customer decides to use just one number range for all its vendors, the configuration would show one number range assigned to all account groups.

Group	Name	Number range
0001	Vendors	XX
0002	Goods supplier	XX
0003	Alternative payee	XX
0004	Invoice presented by	XX
0005	Forwarding agent	XX
0006	Ordering address	XX
0007	Plants	BP
0012	Hierarchy nodes	01
0100	Vendor distribution center	BP

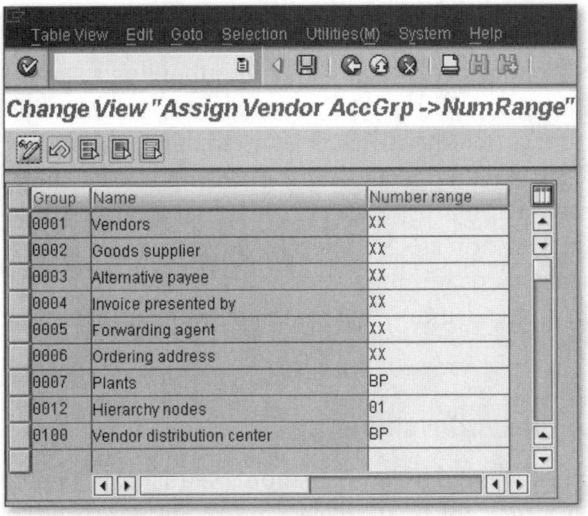

Figure 3.11 Vendor Account Groups and Assigned Number Ranges

3.3   Purchasing Information Data

The purchasing information record allows additional information to be held on a specific material that is purchased from a specific vendor.

3.3.1   Purchasing Information Record

The purchasing information record is where information specific to a material and a vendor is held. This can then be further specified for a particular purchasing organization.

The purchasing information record is used in the purchase order (PO) where information from the record is defaulted into the PO. Information such as purchasing group, net price, Invoice Verification indicators, and delivery tolerances all can be entered into the purchasing information record.

Four categories of purchasing information records can be created:

▶ Standard
▶ Pipeline
▶ Consignment
▶ Subcontracting

It is important to identify the correct category before creating a purchasing information record.

3.3.2   Purchasing Information Record for a Non-Stock Material

The purchasing information record usually applies to a vendor and a specific material that it supplies. However, the vendor occasionally may be supplying a service to a non-stock material. For example, there may be an operation in a production order where material is sent out for a treatment. There is no material number at that point for the material in the production order, but there is a purchase information record for a group of materials, that is, a specific material group such as certain raw materials or semi-finished non-stock items. In the system, it is possible to create a purchasing information record for a vendor and a material group. This contains the same information that a vendor/material purchasing information record would have.

3.3.3   Purchasing Information Record Numbering

The fact that there are different types of purchase information records makes number ranges necessary. The number ranges for the purchase information record can be assigned either externally or internally.

The number ranges for the purchase information records can be predefined in SAP ERP, and SAP recommends that the customer accept the given number ranges. The system does allow the number ranges to be changed if the customer requires it.

The transaction to define the purchasing information record number ranges is OMEO, or you can use the navigation path, IMG • MATERIALS MANAGEMENT • PURCHASING • PURCHASING INFORMATION RECORD • DEFINE NUMBER RANGES.

The predefined number ranges for the purchase information records are the following:

▶ Stock material – internally assigned 5300000000 to 5399999999

▶ Stock material – externally assigned 5400000000 to 5499999999

▶ Non-stock material – internally assigned 5500000000 to 5599999999

▶ Non-stock material – externally assigned 5600000000 to 5699999999

3.3.4 Purchasing Information Record-Screen Layout

The screens in the purchasing information record transactions can be modified to allow field changes. The navigation path for this transaction is IMG • MATERIALS MANAGEMENT • PURCHASING • PURCHASING INFORMATION RECORD • DEFINE SCREEN LAYOUT.

The screen shown in Figure 3.12 allows you to choose the modifications for each transaction. To select a transaction, double-clicking on the transaction will take you to a screen where you can modify the screen layout, found in Table T162. You then can select one of the field-selection groups to modify the individual fields.

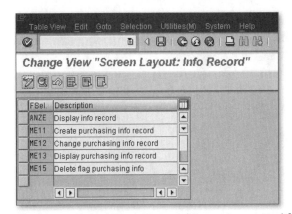

Figure 3.12 Record Transactions and Screen-Layout Modifications

Figure 3.13 shows the field selection groups available to select from for the purchasing information record transaction. Figure 3.14 shows the individual fields of the QUANTITIES field selection group for Transaction ANZE.

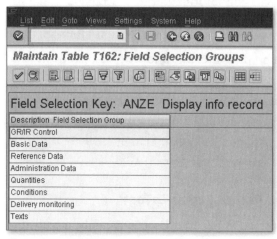

Figure 3.13 Field Selection Groups Available for the Purchasing Information Record Transaction

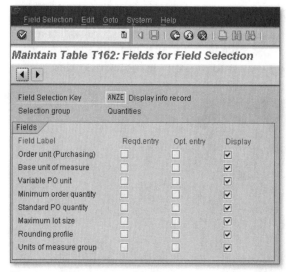

Figure 3.14 Quantities Field-Selection Group for Transaction ANZE

3.4   Batch Management Data

A batch of material is an important feature that allows a group of one material to have the same characteristics, identified by the batch number. This may be due to production or purchasing.

3.4.1   What Is a Batch?

A batch is a quantity of material that is grouped together for various reasons. It is often determined that the materials have the same characteristics and values. For instance, in the chemical industry, a certain number of containers of a certain product may be considered a batch because they were produced at the same time and have the same physical and chemical characteristics. These characteristics may differ from those of another batch of material produced on the same day.

The pharmaceutical industry is one sector where material batches are extremely important. Each batch of material is recorded throughout the product and distribution process. In the case of product recall, the batch number stamped on the pack or bottle of material is the identification that is needed.

To understand how important batch recording has become, consider the regulations within the European Union. The EU requires that each batch of pharmaceutical material imported into the EU must be accompanied by a batch certificate. This must contain the testing specifications of the product, analytical methods and test results, statements that indicate that it conforms to current Good Manufacturing Procedures (cGMP), and sign-off by a company official.

3.4.2   Batch Level

In the SAP system, the batch number can be determined at different levels. This determination needs to made early in any implementation project. Batches can be determined at client level, plant level, and material level.

Client Level

If the batch level is configured at the client level, then the batch number can only be assigned once throughout the whole client. One batch number will exist for one batch regardless of material or location. There is no issue when batches are moved from plant to plant because the batch number would not exist in the receiving plant. This is a level where, in some countries, batch numbers are unique to a company and not to a material.

Plant Level

Batch level at the plant level is the SAP default. This means that the batch is unique to a plant and material but not applicable across the company. Therefore, a batch of material at a different plant within the company could have the same batch number with different characteristics. When transferring batch material from one plant to another, the batch information is not transferred, and the batch information needs to be re-entered at the receiving plant.

Material Level

Batch level at the material level means that the batch number is unique to a material across all plants. Therefore, if a batch of material is transferred to another plant, the batch information will be adopted in the new plant without re-entering the batch information because that batch number could not have been duplicated for that material in the receiving plant.

3.4.3   Changing the Batch Level

The batch level should be decided on early in any implementation. However, due to unforeseen circumstances, you may need to change the batch level.

The batch level can be changed using Transaction OMCE. The navigation path is IMG • Logistics - General • Batch Management • Specify Batch Level and Activate Status Management • Batch Level.

In this transaction, the level can be changed between client, plant, and material. When changing the batch level, and prior to configuration, be aware of the following:

▶ To change the batch level from plant level to material level, the material has to be batch-managed in all plants.

▶ Any change in batch level requires significant testing before transporting the change to a production system.

▶ Batch-level configuration affects batch-status management functionality.

3.4.4   Batch-Status Management

Batch-status management is simply the ability to make a batch either restricted or unrestricted. The transaction for this configuration is OMCS, or you can use the navigation path, IMG • Logistics - General • Batch Management • Specify Batch Level and Activate Status Management • Batch Status Management.

The configuration is simply an option to make batch-status management active or not active. However, the batch-level configuration does affect the way in which batch-status management works, as described here:

▶ If the batch-level configuration occurs at the material or client level, then the batch-status management is effective for all plants in the client

▶ If the batch-level configuration is at the plant level, then you can configure the system to determine at which plant you require batch-status management to be active. The transaction to configure this is OMCU and can be accessed using the navigation path, IMG • Logistics - General • Batch Management • Specify Batch Level and Activate Status Management • Plants with Batch Status Management

3.4.5 Initial Batch Status

After defining the batch-status management, there is additional configuration that may be important to an SAP customer. If you have configured that batch-status management is active and that each batch will have a restricted or an unrestricted status, it is possible to configure the system to set the initial status when a batch is created.

This transaction code to set the initial status of a batch to restricted or unrestricted status is OMAB. The navigation path is IMG • Logistics - General • Batch Management • Specify Batch Level and Activate Status Management • Initial Status of New Batch.

The configuration for this is based on the material type. For example, it is possible to configure for all semi-finished goods, material type HALB, to have a batch status of restricted when the batches are created for materials with that material type.

3.4.6 Batch-Number Assignment

The batch number range is predefined in SAP. The predefined range 01 is defined as 0000000001 to 9999999999. The number range object for this is BATCH_CLT. This can be changed in configuration using Transaction OMAD or by using the navigation path IMG • Logistics - General • Batch Management • Batch Number Assignment • Maintain Internal Batch Number Assignment Range.

There are two configuration steps that can be carried out if the customer requires it. First, you can allow the batch number to be assigned internally using the internal number range. To configure this, use Transaction OMCZ or the navigation path, IMG •

LOGISTICS - GENERAL • BATCH MANAGEMENT • BATCH NUMBER ASSIGNMENT • ACTIVATE INTERNAL BATCH NUMBER ASSIGNMENT • ACTIVATE BATCH NUMBER ASSIGNMENT.

Second, you can configure the system to allow the automatic numbering of batches on a goods receipt with account assignment. The navigation path for this transaction is IMG • LOGISTICS - GENERAL • BATCH MANAGEMENT • BATCH NUMBER ASSIGNMENT • ACTIVATE INTERNAL BATCH NUMBER ASSIGNMENT • INTERNAL BATCH NUMBER ASSIGNMENT FOR ASSIGNED GOODS RECEIPT.

3.5 Serial Number Data

As we have just discussed, some materials are grouped in batches. If we want to identify a single unit of material uniquely, then the unit would have to be identified by a serial number.

3.5.1 What Is a Serial Number?

A serial number is given to a unique item to identify it and to record information about it. The serial number is different from a batch number: While a batch number is given to a number of items, a serial number is unique to one. The serial number is most often found to refer to equipment, such as motors, lathes, drills, or vacuums. For the SAP customer, there may be many areas where serial numbers need to be addressed. If the SAP customer produces items that should be uniquely defined, then serial numbers may be used. If that customer uses machines in production, it may regularly purchase maintenance items that are serialized. The Plant Maintenance functionality frequently uses serial numbers because the functionality includes use data for equipment that is most often serialized.

3.5.2 Serial Number Profile

The serial number profile is created to define attributes for the serial number. The serial number profile is a four-character alphanumeric field defined in Transaction OIS2. The transaction can also be accessed using the navigation path, IMG • PLANT MAINTENANCE AND CUSTOMER SERVICE • MASTER DATA IN PLANT MAINTENANCE AND CUSTOMER SERVICE • TECHNICAL OBJECTS • SERIAL NUMBER MANAGEMENT • DEFINE SERIAL NUMBER PROFILES • SERIAL NUMBER PROFILE.

The fields in Figure 3.15 show what is needed for configuring serial number profiles. The first field is the PROFILE, the four-character field, followed by a profile description. The EXISTREQ indicator, when not set, allows the user to create the serial number master record during a business transaction. If the indicator is set, the serial number master record must exist before the transaction can take place.

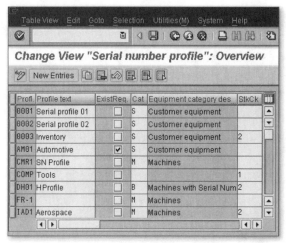

Figure 3.15 Configuration Screen for Serial Number Profiles

The CAT field is for the equipment category, a Plant Maintenance item, which defines the type of equipment for which this serial number profile is used. For example, A is for machines, while S is for customer equipment.

The STKCHK field is used to indicate whether the system should perform a stock check when the serial number is assigned.

The configuration of the serial number profile should be performed with the aid of a Plant Maintenance consultant, who will ensure that the customer's requirements for Plant Maintenance are taken into account.

3.5.3 Serializing Procedures

Serial numbers are used in many areas of SAP. Using Transaction OIS2, you can define whether a serial number is optional, required, or automatic for a number of serializing procedures. The navigation path for this transaction is IMG • PLANT MAINTENANCE AND CUSTOMER SERVICE • MASTER DATA IN PLANT MAINTENANCE AND CUSTOMER SERVICE • TECHNICAL OBJECTS • SERIAL NUMBER MANAGEMENT • DEFINE SERIAL NUMBER PROFILES • SERIALIZING PROCEDURES.

In Figure 3.16, the serial number profile 0001 is assigned a number of procedures. For each of these procedures, there are configuration items for serial number usage. The SERUSAGE field can be configured to be none, optional, obligatory, and automatic. The other field, EQREQ, enables serial numbers to be allowed with or without Plant Maintenance equipment.

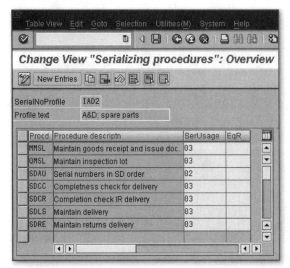

Figure 3.16 Serializing Procedures for Serial Number Profile 0001

The procedures that can be assigned to each serial number profile are defined in SAP. Table 3.1 identifies the procedure and its business meaning with relation to serial numbers (SN).

Procedure	Business Meaning
HUSL	Enables SN to be assigned in Handling Unit Management
MMSL	Enables SN to be assigned in Goods Receipt, Goods Issue, Stock Transfers, Stock Transport Orders, and Physical Inventory
PPAU	Enables SN to be assigned in Production & Refurbishment orders
PPRL	Enables SN to be assigned in Production & Refurbishment orders when they are released
QMSL	Enables SN to be assigned when entering the original value in a QM Inspection Lot
SDAU	Enables SN to be assigned in Sales Orders, Inquiries, and Quotations
SDCC	Enables SN to be assigned when performing completeness checks for deliveries
SDCR	Enables SN to be assigned when performing completeness checks for return deliveries
SDLS	Enables SN to be assigned for deliveries
SDRE	Enables SN to be assigned for return deliveries

Table 3.1 Business Procedures and Meaning for Serial Number Profiles

3.6 Business Examples – Master Data in Materials Management

In MM, there are a number of master data files that are fundamental to the functionality. The Material Master contains all of the information that is required for a material with regards to each area the material is used, for example, sales, finance, manufacturing, quality, and so on. The Vendor Master contains the information that is required for purchasing any item or service. The purchasing information record is used when purchasing specific items for a vendor. Batch data is held for each batch of material that is defined in the system. That data can be used to determine which batch is used or sold. Serial number data is used for items that need to be uniquely identified, for example, if each piece is purchased with a warranty.

3.6.1 Material Master Data

The Material Master data is comprised of data that relates to a number of different areas. For materials to be used successfully, the data has to be collected and entered into the Material Master record. Not only does the data have to be entered for those areas but also for the specific organizational areas: plants, storage locations, sales organizations, and so on. For example, a material cannot be purchased without the relevant purchasing data being entered.

Example

Prior to its SAP ERP implementation, an Irish beverage company had developed a process for creating new materials. When a finished good was developed, it had to be approved by a product board. After approval, the finished good then passed on to a product manager who collected all of the relevant information required for the manufacturing, inventory, sales, and finance systems. This process often took longer than expected, and goods had to be shipped without being recorded in all of the systems because information was still missing. When SAP ERP was implemented, the process was changed as management realized the product would not be shipped until the Material Master was created and that the current process was too slow. The company kept the role of the product board for approvals, but instead of the product manager entering the data, the individual departments entered the data relevant to their areas. Using this method, the departments became responsible if data was missing and the product could not be shipped.

3.6.2 Vendor Master Data

The Vendor Master record contains data that is used in purchasing. The Vendor Master has three distinct sections: general data, purchasing data, and accounting data. The general data has basic information on the vendor such as name, address, and telephone number. The purchasing data is entered for the vendor at a purchasing organizational level and includes control data required in purchasing, partner functions, and purchasing defaults. The accounting data is the financial data that is entered at the company code level. This data includes tax information, bank details, and payment methods.

Example

A specialty chemicals manufacturer in New Mexico operated a simple production process where it produced five finished goods. The purchasing process was also simple with fewer than 50 items purchased. There were fewer than 40 vendors, and each vendor's information was kept on an index card in the purchasing clerk's office. The purchasing process was not automated, and POs were handwritten on carbonated preprinted forms. A larger specialty chemicals company from Alabama purchased the New Mexico manufacturer. As an SAP customer, the company deployed its standard functionality at the New Mexico location, which meant that the purchasing data had to be re-created in SAP ERP. The information on the index cards was so sparse that the company sent a questionnaire to vendors to get enough basic information to create Vendor Master records in the SAP ERP system.

3.6.3 Purchasing Data

The Material Master will contain some purchasing data at the purchasing organization level, which means that the material data may be different for one purchasing organization to the next. However, it is the purchasing information record that contains data to a unique combination of vendor and material. This means that the same material can be purchased from two different vendors, and the price offered by each vendor may be different.

Example

The headquarters for an oil company in Texas implemented only the Finance and Purchasing components, rather than the full suite that was deployed at the oil facilities. At the head office, the majority of purchases were for services, office equipment, and office supplies. Before the SAP ERP implementation, the purchasing function at the head office was performed by two purchasing clerks who filled in POs once a week after collecting requisitions from employees. Vendors offered no price incentives, and purchasing clerks made no attempt to shop around different vendors for better prices. As part of the implementation, the purchasing clerks were asked to review every material purchased at the head office and identify whether it was a material that could be offered out for a competitive bid. The review found that 80% of items purchased at the head office could be put out to bid. Over the next six months, the company sent out RFQs and then selected the top two vendors for each item. The company created purchase information records with pricing information for the vendor and material combination, including price discounts and scale discounts.

3.6.4 Batch Management

Batch Management is used when items of the same material number have the same attributes and can be identified using those attributes. For example, for a chemical company, a batch of chemicals will be made at one time and that batch will have values for a number of attributes that will be different from a different batch. The batch values can determine whether a batch is suitable to be used, sold, or stored in a certain way.

Example

A New Jersey manufacturer of paint additives had used a desktop-based program to record information about the batches. As a part of the SAP ERP implementation, the company moved the information from the desktop program to Batch Master records as the product was produced. The additives manufacturer won business with a new customer and started supplying product to the customer. However, the product was returned because the company failed to identify an expiry date for the batch. This was one data element that had never been recorded for each batch, so to keep the new customer, the company had to develop a formula to determine an expiry date for each batch. The company developed the formula, which was calculated and entered by production personnel at the end of each batch run.

3.6.5 Serial Numbers

A serial number is used to uniquely distinguish items of the same material number. This is important for companies that use materials that are purchased with a warranty or materials that must be uniquely identified. For example, aircraft parts are serialized so that maintenance personnel can record data against that serialized part and replace it when it has performed a certain number of cycles.

Example

A Spanish vacuum cleaner manufacturer used a motor in its machines that was made by a subsidiary company. The vacuum cleaners were of good quality and had a high level of customer satisfaction for many years. The company implemented SAP ERP in its Spanish plants, and a year later, sold its motor manufacturing plant to a Chinese company who moved production overseas. The vacuum cleaner manufacturer continued to source its motors from China because the price per unit was less than 50% of what it was costing from its own subsidiary. After a few months, the company found that customer complaints had increased dramatically. Consumers complained that the vacuum would lose suction and then stop completely. The vacuum manufacturer examined the returned machines and found that the motors were defective. After contacting the vendor, the company found that motors within a certain serial number range could be subject to overheating. The problem for the vacuum manufacturer was that it did not serialize the motor in its system, so the manufacturer could not identify which vacuum had the defective motor. After this incident, the company started to serialize a number of key components to ensure that if it had defective parts in the future, the company would be able to quickly pass on the information to consumers.

3.7 Summary

This chapter has described the major elements that define the master files of the Material Master. Many companies use batch management and serial numbers, so it is important that if you are involved with these that you understand how each works. Both batches and serial numbers are important to industries such as pharmaceutical and chemical, where each batch or serial number may have very different characteristics.

Let's move on to Chapter 4, Part 1 of the Material Master Data coverage.

Data entered into the Material Master is extremely important to an SAP implementation. Incorrect or missing data can cause companies to halt operations. Understanding how to enter correct data into the Material Master is vital for all SAP components.

4 Material Master Data – Part 1

In the first of these two chapters on the Material Master file, we will show the basic structure of the Material Master and the data-entry screens for Basic Data, Classification, Purchasing, Forecasting, Work Scheduling, Sales Organization, and General Sales data. It is important that you understand what a field in the Material Master means and how it relates to the data in a customer's legacy system.

Data conversion is not often treated with the importance that it deserves. The earlier in the implementation the team works on understanding the data in the SAP master files, the more time there will be to correctly convert legacy data and create data that is not in the customer's legacy files.

Prior to the start of any implementation, it is a good idea for customers to start parallel projects of cleansing their legacy data and eradicating duplicate and redundant records. Often companies have many duplicate records for one vendor, which should be identified and corrected before any data is loaded into SAP.

The customer may have more than one legacy system and may be combining master data from several systems to be loaded into SAP. The more complicated the data-rationalization task, the earlier this needs to begin to ensure successful loading of data into SAP before an implementation goes live.

Before entering the first material into the Material Master, a certain amount of configuration must be completed. First, we will look at the industry sector assignment.

4.1 Industry Sector

The industry sector has to be assigned for each Material Master record added. In general, SAP customers use just one industry sector for all their Material Master records, but this is not mandatory.

To configure the industry sectors, use Transaction OMS3 or the navigation path, IMG • Logistics - General • Material Master • Field Selection • Define Industry Sectors and Industry Sector-Specific Screen Selection.

The SAP system has four predefined industry sectors:

- ▶ **P:** For the pharmaceutical sector.
- ▶ **C:** For the chemical industry sector.
- ▶ **M:** For the mechanical engineering sector.
- ▶ **A:** For plant engineering and construction.

Defining a new industry sector requires the choice of a single character for the industry sector and a description. The new industry sector needs to be linked to a field reference. This field reference is defined in Transaction OMS9 or by using navigation path, IMG • Logistics - General • Material Master • Field Selection • Maintain Field Selection for Data Screens.

The field reference is made up of a list of Material Master fields and whether the individual field is Hidden, Displayed, Optional Entry, or Required Entry. Exercise careful consideration when configuring a new field reference.

4.2   Material Type

A material type is group of materials with similar attributes. The material type allows the management of different materials in a uniform manner. For example, the material type can group together materials that are purchased or produced internally, or are non-valuated. SAP delivers a set of standard predefined material types, but your clients may decide to create their own material types.

4.2.1   Standard Material Types

A number of SAP-delivered material types can be used without having to configure any new material types. The standard material types are defined in this section, but your clients may decide to configure their own. This does come with the added complication of additional configuration steps and testing.

CONT – KANBAN Container

This is a material type delivered by SAP to use for creating KANBAN containers. A KANBAN container is used in the KANBAN container-based system sometimes implemented at a manufacturing plant for just-in-time (JIT) replenishment of parts on the production line. The KANBAN container is used to transport the material from the supply area to the manufacturing location. These materials used as KAN-BAN containers only have the basic data view.

DIEN – Services

Services are either internally supplied or externally supplied by a vendor. Service Material Master records will not have storage information. The services can involve activities such as consulting, garbage collection, or legal services.

ERSA – Spare Parts

Spare parts are materials used for equipment maintenance in the plant. The material is purchased and stored like any other purchased item, but a spare part is not sold and therefore does not contain sales information. If a maintenance item is sold, then it should use a different material type such as a trading good.

FERT – Finished Good

A finished good is a material that has been manufactured by some form of production from items, such as raw materials. The finished good is not purchased, so it does not contain any purchasing information.

FHMI – Production Resources/Tools (PRT)

Production resources/tools (PRTs) are purchased and used by the plant maintenance department. This material type is assigned to items used in the maintenance of plant equipment, such as test machines, drill bits, or calibrating tools. The material type for PRTs does not contain sales information because the PRTs are not purchased to sell. In addition, PRTs are only managed on a quantity basis.

HALB – Semi-Finished Goods

Semi-finished products are often purchased and then completed and sold as finished goods. The semi-finished products could come from another part of the company or from a vendor. The semi-finished material type allows for purchasing and work scheduling but not sales.

HAWA – Trading Goods

Trading goods are generally materials that are purchased from vendors and sold. This kind of material type only allows purchasing and sales information because there are no internal operations carried out on these materials. An example of a trading good can be found at many computer manufacturers, where they sell their manufactured goods (computers) but also sell printers and routers. These trading goods are not manufactured by the company but bought from the manufacturer and sold alongside their own manufactured computers.

HERS – Manufacturer Parts

Manufacturer parts are materials that can be supplied by different vendors that use different part numbers to identify the material. This type of material can be found in many retail stores. For example, a DIY retail store may sell a three-step ladder for $20, but the ladder can be made by three different manufacturers, each of which have a different part number. The store will then have three part numbers for the ladder, but the consumer will not be aware of this fact.

HIBE – Operating Supplies

Operating supplies are vendor-purchased and used in the production process. This HIBE material type can contain purchasing data but not sales information. This type of product includes lubricants, compressed air, or solder.

IBAU – Maintenance Assembly

Maintenance assembly is not an individual object but a set of logical elements to separate technical objects into clearly defined units for plant maintenance For example, a car can be a technical object, and the engine, transmission, axles, and so on are the maintenance assemblies. An IBAU material type contains basic data and classification data.

KMAT – Configurable Material

Configurable materials form the basis for variant configuration. The KMAT material type is used for all materials that are variant configuration materials. A material of this type can have variables that are determined by the user during the sales process. For example, automotive equipment produced by a manufacturer may have variable attributes that each car manufacturer needs to be different for each car, such as length of chain or height of belt.

LEER – Empties

Empties are materials consisting of returnable transport packaging and can be subject to a nominal deposit. Empties can be made from several materials grouped together in a bill of material (BOM) that is assigned to a finished material. Examples of empties include crates, drums, bottles, or pallets.

LEIH – Returnable Packaging

Reusable packaging material is used to pack finished goods to send to the customer. When the finished good is unpacked, the customer is obliged to return the returnable packaging material to the vendor.

NLAG – Non-Stock Material

The non-stock material type is used for materials that are not held in stock and not inventoried. These materials can be called consumables and include items such as maintenance gloves, safety glasses, or grease. Items like this are purchased when needed.

PIPE – Pipeline Material

The pipeline material type is assigned to materials that are brought into the production facility by pipeline. Materials like this are not planned for because they are always at hand. This type of material type is used, for example, for oil, water, electricity, or natural gas.

ROH – Raw Materials

Raw material is purchased material that is fed into the production process and may result in a finished good. There is no sales data for a raw material because it is not sold. If the company wanted to classify a material that would normally be a raw material, then it should be considered a trading good.

UNBW – Non-Valuated Material

The non-valuated material type is similar to the NLAG (non-stock material) except that the non-valuated material is held by quantity and not by value. Examples of this are often seen in plant maintenance, where materials are extremely important to the plant equipment but of little or no other value. Therefore, the plant maintenance department will monitor inventory to allow for planned purchases.

VERP – Packaging Material

Unlike LEER (empties), the packaging material type is for materials that are packaged but are free of charge to the customer in the delivery process. This does not mean that the packaging material has no value; often, the packaging material has a value, and a physical inventory is recorded.

WETT – Competitive Products

The sales department uses WETT to monitor competitor's goods. The material type is used to identify these types of products. Only basic data is held for these materials.

> **Note**
>
> In addition to these material types, a number of additional material types are used for SAP Retail customers. These types include FRIP (perishables), NOF1 (non-food items), FOOD (food except perishables), FGTR (beverages), MODE (apparel), VKHM (additional items, such as clothes labels), and WERB (advertising material).

4.2.2 Configuring Material Types

The material type can be configured in Transaction OMS2 using the navigation path, IMG • LOGISTICS - GENERAL • MATERIAL MASTER • BASIC SETTINGS • MATERIAL TYPES • DEFINE ATTRIBUTES FOR MATERIAL TYPE.

The method for creating a new material type is to select an existing material type and copy to a new one. Copying from an existing material type reduces the amount of configuration required. Figure 4.1 shows the configurable fields for the material type. The four-character MATERIAL TYPE should always start with a "Z" for a user-defined material type.

After a new material type is configured, the valuation areas defined for that material type can also be configured. The valuation area is the level at which material is valuated. The valuation area can be defined as being at the plant level or the company code level. A number of valuation areas can be defined for a material type, as shown in Figure 4.2.

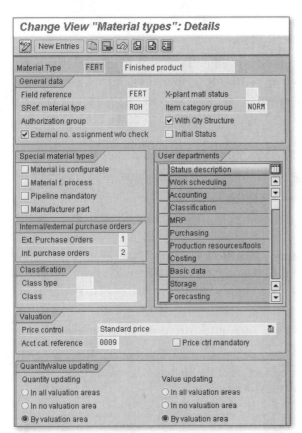

Figure 4.1 Configurable Fields for Material Type

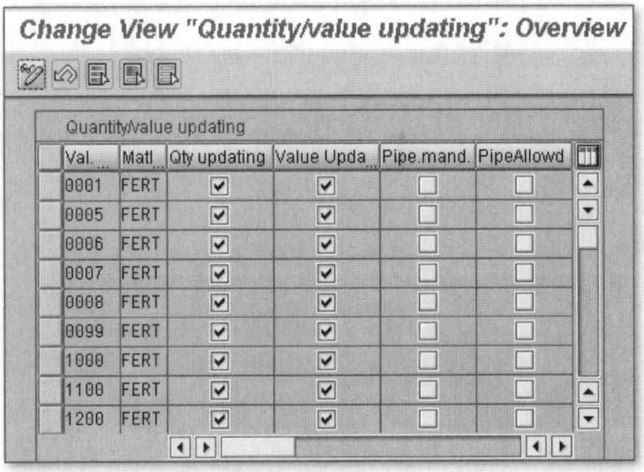

Figure 4.2 Valuation Areas for Material Type

The four fields that can be configured for the valuation area (VAL. AREA)/material type (MATL TYPE) combination are the following:

▶ QTY UPDATING: This field can specify whether a material assigned this material type can be managed on a quantity basis for this valuation area.

▶ VALUE UPDATE: This field can specify whether a material assigned this material type can be managed on a value basis for this valuation area.

▶ PIPE.MAND: This field can specify whether a material assigned this material type is subject to mandatory pipeline handling for this valuation area.

▶ PIPEALLOWD: This field can specify whether a material assigned this material type is allowed to be subject to pipeline handling for this valuation area.

4.2.3 Changing a Material Type

The material type of a material may need to be changed. For example, if a raw material that has only been used for in-house production has a requirement to be sold, the material type may need to be changed from ROH to HAWA, (trading good).

There are a number of caveats regarding unrestricted material type changes as shown in Tables 4.1 and 4.2.

In addition, there are a number of caveats if the material has any stock, reservations, or purchasing documents against it.

Material with Old Material Type	Material with New Material Type
No price control specification	Can only allow standard price
PRT view maintained	PRT view must be maintained
Not a configurable material	Must not be a configurable material
Allows inspection plans	Must allow inspection plans
Material for process indicator	Must be the same setting
Manufacturer part indicator	Must be the same setting

Table 4.1 Changing a Material Type

Material with Old Material Type	Material with New Material Type
Stock value updated in GL account	Must be the same GL account
Quantity and value updating	Must be the same as previously
WM transfer request open	WM view must be maintained
Batch managed	Must be batch managed

Table 4.2 Changing a Material Type

4.3   Basic Data

The basic data screen is the initial screen that is displayed when a Material Master record is created. The basic data screen contains data that is common across the client, such as material description and basic unit of measure.

4.3.1   Creating a Material Master Record - Immediately

The Material Master record can be created in a number of different ways. The most common ways for a Material Master record to be created is via Transaction MM01 or via the navigation path, SAP MENU • LOGISTICS • MATERIALS MANAGEMENT • MATERIAL MASTER • MATERIAL • CREATE (GENERAL) • IMMEDIATELY.

Figure 4.3 shows the fields needed to initially create the record:

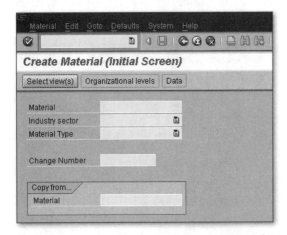

Figure 4.3   Initial Fields Required to Create Material Master Record

▶ MATERIAL: Leave blank for internal numbering, or enter a material number.

▶ INDUSTRY SECTOR: Enter the selected industry sector.

▶ MATERIAL TYPE: Enter a defined material type or a user-defined material type.

▶ CHANGE NUMBER (optional): Enter a change number if the customer is using Engineering Change Management.

▶ COPY FROM MATERIAL (optional): Enter a material number of a material that provides the information required for the new material.

4.3.2 Creating a Material Master Record - Schedule

If you decide to schedule the creation of the Material Master, you can use Transaction MM11 or use the navigation path, SAP MENU • LOGISTICS • MATERIALS MANAGEMENT • MATERIAL MASTER • MATERIAL • CREATE (GENERAL) • SCHEDULE.

This has the same entry fields as MM01, as shown in Figure 4.3, but it also has a field that requires the material user to enter a date on which the material is scheduled to be created.

4.3.3 Creating a Material Master Record – Special

This particular way of creating the Material Master record is to have the material type already defined. For example, if you want to create a Material Master record for the ROH material type (raw material), then you can use Transaction MMR1 or the navigation path, SAP MENU • LOGISTICS • MATERIALS MANAGEMENT • MATERIAL MASTER • MATERIAL • CREATE (SPECIAL) • RAW MATERIAL.

Table 4.3 shows the transactions for creating Material Masters for the various material types.

Material Type	Transaction
Raw materials (ROH)	MMR1
Semi-finished materials (HALB)	MMB1
Finished products (FERT)	MMF1
Operating supplies (HIBE)	MMI1
Trading goods (HAWA)	MMH1
Non-valuated material (UNBW)	MMU1
Non-stock material (NLAG)	MMN1
Packaging (VERP)	MMV1

Table 4.3 Transactions for Creating Materials by Material Type

Material Type	Transaction
Empties (LEER)	MML1
Services (DIEN)	MMS1
Configurable material (KMAT)	MMK1
Maintenance assembly (IBAU)	MMP1
Competitor product (WETT)	MMW1
Returnable packaging (LEIH)	MMG1

Table 4.3 Transactions for Creating Materials by Material Type (Cont.)

4.3.4 Organizational Levels

After the material type, industry sector, and external material number are entered (if applicable), a dialog box will show the views applicable to the particular material type. Users then can choose in which views they want to enter information.

After the views have been selected, a dialog box appears with the organizational levels required for this Material Master record, as shown in Figure 4.4.

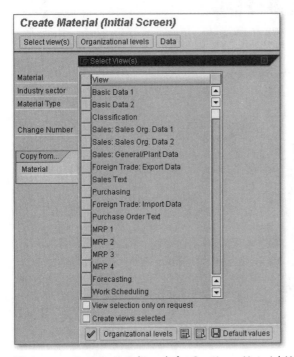

Figure 4.4 Organizational Levels for Creating a Material Master Record

The organizational levels relate to the level at which Material Master information is held. DISTR. CHANNEL is required for Sales and Distribution screens, WAREHOUSE NO. for Warehouse Management screens, and other items.

Figure 4.4 shows that the data entry user can enter the PLANT, STOR. LOCATION, SALES ORG., DISTR. CHANNEL, WAREHOUSE NO., and STORAGE TYPE. In the PROFILES section, the other two fields are MRP PROFILE for material requirements planning (MRP) and FORECAST PROF. for forecasting.

MRP Profile

The MRP profile is a key that provides a set of field values for MRP screens that save you from having to make data-entry decisions.

The MRP profile is not part of configuration and can be defined by authorized end users via Transaction MMD1 or through the navigation path, SAP MENU • LOGISTICS • MATERIALS MANAGEMENT • MATERIAL MASTER • PROFILE • MRP PROFILE • CREATE.

Figure 4.5 shows some of the fields that can be defaulted for the MRP profile.

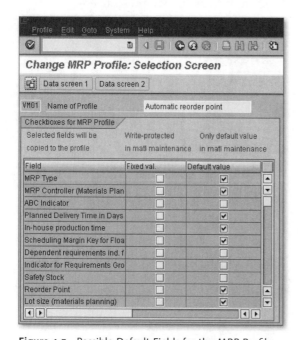

Figure 4.5 Possible Default Fields for the MRP Profile

The MRP profile allows you to highlight a field from the list of fields on the MRP screens. You can choose one of two options. The data from the field is entered into the Material Master either as a fixed value that cannot be overwritten or as a default value that can be changed. After you determine which fields are going to be part of the MRP key, the values need to be entered. The MRP profile can be changed using Transaction MMD2, or it can be deleted.

Forecast Profile

The forecast profile is very similar to the MRP profile because it is a key that provides a set of field values for the FORECASTING screen.

The forecast profile can be defined by authorized end users via Transaction MP80 or through the navigation path, SAP MENU • LOGISTICS • MATERIALS MANAGEMENT • MATERIAL MASTER • PROFILE • FORECAST PROFILE • CREATE.

4.3.5 Basic Data Screen

After the views have been selected and the organizational levels entered, the first screen that appears is the BASIC DATA screen, as shown in Figure 4.6.

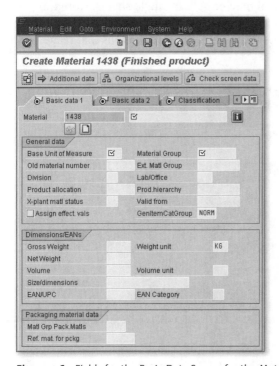

Figure 4.6 Fields for the Basic Data Screen for the Material Master

The Basic data screen allows data entry for non-organizational level fields. This screen does not require a plant or sales organization to be defined but allows the data entry user to enter basic information about the material. The mandatory fields on this screen, as defined by configuration, are the minimum information that can be added to create a Material Master. If the complete Material Master is created by a number of different departments, each entering its own information, then this basic data is used to enter material at the client level. The following sections describe the fields in the Basic data screen.

Material Description

The first field to be entered is the material description next to the Material field. We can add different descriptions of the material based on the language, with EN is English, DA as Danish, or NL as Dutch, for example. The material description is only 40 characters long, so it is good practice defining a material description policy. Abbreviations and standard wording should be used where possible.

Base Unit of Measure

The Base Unit of Measure field is the unit of measure that is the lowest level for the material. For example, sheet metal may be sold in single sheets, stored in pallets of sheets, and purchased by the truckload, but the base unit of measure may be a square foot. Figure 4.7 shows the unit of measure conversions that relate back to the base unit of measure.

Figure 4.7 Base Unit of Measure and Conversion Factors to Alternative Units of Measure

Material Group

The MATERIAL GROUP field reflects a method of grouping similar materials. The material group can be defined either by using classification or by configuration. The material group is important not only for searching for materials but also in other areas such as Purchasing. For example, a purchase information record can be created without a material number but must require a material group and a vendor. This material group/vendor purchase information record is used in production orders where in-process material is sent to vendors for outside processing.

The material group is configured in Transaction WG21 or through the navigation path, IMG • LOGISTICS – GENERAL • MATERIAL GROUP • CREATE MATERIAL GROUP.

You can also create a material group hierarchy. This is difficult and time-consuming, so the best practice is to use an existing hierarchical material structure already defined in the implementing organization.

Changes to the material group hierarchy after the project has been implemented can be very complicated and have far-reaching implications. Therefore, it is important to define material groups and hierarchies early in the project.

Old Material Number

The OLD MATERIAL NUMBER is useful to customers because it allows them to enter a number that the material was referred to in legacy systems or systems that they are still interfacing with SAP. This field is 18 characters in length. For example if a company is using a legacy warehouse system for shipping material, the material number used on that system could be entered into the OLD MATERIAL NUMBER field in SAP.

Division

Each material can only be assigned to one division, primarily at a sales-and-distribution organizational level, which is entered in the DIVISION field. It can be used to distinguish different areas of the distribution channel. The division allows a company to organize its sales structure to work with groups of similar materials. Divisions can be configured using Transaction VOR2 or via the navigation path, IMG • SALE AND DISTRIBUTION • MASTER DATA • DEFINE COMMON DIVISIONS.

Laboratory/Design Office

The LAB/OFFICE field is defined to be the laboratory or design office that is responsible for the material. It is used more frequently in PP to identify the persons responsible for a BOM. The field can be configured using the navigation path,

IMG • Logistics – General • Material Master • Settings for Key Fields • Define Laboratories/Offices.

Cross-Plant Material Status

The material status can be entered in a number of areas. The cross-plant material status (X-Plant Matl Status) field on the Basic Data screen allows the data entry user to enter a status that will be valid across the client. The material statuses are defined using Transaction OMS4 or via the navigation path, IMG • Logistics – General • Material Master • Settings for Key Fields • Define Material Statuses.

A two-character field defines the material status. The user can configure new material statuses. The material status shown in Figure 4.8 is user-defined and shows the process areas where either a warning message is given, A, or an error message, B.

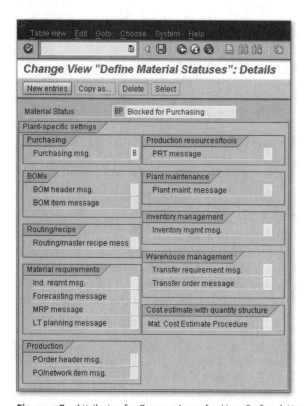

Figure 4.8 Attributes for Process Areas for User-Defined Material Status

Product Hierarchy

The product hierarchy is used in the SD area for analyses and price determination. The PROD.HIERARCHY field is an alphanumeric character string that groups together materials by combining different characteristics. In standard SAP, the product hierarchy can have up to three levels. Levels one and two have five characters each, and level three has eight. The product hierarchy is defined in Table T179 using Transaction V/76.

General Item Category Group

The GENITEMCATGROUP field allows the system to automatically generate an item type in the sales document being created. This depends on the type of sales document and the general item category group. The item category group can be configured using the navigation path, IMG • SALES AND DISTRIBUTION • SALES • SALES DOCUMENTS • SALES DOCUMENT ITEMS • DEFINE ITEM CATEGORY GROUPS.

Dimensions

This section of the BASIC DATA screen enables you to enter information in the GROSS WEIGHT, NET WEIGHT, and VOLUME fields. The SIZE/DIMENSIONS text field allows a text description that may be required on a document. The dimensions of material may be relevant to shipping companies when they are deciding how to pack and ship material. The dimensions may determine how the material is to be shipped.

EAN/UPC

The European Article Number (EAN) is assigned by the manufacturer of the particular material. The EAN identifies the manufacturer uniquely. In the United States, the equivalent to the EAN is the Universal Product Code (UPC). An SAP customer can configure EANs to be used internally.

Some configuration items can be found for EAN/UPC items using the navigation path, IMG • LOGISTICS - GENERAL • MATERIAL MASTER • SETTINGS FOR KEY FIELDS • INTERNATIONAL ARTICLE NUMBERS (EANs):

- Internal and external number ranges for EAN (Transaction W4EN)
- Number ranges for perishables for EAN (four-digit and five-digit)
- Prefixes for EAN/UPCs
- Attributes for EAN/UPCs

The following fields are not displayed in Figure 4.6 but can be displayed depending on how the screen layout is configured. Each of your client's Material Master screens may appear slightly different.

Product/Inspection Memo and Industry Standard Description

These fields are for information only. The PRODUCT/INSPECTION field allows you to enter a product or inspection memo for the material. The INDUSTRY STANDARD field allows the entry of the industry standard description of the material. If there is an International Organization for Standardization (ISO) or American National Standards Institute (ANSI) standard name for the material, then this can be added.

Basic Material

In the BASIC DATA screen, THE BASIC MATERIAL field allows a basic material to be chosen that the material being entered can be grouped under. The BASIC MATERIAL field has no specific control function but is often used in custom reports where end users want to see the activity of material at a basic material level. The basic material is found in Table TWSPR.

The basic material can be configured using the navigation path, IMG • LOGISTICS - GENERAL • MATERIAL MASTER • SETTINGS FOR KEY FIELDS • DEFINE BASIC MATERIALS.

Dangerous Goods (DG) Indicator Profile

This field is defined in the SAP Environment, Health, and Safety Management (SAP EHS Management) component. A DG indicator profile can be selected if the material being added is relevant for dangerous goods and for any documentation that accompanies that type of material.

The DG indicator profile can be configured in SAP EHS Management using the navigation path, IMG • ENVIRONMENTAL HEALTH AND SAFETY • DANGEROUS GOODS MANAGEMENT • DANGEROUS GOODS CHECKS • COMMON SETTINGS • SPECIFY INDICATOR PROFILES FOR MATERIAL MASTER.

Environmentally Relevant

This field is relevant for safety-data shipping. If this field is checked, then during the delivery-creation process, an output type of SDS (Safety Data Sheet) is selected via the SD condition table. The output for this delivery will include an MSDS and other documentation that may be defined in SAP EHS Management Product Safety.

Highly Viscous and In Bulk/Liquid

These two indicators do not have any control features in standard SAP. These can be used to influence the text or documentation of transportation documents, if custom reports are developed.

Design Drawing Fields

The DOCUMENT TYPE, DOCUMENT VERSION, PAGE NUMBER, DOCUMENT CHAPTER PAGE FORMAT, and NUMBER OF SHEETS fields are all used if there is a design document that is not controlled under the SAP Document Management System (DMS). If there is a design document that the users need to add to the Material Master, then these are the fields that need to be entered.

Cross-Plant Configurable Material

This field is used in variant configuration to identify a configurable material that is relevant for the client, not just one plant.

Material Group: Packaging Materials

A packaging material group can be entered for a material that groups similar packaging materials. The packaging material group can be found in Table TVEGR. The fields can be configured using the navigation path, IMG • LOGISTICS – GENERAL • HANDLING UNIT MANAGEMENT • BASICS • TECHNICAL BASICS • DEFINE MATERIAL GROUPS FOR PACKAGING MATERIALS.

4.4   Classification Data

The classification data is used primarily when searching for materials. The characteristic values entered into the classes for each material can be used to search for material with that set of characteristics. This functionality is very powerful when the customer has allocated significant effort into identifying and creating characteristics and classes, as well as entering the characteristic values for materials and other objects, such as vendors or batches.

4.4.1   Class Type

The CLASSIFICATION entry screen after the basic data entry allows information to be entered into user-defined characteristics and classes that can be assigned to a material.

Figure 4.9 shows that for this material, the material user can choose to find a class that has been assigned to one of four class types. The class type is a predefined grouping in SAP. When a class is created, it is assigned to a class type depending on its function. Figure 4.9 shows class type 001, which is a grouping of classes associated with a material. Class type 023 is for batch records. The class contains the characteristics for which values are entered. The material user can view the classes of a particular class type by choosing that class type in the screen, as shown in Figure 4.9. The classification system is defined in detail later in this book.

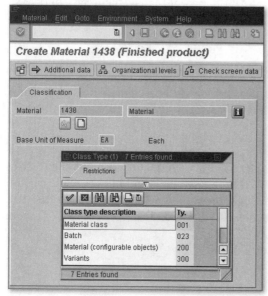

Figure 4.9   Class Types Accessible from the Material Master Data Entry Screen

4.4.2   Classes

After the class type has been chosen for the material, in this case, class type 001, individual classes can be selected. These classes have been set up to group together characteristics that describe the material further than do the fields in the Material Master.

4.4.3   Characteristics

The characteristics are the lowest level of the classification structure. Information or a value is entered in the characteristic level. In Figure 4.10, two classes, DETER-

GENT and 200, have been selected for this material. The characteristics for the first class, DETERGENT, are shown and are available for entering values.

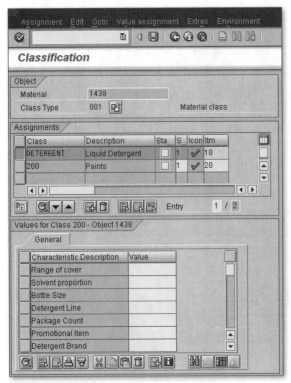

Figure 4.10 Two Classes Selected for Material, and Characteristics for One of the Classes

The characteristic can be configured to accept certain values or a range of values, and entry can be mandatory or optional.

4.5 Purchasing Data

The Purchasing data screen, shown in Figure 4.11, is displayed when the material being entered is assigned to a material type that allows purchasing. For example, it is normal to have a Purchasing data screen for trading goods (HAWA), raw materials (ROH), and PRT (FHMI). Some of the fields shown have already been described in other Material Master screens.

— For material types that allow purchasing.

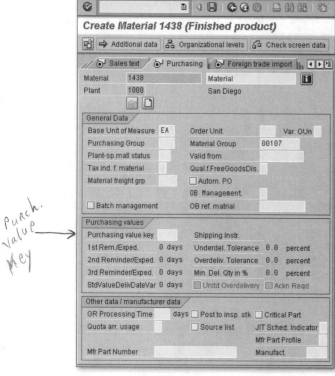

Purch. value key →

Figure 4.11 Purchasing Data Screen of the Material Master Creation Transaction

4.5.1 General Data

The GENERAL DATA area contains the various units of measure and other basic data that can be entered on the PURCHASING screen of the Material Master.

Base Unit of Measure

The BASE UNIT OF MEASURE field has been defaulted from the BASIC DATA screen and will be defaulted through to the other data screens. After a BASE UNIT OF MEASURE is entered, this will appear as the unit of measure for all instances. For example, if a material has a base unit of measure of kilograms (Kg), then this will be defaulted as the unit of measure for purchasing, warehousing, production, and so on. This will occur unless another unit of measure is entered in those screens, for example, if the PURCHASING UNIT OF MEASURE is entered as pounds (Lb).

Base units of measure.

[Order Unit]

→ coordination with Base unit of measure, or Blank

The purchasing ORDER UNIT of measure is the unit of measure that the material can be purchased in. Therefore, a material that has a BASE UNIT OF MEASURE of EACH (EA) may be purchased from a vendor in the ORDER UNIT OF CARTON (CAR). If the ORDER UNIT field is blank, then the BASE UNIT OF MEASURE is used as the purchasing ORDER UNIT of measure.

Variable Order Unit

Checking this field allows the purchasing unit of measure to be variable. The purchasing unit of measure can be changed for a PO or the source list.

Plant-Specific Material Status

The plant-specific material status (PLANT-SP.MATL STATUS) field on the PURCHASING screen uses the same status fields that are used for the X-PLANT MATL. STATUS field in the BASIC DATA screen shown earlier in Figure 4.6. The field in this screen defines the material status at the plant level.

Tax Indicator for Material

The TAX IND. F. MATERIAL field is used for the automatic determination of the tax code in purchasing. The tax code can be determined automatically by price determination using purchasing conditions.

Qualify for Free Goods Discount

This indicator (QUAL.F.FREEGOODSDIS.) specifies whether a material qualifies for a discount in kind. A value should appear if the material does qualify for a discount in kind from vendors.

(Material Freight Group) —

Provide Transportation info to transporters.

The MATERIAL FREIGHT GRP field is used to classify materials to provide transportation information to the forwarding agents and rail transportation companies.

The configuration for the freight groups and codes is completed in the transportation area of SD. The table containing this information is TMFG. The navigation path for configuring the freight groups is IMG • LOGISTICS EXECUTION • TRANSPORTATION • BASIC TRANSPORTATION FUNCTIONS • MAINTAIN FREIGHT CODE SETS AND FREIGHT CODES.

Automatic Purchase Order

The AUTOM. PO indicator allows the customer to have POs generated automatically when purchase requisitions are converted to POs. To make the generation automatic, a further indicator must be set in the Vendor Master record of the vendor associated with the PO.

Batch-Management Requirement Indicator

The BATCH MANAGEMENT indicator configures the material to allow batches to be created for the material. This indicator is found in screens where the batch information is required, such as the MRP screen.

4.5.2   Purchasing Value Key

The PURCHASING VALUE KEY field is configured to allow the entry of the purchasing values of tolerance limits; reminder days, which are the days elapsed before the vendor is contacted regarding the outstanding POs; or similar information by using one entry. The purchase value key information is found in Table T405. Figure 4.12 shows the purchasing value key (PUR.VAL.KEY) and the attributes that can be configured.

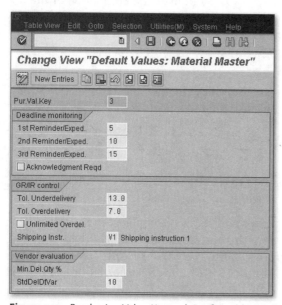

Figure 4.12   Purchasing Value Key and Configurable Attributes

The configuration of the purchase value key can be selected via the navigation path, IMG • MATERIALS MANAGEMENT • PURCHASING • MATERIAL MASTER • DEFINE PURCHASING VALUE KEYS.

Deadline Monitoring – Reminders

— LeTTeas To Vendor - coRRespondeie.

In the reminder fields, you enter the number of days at which you want reminder or urging letters or messages generated and sent to the vendor. If the figure entered is a positive number, then reminders are sent that many days after the due date given by the purchasing document. If the figure entered is a negative number, the reminder is sent that many days before the due date.

The number of days for the 1ST REMINDERS/EXPED, 2ND REMINDER/EXPED, and 3RD REMINDER/EXPED fields are used from the purchase information record. If there is no record, then information in the Material Master record is used.

Deadline Monitoring – Acknowledgement Required

If the ACKNOWLEDGMENT REQD indicator is checked, then the vendor is expected to supply an acknowledgement that it has received the purchasing document.

GR/IR Control – Under-Delivery Tolerance

In this field, the customer can enter a percentage figure for the under-delivery tolerance (TOL. UNDERDELIVERY) for this material. For instance, if the tolerance is 13%, then on a PO to a vendor for 20 units, the customer will accept a delivery for 18 units (10%) but not 17 units (15%).

GR/IR Control – Over-Delivery Tolerance

In this field, the customer can enter a percentage figure for the over-delivery tolerance (TOL. OVERDELIVERY) for this material. For example, if the tolerance is 7%, then on a PO to a vendor for 340 units, the customer will accept a delivery for 363 units (6.8%) but not 364 units (7.1%).

GR/IR Control – Unlimited Over-Delivery Allowed

The UNLIMITED OVERDEL. indicator allows the customer to accept any over-delivery from the vendor. This may not be acceptable for some materials and some vendors, so the purchasing department should understand the ramifications of the unlimited over-delivery.

GR/IR Control – Shipping Instructions

The SHIPPING INSTR. field allows a shipping instruction indicator to be chosen. The instructions regarding shipping and packaging requirements are sent to the vendor if configured. The shipping instruction indicator is found in Table T027A and configured via the navigation path, IMG • MATERIALS MANAGEMENT • PURCHASING • MATERIAL MASTER • DEFINE SHIPPING INSTRUCTIONS.

Vendor Evaluation – Minimum-Delivery Quantity Percentage

In this field (MIN.DEL.QTY %), you can enter the minimum percentage of the PO quantity that must be delivered for the goods receipt to be included in the vendor evaluation. This field prevents the vendor from receiving a good score for on-time delivery when the delivery quantity was insufficient.

[handwritten margin note: Vendor eval? include?]

Vendor Evaluation – Standardizing Value for Delivery-Time Variance

The value is entered to determine how many days from the planned delivery date will constitute 100% variance for vendor evaluation. If the entry in this field is 10, then the vendor evaluation system calculates that the vendor will receive a 100% variance if the PO is delivered 10 or more days after the expected delivery date.

4.5.3   Other Data/Manufacturer Data

The OTHER DATA/MANUFACTURER DATA section on the PURCHASING screen, as shown earlier in Figure 4.11, contains other data required for the purchasing view of the Material Master.

Goods-Receipt Processing Time in Days

The GR PROCESSING TIME refers to the number of working days required after receiving the material for any quality inspection and movement into storage.

Post to Inspection Stock

The POST TO INSP. STK indicator allows the user to indicate whether the material is subject to inspection and the material needs to post to inspection stock.

Critical Part

The CRITICAL PART indicator is only used in inventory sampling and is for information purposes only. Discuss with the customers how or if they need to use this indicator.

check mark required
a source list
before PO.

Source List

The SOURCE LIST indicator is important to the purchasing department. If this indicator is checked, there is a requirement to maintain a source list for procurement for the plant. The source list has to have been created before a PO can be entered. Maintenance of source lists is described more fully later in this book.

Quota Arrangement Usage

The QUOTA ARR. USAGE field is a key that defines how quota arrangements are used in purchasing. The information for the quota-arrangement usage key is found in Table TMQ2 and configured via the navigation path, IMG • MATERIALS MANAGEMENT • PURCHASING • QUOTA ARRANGEMENT • DEFINE QUOTA ARRANGEMENT USAGE. Figure 4.13 shows the purchasing functions that can be assigned to a quota arrangement usage key.

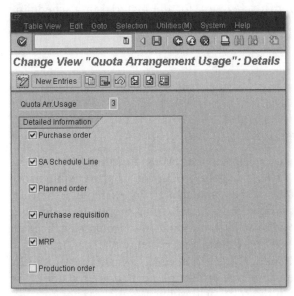

Figure 4.13 Purchasing Functions Assignable to a Quota Arrangement Usage Key

The quota arrangement usage key controls how the total order quantity is calculated in the quota arrangement and which source of supply is determined for the material. The key can be configured for the following purchasing functions:

▶ PURCHASE ORDER: Quantity of the material ordered is included in the quota arrangement.

▶ PURCHASE REQUISITION: Total quantity requested in purchase requisitions for this material is included.

▶ SCHEDULING AGREEMENT: Quantity scheduled in delivery schedules for this material is included.

▶ PLANNED ORDER: Quantity planned in planned orders for this material is included.

▶ MRP: Planned orders and purchase requisitions created by MRP are included in the quota arrangement.

▶ PRODUCTION ORDER: Quantity of all production orders for this material is included.

Item Relevant to JIT Delivery Schedules

The JIT SCHED. INDICATOR determines whether the system can generate a JIT delivery schedule, as well as the forecast schedules, for the material in a scheduling agreement.

4.5.4 Manufacturer Parts

This section includes the MFR PART NUMBER and name of the manufacturer (MANUFACT.).

Manufacturer Part Number

This field is part of the Manufacturer Part Number (MPN) functionality. The vendor who supplies a material that is used in your production or plant maintenance may be the supplier of the part but not the manufacturer. For example, if there are a number of manufacturers that produce oil filters that fit a shop-floor lathe, your company may require that the vendor sell you a specific filter from a specific manufacturer. In turn, that manufacturer may make better quality filters at its plant in Latvia than at its plants in Latin America. Therefore, you as a customer can specify that information with a specific manufacturer part number to your vendor. The way to store that information is in the MPN field in the Material Master.

Manufacturer

This is the manufacturer corresponding to the MPN number that has been entered in that field.

4.5.5 Foreign Trade Data

This section examines the fields in the FOREIGN TRADE IMPORT section of Figure 4.14.

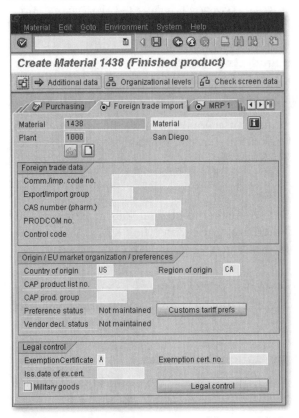

Figure 4.14 Foreign Trade Data Screen of the Material Master Creation Transaction

Commodity Code/Import Code Number for Foreign Trade

This field relates to the harmonized system for the description and coding of merchandise. If selected, the commodity code is used for statistical purposes and must be declared to the authorities for foreign trade transactions. Examples of this are INTRASTAT and EXTRASTAT in the European Union and the Automated Export System (AES) in the United States.

The commodity code is defined in Table T604 and is configured via the navigation path, IMG • SALES AND DISTRIBUTION • FOREIGN TRADE/CUSTOMS • BASIC DATA FOR FOREIGN TRADE • DEFINE COMMODITY CODES/IMPORT CODE NUMBERS BY COUNTRY.

Export/Import Group

This four-character field is a grouping for similar materials based on import and export attributes. The export/import group information can be found in Table TVFM and can be configured via the navigation path, IMG • SALES AND DISTRIBUTION • FOREIGN TRADE/CUSTOMS • BASIC DATA FOR FOREIGN TRADE • DEFINE MATERIAL GROUPS FOR IMPORT/EXPORT.

CAS Number for Pharmaceutical Products

This field is only required if the material has a CAS number that is a key to descriptions given by the World Health Organization (WHO) for customs-free materials.

The CAS number can be defined using Transaction VI36 or via the navigation path, IMG • SALES AND DISTRIBUTION • FOREIGN TRADE/CUSTOMS • SPECIFIC DATA FOR CUSTOMS PROCESSING • DEFINE CAS NUMBERS.

PRODCOM Number for Foreign Trade

This field is used to enter a PRODCOM number in EU countries. It allows for harmonized production statistics in the European Union. The PRODCOM numbers can be configured by using Transaction VE47.

Control Code for Consumption Taxes in Foreign Trade

This field is used for consumption taxes in foreign trade. The values can be updated in Table T604F.

4.5.6 Origin/EU Market Organization/Preferences

This section refers to the country of origin and region of origin fields. This is particularly relevant when using a Certificate of Origin (COO) document.

Country of Origin

A country of origin must be specified for export documentation. The material will often require a COO to be printed and included in the shipping documents. This field uses the country abbreviations in Table T005.

Region of Origin

The region of origin — a state in the United States, a county in the United Kingdom, a province in Australia, and so on — can provide more information for documentation of where the material originated. This field uses the region abbreviations from Table T005S.

CAP Product List Number

The CAP product list number is the number of the material as defined in the EU market products group list. The product list numbers are defined in Table T618M and can be configured using Transaction VI67.

CAP Product Group

Similar materials can be grouped under a CAP product group. This is for use in the European Union only. The product groups are defined in Table T618G and can be configured using Transaction VI69.

Preference Status

This field specifies whether the preference status is allowed at a plant level. The preference status identifies whether a material is eligible to receive any special or preferential treatment under the terms of a trade agreement between countries.

Vendor Declaration Status

This field specifies whether the vendor declaration status is allowed at the plant level. A vendor declaration states where the material was manufactured. The origin of the material is determined with this declaration.

4.5.7 Legal Control

The LEGAL CONTROL section relates to the details required for the exemption certificate.

Exemption Certificate/Certificate Number/Issue Date

This field is defined as an indicator for export-certification information. The values for the export-certification are given here:

▶ **A – Applied for:** The material does not require a license for import or export.

▶ **B – Accepted:** The material does not require a license for import or export because a certificate has been obtained.

▶ **C – Rejected:** Application for an exemption certificate has been rejected.

▶ **Blank – Not relevant:** The material has no exemption and requires an import or export license.

If the indicator has been set to "B," then the certificate number and the issue date need to be entered using the two fields, EXEMPTION CERT. NO. and ISS. DATE OF EX. CERT.

Military Goods

This field is for use only in Germany, due to weapons regulations. It can be used as an information-only field outside of Germany.

The next section examines the Material Master fields that are used for forecasting purposes.

4.6   Forecasting Data

The FORECASTING data screen shown in Figure 4.15 is displayed when the material being entered is assigned to a material type that is applicable to forecasting. A forecast profile can be entered at the organization level screen, if available. The forecasting data that can be entered into the Material Master comprises the initial calculated forecast and consumption values.

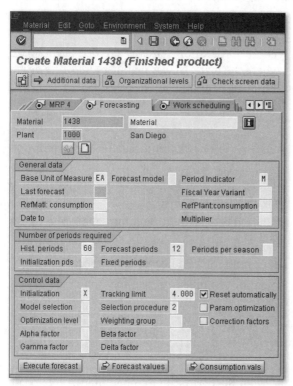

Figure 4.15   Forecast Screen of the Material Master Creation Transaction

4.6.1 General Data

The GENERAL DATA section on the FORECAST screen includes a number of fields such as the FORECAST MODEL to be used for the material, the PERIOD INDICATOR used for forecasting the material, and the FISCAL YEAR VARIANT.

Forecast Model

The forecast model calculates the requirements forecast for the material. The forecast models and analysis of forecasting in general will be discussed later in this book.

Period Indicator

The PERIOD INDICATOR field specifies the time period for which the consumption values are held for forecasting. The normal time period is one month, and this is the SAP default if this field is left blank.

Fiscal Year Variant

The FISCAL YEAR VARIANT is an accounting defined field, which describes the variant for the fiscal year, that is, the number of posting periods. The fiscal year variant can be seen in Table T009 and configured using Transaction OB37 or via the navigation path, IMG • FINANCIAL ACCOUNTING • FINANCIAL ACCOUNTING GLOBAL SETTINGS • FISCAL YEAR • MAINTAIN FISCAL YEAR VARIANT.

Reference Material for Consumption

If the material you are entering has no historical data from which to create a forecast, you can define a material that may be of similar characteristics to be used as reference material (REFMATL:CONSUMPTION). The system then uses the consumption figures for the reference material to create a forecast for the new material.

Reference Plant

The reference plant (REFPLANT:CONSUMPTION) is the plant from which to drive the consumption figures. This field is used for new materials and used in combination with the REFMATL:CONSUMPTION field. This field points to the plant from which you require the material to copy the consumption figures.

Date To

This is the furthest date to which the figures for the reference material should be taken. This field is used with the REFMATL:CONSUMPTION and the REFPLANT:CONSUMPTION fields.

Multiplier

The MULTIPLIER field is a number between 0 and 1 where the value relates to the percentage of the consumption of the reference material that should be used for the new material. For example, 1 means 100% of the reference-material consumption is used, whereas 0.6 indicates that 60% of the reference-material consumption is used.

4.6.2 Number of Periods Required

The fields in this section include the historical periods, forecast periods, and the number of periods per seasonal cycle.

Historical Periods

The number of historical periods entered into the HIST. PERIODS field is used to calculate the forecast. If it is blank, no periods are used.

Forecast Periods

The number entered in the FORECAST PERIODS field is the number of periods over which the forecast is calculated.

Number of Periods for Initialization

This number is for the historical values that you want to be used for the forecast initialization. If the INITIALIZATION PDS field is blank, no historical values are used to initialize the forecast.

Fixed Periods

The FIXED PERIODS field is used to avoid fluctuations in the forecast calculation or because production can no longer react to changed planning figures. The forecast will be fixed for the number of periods entered.

Number of Periods per Seasonal Cycle

If the customer uses a seasonal forecast model, then the PERIODS PER SEASON field can be used to define the number of periods that make up a season for this material.

4.6.3   Control Data

The CONTROL DATA section of the FORECASTING screen includes the INITIALIZATION indicator, TRACKING LIMIT, WEIGHTING GROUP, and MODEL SELECTION fields, among others.

Initialization Indicator

If the forecast needs to be initialized, then this indicator can be set to allow the system to initialize the forecast or allow manual initialization.

Tracking Limit

The TRACKING LIMIT field holds the value that specifies the amount by which the forecast value may deviate from the actual value. This figure can be entered to three decimal places.

Reset Forecast Model Automatically

If the RESET AUTOMATICALLY indicator is set, the forecast is reset if the tracking limit is exceeded.

Model Selection

This field is only active if the user did not enter a value in the FORECAST MODEL field. This means that the user requires the system to select a model automatically. To assist the system in choosing a forecast model, the MODEL SELECTION field can be set to one of the following three indicators:

- ▶ **T:** Examine for a trend.
- ▶ **S:** Examine for seasonal fluctuations.
- ▶ **A:** Examine for a trend and seasonal fluctuations.

Selection Procedure

The SELECTION-PROCEDURE field is used when the system is selecting a forecasting model. There are two selection procedures to select from:

- ▶ Procedure 1 performs a significance test to find the best seasonal or trend pattern.
- ▶ Procedure 2 carries out the forecast for all models and then selects the model with the smallest mean absolute deviation.

Indicator for Parameter Optimization

If the PARAM. OPTIMIZATION indicator is set, then the system will use the smoothing factors for the given forecast model.

Optimization Level

This indicator can be set to fine, middle, or rough. The finer the optimization level, the more accurate the forecast becomes but at the expense of processing time.

Weighting Group

This key is used with the weighted moving average forecast model. The weighting group can be configured via the navigation path, IMG • MATERIALS MANAGEMENT • CONSUMPTION-BASED PLANNING • FORECAST • WEIGHTING GROUPS FOR WEIGHTING MOVING AVERAGE.

Correction Factor Indicator

The CORRECTION FACTORS indicator allows the user to decide whether the forecast should include the corrector factors.

▶ ALPHA FACTOR: This is the smoothing factor for the basic value. If left blank, the default for the ALPHA factor is 0.2.

▶ BETA FACTOR: This is the smoothing factor for the trend value. If left blank, the default for the BETA factor is 0.1.

▶ GAMMA FACTOR: This is the smoothing factor for the seasonal index. If left blank, the default for the GAMMA factor is 0.3.

▶ DELTA FACTOR: This is the smoothing factor for the mean absolute deviation. If left blank, the default for the DELTA factor is 0.3.

This section has discussed in great detail the forecast data required for the Material Master record. The next section goes on to examine the data required for the WORK SCHEDULING screen.

4.7 Work Scheduling Data

The WORK SCHEDULING screen shown in Figure 4.16 allows the user to enter information relevant to a particular plant. The material may be used in many plants. Some of the fields in this screen will be defaulted from other entry screens, such as BASE UNIT OF MEASURE.

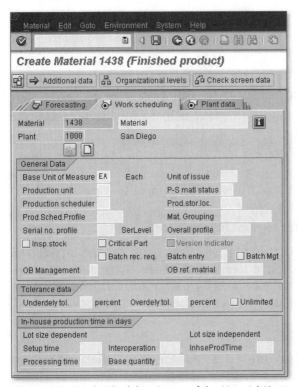

Figure 4.16 Work Scheduling Screen of the Material Master

4.7.1 General Data

The GENERAL DATA refers to the production unit, production storage location, and the production scheduling profile.

Production Unit

The PRODUCTION UNIT field reflects the unit of measure that is used for the material in the production process. If no production unit is entered, then the base unit of measure is assumed for the production unit of measure.

Production Scheduler

The PRODUCTION SCHEDULER has an important position in production and has to play many roles, including the following:

- Generating a collaborative production schedule
- Maximizing plant efficiency through the effective use of equipment and personnel
- Determining short-term labor requirements necessary to support the plan
- Creating a production plan that meets stated goals for on-time delivery
- Monitoring schedule adherence and schedule attainment to identify corrective actions for addressing shortfalls
- Working with management to report current order status and maintain order accuracy
- Coordinating project schedules and incorporating them into the commercial production schedule
- Identifying and resolving potential capacity constraints

In the Material Master, the production schedule is entered at each plant level. The field is a three-character string found in Table T024F. The production scheduler can be configured using Transaction OPJ9 or using the navigation path, IMG • PRODUCTION • SHOP FLOOR CONTROL • MASTER DATA • DEFINE PRODUCTION SCHEDULER.

Production Storage Location

This PROD.STOR.LOC field is the key to the production of a material in a plant. This is the storage location used as the issuing storage location for the backflushing process for a material that is a component for a finished good. If the material is a finished good, then this storage location is where the finished goods will be received after production.

Production Scheduling Profile

The production scheduling profile can be configured using Transaction OPKP or via the navigation path, IMG • PRODUCTION • SHOP FLOOR CONTROL • MASTER DATA • DEFINE PRODUCTION SCHEDULING PROFILE.

The PROD.SCHED.PROFILE field can be configured to perform automatic actions on either release or creation of a production or process order. The profile also provides configuration for capacity planning, availability check goods receipt, Batch Management, and transport and order type.

4.7.2   Tolerance Data

The TOLERANCE DATA section includes the fields that describe the under-delivery and over-delivery tolerances.

Under-Delivery Tolerance

The UNDERDELY TOL. field allows you to define an under-delivery tolerance percentage for the material. This means that if a goods receipt for a production order differs from the expected amount by more than the under-delivery tolerance, then the goods receipt will not be allowed.

Over-Delivery Tolerance

The OVERDELY TOL. field allows you to define an over-delivery tolerance percentage for the material. This means that if a goods receipt for a production order differs from the expected amount by more than the over-delivery tolerance, then the goods receipt will not be allowed.

Unlimited Over-Delivery

If the UNLIMITED indicator is set, then the goods receipt from a production order for this material will accept any amount over the expected goods receipt total.

4.7.3　In-House Production Time in Days

The fields in the IN-HOUSE PRODUCTION TIME IN DAYS section include SETUP TIME, PROCESSING TIME, BASE QUANTITY, and INTEROPERATION.

Setup Time

The SETUP TIME field is used to determine the dates for planned orders. The setup time is the number of days required to configure the work centers used in the production of the material. For example, if production for material ABC in a machine shop has finished, the equipment must have the parts used for material ABC removed. After the machines have been torn down, and the setup for the next production has been run, material XYZ will start. After the run for XYZ has finished, the machines will be torn down before the next production run. The setup time for material XYZ is the setup time plus the tear-down time.

This setup time does not take into account the quantity of the material being produced. The setup time may be a standard figure that has been calculated or negotiated. The field can be defined up to two decimal places for partial days.

Processing Time

The PROCESSING TIME field reflects the amount of time the material consumes at the work centers used in the production order. The processing time will take into account the BASE QUANTITY that is entered.

Base Quantity

This processing time is entered for the base quantity and can be defined up to three decimal places.

Interoperation Time

The INTEROPERATION field reflects the time that a material is in the state between operations in the production order. Many situations can make up the total interoperation time:

▶ **Move time:** Time that is accumulated as the material is moved from one work center to the next.

▶ **Wait time:** Time the material has to be left after the operation and before the move can take place on the material, for example, curing and temperature reduction.

▶ **Queue time:** Time that materials are queued for work centers that are bottlenecked or because of production delays in the operations. This queue time can be calculated by production staff.

▶ **Float before production:** The number of days between the start date or the production order and the scheduled start date (entered by the production scheduler).

▶ **Float after production:** The number of days from the end of the production order to the scheduled end date (entered by the production scheduler).

In-House Production Time

This field, shown as INHSEPRODTIME, is number of days that relates to all of the individual elements of in-house production, including floats and interoperation. This figure is used in the material-planning functionality and is lot size independent.

This section has discussed the data used to define the WORK SCHEDULING screen. The next section goes into detail with regards to the Material Master screen for sales organizational data.

4.8 Sales Organizational Data

These screens allow the user entering the sales information to enter data relevant to the particular sales organization. The material may be sold by various sales organizations, and the data for each may differ. Many of the fields in these screens will default from other entry screens, such as BASE UNIT OF MEASURE. Some of the fields shown in Figure 4.17 and Figure 4.18 already have been described in other Material Master screens.

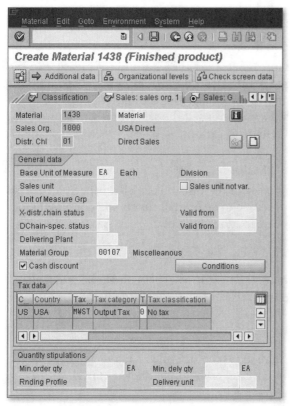

Figure 4.17 Sales Organization Screen 1 for the Material Master

4.8.1 General Data

The GENERAL DATA for the first sales organization screen in the Material Master describes some basic data used in sales processing of materials. The general data includes the sales unit, variable sales unit not allowed indicator, cross-distribution chain material status, and delivering plant.

Sales Unit

The unit of measure in which the material is sold is known as the sales unit of measure. For each sales organization, the material can be specified in a sales unit of measure that is used for the sales orders. This unit of measure can be the same as the base unit of measure or a multiple of the base unit of measure. An example would be a material that has bottle as its base unit of measure, but that could be sold in the sales organization for the United States as cartons and sold through the sales organization for France as pallets.

Variable Sales Unit Not Allowed Indicator

If the SALES UNIT NOT VAR. indicator is set, then the sales unit of measure in the Material Master cannot be changed in the sales order. For example, if the indicator is not set, then the sales representative can change the sales unit of measure in the order from carton to pallet. With the indicator set, the sales representative cannot change the sales unit, and it will remain as cartons.

Cross-Distribution Chain Material Status

The X-DISTR.CHAIN status field, along with the distribution chain-specific material status (DCHAIN-SPEC. STATUS) field, is used in SAP Retail clients and checks whether material can be used in different distribution channels.

Delivering Plant

This field is used to designate the default plant where this material is delivered. This field is automatically copied into the sales order as the delivery plant.

4.8.2   Tax Data

The tax data can be entered for a number of countries that a material is sold in. The country is entered along with the tax category and the relevant tax classification. There can be a number of tax categories per country.

Tax Category/Tax Classification

The TAX CATEGORY for materials is specific to the sales organization/division/plant level that defines the country-specific taxes during pricing. The configuration of the access sequences in the tax-condition tables for sales and use tax is made in the Financial Accounting Global Settings section of the IMG. That part of the IMG is cross-client and requires careful consideration before any access sequences are added. Consult with the Financial Accounting specialist when considering any changes to the tax-calculation procedures.

The tax category/classification is defined in the IMG using Transaction OVK4 or via the navigation path, IMG • SALES AND DISTRIBUTION • BASIC FUNCTIONS • TAXES • DEFINE TAX RELEVANCY OF MASTER RECORDS.

4.8.3 Quantity Stipulations

The fields in the QUANTITY STIPULATIONS section describe the minimum and maximum values used for the material for the particular sales organization.

Minimum Order Quantity ◀

The MIN. ORDER QTY value is the minimum quantity that a customer can order for this material/sales organization combination.

Minimum Delivery Quantity

The MIN. DELY QTY value is the minimum quantity that a customer can have delivered for an order for this material/sales organization combination.

Delivery Unit

The DELIVERY UNIT is the minimum unit of quantity for a delivery. The second field is for the unit of measure. For example, if the delivery unit is 50 cartons, then the delivery quantity to the customer can only be 50, 100, 150, and so on. The delivery quantity should not be 125 because it is not a multiple of 50.

Rounding Profile

The RNDING PROFILE field defines how a quantity is rounded up to a given value, depending on whether a static or dynamic profile is defined. The configuration for a rounding profile allows the user to define the rounding quantities for different thresholds. Table 4.4 shows an example of a static rounding profile.

Threshold Value	Rounding Value
1.000	70.000
211.000	300.000
301.000	450.000
451.000	1000.000

Table 4.4 Configuration for a Rounding Profile in Transaction OWD1

Table 4.5 shows the actual rounding of quantities 1 to 1000 based on the rounding value in Table 4.4. The configuration for rounding profiles can be found in Transaction OWD1 or via navigation path, IMG • PRODUCTION • MATERIAL REQUIREMENTS PLANNING • PLANNING • LOT-SIZE CALCULATION • MAINTAIN ROUNDING PROFILE.

Value From	Value To	Rounded Value
1.000	70.000	70.000
71.000	140.000	140.000
141.000	210.000	210.000
211.000	300.000	300.000
301.000	450.000	450.000
451.000	1000.000	1000.000

Table 4.5 Actual Rounding of Quantities

4.8.4 Grouping Items

There are a number of groups that a material can be assigned to for a sales organization for use in the information systems as shown in Figure 4.18.

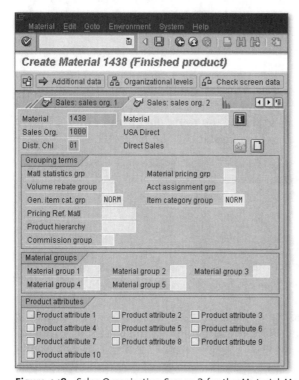

Figure 4.18 Sales Organization Screen 2 for the Material Master

Material Statistics Group

The material statistics group is a grouping used in the Logistics Information System (LIS). This field is found in Table TVSM. The values can be configured using Transaction OVRF or by using the navigation path, IMG • LOGISTICS INFORMATION SYSTEM (LIS) • LOGISTICS DATA WAREHOUSE • UPDATING • UPDATING CONTROL • SETTINGS: SALES AND DISTRIBUTION • STATISTICS GROUPS • MAINTAIN STATISTICS GROUPS FOR MATERIAL.

Volume Rebate Group

The VOLUME REBATE GROUP field is just a way of grouping similar materials for rebate-agreement processing. The field can be configured using navigation path, IMG • LOGISTICS GENERAL • SALES AND DISTRIBUTION • BILLING • REBATE PROCESSING • DEFINE MATERIAL REBATE GROUP.

Commission Group

The COMMISSION GROUP field can group together materials that offer similar commissions. The commission group can be used in pricing procedures. This field can be configured via the navigation path, IMG • LOGISTICS - GENERAL • MATERIAL MASTER • SETTINGS FOR KEY FIELDS • DATA RELEVANT TO SALES AND DISTRIBUTION • DEFINE COMMISSION GROUPS.

Material Pricing Group

The MATERIAL PRICING GRP is another available field that groups materials for pricing conditions. The field is found in Table T178.

Account Assignment Group

The ACCT ASSIGNMENT GRP can be selected to group together materials that have similar accounting requirements. For example, you can select a group for service revenues or a group for trading goods revenues. This field is used in sales billing documents. This field can be found in Table TVKM. The account assignment groups can be defined in configuration steps. The navigation path is IMG • SALES AND DISTRIBUTION • BASIC FUNCTIONS • ACCOUNT ASSIGNMENT/COSTING • REVENUE ACCOUNT DETERMINATION • CHECK MASTER DATA RELEVANT FOR ACCOUNT ASSIGNMENT • MATERIALS: ACCOUNT ASSIGNMENT GROUPS.

4.8.5 Material Groups

The material groups that can be entered on this SALES ORGANIZATION screen are not used in standard SAP ERP processing. The sales department can use the five material group fields to further define the material based on the sales organization. These fields are available for sales department analysis.

The definition of these five material groups can be configured via the navigation path, IMG • LOGISTICS - GENERAL • MATERIAL MASTER • SETTINGS FOR KEY FIELDS • DATA RELEVANT TO SALES AND DISTRIBUTION • DEFINE MATERIAL GROUPS.

4.8.6 Product Attributes

The product attribute indicators are available to the sales department for analysis. The 10 product attribute fields are found in Table MVKE, which can be viewed using Transaction SE11.

This section has discussed the data used to define the SALES ORGANIZATIONAL data screen on the Material Master record. The next section goes into detail with regards to the Material Master screen for the sales general data.

4.9   Sales General Data

The SALES GENERAL data section is specific to a material and a particular plant as shown in Figure 4.19.

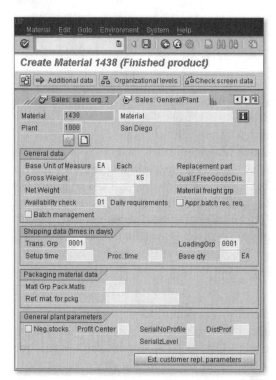

Figure 4.19   Fields on the Material Master's Sales General Data Screen

4.9.1 General Data

The GENERAL DATA section for the material as it refers to sales functionality includes the fields for REPLACEMENT PART and AVAILABILITY CHECK, and the approved batch record required indicator.

Replacement Part

This indicator allows the sales department to specify whether the material is a replacement part. The options are to indicate that this is not a replacement part, that it must be a replacement part, or that there is an optional replacement part.

Availability Check

The AVAILABILITY CHECK field is important to the sales department because it defines how an availability check is defined. The configuration can be found using Transaction OVZ2 or via the navigation path, IMG • SALES AND DISTRIBUTION • BASIC FUNCTIONS • AVAILABILITY CHECK AND TRANSFER OF REQUIREMENTS • AVAILABILITY CHECK • AVAILABILITY CHECK WITH ATP LOGIC OR AGAINST PLANNING • DEFINE CHECKING GROUPS.

New availability checks can be defined based on the sales department's requirements.

Approved Batch Record Required Indicator

The APPR.BATCH REC. REQ. indicator is only valid when the batches are from a process order. It specifies that certain activities can only be performed after a batch record has been entered.

4.9.2 Shipping Data

The many fields used in the shipping processes are described next.

Transportation Group

The TRANS. GROUP field is used to group together those materials that have similar transportation requirements, such as truck, tanker, train, and so on. This field can be used in the automatic route-scheduling function in sales order and delivery. The transportation group can be configured using the navigation path, IMG • LOGISTICS EXECUTION • SHIPPING • BASIC SHIPPING FUNCTIONS • ROUTES • ROUTE DETERMINATION • DEFINE TRANSPORTATION GROUPS.

Loading Group

The LOADINGGRP field allows the sales departments to group together materials that have similar loading requirements, such as crane, forklift, trolley, and so on. This field is required if shipping point determination will be used. The field contents can be configured via the navigation path, IMG • LOGISTICS EXECUTION • SHIPPING • BASIC SHIPPING FUNCTIONS • SHIPPING POINT AND GOODS RECEIVING POINT DETERMINATION • DEFINE LOADING GROUPS.

Setup Time

The SETUP TIME for shipping is similar to the setup times in other Material Master screens such as the WORK SCHEDULING screen. This setup time is strictly the setup time for getting the equipment, such as a forklift or a trolley cart, ready to move the material.

Processing Time/Base Quantity

The processing time (PROC. TIME) for shipping is the actual time it takes to load the material from its location onto the transportation vehicle. This processing time is valid for the amount of material that is entered into the base quantity (BASE QTY) field.

4.9.3   General Plant Parameters

A number of plant parameters are used in sales processing as described next.

Negative Stock in Plant

The NEG.STOCKS indicator can be set if there is a requirement to allow stocks of this material to be in a negative stock situation. The negative stock occurs when there is actual physical stock, but that stock has not been receipted into inventory. If a goods issue is made from inventory, then the stock will go negative until the missing goods receipt is made. This allows stock to be shipped without waiting for paperwork to be completed. However, this situation is dependent on the policy of the company.

Profit Center

A profit center is a function of the Controlling area (CO) of SAP. The profit center is a way of internally managing the company. The company has to manage and analyze the financials for profit center accounting. The PROFIT CENTER field in this screen can be used if profit centers will be used.

Serial Number Profile

The serial number profile (SERIALNOPROFILE) is used for materials that are required to be serialized. For example, a fuel indicator that is sold for use on an aircraft is required to have a unique serial number. The serial number profile determines the conditions and business transactions for issuing serial numbers.

Distribution Profile

Clients using the SAP Retail solution use the distribution profile for materials in a plant (DISTPROF) as a control profile for merchandise distribution.

Level of Explicitness for Serial Number

This field (SERIALIZLEVEL) describes the level on which the serial number is unique. A number of different levels can be assigned. Serial numbers can be made unique across the SAP client by setting this indicator with a "1" for every material. This will also create an equipment number with the same number as the serial number. If the indicator is blank, then the serial number is unique to the material only.

This section has discussed the SALES GENERAL DATA screen on the Material Master. Discussion of the remaining Material Master screens can be found in the next chapter.

4.10 Business Examples – Material Master Data

Material Master data is important for any company to ensure that it is accurate and current. When a business is implementing an SAP solution and decommissioning a legacy system, it is vitally important to allocate sufficient time and resources to the migration of data. If the data migrated to Material Master records are not accurate, this can cause a high degree of inefficiency and inconsistency for the company.

Often, the master files used on the legacy system do not contain all of the fields required on each SAP Material Master record. This then requires additional time and resources to investigate each item and develop the data needed for an accurate master record.

4.10.1 Material Type

A material type groups materials with similar attributes and allows the management of different materials in a uniform manner. When the SAP system is delivered, a company can decide to use the predefined material types, such as finished goods, trading goods, raw material, and so on, but the company can also define custom material types if necessary.

Example

A small domestic appliances manufacturer was implementing a new SAP ERP system and decommissioning an inventory system that was developed in-house. The legacy item master file had been adapted over time to include a number of fields that were required by systems interfaced into the original inventory software. As part of the SAP implementation plan, the company created a team to migrate the data from the legacy item master file to SAP ERP. Immediately, it became clear that the existing material types predefined in SAP ERP offered many more screens and fields than were necessary for the company. The company found that it would only use two of the predefined material types: finished goods and trading goods.

A team was tasked with identifying whether the company could reduce the number of screens a user would have seen during a Material Master creation by creating new material types based on finished goods and trading goods. The team concluded that the company could indeed create new material types for both finished and trading goods, thus reducing the number of screens a user would see, but this came with restrictions. If the company required the excluded screens in the future, this would require significant work to change material types. Although the company did not believe the excluded screens would be needed, it decided against creating new material types to maintain a "vanilla" SAP implementation.

4.10.2 Classification Data

Each material has the ability to be classified, which means that a company can enter characteristic values that can be used to search for material with that set of characteristics. This functionality is useful to a company when it is assisting customers to find a specific item based on a set of specific criteria. Because the characteristics assigned to a material can be very specific, this is a value-added benefit to customers when they need to purchase the correct material.

Example

A specialty chemicals company in India had a very narrow range of products that were used in paint manufacturing. The R&D department created the individual materials, which differed only slightly from other materials sold by the company. To a casual observer, it would appear that the chemicals were identical; however, the subtle differences between the various items were important to manufacturers. The company used text fields on its legacy item master file to describe the differences and the unique chemical composition. The sales team would have to read the text to sell the correct item to customers. After the initial implementation of SAP ERP, the text fields on the Material Master were again used to highlight the differences between materials. After a number of months, the sales staff reported to management that the SAP ERP system had not improved their ability to better serve the customer.

The chemicals company employed a consulting company to help increase productivity in the sales area and improve customer satisfaction. The consulting team proposed the use of classification to allow the sales staff to search for specific materials based on the customer's unique requirements. The company initiated a project to identify a list of characteristics that could be assigned to the material and then develop the data for current materials. The company, with input from its customers, identified more than 30 characteristics that covered the requirements its customers needed when ordering chemicals. A month after the classification project was implemented, the sales staff reported that productivity had increased and comments from the customers had been very positive.

4.10.3 Purchasing Data

The purchasing data on the Material Master record permits a company to enter data that is specifically used when the material is purchased. In addition, the company can enter a configurable purchasing value key so that when the key is entered, a number of other fields are automatically defined, such as over-delivery and under-delivery tolerances, shipping instructions, and reminder days.

Example

A children's toys manufacturer implemented an SAP ERP system for the business that manufactured electronic toys. Although most of the toys were manufactured in China, some modifications and quality checks were performed in the United States, as well as the application of decals and other accessories. The company purchased several thousand different decals for their toys from a small number of vendors. When the company started the migration of data from its legacy system, the company identified the need to reduce the data-entry effort. The team working on the Material Master data found that for a large number of materials, the purchasing data was very similar. After further analysis, the team decided that they could configure a small number of purchasing value keys to be used in the Material Master. Using the purchasing value keys reduced the amount of data entry.

4.10.4 Sales Data

The sales data on the Material Master allow the user to enter information pertinent to a particular sales organization. The material may be sold by various sales organizations, and the data for each organization may differ. The sales data includes tax information, shipping data, and sales groupings.

Example

An aircraft spare parts company based in Florida implemented SAP ERP to replace a custom-built sales and inventory solution. The legacy system was customized heavily to facilitate the way the company identified and sold its products. The legacy business process began with used and salvaged aircraft parts arriving at the facility where they were identified and entered into the system. Each part was identified by a number of attributes that were used by the sales staff to help customers select the correct part.

During the SAP implementation, the project team had to develop a solution that allowed the sales staff access to the item attributes. The team initially considered using characteristics in the classification system to contain the material attributes. The attributes for 10 materials were entered into the classification system as characteristics, and the sales staff was asked to perform a number of sales order tests. The results were that the staff felt that they were spending too much time finding the correct attributes on the Material Master file.

The project team revisited the problem, and using the comments from the sales staff, they looked at configurable material attributes fields on the Material Master. The project team members were concerned that there were only 10 configurable attributes and 5 configurable material groups. This limited the number of attributes that could be used for each material, but an analysis of existing items on the legacy system found that no material had more than 15 attributes. The project team configured the attributes on the Material Master, and 10 materials were defined using those attributes. The sales staff repeated the tests that they carried out previously, but this time the feedback was positive, and the company decided to use the configurable attributes for all sales materials.

4.11 Summary

This chapter on the Material Master discussed the elements that make up the Material Master file for a number of screens, including the BASIC DATA, CLASSIFICATION, PURCHASING, FORECASTING, WORK SCHEDULING, SALES ORGANIZATION, and GENERAL SALES DATA.

Chapter 5, the second chapter on the Material Master file, will describe the production resources and tools data, plant data/storage location data, warehouse management data, quality management data, material requirements planning (MRP), accounting, and costing.

Data entered into the Material Master is extremely important to an SAP implementation. Incorrect or missing data can cause companies to halt operations. Understanding how to enter correct data into the Material Master is vital for all SAP components.

5 Material Master Data – Part 2

In this second chapter on the Material Master file, we will show the data-entry screens for the production resources and tools data, plant data/storage location data, Warehouse Management (WM) data, Quality Management (QM) data, material requirements planning (MRP), Accounting, and Costing. It is important that you understand the fields in the Material Master and how they relate to the data in a customer's legacy system.

5.1 Production Resources/Tools (PRT) Data

The PRT screen, as shown in Figure 5.1, allows the plant maintenance department to enter the data for the PRT material. Some of the fields shown have already been described in other Material Master screens.

5.1.1 General Data

The GENERAL DATA on the PRT screen allows the user to enter basic plant-specific data such as task list usage and grouping keys.

Task List Usage

This field determines on what task lists the PRT is valid for the particular plant. This field can be found in Table TC23. The configuration for the TASK LIST USAGE field is found in Transaction OP47 or via the navigation path, IMG • PLANT MAINTENANCE AND CUSTOMER SERVICE • MAINTENANCE PLANS, WORK CENTERS, TASK LISTS AND PRTS • PRODUCTION RESOURCES/TOOLS • GENERAL DATA • DEFINE TASK LIST USAGE KEYS.

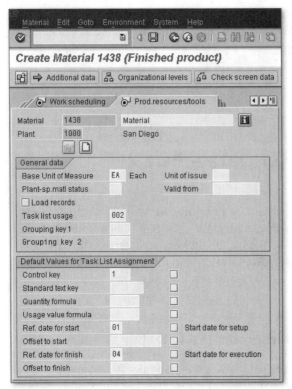

Figure 5.1 Available Fields on the Material Master PRT Screen

Grouping Keys 1 and 2

These fields allow the plant maintenance department to define groupings for their PRTs. The grouping keys can be defined in configuration and are found in Table TCF12. The configuration for the grouping keys is found via the navigation path, IMG • PLANT MAINTENANCE AND CUSTOMER SERVICE • MAINTENANCE PLANS, WORK CENTERS, TASK LISTS AND PRTS • PRODUCTION RESOURCES/TOOLS • GENERAL DATA • DEFINE PRT GROUP KEYS.

5.1.2   Default Values for Task List Assignment

The default values for the task list assignments include the control keys for the management of the PRTs, standard text key, and quantity formula.

Control Key for the Management of PRTs

The CONTROL KEY field specifies how the PRT is used in the maintenance order or the task list. The PRT control key can be found in Table TCF10. The control key defines in what parts of the task list the PRT can be used. This field allows the user to select a control key that has been configured. During the configuration of a control key, five indicators can be selected for the control key that are deemed to be appropriate. The five indicators that can be selected during the configuration of the control key are SCHEDULE, CALCULATE, CONFIRM, EXPAND, and PRINT. The control key can be configured via the navigation path, IMG • PLANT MAINTENANCE AND CUSTOMER SERVICE • MAINTENANCE PLANS, WORK CENTERS, TASK LISTS AND PRTS • PRODUCTION RESOURCES/TOOLS • PRODUCTION RESOURCE/TOOL ASSIGNMENTS • DEFINE PRT CONTROL KEYS.

Standard Text Key

The STANDARD TEXT KEY allows the plant maintenance department to enter a key on the Material Master that defines a standard text for the PRT, which is then used as a default in the task list or maintenance order. The standard texts are maintained in Transaction CA10 or via the navigation path, IMG • QUALITY MANAGEMENT • QUALITY PLANNING • INSPECTION PLANNING • OPERATION • WORK CENTER • MAINTAIN STANDARD TEXT KEYS.

The standard text has to be maintained in the correct language. For example, the standard text key P000010 for PRTs can be defined in a number of different languages.

Quantity Formula

This field is the formula for calculating the total of the PRTs required. This field is copied into the maintenance order or task list. The formula can be defined in configuration Transaction OIZM or via the navigation path, IMG • PLANT MAINTENANCE AND CUSTOMER SERVICE • MAINTENANCE PLANS, WORK CENTERS, TASK LISTS AND PRTS • PRODUCTION RESOURCES/TOOLS • PRODUCTION RESOURCE/TOOL ASSIGNMENTS • FORMULAS • CONFIGURE FORMULA DEFINITION.

All formulas are defined in this transaction. For a formula to be selected in the QUANTITY FORMULA field in the PRT screen, the formula must have set the indicator PRT ALLOWED FOR REQUIREMENT, which is found on the configuration screen, Transaction OIZM.

Usage Value Formula

This field calculates the total usage value of the PRT. This field is selected from the same formulas as the QUANTITY FORMULA field.

Reference Date to Start of PRT Usage

The REF. DATE FOR START field is used in calculating the start date/time for the PRT usage. It is used with the OFFSET TO START field, which is the next field in the Material Master and used in the task list or maintenance order. The start date can be selected from entries in Table TCA54.

Offset to Start

This field is used in conjunction with the REF. DATE FOR START field for PRT scheduling. The numeric value can be positive or negative. A negative value indicates a start time before the reference date. A positive value indicates a time after the reference date. The numeric value can have a unit of measure that indicates hours, minutes, days, and so on.

Reference Date for Finish/Offset to Finish

These fields are similar to those in the OFFSET TO START field, except they are to determine the finish date rather than the start date.

5.2   Plant Data/Storage Location

The plant data/storage location screens, shown in Figure 5.2 and Figure 5.3, allow the inventory staff to enter information relevant to storage location and to shelf-life characteristics, including storage bin, container requirements, maximum storage period, and total shelf life of the material.

5.2.1   General Data

The fields in this section of the PLANT DATA/STOR. 1 screen allow the entry of material data specifically for the storage location, such as STORAGE BIN and cycle counting indicator (CC PHYS. INV. IND). These are referred to as general data items.

Storage Bin

The STORAGE BIN field can be entered by the warehouse staff to identify a location within the storage location where the material is always stored. This is used when WM is not implemented. The STORAGE BIN is a 10-character field that is not configurable because it has no functional purpose and is only used as a reference field. The STORAGE BIN field does not have any functionality within Inventory Management.

> **Note**
>
> There can only be one storage bin defined for each material per storage location.

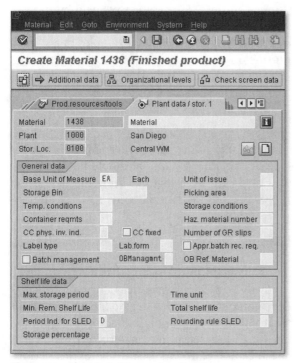

Figure 5.2 Plant Data/Storage Location Screen 1

Picking Area

The PICKING AREA field represents a group of WM storage bins that are used for picking in Lean WM. The PICKING AREA field is similar to the definition of storage section on the WAREHOUSE MANAGEMENT screen. The picking area can be configured using the navigation path, IMG • LOGISTICS EXECUTION • SHIPPING • PICKING • LEAN WM • DEFINE PICKING AREAS.

Temperature Conditions

TEMP. CONDITIONS is simply the temperature at which the material should be stored. Certain chemicals and metals need to be stored at low temperatures to avoid chemical reactions. The TEMP. CONDITIONS field is stored at the client level, so it is valid for all plants. The TEMP. CONDITIONS field can be configured using the navigation path, IMG • Logistics - General • Material Master • Settings for Key Fields • Define Temperature Conditions.

Storage Conditions

The Storage conditions field is similar to the Temp. conditions field in that it is a client-wide field and is valid for all plants. The storage conditions can be defined by the company to be relevant for its specific requirements. Examples of a storage condition may be refrigeration, outside only, or hotbox. The Storage conditions field can be configured using the navigation path, IMG • Logistics - General • Material Master • Settings for Key Fields • Define Storage Conditions.

Container Requirements

Container reqmts is another field that works at the client level and is the same for all plants. It is a field that defines what container a material should be stored and shipped in. The Container reqmts field can be configured using the navigation path, IMG • Logistics - General • Material Master • Settings for Key Fields • Define Container Requirements.

Hazardous Material Number

A hazardous material number can be assigned to the material at the client level. This links the material number with the hazardous material information that is defined for that hazardous material number, such as water pollutant, hazardous storage class, or warnings. The hazardous material is not defined in configuration but in the Logistics Execution functionality. A hazardous material can be created using Transaction VM01 or via the navigation path, SAP Menu • Logistics • Logistics Execution • Master Data • Material • Hazardous Material • Create.

Cycle Counting Physical Inventory Indicator

CC phys. inv. ind. (cycle counting indicator) is set if the material is to be cycle counted. The indicator can also determine how the count is taken and how often. The cycle count indicator usually is an A, B, C, or D to coincide with the ABC indicators. The cycle counting indicator is defined by four characteristics:

▶ Numbers of physical inventories per fiscal year to be performed

▶ Maximum interval of days between counts

▶ Float time that is allowed for the planned count date after the required date

▶ Percentage of consumption allocated to each of the indicators (A, B, C, etc.)

The cycle counting indicator can be configured using Transaction OMCO or the navigation path, IMG • MATERIALS MANAGEMENT • INVENTORY MANAGEMENT AND PHYSICAL INVENTORY • PHYSICAL INVENTORY • CYCLE COUNTING.

Cycle Counting Indicator Is Fixed

If the CC FIXED indicator is set, then CC PHYS. INV. IND., defined previously, cannot be changed by the ABC functionality that can be run periodically. If the indicator is not set, CC PHYS. INV. IND. will be changed if the ABC functionality determines that the material has changed status. If the indicator is set, and no changes can be made via the ABC functionality, then CC PHYS. INV. IND. can still be set by changing it in the Material Master.

Number of Goods Receipt Slips

The NUMBER OF GR SLIPS field allows the receiving department to enter a figure that determines the number of goods receipt documents that will be printed. If the field is blank, the system assumes that one material document will be printed.

Label Type

Some materials require labels to be printed and affixed to the product or packaging. The LABEL TYPE field defines which labels are printed for which goods movement, how many labels are printed, and which printer they are printed on. The label type can be configured in Transaction OMCF or via the navigation path, IMG • MATERIALS MANAGEMENT • INVENTORY MANAGEMENT AND PHYSICAL INVENTORY • PRINT CONTROL • SET LABEL PRINTOUT • LABEL TYPE.

Label Form

The LAB.FORM field can be used when the LABEL TYPE has been entered for a material. The LAB.FORM field defines the dimensions and characteristics of the label. The label form can be defined in Transaction OMCF, as the label type, or via the navigation path, IMG • MATERIALS MANAGEMENT • INVENTORY MANAGEMENT AND PHYSICAL INVENTORY • PRINT CONTROL • SET LABEL PRINTOUT • LABEL FORM.

5.2.2 Shelf Life Data

The SHELF LIFE DATA section allows the entry of data that is used in shelf-life date functionality. For example, some companies use, store, and sell material that can only be used before its shelf life expires, such as food items, chemicals, and pharmaceuticals.

Maximum Storage Period

This field is for information and reporting only and does not have any functionality. The users can define the maximum storage period for a material before it expires.

Time Unit

This is the unit of measure of the maximum storage period, that is, days, months, and years. For example, many foodstuffs will have a shelf life of days, whereas pharmaceuticals may have a shelf life of a year or more.

Minimum Remaining Shelf Life

The MIN. REM. SHELF LIFE field determines whether a material can be received via goods receipt based on the remaining shelf life of the material to be receipted. If this field has the value 100 days, and the material to be goods receipted has only 80 days of shelf life left, then the goods receipt will not be accepted. The MIN. REM. SHELF LIFE field works at the client level and is the same for the material across all plants.

Total Shelf Life

The TOTAL SHELF LIFE figure is at the client level and does not vary by plant. The total shelf life is the time for which the materials will be kept, from the production date to the shelf life expiration date. The shelf life is only checked if the expiration date check has been activated. The activation is configured at plant level or movement type level in Transaction OMJ5 or via the navigation path, IMG • LOGISTICS – GENERAL • BATCH MANAGEMENT • SHELF LIFE EXPIRATION DATE (SLED) • SET EXPIRATION DATE CHECK.

Period Indicator for Shelf-Life Expiration Date

The PERIOD IND. FOR SLED field is defined for the shelf life expiration date (SLED) fields used in this Material Master screen. The period can be defined as months, days, and so on. The period indicator can be configured in Transaction OO2K or through the navigation path, IMG • LOGISTICS – GENERAL • BATCH MANAGEMENT • SHELF LIFE EXPIRATION DATE (SLED) • MAINTAIN PERIOD INDICATOR.

Rounding Rule SLED

The ROUNDING RULE SLED allows the SLED dates to be rounded up to the nearest unit of the time defined in the period indicator. For example, if the period indicator were months, then the rounding rule either would be the first day of the month, or the last day of the month, or no change if there were no rounding rule. The rounding rule is for calculated dates rather than dates entered into the record.

Figure 5.3 shows the second plant data/storage location screen. The fields displayed on the screen, weight/volume fields, such as GROSS WEIGHT and NET WEIGHT, and general plant parameter fields, such as SERIAL NO. PROFILE and PROFIT CENTER, can found on other Material Master screens.

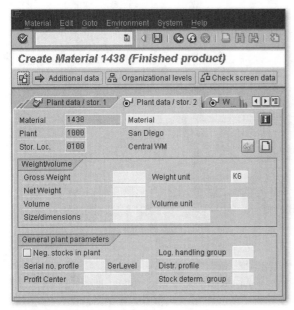

Figure 5.3 Plant Data/Storage Location Screen 2

The next section examines the Material Master screens for WM and the data that can be entered if the WM functionality is used at your client.

5.3 Warehouse Management Data

The Warehouse Management screens of the Material Master allow the user to enter information at the warehouse/storage type level, as shown in Figure 5.4 and in Figure 5.5.

5.3.1 General Data

The GENERAL DATA section of Figure 5.4 allows the entry of specific WM data, including BASE UNIT OF MEASURE and PICKING STORAGE TYPE.

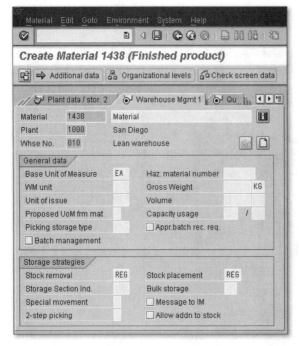

Figure 5.4 Fields of the Warehouse Management 1 Screen in the Material Master

Warehouse Management Unit of Measure

Like the other units of measure, this WM UNIT field is the unit of measure defined for the material as it is relates to its movements through the warehouse.

Unit of Issue

This UNIT OF ISSUE field allows the warehouse department to define a different unit of measure for items issued from the warehouse, as an alternative to the base unit of measure.

Picking Storage Type

This PICKING STORAGE TYPE field is used by planning as the storage type that will contain material that can be used in rough-cut planning.

5.3.2 Storage Strategies

The data in this section relates to the stock placement and stock removal strategies in WM that can be attributed to the material during the Material Master creation.

Stock Removal

This field allows the warehouse staff to enter the storage type indicator that defines the sequence in which storage types are searched for the material to be picked in the warehouse. The storage type indicator can be defined in Transaction OMLY. The navigation path is IMG • Logistics Execution • Warehouse Management • Strategies • Activate Storage Type Search.

Stock Placement

The Stock placement field acts in a similar manner to the Stock removal field, except that the strategy defined in the storage type search is for a placement strategy rather than a removal strategy.

Storage Section

The storage section search is a more specific strategy for stock placement because it defines one level below the storage type search for stock placement. The Storage section Ind. must be defined for each warehouse and storage type. The strategy allows up to 10 storage sections to be defined in sequence for the placement strategy. The configuration can be found in Transaction OMLZ or the navigation path, IMG • Logistics Execution • Warehouse Management • Strategies • Activate Storage Section Search.

Bulk Storage

Within the placement strategies, you can define how bulk materials should be placed in stock. The Bulk storage indicator can be used if the bulk storage placement strategy has been activated in WM. The Bulk storage indicator can indicate height or width of a particular storage type. The configuration can be found in Transaction OMM4 or the navigation path, IMG • Logistics Execution • Warehouse Management • Strategies • Putaway Strategies • Define Strategy for Bulk Storage.

Special Movement

The Special movement indicator allows the material to be identified as requiring a special goods movement. The Special movement indicator is configured in WM to allow special processing for a group of materials. The configuration is found using the navigation path, IMG • Logistics Execution • Warehouse Management • Master Data • Material • Define Special Movement Indicators.

After the SPECIAL MOVEMENT indicator has been defined, it can be used in the LE-WM interface to Inventory Management, where the configuration determines the WM movement type. The SPECIAL MOVEMENT indicator can allow certain materials assigned with that indicator to behave differently during goods movements. The configuration for the warehouse goods movements can be found using the navigation path, IMG • LOGISTICS EXECUTION • WAREHOUSE MANAGEMENT • INTERFACES • INVENTORY MANAGEMENT • DEFINE MOVEMENT TYPES.

Message to IM

This field is used if the WM system is decentralized. If the indicator is set, it allows the WM information for this material to be sent to Inventory Management immediately.

Two-Step Picking

In WM, you can choose between one-step and two-step picking for materials. If the material were large and bulky, then a one-step removal would be optimal. However, if the materials to be picked are small and numerous, then one-step picking may not be an efficient use of warehouse resources. Therefore, two-step picking is used to minimize workload. The two-step process defines an interim storage type, which is normally 200, where items are picked and transferred to; from there, the final pick takes place. The configuration for two-step picking is found using the navigation path, IMG • LOGISTICS EXECUTION • WAREHOUSE MANAGEMENT • INTERFACES • SHIPPING • DEFINE 2-STEP PICKING.

Allow Addition to Stock Indicator

Setting this indicator allows material to be added to the existing stock of the same material in the same storage bin. This is only true if the characteristics of the two quantities of material are the same. If the storage-type table does not allow additions to existing stock for this storage type, the indicator is redundant.

Figure 5.5 shows the data relating to palletization and storage bin stock, which are described in further detail next.

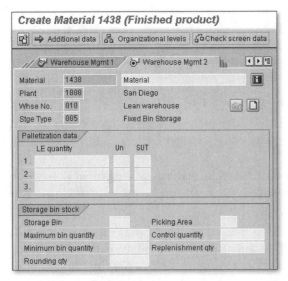

Figure 5.5 Fields of the Warehouse Management 2 Screen in the Material Master

5.3.3 Palletization Data

Palletization is used in storage unit handling within WM. The process uses pallets to store and move material in the warehouse. The PALLETIZATION DATA section determines how the material should be entered into stock. The material may be able to be placed into storage in different ways depending on what storage unit type is being used.

Loading Equipment Quantity/Unit of Measure

The LE QUANTITY entered here is the amount of material to be placed on to the storage unit type. The storage unit type (SUT), described in this section, is the entity used to store some material in the warehouse. This field determines the quantity of material that can be stored in it.

Storage Unit Type

The storage unit type (SUBT) is a description of how the material is stored in the storage bin. For example, some bins may not be able to allow a full pallet due to height restrictions, but a half-pallet may fit. Therefore, the warehouse can define a storage unit type that defines a half-pallet and the quantity of the material that can fit on that half-pallet.

Suppose that for material XYZ, 30 boxes are equivalent to one half-pallet. The storage unit type is configured in the IMG and has to be activated in each warehouse before it can be used. There is a definition of the storage unit type for each plant. The configuration can be made using the navigation path, IMG • Logistics Execution • Warehouse Management • Master Data • Material • Define Storage Unit Types.

5.3.4 Storage Bin Stock

The Storage bin stock information entered in the warehouse screen is used for calculation in WM bin replenishment.

Storage Bin

The storage bin is the lowest level of storage defined in the warehouse. The Storage Bin field allows the warehouse user to enter a storage bin that this material will be added to for the plant/storage type combination. Selecting F4 shows the options for the empty storage bins.

Maximum Bin Quantity

This value can be entered to define the maximum quantity of this material that can be entered into any storage bin defined in the storage type. The quantity is defined in the base unit of measure, not the WM unit of measure.

Control Quantity

The Control quantity can be entered to define for this storage type the amount of material that reaches the level where stock removal can take place. Similar to the Maximum bin quantity, this Control quantity is in the material base unit of measure.

Minimum Bin Quantity

This field allows the warehouse users to define a minimum quantity that can be stored in the bin locations for this storage type. This makes efficient use of storage bins. For example, if the material is small, the maximum bin quantity is high, and no minimum quantity is set, then there could be many bins containing small amounts of stock. Entering a minimum bin quantity allows the bin to be used efficiently and minimizes picking. Like the other quantities, the Minimum bin quantity is recorded in the base quantity unit.

Replenishment Quantity

The REPLENISHMENT QTY field is defined to suggest the quantity that should be placed in the storage bin. Like the other quantities, the REPLENISHMENT QTY is recorded in the base quantity unit.

Rounding Quantity

This quantity is used if the material is subject to the quantity-dependent picking strategy. The ROUNDING QTY field is the figure that the picking quantities are rounded down to for this material/storage type combination. This quantity is also defined in the base unit of measure.

The next section examines the Material Master screens that contain the QM fields. Data on these screens should only be entered if your client is using the QM functionality.

5.4 Quality Management Data

QM
at Plant
Levels

The QUALITY MANAGEMENT data screen allows the quality department to define the basic quality requirements for the material at each plant level. Figure 5.6 shows the fields of the QUALITY MANAGEMENT screen for the Material Master.

5.4.1 General Data

The GENERAL DATA section of the screen shown in Figure 5.6 allows the entry of specific quality management data, including unit of measure, inspection interval, and the documentation indicator.

Figure 5.6 Quality Management Screen for the Material Master

Inspection Setup

The INSPECTION SETUP indicator is set if a QM inspection setup already exists for this material/plant combination. If the quality inspection user wants to enter the inspection setup information for this material at this plant, there is a button to the right of the indicator that will bring up the inspection entry screen. The screen allows a number of inspection types to be entered, such as GOODS RECEIPT INSPECTION and STOCK TRANSFER INSPECTION.

Post to Inspection Stock Indicator

This indicator can be set to force material to be posted to inspection stock. This indicator is copied into the purchase order (PO). However, this indicator is ignored if an inspection type that is stock-relevant—in other words, an inspection due to stock movement—has been entered in the inspection setup.

Material Authorization Group for Activities in QM

The QM MATERIAL AUTH. field allows the quality department to add a layer of security to the quality information of each material. The authorization group that can be entered in the field will check to see if a quality inspection user has the correct authorization to view the information. The authorization group is defined in configuration via the navigation path, IMG • QUALITY MANAGEMENT • ENVIRONMENT • CENTRAL FUNCTIONS • AUTHORIZATION MANAGEMENT • DEFINE AUTHORIZATION GROUP AND DIGITAL SIGNATURE.

Document Required Indicator

After the indicator is set, it causes the system to record any changes to inspection lots or usage decisions. These status changes are recorded in change documents and can be viewed in the status history for the material. The status can be viewed by pressing Shift + F4 .

Inspection Interval

This field allows the quality department to enter the number of days required between inspections of the material at this plant. This figure is copied to the batch record when a batch is created.

Catalog Profile

This field reflects a value that is relevant in quality notifications. The catalog profile is defined in configuration using the navigation path, IMG • QUALITY MANAGEMENT • QUALITY NOTIFICATIONS • NOTIFICATION CREATION • NOTIFICATION CONTENT • DEFINE CATALOG PROFILE.

[handwritten: Procurement data from the QM screen.]

5.4.2 Procurement Data

The procurement data on the QUALITY MANAGEMENT screen of the Material Master allows the material to be flagged for quality checks in procurement.

QM in Procurement Indicator

The QM PROC. ACTIVE indicator switches on the quality-management aspect of procurement. This can be activated at a plant level or a client level. If activated at a client level, then the QM CONTROL KEY field should be defined also.

[handwritten: QM control key determines]

QM Control Key

The QM CONTROL KEY can be defined during configuration and determines how a material is affected by quality during the procurement cycle. The control key can determine the following:

► If technical delivery terms must exist as a document

► If a quality assurance document must exist between the company and the vendor

► If a valid purchasing information record must exist

► If a quality certificate is required from the vendor on each shipment

► If a block can be put in place against the invoice

Certificate Type

The quality certificate can be required by the quality department for each goods receipt item or PO item concerning certain materials from the vendor. There can be many different certificate types defined in configuration. The navigation path is IMG • QUALITY MANAGEMENT • QM IN LOGISTICS • QM IN PROCUREMENT • DEFINE KEYS FOR CERTIFICATE PROCESSING • DEFINE CERTIFICATE TYPES.

Target QM System

The TARGET QM SYSTEM field allows the quality department to define the type of QM system it requires from vendors. For example, the quality department may require that the vendors for the material have an ISO 9001 certification for their sites. The configuration in QM can define the requirements and in addition determine what rating vendors can achieve through the quality department's evaluation.

The configuration for the target QM system can be found in Transaction OQB7 or via the navigation path, IMG • QUALITY MANAGEMENT • QM IN LOGISTICS • QM IN PROCUREMENT • DEFINE QM SYSTEMS.

The following section describes the fields entered on the Material Master when the material is to be produced. The material requirements planning (MRP) screens allow the production staff to enter the basic data required for the production of this material specific to the plant.

5.5 Material Requirements Planning Data

The MRP data is divided over a number of screens in the Material Master. Figure 5.7 shows the first of these screens. The number of screens may depend on the version of SAP you are working on.

The information on the MRP screens is important in how material is made, planned, and produced within the plant. Some of the fields from the screens have been discussed in previous sections.

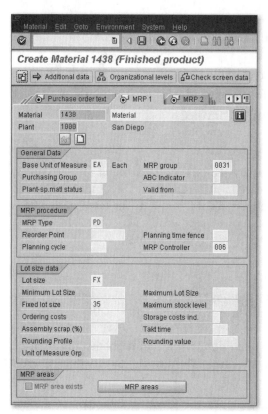

Figure 5.7 First MRP Data-Entry Screen

Figure 5.7 shows the MRP 1 screen for the Material Master. This screen allows data to be entered for the material/plant combination.

5.5.1 General Data

The GENERAL DATA section contains some fields already entered such as unit of measure, but it also includes the MRP GROUP and the ABC INDICATOR fields.

MRP Group

The MRP GROUP field is a combination of special control parameters specific to the total planning run. The MRP group is created at plant level and assigned to materials with similar needs for these parameters.

The MRP group is created in Transaction OPPR or via the navigation path, IMG • PRODUCTION • MATERIAL REQUIREMENTS PLANNING • MRP GROUPS • CARRY OUT OVERALL MAINTENANCE OF MATERIAL GROUPS.

Figure 5.8 shows the fields available to modify for the MRP group.

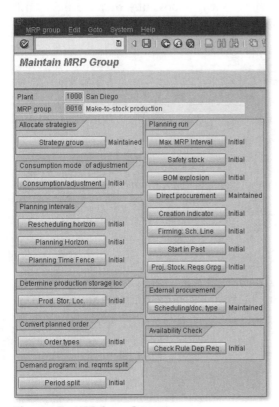

Figure 5.8 MRP Group Parameters

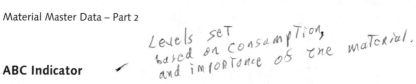

ABC Indicator

The ABC INDICATOR field allows a determination to be made based on consumption criteria. The higher the consumption, the more important the material is and the earlier in the alphabet is its indicator. The SAP system predefines the indicators A, B, and C, but it is possible to define other indicators.

The ABC INDICATOR can be configured using the navigation path, IMG • LOGISTICS – GENERAL • MATERIAL MASTER • SETTINGS FOR KEY FIELDS • DEFINE ABC INDICATOR.

5.5.2   MRP Procedure

The MRP PROCEDURE fields allow the entry of the MRP TYPE, MRP CONTROLLER, and other fields necessary for the MRP function.

MRP Type

The MRP TYPE field is a key to a procedure that is used to plan a material and to control which MRP parameters can be maintained for the material.

SAP predefines a number of MRP types, but it is possible to create new MRP types in configuration. Table 5.1 shows these standard MRP types and their descriptions.

MRP Type	Description
PD	Standard MRP
VB	Manual reorder point planning
VM	Automatic reorder point planning
V1	Automatic reorder point planning (including external requirements)
V2	Automatic reorder point planning (without external requirements)
VV	Forecast-based planning
ND	No planning

Table 5.1   SAP Standard MRP Types

The planning department can create new MRP types using configuration via the navigation path, IMG • PRODUCTION • MATERIAL REQUIREMENTS PLANNING • MASTER DATA • CHECK MRP TYPES.

Reorder Point

This field is used <u>only for reorder point planning.</u> Reorder point planning uses the reorder point to indicate to MRP that the material needs to be included in the next planning run when a requirement will be produced. The production staff will determine the reorder level and enter it into the Material Master. The reorder level can be calculated in a number of ways. For example, the reorder point can be calculated as the safety stock level plus the forecasted demand for the material during its replenishment lead-time.

Planning Time Fence

The planning department, to create a period of time when there are no automatic changes to the master plan, enters a value for the PLANNING TIME FENCE.

Planning Cycle

The PLANNING CYCLE field reflects a planning calendar that determines when material is ordered and planned. For this data to be relevant, the material must be assigned an MRP type that allows time-phased planning. The planning cycle can be configured for the specific planning department. To configure the planning calendar, use the navigation path, IMG • PRODUCTION • MATERIAL REQUIREMENTS PLANNING • MASTER DATA • MAINTAIN PLANNING CALENDAR.

MRP Controller

The MRP CONTROLLER field reflects a person or persons who are responsible for the planning of the material. The MRP controller can be configured via the navigation path, IMG • PRODUCTION • MATERIAL REQUIREMENTS PLANNING • MASTER DATA • DEFINE MRP CONTROLLERS.

5.5.3 Lot Size Data

A number of lot size fields can be entered on this screen, such as minimum and maximum lot sizes, if these are relevant for the material.

Lot Size

The LOT SIZE field defines the lot-sizing procedure. The procedure calculates the reorder quantity in the planning run. The lot size can be defined for short-term and long-term periods. The production department will determine what lot-size calculation is required for the material. The lot-size calculation can be configured in Transaction OMI4 or via the navigation path, IMG • PRODUCTION • MATERIAL

REQUIREMENTS PLANNING • PLANNING • LOT-SIZE CALCULATION • CHECK LOT-SIZING PROCEDURE.

Minimum Lot Size

The planning department can enter this field to determine this material's minimum lot size for procurement.

Maximum Lot Size

This is the material's maximum lot size for procurement. This value is used in the lot-size calculation for production orders.

Fixed Lot Size

The FIXED LOT SIZE field is the amount of the material that is ordered if there is a shortage of the material. If the fixed lot size is less than the shortage, then multiples of the fixed lot size will be ordered to cover the shortage.

Maximum Stock Level

This field is only used if the LOT SIZE field value "HB" (replenish to maximum) has been entered for this material. This field determines the maximum level of stock for this material at the plant.

Ordering Costs

These costs are only used with the optimum lot-sizing procedure and represent the cost of producing or purchasing the material above the normal purchasing costs. The system assumes the currency is the same as the currency used for the plant.

Storage Costs Indicator

This field is used only with the optimum lot-sizing procedure. It is defined as the cost of storing material based on the quantity and the unit price.

Assembly Scrap

The ASSEMBLY SCRAP (%) field allows entry of the amount of scrap that normally occurs during the assembly of a material. The percentage scrap will allow the lot-size calculation to increase to allow for the scrap. A value should only be entered if this material is an assembly.

Takt Time

TAKT is the German word for the baton used by an orchestra conductor to regulate the speed at which musicians play. Production uses TAKT time as the rate that a material is completed. If the TAKT TIME field is defined as four hours, which means every four hours a complete material is produced.

The second MRP screen, as shown in Figure 5.9, allows the entry of material data for procurement, such as PROCUREMENT TYPE and the BACKFLUSH indicator; scheduling, such as IN-HOUSE PRODUCTION and PLANNING CALENDAR; and net requirements calculations, such as SAFETY STOCK of the material.

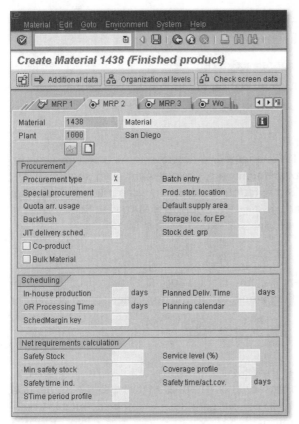

PROCUREMENT section
os MRP screen

Figure 5.9 Second MRP Data Entry Screen

5.5.4 Procurement

The first section of data fields on the second MRP screen in the Material Master refer to how material can be procured for production.

Procurement Type

The PROCUREMENT TYPE field describes how a material is procured. The material can be purchased externally from a vendor, be produced in-house via a production order, or be both produced and purchased.

Batch Entry

The BATCH ENTRY key is used to identify where the batches have to be entered in the production process. Three options are available for the BATCH ENTRY field:

▶ Manual Batch Determination at release of order

▶ Batch Not Required in Order; confirmation required

▶ Automatic Batch Determination upon release of order

Special Procurement

The SPECIAL PROCUREMENT field is configured to describe a procurement scenario. The key can determine the procurement type, procurement from another plant, and BOM characteristics. The configuration of the SPECIAL PROCUREMENT field can be found via the navigation path, IMG • PRODUCTION • MATERIAL REQUIREMENTS PLANNING • MASTER DATA • DEFINE SPECIAL PROCUREMENT TYPE.

Production Storage Location

If the material is produced in-house, the storage location entered in the PROD. STOR. LOCATION field is used in the planned or production order. It also is used for backflushing purposes.

Default Supply Area

The DEFAULT SUPPLY AREA field is used for KANBAN operations. The default supply area is a defined interim storage area that supplies material to the production operation. The supply area is not part of configuration and can be defined in Transaction PK05 or via the navigation path, SAP MENU • LOGISTICS • PRODUCTION • KANBAN • SUPPLY AREA • MAINTAIN.

Storage Location for External Procurement

The storage location for external procurement (STORAGE LOC. FOR EP) field is used as the storage location defaulted into the planned order for material procured externally.

JIT Delivery Schedule

This indicator can be set to allow a JIT delivery schedule to be generated as well as the forecast schedules for this material.

Co-Product Indicator

A co-product is a material generated by the production process that has the composition or characteristics of a manufactured product or raw material. The CO-PRODUCT field indicates whether this material can be used as a co-product.

Bulk Material Indicator

This indicator, if set, defines the material as a bulk material for BOM purposes.

5.5.5 Net Requirements Calculations

The net requirement calculations are for the safety stock amounts that are active for a material at a specific plant. For example, depending on the specific production facilities at each plant and the location of key vendors, the values of safety stock, minimum safety stock, and service level may be very different for each plant in the company.

Safety Stock

The purpose of SAFETY STOCK is to ensure that there is no material shortage for production. The safety stock level is designed to offset any unexpected increase in demand.

Service Level

This percentage field is used in the calculation of safety stock. A low SERVICE LEVEL percentage will reflect in a low safety stock level.

Minimum Safety Stock

The minimum safety stock level (MIN. SAFETY STOCK) is the lower limit of the safety stock range. This should only be used by the planning department in forecasting and calculating of safety stock.

Coverage Profile

The COVERAGE PROFILE field defines parameters used in the calculation of dynamic safety stock. The dynamic safety stock is calculated using daily average requirements and the range of coverage. The coverage profile can be found in Table T438R. The coverage profile can be configured via the navigation path, IMG • MATERIALS MANAGEMENT • CONSUMPTION-BASED PLANNING • PLANNING • MRP CALCULATION • DEFINE RANGE OF COVERAGE PROFILE.

Safety Time Indicator

The safety time indicator (SAFETY TIME IND.) allows the user to define the mechanism for safety time. Two indicators can be used. The first allows the safety time to be active for all requirements; the second is just for independent requirements. The safety time is when the MRP requirements can be brought forward. This inserts a time buffer to allow more time for the delivery of materials, among other things.

Safety Time/Actual Coverage

The SAFETY TIME/ACT.COV field contains the value representing the actual time that the MRP requirements are brought forward. The figure is the number of actual coverage in workdays.

Period Profile for Safety Time

In defining safety time, it can be more useful to employ a period profile, given that requirements fluctuate at different times of the year. In configuration, the user can create a safety time based on the dates the user enters for each period. The user can also create a number of safety time-period profiles.

The configuration can be completed in Transaction OM0D or via the navigation path, IMG • MATERIALS MANAGEMENT • CONSUMPTION-BASED PLANNING • PLANNING • MRP CALCULATION • DEFINE PERIOD PROFILE FOR SAFETY TIME.

The third MRP screen on the Material Master, shown in Figure 5.10, allows the entry of forecast, planning, and availability check information.

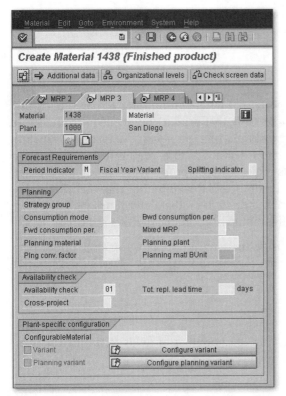

Figure 5.10 Third MRP Data Entry Screen

5.5.6 Forecast Requirements

The FORECAST REQUIREMENTS section contains three fields: PERIOD INDICATOR, FIS-CAL YEAR VARIANT, and SPLITTING INDICATOR.

Period Indicator

The PERIOD INDICATOR field specifies the time period for which the consumption values are held for forecasting. The normal time period is one month, which is the SAP default if this field is left blank. This field is also displayed on the FORECAST-ING DATA screen.

Fiscal Year Variant

The FISCAL YEAR VARIANT is an accounting-defined field that describes the variant for the fiscal year, that is, the number of posting periods. The fiscal year variant can be seen in Table T009 and configured using Transaction OB37 or via the navigation path, IMG • FINANCIAL ACCOUNTING • FINANCIAL ACCOUNTING GLOBAL SETTINGS • FISCAL YEAR • MAINTAIN FISCAL YEAR VARIANT. This field is also displayed on the FORECASTING DATA screen.

Splitting Indicator

The SPLITTING INDICATOR is an important function within forecast-based planning. The forecast for a material may determine that production needs to manufacture 1,000 units per month for the next six months. However, the planning function needs to split this into smaller time intervals. It may require the planning run to determine the number of units required to be produced each day for the first month, then weekly for the second month, and then monthly after that. To do this, a splitting indicator can be defined in configuration that determines the number of days, the number of weeks, and the number of forecast periods required.

This configuration can be found using the navigation path, IMG • PRODUCTION • BASIC DATA • MATERIAL REQUIREMENTS PLANNING • FORECAST • DEFINE SPLITTING OF FORECAST REQUIREMENTS FOR MRP.

5.5.7 Planning

This part of the screen allows the entry of a number of fields regarding the planning of the material at the specific plant.

Strategy Group

STRATEGY GROUP is a field that groups planning strategies. The strategies used in planning are usually predefined in SAP. Examples of strategies include 20 - Make to Order Production, 30 - Production by Lot Size, and 70 - Planning at Assembly Level.

The strategy group is defined with a main strategy and then can have up to seven other strategies as part of that group. For instance, the strategy group 33 may have its main planning strategy defined as 30 – Production by Lot Size, and then have 40 – Planning with Final Assembly defined as part of the group. The configuration for the strategy group can be found using the navigation path, IMG • PRODUCTION • BASIC DATA • MATERIAL REQUIREMENTS PLANNING • MASTER DATA • INDEPENDENT REQUIREMENTS PARAMETERS • PLANNING STRATEGY • DEFINE STRATEGY GROUP.

Consumption Mode

The CONSUMPTION MODE is simply the direction in which the system consumes requirements. In backward consumption, the consumption of the planned requirements occurs before the requirement date. In a forward-consumption system, consumption occurs after the requirement date.

Backward Consumption Period

The BWD CONSUMPTION PER. field is a figure that relates to consumption mode. If the consumption mode is defined as backward consumption, then this field can be defined to the number of workdays that consumption should be carried out. The backward-consumption period can last up to 999 workdays from the current date.

Forward Consumption Period

The FWD CONSUMPTION PER. field also relates to consumption mode. If the consumption mode is defined as forward consumption, then this field can be defined to the number of workdays that consumption should be carried out. The forward-consumption period can last up to 999 workdays from the current date.

Mixed MRP

The MIXED MRP field can identify the material as being available to one of three options: subassembly planning with final assembly, gross requirements planning, or subassembly planning without final assembly.

Planning Material

The PLANNING MATERIAL field can be used when the material has a BOM that contains variant and non-variant parts. Using another material (the planning material), the planning department can plan the non-variant parts. When planning runs, the planning material is not produced but is only used to plan the non-variant parts. This planning strategy is called planning with a planning material.

Planning Plant

The PLANNING PLANT field reflects the plant that is associated with the planning of the material. The material is planned to be goods receipted into this plant.

Conversion Factor for Planning Material

If the regular material and the planning material do not have the same unit of measure, a conversion is needed. The PLNG CONV. FACTOR field holds a 10-character string and can be defined as appropriate. If the field is blank, the system assumes that the conversation factor is one.

5.5.8 Availability Check

This section allows the review of the availability check that has been identified on other entry screens and the addition of total replenishment lead time and cross project materials.

Total Replenishment Lead Time

The Tot. repl. lead time field reflects the time, in workdays, that it will take before the material is available to be used or sold. This field is not a system calculation but should be the sum of the total in-house production times and the planned delivery times. This field should be entered if the planning department wants it to be part of the availability check.

Cross-Project Material Indicator

This indicator allows the user to take into account all project stock or just the one project segment.

The fourth MRP screen, shown in Figure 5.11, shows the BOM explosion data, such as Component scrap percentage; information for discontinued parts, such as Follow-up matl; repetitive manufacturing, assemblies, and deployment strategy, such as REM profile; and storage location MRP, such as SLoc MRP indicator.

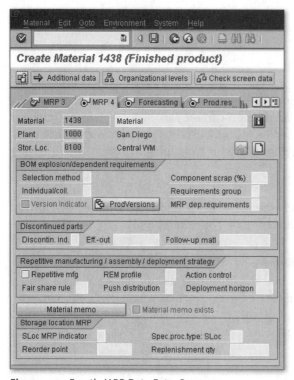

Figure 5.11 Fourth MRP Data Entry Screen

5.5.9 Bill of Materials Explosion/Dependent Requirements

The information in the BOM EXPLOSION/DEPENDENT REQUIREMENTS section includes the selection method, component scrap, and requirements group.

Selection Method

The SELECTION METHOD determines the way in which the alternate BOM is selected during MRP. There are four selection methods to choose from:

▶ **Selection by Order Quantity:** Alternative BOM is chosen by lot size.

▶ **Selection by Explosion Date:** Alternative BOM is chosen by date.

▶ **Selection by Production Version**: Alternative BOM is defined in production version.

▶ **Selection by Only Production Version:** If no production version exists, then no production orders are created.

Component Scrap

The COMPONENT SCRAP percentage is needed to calculate the correct figure for component stock in MRP. This field is needed if the material is a component in a BOM. If a BOM for a finished material needs 400 units of material X, and material X has a component scrap figure of 10%, then the actual figure needed is 110%, that is, 440 units of material X. This figure is not used if it is defined in the BOM.

Individual or Collective Requirements

The INDIVIDUAL/COLL. indicator allows the planning department to determine whether this material is relevant for individual or collective requirements, or for both. Individual requirements are the quantities of the material that are shown separately. The collective requirements are quantities of the material that are grouped together.

Requirements Group

The REQUIREMENTS GROUP field can be set to allow the system to group together the material requirements for the material on a daily basis.

MRP Dependent Requirements

This indicator is used for make-to-stock materials and assemblies. The indicator can be set to indicate that the materials-dependent requirements are relevant for MRP.

5.5.10 Discontinued Parts

If the material is to be discontinued, data regarding the discontinuation can be added in this section. In many industries, you will find materials that are discontinued. For example, companies that manufacture and sell computer network cards are continually updating and improving technology. Their products are frequently discontinued, and replacement products are introduced.

Discontinuation Indicator

The DISONTIN. IND. indicator is used when a material is being discontinued. For MRP purposes, the system needs to know whether this material has dependent requirements. This indicator can be set to "1" for a single-level material and to "3" for dependent requirements.

Effective-out Date

The EFF.-OUT field reflects the date by which the inventory of the discontinued material will be at zero. At this time, the follow-up material will be used in its place.

Follow-Up Material

This is the material number of the material that will take the place of the discontinued material on the effective-out date.

5.5.11 Repetitive Manufacturing/Assembly/Deployment Strategy

Information in this section relates to the repetitive manufacturing, assemblies, and deployment strategy.

Repetitive Manufacturing Indicator

This indicator allows the material to be considered in repetitive manufacturing. If this indicator is set, a repetitive manufacturing profile also must be entered for the material.

Repetitive Manufacturing Profile

The repetitive manufacturing profile (REM PROFILE) is configured but allows the production user to determine some of these issues:

▶ Error correction for use during backflushing

▶ Goods issue backflushing at goods receipt

- Planned order reduction
- Which movement types are used

The repetitive manufacturing profile can be configured using the navigation path, IMG • PRODUCTION • REPETITIVE MANUFACTURING • CONTROL DATA • DEFINE REPETITIVE MANUFACTURING PROFILES.

Action Control

The ACTION CONTROL field defines what actions occur and in what sequence they will occur for a planned order. The planning department can define this field in configuration to create actions that can occur during the planned order.

The action keys combined to make up the action control are defined in configuration using the navigation path, IMG • PRODUCTION • MATERIAL REQUIREMENTS PLANNING • PROCUREMENT PROPOSALS • PLANNED ORDERS • ACTION FOR PLANNED ORDER • DEFINE ACTION KEYS.

Table 5.2 shows the keys and actions predefined in SAP.

Key	Action
BOME	Explode BOM
BEMA	Explode BOM, check material availability
NEMA	Check material availability; no BOM explosion
MAAV	Check material availability; BOM explosion if necessary
RSMA	Reset availability check
SCHE	Schedule planned order
CPOD	Change planned order
PRNT	Print component list
ZZxx	User-defined action

Table 5.2 Action Keys Predefined in SAP

The action control can be defined by selecting these action keys. The configuration can be found using the navigation path, IMG • PRODUCTION • MATERIAL REQUIREMENTS PLANNING • PROCUREMENT PROPOSALS • PLANNED ORDERS • ACTION FOR PLANNED ORDER • DEFINE ACTION CONTROL.

Fair Share Rule

This field is maintained if the company has implemented, or will implement distribution requirements planning (DRP). This field allows the planners to determine a rule for materials deployment when demand exceeds supply.

Push Distribution

This field is maintained for DRP. If the material is in surplus, the planners can define whether the material is to be subject to push or pull distribution.

5.5.12 Storage Location MRP

The data in this section relates to when a storage location is planned separately or excluded from plant MRP.

Storage Location MRP Indicator

The SLoc MRP INDICATOR field allows the entry of an indicator to exclude the material in this storage location from MRP procedures. If this field is left blank, then the stock, requirements, and receipts are included in MRP at plant level. If storage location stock is planned separately, the storage location is replenished with goods if the stock falls below the reorder point, which is entered in this section.

Special Procurement Type at Storage Location Level

The SPEC.PROC.TYPE: SLoc field defines the procurement type for the material specifically at the storage location level. The values in this field are found in Table T460A. The configuration for the values used in this field can be found using the navigation path, IMG • PRODUCTION • MATERIAL REQUIREMENTS PLANNING • MASTER DATA • DEFINE SPECIAL PROCUREMENT TYPE.

Reorder Point for Storage Location MRP

Unlike other reorder points, this is specifically for storage location MRP. If the material falls below this reorder quantity, SAP will enter the material in the planning file at the storage location level.

Replenishment Quantity for Storage Location MRP

This field is the quantity that must be ordered or produced in the case of a storage location shortage. This process will lead to a stock transfer reservation within the plant when a planning run is carried out, and the replenishment quantity is transferred from the plant to the storage location.

The MRP screens examined in this section contain a large amount of information that may be required when material is to be produced in-house. Check with the production staff to ensure that the correct information is entered. The next section examines the information entered into the ACCOUNTING data screen of the Material Master.

5.6 Accounting Data

The first ACCOUNTING data entry screen in the Material Master (shown in Figure 5.12) allows the accounting department to enter the valuation and price data needed for inventory transactions.

Figure 5.12 Accounting Data Screen 1 in the Material Master

5.6.1 General Data

The GENERAL DATA on the first accounting screen displays some information that has been entered on other Material Master screens, such as BASE UNIT OF MEASURE.

Valuation Category

This field determines whether the material is subject to split valuation. Split valuation means that the material can be valuated in different ways. An example of split valuation is the valuation of batches separately, such as in the chemical industry where batches of the same material may have a different number of days left before the batches expire. A batch with only 10 days before expiry may be valuated differently from a batch that has 100 days left before expiry because the batch with only 10 days left of shelf life could only be sold at a discount price.

ML Active

The ML ACT. indicator shows if the material ledger has been activated for this material. The material ledger is the basis of actual costing. It enables material inventories to be valuated in multiple currencies and allows the use of different valuation approaches.

5.6.2   Current Valuation

The CURRENT VALUATION section is where the valuation class is determined for the material at the specific plant and the price of the material, either standard or moving average.

Valuation Class

The VALUATION CLASS field is a mechanism to assign a material to the GL accounts. These GL accounts are updated when material movements occur that are relevant to accounting. The valuation class is assigned to a material type, via configuration.

The valuation class can be configured in Transaction OMSK or via the navigation path, IMG • MATERIALS MANAGEMENT • VALUATION AND ACCOUNT ASSIGNMENT • ACCOUNT DETERMINATION • ACCOUNT DETERMINATION WITHOUT WIZARD • DEFINE VALUATION CLASS.

Valuation Class for Sales Order Stocks

The accounting department has the option of entering a different valuation class for sales-order stock in the VC: SALES ORDER STK field.

Valuation Class for Project Stock

As with the valuation class for sales-order stock, the accounting department can enter a different valuation class for project stock in the Proj. stk val. class field.

Price Control

The Price control field is used in the valuation of the stock. The two options are average moving price (V) and standard price (S).

Price Unit

The number entered in the Price Unit field is the number of units that the moving price or standard price relates to. Therefore, if the standard price for material XYZ is USD 3.24, and the price unit is 1000, then the actual cost per unit is USD 0.00324. The price unit is important when entering materials with very small prices because it can prevent rounding errors if the number of decimal places in a report is not sufficient.

Moving Price

The moving price, more often called the moving average price, is calculated by dividing the material value by the total stock. This price changes with each goods movement that is relevant for valuation. The accounting department can make an initial price entry if the Price control indicator is set to "V" for Moving price. This field is also referred to as the periodic unit price if the material ledger is active.

Standard Price

The Standard price field is a constant; once entered, it does not fluctuate. It does not take into account invoice prices or any other price-altering movements. The standard price can be entered when the Price control indicator is set to "S" for Standard price.

Future Price

The Standard price can be changed through an entry in the Future price field. The future price is entered in the field and will become valid from the date that it is entered in the Valid from field.

The second accounting screen (see Figure 5.13) shows the Determination of lowest value and LIFO data sections.

Figure 5.13 Accounting Data Screen 2 in the Material Master

5.6.3 Determination of Lowest Value

This section contains the fields for three TAX PRICE and three COMMERCIAL PRICE fields, as well as the DEVALUATION IND. and PRICE UNIT fields.

Tax Price

This field is not used in the United States but is used in some countries. Ask your accounting department if this field is used in your particular country. This field is available for entering the price of the material for tax purposes.

Commercial Price

This field is also not used in the United States but is used in some countries. Ask your accounting department if this field is used in your particular country. This field is available for entering the price of the material for commercial valuation purposes.

Devaluation Indicator

The DEVALUATION IND. value can be entered into a Material Master if the company feels that the material is a slow or non-moving item. The accounting department can configure a number of indicators for each material type per company code that has a devaluation percentage attached.

The indicator can be changed to increase or decrease the devaluation percentage depending on the movement of the material stock. The indicators can be configured through Transaction OMW6 or via the navigation path, IMG • MATERIALS MANAGEMENT • VALUATION AND ACCOUNT ASSIGNMENT • BALANCE SHEET VALUATION PROCEDURES • CONFIGURE LOWEST-VALUE METHOD • PRICE DEDUCTIONS BASED ON NON-MOVEMENT • MAINTAIN DEVALUATION BY SLOW/NON-MOVEMENT BY COMPANY CODE.

5.6.4 LIFO Data

The two fields in this section are the LIFO/FIFO-RELEVANT indicator and the LIFO POOL field.

LIFO/FIFO-Relevant

If this indicator is set, it means that the material is subject to LIFO and FIFO valuation.

LIFO (last in, first out) valuation for stock implies that as new stock comes in and then moves out first, the old stock does not change in value, and there is no overvaluation of the older stock.

FIFO (first in, first out) valuation calculates the valuation of the stock based on the price of the last receipt. Although this is the most realistic valuation, it can overvaluate older stock.

LIFO Pool

The LIFO POOL field is ignored if the material is not LIFO relevant. The LIFO POOL field can be configured to define a group of materials that can be valued together. The LIFO pools can be configured in Transaction OMW2 or via the navigation path, IMG • MATERIALS MANAGEMENT • VALUATION AND ACCOUNT ASSIGNMENT • BALANCE SHEET VALUATION PROCEDURES • CONFIGURE LIFO/FIFO METHODS • LIFO • CONFIGURE LIFO POOLS.

The accounting screens examined in this section contain specific information that is important when the material is valuated. Check with the accounting staff to ensure that the correct information is entered. The next section examines the information entered into the COSTING screen of the Material Master.

5.7 Costing Data

The COSTING data screens of the Material Master, shown in Figures 5.14 and 5.15, allow the costing department to enter costing information for the material. Some of the fields on these screens have been discussed in previous sections.

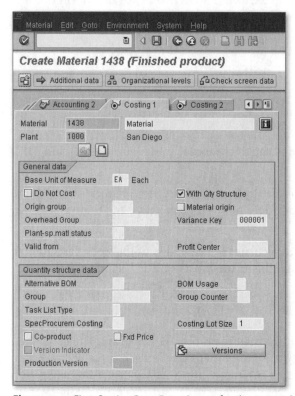

Figure 5.14 First Costing Data Entry Screen for the Material Master

5.7.1 General Data

The GENERAL DATA section contains the following fields.

Do Not Cost

This field should be selected if the material will not have a material cost estimate, a sales order cost estimate, or a procurement alternative. The material will also be unable to be part of a BOM's explosion.

With Quantity Structure

The costing of materials can be performed with or without a quantity structure. If your client costs materials with quantity structure, turn on the WITH QTY STRUCTURE indicator. If your client costs materials without quantity structure, do not turn on this indicator. If this indicator is not set, the planned costs for the material are calculated using the cost estimate without quantity structure. Check with the client's staff working on costing of materials to ensure this field is set correctly.

Origin Group

The ORIGIN GROUP field is used to subdivide overhead and material costs. The material can be assigned to an origin group, and overhead costs are assigned to different origin groups at different percentage rates or at a flat cost.

Material Origin

The MATERIAL ORIGIN indicator should be set when the costs incurred need to be updated under a primary cost element and with reference to the material number.

Overhead Group

The costing OVERHEAD GROUP field applies overhead costs from the costing sheet of a production order to materials in that group.

5.7.2 Quantity Structure Data

Some of the fields in the QUANTITY STRUCTURE DATA section have been explained in the descriptions of previous screens, such as BOM USAGE and ALTERNATIVE BOM.

Group

A GROUP or sometimes called a task list group, can combine production processes that are similar and are for similar materials. It can be used to group task lists for varying lot sizes.

Group Counter

Combined with the group, the GROUP COUNTER identifies a unique task list for the material. A task list describes the steps needed to produce a material or perform an activity without reference to an order. The task list is comprised of a header, operations, material component allocations, PRT, and inspection characteristics.

Task-List Type

This field identifies the task list type, that is, whether the task list is for routings, rate routings, standard networks, and so on. The task list type can be maintained using Transaction OP8B or via the navigation path, IMG • Production • Basic Data • Routing • Control Data • Maintain Task List Types.

Costing Lot Size

This field allows the product costing department to enter a lot size for the material that would be used in the product cost estimate.

The first section of the second costing screen (see Figure 5.15) is the Standard Cost Estimate, which shows future, current, and previous prices.

Figure 5.15 Second Costing Data Entry Screen for the Material Master

5.7.3   Standard Cost Estimate

The standard cost estimate is the most important type of cost estimate in material costing. This type of cost estimate forms the basis for profit planning or product costing. The standard cost estimate is created for each material at the beginning of the company's fiscal year.

Planned Price

The PLANNED PRICE field allows the entry of a marked standard cost estimate for a future price for the material. When a standard cost estimate for a material is marked, the cost calculated in the standard cost estimate is written to the Material Master record as the future planned price. A standard cost estimate must be marked before it can be released to the material. This is not the same as the three planned price fields in the PLANNED PRICES section.

Standard Price

The value in the STANDARD PRICE field means that all goods movements are valuated at that same price.

5.7.4 Planned Prices

This part of the screen allows the costing user to add three planned prices to the Material Master and the dates on which those prices become valid.

Planned Price 1

Subsequent to the planned price from the standard cost estimate, three other planned prices can be added to the Material Master that can be used for product costing. When the price becomes valid, by date, the price is used in product costing.

Planned Price Date 1

This is the date on which the planned price 1 becomes valid to be used by product costing.

The COSTING screens contain a number of fields that are not familiar to the MM consultant, so you should contact the costing analyst to ensure that the data entered in the Material Master is correct.

5.8 Business Examples – Material Master Data

As you've noticed in this and the previous chapter, it's important for Material Master data at any company to be accurate and current. During the implementation of a new SAP system, it's vitally important to allocate sufficient time and resources to the migration of data. If the data migrated to Material Master records are not accurate, this can cause a high degree of inefficiency and inconsistency for the company.

5.8.1 Plant and Storage Location Data

Some data fields on the Material Master record are specific to a plant and a storage location. These include the material's shelf-life characteristics, storage bin, container requirements, maximum storage period, and total shelf life of the material.

Example

A small Canadian manufacturing company had implemented SAP ERP as part of a wider implementation by its German parent company. Because the company operated with few employees, the company decided not to implement WM but to use the Inventory Management functionality, despite the fact that before SAP ERP, the company used a PC warehouse package interfaced to its in-house system. After two months of operating SAP ERP, the company found that the time it took to locate and ship products had significantly increased. Management immediately identified the lack of a warehousing system as the primary reason for the decline in customer service. An SAP team from the head office was brought in to see what could be done to increase productivity and perform re-training if necessary.

The team soon realized that the data in the Material Master at the plant and storage location level did not include any information on where material was stored in the warehouse. Although the decision had been made not to implement WM, the company had not loaded any information about the static location in the warehouse of where material was stored. The team entered the storage bin location of each material on the Material Master, along with other missing data such as cycle counting information and maximum storage period. Subsequent to this change, the time it took to locate and ship product to a customer did return to around the pre-SAP level.

5.8.2 Warehouse Data

Not all companies implement WM, and some find that the functionality contained in the Inventory Management process is quite adequate for the materials their company deals with. However, when WM is implemented, a certain amount of data needs to be entered.

Example

When a company decides to implement WM, it is important to ensure that the warehouse data in the Material Master are accurate. Entering the correct information in the warehouse screens for stock removal and stock placement allows the automatic strategies to work successfully. Using the automatic search and confirmation processes in SAP ERP can save significant time and effort.

A U.S. manufacturer of industrial tools implemented SAP ERP and was using the WM functionality. The company had configured some of the automatic processes but hadn't entered the correct information for all materials. This meant some transfer orders had to be manually created and confirmed. The warehouse operators required the shift manager to create the necessary transfer orders, which resulted in a bottleneck when the goods receiving area needed to be cleared. The company decided to try to alleviate this problem by examining the Material Master records for items in the warehouse and updating the correct information for the stock removal and stock placement fields. After the updates were complete, the bottleneck was removed because warehouse operators no longer waited for transfer orders to be created.

5.8.3　Quality Management Data

The QUALITY MANAGEMENT screen contains data that is used by member of the quality department when they have to perform processes on the material. Quality is important when raw materials are received prior to being used in the manufacturing process or during the manufacturing process. Quality is also important before finished goods are sent to customers.

Example

A manufacturer of injection plastic molds had been using the same local supplier of polyethylene beads for more than 10 years. Over that time, there were no issues with the quality of the product. The company received a notice from the supplier that it had been acquired by a larger company from out of state, but the products would still be manufactured at the local site. The next shipment from the supplier did not arrive in the same packaging, but because the company did receive a notice from the supplier, no additional checks were made on the product. When the polyethylene beads were used in the molds, it became clear that the product was not performing as usual. The beads melted too quickly, and the resulting molds were damaged.

The company performed a quality analysis on the raw material and found it to be significantly different from the previous material, although it was just barely within the tolerances for the product. The company decided to tighten the tolerances of the raw material it would accept, and this was relayed to the supplier. In addition, the company decided to inspect all material from the supplier at goods receipt, and the Material Master records were updated to reflect this.

5.8.4　Material Requirements Planning Data

The information on the MRP screens is important in how material is made, planned, and produced within the plant. Without this information, the production planning of items within a plant will not be efficient and resources will not be used to their optimum level.

Example

A large automotive parts manufacturer in the middle of implementing a new version of SAP ERP purchased an elevator parts manufacturer. The elevator parts manufacturer thought this would be an ideal opportunity to upgrade its aging software and to be on the same platform as its new owners. The AS/400 software used by the company had been customized to the way it operated and was focused mainly on finance and sales, rather than manufacturing. The planning for the production of parts was first created on the AS/400 software and then manually changed by the production manager based on his experience of the process. This manual intervention allowed the company to react quickly to changes due to problems with the supply of raw materials. However, this was problematic for the sales staff because they were unaware of the changes when dealing with customers.

The migration of data from the AS/400 to the SAP ERP system was a relatively smooth process with a lot of data having to be created because it wasn't available on the legacy system. During testing, the team found that the production planning tests created purchasing requisitions that were far short of what was normally created. In addition, the tests found that stockouts would occur on the company's most popular items. When the production manager was asked if he could help explain these events, he indicated that, as a rule, he would manually change the POs to suppliers because they were always short. After the production manager explained the manual changes he normally made, the team was able to adopt those changes into the Material Master data. The integration tests were re-run with more successful results.

5.8.5   Accounting Data

The accounting information in the Material Master allows the accounting department to enter the valuation and price data needed for inventory transactions. Although as a logistics-focused consultant you may not fully comprehend the processes in the accounting functionality, it's important to understand the accounting data in the Material Master.

Example

A small whiskey manufacturer was looking to replace its in-house developed systems and had told prospective ERP vendors of an issue that it has to deal with on a daily basis. When a finished product was produced, it was free of any taxes inside of the factory gates. As soon as the product left the facility, it was subject to tax.

So, if product was returned to the facility for any reason, such as rejected by the customer or if the truck broke down and had to be towed back to the plant, the returned product would be valuated at a different amount. This meant that there would be split valuation; some batches of material that had been returned would be valued at a higher amount, while other batches that had never left the facility would be valued at a lower amount. While some ERP vendors don't have the capabilities to deal with this scenario, split valuation can be dealt with within Material Master records in SAP ERP.

5.9 Summary

This chapter discussed the elements that make up the Material Master file. When you first encounter the SAP Material Master file, it might seem daunting. Other inventory or integrated systems have item master files that are a fraction of the size of the Material Master. This is important when bringing on legacy systems.

When converting item master files into the SAP Material Master, it is common for the legacy master files to only hold a small number of the necessary fields for the Material Master. Most companies spend a great deal of time constructing data for the Material Master.

Therefore, if you intend to be involved in the Material Master and assisting in this type of project, it is prudent to learn about the Material Master structure and the implications of entering or not entering information into Material Master fields.

Another master file is examined in Chapter 6: the Vendor Master file. The vendor is the company who supplies materials and services. The information contained in the Vendor Master file allows the purchasing department to purchase from and pay the vendor.

The Vendor Master is as important to the accounting staff as it to those in purchasing. The vendor's relationship with any company is twofold: negotiating price and supplying material through purchasing, while invoicing and receiving payment through accounts payable.

6 Vendor Master Data

The Vendor Master is a collection of data that fully describes the vendor's relationship with the company. The vendor normally will have an initial relationship with the purchasing department. Purchasing may have selected the vendor through its response to a request for quotation (RFQ) or because it is the sole vendor for a required material. However, before a vendor is authorized, the accounting department will ensure that the information it requires is available and satisfactory.

Just as a Material Master record is not complete until all relevant departments have entered their data, the Vendor Master is not complete until both the accounting and purchasing departments have entered their information.

The Vendor Master can be created using three transactions, each of them giving different views of the data to be entered for the vendor:

- **XK01**: Create Vendor Centrally.
- **FK01**: Create Vendor via Accounting.
- **MK01**: Create Vendor via Purchasing.

6.1 General Data

Transaction XK01 enables accounting users to enter the ACCOUNT GROUP for the vendor and either the COMPANY CODE or PURCHASING ORGANIZATION, or both as shown in Figure 6.1. The vendor number may need to be entered if the account group is defined as allowing only external number assignment.

The Vendor Master can be created by referencing an existing vendor. To do this, use the REFERENCE section below the ACCOUNT GROUP field. This can be an efficient method of creating vendors that may have the same or similar data.

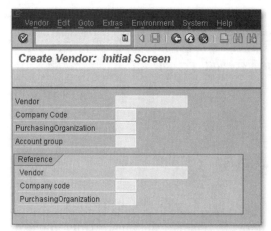

Figure 6.1 Entry Screen for Transaction XK01, Create Vendor

6.1.1 Address Screen

The initial screen of the Vendor Master is the ADDRESS screen, shown in Figure 6.2. The information to be entered includes the vendor's NAME and address and communications data, including TELEPHONE, FAX, and EMAIL.

Title

This is the title for the vendor. If it is a company, then select the COMPANY option; otherwise, select the appropriate salutation. The titles for the business address forms can be configured in the IMG via the navigation path, IMG • FLEXIBLE REAL ESTATE MANAGEMENT • ADDRESS MANAGEMENT • MAINTAIN TEXTS FOR FORM OF ADDRESS.

Name

The NAME of the vendor should be consistent to avoid duplicate vendor entries. The purchasing department should create a template to follow so that the vendor name always appears the same way as it is entered into the Vendor Master. This will benefit the purchasing users during vendor searches.

Search Terms

The search term is used to find vendors. The entry of data into the SEARCH TERM 1/2 field can be structured so that purchasing users can easily remember the criteria for this type of search. For example, the policy may be to enter a search term that is the first five characters of the vendor name plus the two-letter country code for the vendor's country location. For these criteria, the search term for Smith Brothers of London, England would be SMITHGB, and Lakshmi Machine of Coimbatore, India would be LAKSHIN. There is no case sensitivity for this field.

Street Address

The STREET ADDRESS is the address of the vendor. The COUNTRY, REGION, and POSTAL CODE will be used to calculate the tax jurisdiction code. If connected to an external tax system, such as Vertex or Taxware, the transaction may validate the address information that you enter to ensure that a valid tax jurisdiction code is obtained.

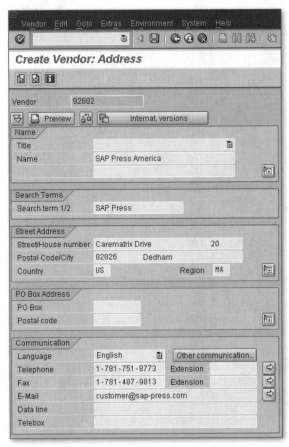

Figure 6.2 Create Address Screen for the Vendor Master

PO Box Address

Many companies use post-office boxes, and these fields allow that information to be added to the Vendor Master.

Communication

The COMMUNICATION fields should be kept up to date, especially because fax numbers and email addresses change at the vendor regularly.

6.1.2 Control Screen

The CONTROL screen as shown in Figure 6.3 as CREATE VENDOR: CONTROL, allows the accounting user to enter some general tax information and reference data.

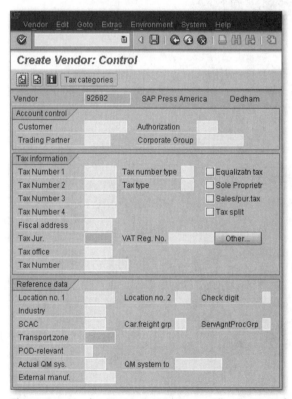

Figure 6.3 Vendor Master Control Screen Allowing Tax Information Entries

Customer

This CUSTOMER field allows the purchasing user to enter the customer number for the vendor, if the vendor is both a vendor and a customer of the company. For example, a paper-pulping company may be a vendor for paper products to a particleboard manufacturer but also may be a customer for scrap particleboard that it can use in pulp creation.

Trading Partner

If the vendor is part of an independent company that has been designated in Financial Accounting for consolidation purposes, then it is possible to enter that company in this field as a trading partner. The companies are configured as internal trading partners in financial accounting. The navigation path is IMG • ENTERPRISE STRUCTURE • DEFINITION • FINANCIAL ACCOUNTING • DEFINE COMPANY.

Corporate Group

The CORPORATE GROUP key is used to combine vendors to enhance the search capability. The group key is a 10-character string and is not configured. Therefore, a policy for entering a group key must be established before any vendor entry commences.

For example, a user might create a group key based on the characters having meaning. This could be defined as the following:

- Characters 1 and 2 – Country of vendor
- Characters 3 and 4 – Industry Code
- Characters 5 through 7 – Minority Indicator
- Character 8 – ABC indicator
- Characters 9 and 10 – Shipping Conditions

Tax Numbers 1 and 2

These fields allow the accounting user to enter the tax identification number, or numbers, of the vendor. In the United States, this would be the Employer Identification Number (EIN), or Social Security number (SSN), if the vendor is an individual. In France, this field would be the SIRET number; in Spain, the NIF number; and so on for various countries.

Tax Type

The TAX TYPE can be assigned to the vendor to identify its position regarding sales- and use-tax responsibility.

Jurisdiction Code

The tax jurisdiction code is either determined in SAP by the information entered in the ADDRESS field or referenced from an external tax package, such as Vertex or Taxware. The tax jurisdiction code is valid only to vendors in the United States.

Country-Specific Tax Fields

Some of the fields on the Vendor Master control screen are specific to certain countries:

▶ TAX NUMBER TYPE: Specific to Argentina.

▶ EQUALIZATN TAX: Specific to Spain.

▶ SOLE PROPRIETR: Specific to 11 countries, including Italy, Peru, and Mexico.

▶ SALES/PUR. TAX: Specific to countries that levy value-added tax (VAT).

▶ VAT REG. NO.: The VAT number for the vendor, which is important in EU countries.

▶ FISCAL ADDRESS: Specific to Italy.

Global Location Number (GLN)

In the CREATE VENDOR: CONTROL screen, the option is to enter the 13-digit GLN of the vendor. In SAP, the number is divided into three fields, LOCATION NO. 1, LOCATION NO. 2, and CHECK DIGIT in the REFERENCES section. The GLN is issued to a company to identify a legal, functional, or physical location within a business or organizational entity. GLNs are governed by strict rules to guarantee that each one is unique worldwide. The identification of locations by GLN is required for an efficient flow of goods and information between trading partners through EDI messages, payment slips, and so on. The GLN is often found as a bar code on documents.

Industry Key

The INDUSTRY key is another grouping to allow similar vendors to be grouped by industry. This field can also be found in Customer Master records. The INDUSTRY key can be configured using the navigation path, IMG • SALES AND DISTRIBUTION • BUSINESS PARTNERS • MARKETING • DEFINE INDUSTRY SECTOR FOR CUSTOMERS.

Standard Carrier Alpha Code (SCAC)

The National Motor Freight Traffic Association (NMFTA) in the United States maintains the Standard Carrier Alpha Code (SCAC). The NMFTA is a nonprofit membership organization with more than 1,000 motor-carrier members, regulated by the U.S. Department of Transportation's Surface Transportation Board and various state and federal agencies.

The SCAC code is a four-letter string used to uniquely identify a shipping carrier. The SCAC code is frequently used in EDI, on the 856 Advance Ship Notice, the 850 Purchase Order, and all motor, rail, and water-carrier transactions where carrier identification is required. SCAC codes are mandatory when doing business with all U.S. government agencies.

Certain groups of SCAC codes are reserved for specific purposes:

▸ Codes ending with the letter U are reserved for the identification of freight containers.

▸ Codes ending with the letter X are reserved for the identification of privately owned railroad cars.

▸ Codes ending with the letter Z are reserved for the identification of truck chassis and trailers used in intermodal service.

Forwarding Agent Freight Group

This forward agent freight group key, identified in Figure 6.3 as Car.freight grp, is assigned to the forwarding agent to group together forwarding agents. For example, the company's transportation department may decide to group its freight forwarders by mode of transport. Therefore, the transportation staff could configure three freight groups: rail, road, and shipping. The freight groups are part of the determination of freight costs. The configuration for freight groups can be found via the navigation path, IMG • Logistics Execution • Transportation • Basic Transportation Functions • Maintain Freight Code Sets and Freight Codes • Define Forwarding Agent – Freight Groups.

Service-Agent Procedure Group

The freight costs can be calculated as part of the pricing procedure. To calculate the correct freight costs, the service-agent procedure group (ServAgntProcGrp) has a range of forwarding agents assigned to it. The service-agent procedure group is then assigned to a pricing procedure to calculate freight costs. The group can be configured using the navigation path, IMG • Logistics Execution • Transportation • Shipping Costs • Pricing • Pricing Control • Define and Assign Pricing Procedures • Define Service Agent Procedure Group.

Vendor's QM System

Many government agencies require that the quality management (QM) systems used by a vendor meet certain levels of verification. These verifications are the level of certification of the system, that is, ISO 9001, ISO 9002, and so on. The verification levels can be configured in Transaction OQB7 or via the navigation path, IMG • Quality Management • QM in Logistics • QM in Procurement • Define QM Systems.

QM System Valid to Date

The date is the expiry date of the certification of the vendor's QM system. For example, a company that has an ISO 9001:2000 certification has to renew it every three years according to ISO certification regulations.

External Manufacturer Code Name or Number

This field can be used to hold a number or reference for the vendor but is not the vendor number. For example, this field could be used to enter a nickname for a company; SCT may be entered as a shortened version of Southwark Clapton and Thomas. The field will allow up to 10 characters.

6.1.3   Payment Transactions

The Payment transactions screen, shown in Figure 6.4, allows the accounting department to add information on the bank details of the vendor and the payment instructions.

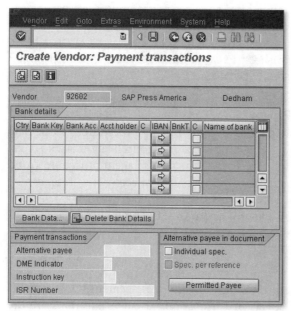

Figure 6.4 Payment Transaction Screen of the Vendor Master

Bank Details

The BANK DETAILS section allows the entry of the bank details of the vendor. More than one bank account can be added for each vendor.

- ▶ CTRY (Country): Enter the country where the vendor's bank is located.
- ▶ BANK KEY: The bank key can be selected from the matchcode with the country code entered. The bank key can be entered as the bank-routing number (U.S.) or the bank-sort code (GB), or other country-specific bank identification. The bank key is not entered through configuration but can be created in Financial Accounting via Transaction FI01. All details for the bank can be created within that transaction. After entering the bank key in the PAYMENT TRANSACTIONS screen, you can see the relevant bank details by clicking on the BANK DATA button beneath the BANK DETAILS table.
- ▶ BANK ACCT: The field allows the accounting department to enter the bank account number for the vendor at the bank. The BANK ACCT field can be entered up to 18 characters in length.
- ▶ ACCT HOLDER: If the bank account is not in the name of the vendor or the vendor company, then the account holder of the bank account can be entered in this field. This field can accommodate a name of up to 60 characters.
- ▶ CK (bank control key:- The CK field is specific to each country. In some countries, there is no information to enter; in others, such as France, Spain, Japan, and the United States, the field is used. In the United States, the field content should be "01" for a checking account and "02" for a savings account. Check with your accounting department to ensure that the correct information is entered into the field for the given country.
- ▶ IBAN (International Bank Account Number): The IBAN was designed because of growing pressure to improve the efficiency of cross-border payments in Europe, with respect to cost, speed, and quality. Such improvements required easier validation of foreign bank account numbers. The IBAN design provided a standard method to enable the cross-border account number formats to be recognized and validated. The IBAN is additional information put on the front of the national account number format of each country:
  - ▶ Check digits and a single simple algorithm perform validation. The algorithm covers the whole IBAN and ensures that individual digits are not transposed.
  - ▶ Recognition is in two parts. The IBAN commences with the ISO 3166 two-letter country code. It is therefore easy to recognize the country in which the account is held. Within the national account identifier part of the IBAN, the ISO standard requires that the bank be unambiguously identified.

▸ The length of the IBAN is not standard across countries. The length can range from 28 characters in Hungary and Cyprus to only 15 characters in Norway.

▸ BNKT (partner bank type): If the vendor has more than one bank account, then this field allows the accounting user to specify in what sequence the accounts are used by entering a value in this key field. This value can then be used in the line-item payments.

▸ REF DETAILS (reference specifications for bank details): This field can be used in countries where additional information or authorization is needed. This information is normally required in Norway and the United Kingdom.

Payment Transactions

The PAYMENT TRANSACTIONS section contains the following fields:

▸ ALTERNATIVE PAYEE: This field can be used to enter another vendor number to whom the automatic payments are made. The alternative payee may be needed if the vendor's bank accounts have been frozen.

▸ DME INDICATOR: This key is only used for data medium exchange (DME) in Germany. The DME engine enables a company to define file formats that meet the requirements of their financial institution. As there is no standard set, each country can have different formats, and the DME allows SAP to read an incoming file that is not in the correct country format.

▸ INSTRUCTION KEY: For DME, this field controls which statements are given to the banks during the payment order. This is used in Germany, Spain, Norway, Japan, and other countries, as well as for the SWIFT format.

> **SWIFT**
>
> The Society for Worldwide Interbank Financial Telecommunication (SWIFT) is a financial industry-owned cooperative. It supplies secure, standardized messaging services and interface software to more than 7,800 financial institutions in more than 200 countries. Many institutions have been using the MT-100 customer transfer format for one-off credit transfers and repetitive instructions, such as lease payments. Since November 2003, the MT-100 has been replaced by the MT-103 Single Customer Credit Transfer.

▸ ISR NUMBER: The ISR number is a special payment procedure of the Swiss Postal Service that is only relevant within Switzerland. Inpayment slip with reference number (ISR) is an electronic debtor service that allows the customer to bill open invoices in Swiss Francs (CHF) and Euros (EUR) in a simple manner and to quickly post incoming payments.

The next section shows the accounting information that can be added for the Vendor Master record using Transaction FK01.

6.2   Accounting Information

Transaction FK01 enables the accounting users to enter the account code for the vendor and the company code. The vendor number may need to be entered if the account group is defined as only allowing external number assignment. The ACCOUNTING screen is shown in Figure 6.5.

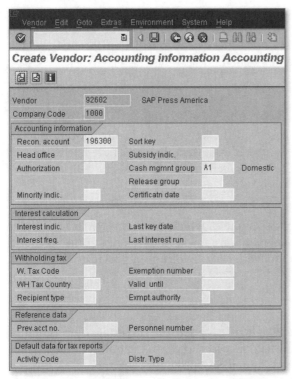

Figure 6.5 Accounting Screen for Transaction FK01, Create Vendor

6.2.1   Accounting Information

The ACCOUNTING screen allows the accounting department to enter relevant data about accounting, interest calculation, and withholding tax as it relates to this vendor within the given company code.

Reconciliation Account

The reconciliation account (RECON. ACCOUNT) is an individual GL account. A reconciliation account is recorded in line-item detail in the subledger and summarized in the GL. The detailed information entered into the reconciliation account is all line-item data from the vendor account. These reconciliation accounts in the sub-ledger are important and must be maintained for vendors, for customers, and for asset accounts.

The reconciliation in the GL is at the summary level and is used to reconcile against the vendor account at the total level. However, the subledger can be used to identify line-item data if necessary.

A reconciliation account can be created using Transaction FS01. When creating a reconciliation account, remember that the account must be a balance-sheet account, the account group must be selected as a reconciliation account, and the RECON. ACCOUNT field must be entered as vendor.

Sort Key

The SORT KEY allows the user to select a sort for the allocation field. The system sorts the document line items based on the key entered in the allocation field. Therefore, if the user selects the SORT KEY 008, then the sort of the line items will be by the allocation 008, which is by cost center.

Head Office

This field allows an entry of a vendor number, which represents the head office or master account for this vendor. Payments are made from the head office account, whereas purchase orders (POs), deliveries, or invoices are posted to the branch account.

Authorization Group

The AUTHORIZATION group is a way of increasing security on certain objects. Entering an authorization group in this field restricts access to the object to those users who have this authorization group in their SAP profiles.

Cash Management Group

In the Cash Management functionality, it is possible to allocate vendors to a planning group. This planning group helps the cash-management department have better information to produce or plan the company's cash forecast.

Release Group

The release-approval group can be defined and configured to allow only those in the group to be able to "release for payment." The RELEASE GROUP can be configured via the navigation path, IMG • FINANCIAL ACCOUNTING • ACCOUNTS RECEIVABLE AND ACCOUNTS PAYABLE • BUSINESS TRANSACTIONS • RELEASE FOR PAYMENT • DEFINE RELEASE APPROVAL GROUPS FOR RELEASE FOR PAYMENT.

Minority Indicator

The MINORITY INDIC. field is only relevant for implementations in the United States. Configuration is required to enter the relevant information because there are no predefined fields in SAP. Many companies are asked by federal and local officials to report on the level of minority vendors supplying material to them.

Virginia Polytechnic Institute's Purchasing Guidelines, 2004, describes a minority vendor as "a business that is owned and controlled by one or more socially and economically disadvantaged persons. Such disadvantage may arise from cultural, racial, chronic economic circumstances or background, or other similar cause. A minority-owned business is at least 51% owned and controlled by one or more such disadvantaged persons. Additionally, the management and daily business operations must be controlled by one or more such individuals. Minority means any African American, Hispanic American, Native American, or Alaskan American, Asian, or a person of Pacific Island descent who is either a citizen of the United States or a permanent resident."

To configure the MINORITY INDIC. field, use the navigation path, IMG • FINANCIAL ACCOUNTING • ACCOUNTS RECEIVABLE AND ACCOUNTS PAYABLE • VENDOR ACCOUNTS • MASTER DATA • PREPARATIONS FOR CREATING VENDOR MASTER DATA • DEFINE MINORITY INDICATORS.

Certification Date for Minority Vendors

The certification expiration date for the minority vendor field is only relevant for implementations in the United States. The certification for a minority vendor has an expiration date. This is required to be entered for the U.S. government.

Interest Calculation Indicator

If this account is suitable for automatic interest, then an interest calculation indicator must be selected. These interest calculations can be configured by the accounting department via the navigation path, IMG • FINANCIAL ACCOUNTING • ACCOUNTS RECEIVABLE AND ACCOUNTS PAYABLE • BUSINESS TRANSACTIONS • INTEREST CALCULATION • INTEREST CALCULATION GLOBAL SETTING • DEFINE INTEREST CALCULATION TYPES.

Interest Calculation Frequency

This field allows the accounting department to select a period that specifies when the interest calculation is run for this vendor. The period can range from monthly to yearly.

Withholding Tax Code

Withholding tax generally refers to an income tax on foreign vendors from country B and applies to those that are not resident in country A but derive incomes from profits, interest, rentals, royalties, and other incomes from sources in country A. The company from country A will be the withholding agent. An income tax of a certain percentage will be withheld on such incomes by the company from country A, which should turn the amount of taxes on each payment over to the local state treasury and submit a withholding income tax return to the local tax authority.

Withholding Tax Country Key

This field can be used in some countries that require this additional country key to calculate or report on withholding tax.

Vendor Recipient Type

In the United States, Form 1042 is the annual taxable return used by withholding agents to report tax withheld on U.S. source income paid to certain non-resident individuals and corporations. The withholding agent issues a Form 1042S, "Foreign Person's U.S. Source Income Subject to Withholding." The 1042 requires that a recipient type be entered. That two-digit code can be configured into SAP. Some examples of this code are 01 – individuals, 02 – Corporations, 06 – Foreign Governments, 11 – U.S. Branch treated as a U.S. person, and so on.

The RECIPIENT TYPE field is also used in Spain for similar reporting. The RECIPIENT TYPE can be configured via the navigation path, IMG • FINANCIAL ACCOUNTING • ACCOUNTS RECEIVABLE AND ACCOUNTS PAYABLE • VENDOR ACCOUNTS • MASTER DATA • PREPARATIONS FOR CREATING VENDOR MASTER DATA • CHECK SETTINGS FOR WITHHOLDING TAX • MAINTAIN TYPES OF RECIPIENT.

Exemption Number

If a vendor is exempt from withholding tax and has an exemption certificate, then that number should be entered on the Vendor Master record.

Validity Date for Exemption

The exemption certificate has an expiration date that should be entered in the VALID UNTIL field. Often, the certificate is extended, so the date of expiry should be updated when necessary.

Exemption Authority

On the IRS form 1042S, a code is required for explaining why there is no withholding tax. This code can be configured into SAP and entered on the Vendor

Master. Examples of this code are 01 – Income effectively connected with a U.S. trade or business, 03 – Income is not from U.S. sources, and 07 – Withholding foreign partnership.

Previous Account Number

This field can be used if the Vendor Master has been renumbered, or you want to store the legacy vendor number.

Personnel Number

If a vendor is also an employee, then this field will accommodate the employee's personnel number.

6.2.2 Payment Transactions

The screen shown in Figure 6.6 allows the accounting user to add vendor information on the automatic payment transaction, such as PAYMENT METHODS, ALTERNAT. PAYEE, and HOUSE BANK, and payment data, such as PAYT TERMS and TOLERANCE GROUP.

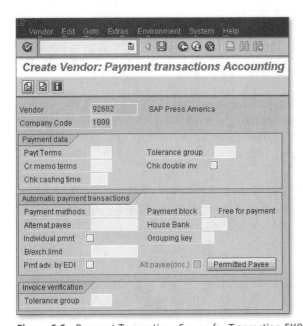

Figure 6.6 Payment Transactions Screen for Transaction FK01, Create Vendor

Payment Terms

The payment terms are defined to allow the vendor to offer cash discounts and favorable payment periods to the company. In many accounts payable departments, before the time of e-commerce, the rule was to pay the vendor as close as possible to the last day of the agreed payment period to maximize the day's payables and keep the cash within the company. However, over the past 10 years, vendors have been offering incentives to companies for fast payment, and purchasing departments have responded by implementing best practices for paying vendors as soon as the invoice arrives, or sooner.

The PAYT TERMS on the Vendor Master record are entered by the accounting department and are configured if the payment terms are not found on the system. The payment terms can be configured via the navigation path, IMG • FINANCIAL ACCOUNTING • ACCOUNTS RECEIVABLE AND ACCOUNTS PAYABLE • BUSINESS TRANSACTIONS • INCOMING INVOICES/CREDIT MEMOS • MAINTAIN TERMS OF PAYMENT.

Tolerance Group

A tolerance is a percentage or a value that is the limit to which an event can deviate. For example, a tolerance of 10% on a line item that is expected to be delivered with 100 units will allow a delivery of 109, which is under the 10% tolerance. A delivery of 111 will not be allowed because it is over the 10% tolerance. A tolerance group is a set of tolerances that are configured and assigned to a vendor if necessary. Each tolerance group is defined for a unique company code as shown in Figure 6.7.

The TOLERANCE GROUP can be configured in Transaction OBA3 or via the navigation path, IMG • FINANCIAL ACCOUNTING • ACCOUNTS RECEIVABLE AND ACCOUNTS PAYABLE • BUSINESS TRANSACTIONS • OPEN ITEM CLEARING • CLEARING DIFFERENCES • DEFINE TOLERANCES FOR CUSTOMERS/VENDORS.

Check Flag for Double Invoices

This indicator should be set if the accounting department wants the system to check for double or duplicate invoices when they are entered.

Check Cashing Time

The value of the check-cashing time is used in Cash Management to calculate the cash outflow. The entry in this field can be calculated by analysis of the issue-to-cash date and an average used.

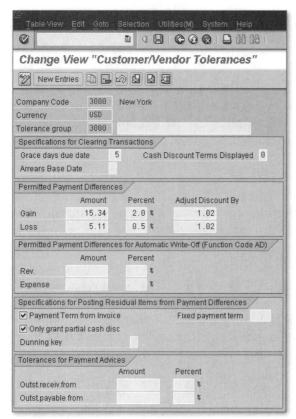

Figure 6.7 Data to be Entered for a Tolerance Group

Payment Methods

The payment method entered here is used if there is no payment method entered in the line item. The options for this field can be configured via the navigation path, IMG • FINANCIAL ACCOUNTING • ACCOUNTS RECEIVABLE AND ACCOUNTS PAYABLE • BUSINESS TRANSACTIONS • OUTGOING PAYMENTS • AUTOMATIC OUTGOING PAYMENTS • PAYMENT METHOD • SET UP PAYMENT METHODS PER COUNTRY FOR PAYMENT TRANSACTIONS.

Payment Block

The accounting department can enter a PAYMENT BLOCK on the Vendor Master that will prevent any open items from being paid. The payment-block keys are defined in configuration via Transaction OB27 or via the navigation path, IMG • FINANCIAL ACCOUNTING • ACCOUNTS RECEIVABLE AND ACCOUNTS PAYABLE • BUSINESS

TRANSACTIONS • OUTGOING PAYMENTS • OUTGOING PAYMENTS GLOBAL SETTINGS • PAYMENT BLOCK REASONS • DEFINE PAYMENT BLOCK REASONS.

House Bank

The HOUSE BANK can be entered if the same bank is always used. This field negates the configuration on the bank-selection screen. The house bank is defined as a business partner that represents a bank through which a company can process its own internal transactions.

Individual Payment Indicator

If this indicator is set, then every item is paid individually rather than having the items combined and paid. Some vendors require that items are individually paid and not combined with other line items on the invoice.

Bill of Exchange Limit

A bill of exchange is a contract entitling an exporter to receive immediate payment in the local currency for goods that would be shipped elsewhere. Time elapses between payment in one currency and repayment in another, so the interest rate would also be brought into the transaction. The accounting department will determine whether the vendor requires a bill-of-exchange limit.

Payment Advice by EDI

If this indicator is set, then all payment advices to this vendor should be sent via EDI.

6.2.3   Correspondence Screen

The CORRESPONDENCE ACCOUNTING screen, shown in Figure 6.8, allows the entry of data for dunning and correspondence.

Dunning Procedure

Normally dunning involves sending reminder letters to customers for payment. However, in this case, dunning relates to reminding vendors to deliver the material from the POs.

The DUNN.PROCEDURE field can be selected to reflect how the dunning should be carried out for this vendor. The dunning procedure can be configured in Transaction FBMP or via the navigation path, IMG • FINANCIAL ACCOUNTING • ACCOUNTS RECEIVABLE AND ACCOUNTS PAYABLE • BUSINESS TRANSACTIONS • DUNNING • DUNNING PROCEDURE • DEFINE DUNNING PROCEDURES.

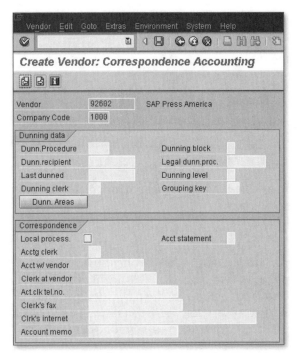

Figure 6.8 Screen for Entering Correspondence and Dunning Information

Dunning Block

If a DUNNING BLOCK is selected, then the vendor is not selected for the dunning run. The DUNNING BLOCK can be entered at any time. The DUNNING BLOCK can be defined via the navigation path, IMG • FINANCIAL ACCOUNTING • ACCOUNTS RECEIVABLE AND ACCOUNTS PAYABLE • BUSINESS TRANSACTIONS • DUNNING • BASIC SETTINGS FOR DUNNING • DEFINE DUNNING BLOCK REASONS.

Dunning Recipient

This field should be completed if the vendor is not the recipient of the dunning notices. If the correspondence should go to a central office or production site, then that vendor number should be entered.

Legal Dunning Procedure

If the dunning procedure that has been undertaken against a vendor has not been successful, then there is the option of legal dunning. Attorneys can carry this out, and documents can be produced through the SAP system. A separate form should be identified for this legal-dunning procedure.

The LEGAL DUNN.PROC. field on the CORRESPONDENCE ACCOUNTING screen allows entry of the date when legal dunning procedures began.

Last Dunned

This is simply the date on which the vendor was last sent a dunning document.

Dunning Level

This field indicates how many times the vendor has been dunned. This field is updated when a new dunning notice is sent.

Dunning Clerk

The dunning clerk is the person in the accounting department who is responsible for the dunning of this vendor. A two-character field identifies the dunning clerk. This DUNNING CLERK field is configured via the navigation path, IMG • FINANCIAL ACCOUNTING • ACCOUNTS RECEIVABLE AND ACCOUNTS PAYABLE • VENDOR ACCOUNTS • MASTER DATA • PREPARATIONS FOR CREATING VENDOR MASTER DATA • DEFINE ACCOUNTING CLERKS.

Account Statement Indicator

This indicator allows the accounting department to define when the vendor will receive its periodic statements. The vendor may receive them weekly, monthly, or yearly.

Accounting Clerk

The ACCTG CLERK field uses the same lookup table as the dunning clerk. The accounting clerk does not necessarily have to be the same as the dunning clerk. However, if the DUNNING CLERK field is not entered, then the dunning clerk is assumed to be the same as the accounting clerk.

Account with Vendor

If known, the account number that the vendor uses to identify the company should be entered here. It is often found on the vendor's invoice.

Vendor Clerk Information

The last fields on this screen relate to information concerning the person at the vendor who has been assigned to manage the day-to-day operations between your company and your vendor.

6.3 Purchasing Data

The purchasing data for the vendor can be entered via Transaction MK01. Figures 6.9 and 6.10 show the purchasing information to be entered in the Vendor Master. Some of the fields on the Purchasing data screens have already been discussed in Sections 6.1, General Data, and 6.2, Accounting Data.

The purchasing information is divided into a number of sections, as shown in Figure 6.9 and 6.10. Figure 6.9 shows the condition data and sales data.

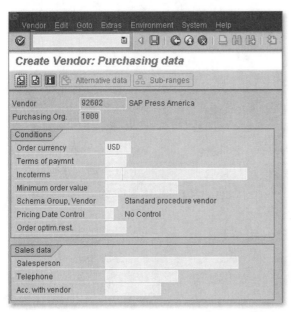

Figure 6.9 First part of the Purchasing Information Screen of the Vendor Master Using Transaction MK01

6.3.1 Conditions

The conditions data includes the Order currency, Terms of paymnt, and other related purchase information using in POs.

used

Order Currency

The ORDER CURRENCY to be used on POs with this vendor can be entered here. The currency is usually that of the vendor's country or that of the purchasing department.

Incoterms

INCOTERMS make international trade easier and help vendors and customers in different countries understand each other. Incoterms are standard trade definitions used in international contracts. The International Chamber of Commerce (ICC) based in Paris, France, devised these. The latest version is Incoterms 2000, which has been translated into 31 languages.

The 13 Incoterms, as shown in Table 6.1, are divided into four groups:

▸ Arrival
▸ Departure
▸ Carriage paid by seller
▸ Carriage not paid by seller

Group	Incoterm	Long Name	Location
E – Departure	EXW	Ex Works	Named Place
D – Arrival	DAF	Delivered at Frontier	Named Place
D – Arrival	DES	Delivered Ex Ship	Port of Destination
D – Arrival	DEQ	Delivered Ex Quay	Port of Destination
D – Arrival	DDU	Delivered Duty Unpaid	Destination
D – Arrival	DDP	Delivery Duty Paid	Destination
C – Paid	CFR	Cost and Freight	Port of Destination
C – Paid	CIF	Cost, Insurance, Freight	Port of Destination
C – Paid	CPT	Carriage Paid To	Destination
C – Paid	CIP	Carriage, Insurance Paid	Destination
F – Unpaid	FCA	Free Carrier	Named Place
F – Unpaid	FAS	Free Alongside Ship	Port of Destination
F – Unpaid	FOB	Free on Board	Port of Destination

Table 6.1 Table of Incoterms 2000

Vendor Schema Group

The calculation schema is used to determine the pricing procedure for the vendor with relation to purchasing documents. The schema group can be configured via the navigation path, IMG • MATERIALS MANAGEMENT • PURCHASING • CONDITIONS • DEFINE PRICE DETERMINATION PROCESS • DEFINE SCHEMA GROUP.

Pricing Date Control

The PRICING DATE CONTROL is used to determine the date on which the pricing determination will take place. For example, if the purchasing department decided to select the PO date, then the new price is calculated at the creation of the PO with the vendor.

Order Optimum Restrictions

This field allows a user to enter a key for PO-based load building. The field identifies whether a vendor is included in optimized load building or whether the target values are to be taken into account in optimized load building.

6.3.2 Sales Data

The SALES DATA refers to the sales department person at the vendor who deals with your company. Most vendors will have a contract person whose information should be entered in this section.

Salesperson

This is the name of the person at the vendor who is the contact for the purchases from your company. This can either be the salesperson or sales clerk.

Telephone

This is the vendor's telephone contact number and is used when a PO is created.

Account with Vendor

This is the customer number that the vendor uses for your company. This can be found on documentation from the vendor.

Figure 6.10 shows the CONTROL DATA, DEFAULT DATA MATERIAL, and SERVICE DATA sections.

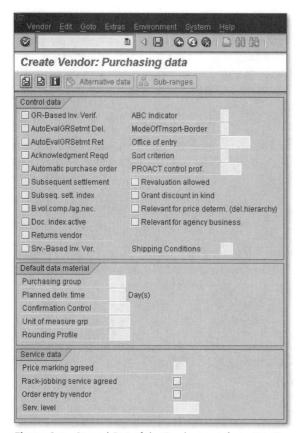

Figure 6.10 Second Part of the Purchasing Information Screen of the Vendor Master Using Transaction MK01

6.3.3 Control Data

The control data for the vendor is made up of a number of indicators that are used in procurement functionality.

Good Receipt-Based Invoice Verification

Setting the GR-BASED INV. VERIF. indicator allows the system to perform Invoice Verification based on the goods receipt amounts. Invoice Verification involves the three-way matching of the PO, goods receipt, and the invoice to ensure that the totals are correct and the invoice can be paid.

Automatic Evaluated Receipt Settlement

The evaluated receipt settlement agreement (identified in Figure 6.10 as Auto-EvalGRSetmt Del.) is created between the vendor and the purchasing department. The agreement allows the purchasing department to send payments for the goods received at the time those materials are posted into stock. The vendor will not send an invoice for the material sent. This method of ERS, sometimes called a two-way match, is designated a best practice by many purchasing experts.

Acknowledgement Required

This indicator determines whether the vendor is supposed to send an acknowledgement that it has received the order. This can be electronically sent via EDI.

Automatic Purchase Order

If a purchase requisition has been created and assigned to this vendor, then an automatic PO can be created if this indicator is set. This reduces work for the purchasing department.

Subsequent Settlement

The vendor may offer some kind of incentive to the purchasing department to purchase more material. This may take two forms. One may be an instant reduction in price — a promotional price — for a given period. The second incentive may take the form of the subsequent settlement. This is an agreement between the vendor and the purchasing department under which, depending on how much material is purchased, a rebate is offered at the end of an agreed period.

For example, an office supply vendor could agree to give a 10% rebate for the total amount of purchases over a three-month period. This may have a provision that the total amount of purchases would be more than 50% greater than for the same period in the previous year. If the purchases were in excess of the 50%, then the subsequent settlement with the vendor would take place at the end of the period. The vendor would give a 10% rebate on all of the purchases over that period.

Business-Volume Comparison/Agreement Necessary

If the B.vol.comp./ag.nec indicator is set, data must be compared between the vendor and the purchasing department before any subsequent settlement is posted. In the example of the office-supply vendor, the agreement may depend on the comparison of the files from both parties.

Document Index Active

The document index is a way of automatically adjusting the purchasing documents if the conditions change.

Service-Based Invoice Verification

Some vendors provide services, and the work performed is entered using service-entry sheets. If the SRV.-BASED INV. VER. indicator is set, the acceptance is carried out at the level of the service-entry sheet.

ABC Indicator

The ABC INDICATOR is used for many objects in SAP. The ABC indicator for vendors relates to the amount of sales the vendor does with the company. The ABC INDICATOR is manually entered.

Mode of Transport for Foreign Trade

This indicator (MODEOFTRNSPRT-BORDER) is used if the vendor is involved in foreign trade. The mode of transport is defined for each country; this field determines how the vendor transports material. The field can be configured via the navigation path, IMG • MATERIALS MANAGEMENT • PURCHASING • FOREIGN TRADE/CUSTOMS • TRANSPORTATION DATA • DEFINE MODES OF TRANSPORT.

Office of Entry

The OFFICE OF ENTRY field defines where the material purchased from this vendor will enter the country or leave in the case of a return. The office of entry is the customs office and is configured via the navigation path, IMG • MATERIALS MANAGEMENT • PURCHASING • FOREIGN TRADE/CUSTOMS • TRANSPORTATION DATA • DEFINE CUSTOMS OFFICES.

Sort Criterion

This field allows the purchasing department to sort the delivery items from the vendor in a specific manner. The default is by Vendor Sub-Range (VSR), but the sort can be by material number, material group, or EAN.

Grant Discount in Kind

A vendor is labeled as granting discount in kind when that vendor offers materials to the purchasing department free of charge as an incentive to purchase.

Relevant for Price Determination for Vendor Hierarchy

If the Vendor Master record represents a node in a customer hierarchy, the pricing indicator determines whether the node is relevant for pricing. If you are maintaining the Vendor Master record for a customer hierarchy node, and you want to create pricing condition records for the node, this indicator must be set.

6.3.4 Default Data Material

This section of vendor data includes the defaults that are used in purchasing processes and documents. These fields include the PURCHASING GROUP who deals with the vendor, the PLANNED DELIV. TIME, and the CONFIRMATION CONTROL key.

Purchasing Group

The PURCHASING GROUP that most often deals with this vendor can be entered. The purchasing group can be associated with one or more vendors.

Planned Delivery Time

This is the average time it takes for a material to be delivered from this vendor. If the vendor supplies many materials, then this field may not be useful if the delivery time differs for each material the vendor supplies.

Confirmation Control Key

A CONFIRMATION CONTROL key can be entered that determines which confirmation categories are expected from a PO item. The CONFIRMATION CONTROL key defines the confirmation sequence that is expected from the vendor. The confirmation sequence specifies the order in which the individual confirmations defined in a CONFIRMATION CONTROL key are expected and which confirmation categories are to be automatically monitored. For example, the CONFIRMATION CONTROL key 0001 can be configured to expect an order acknowledgement and a shipping notification.

The CONFIRMATION CONTROL key is configured in the IMG via the navigation path, IMG • MATERIALS MANAGEMENT • PURCHASING • CONFIRMATIONS • SET UP CONFIRMATION CONTROL.

Unit of Measure Group

The UNIT OF MEASURE GRP is entered to define the allowed units of measure, those defined as part of the unit of measure group. This should be entered when the rounding profile is used.

The unit of measure group is configured in the IMG via the navigation path, IMG • MATERIALS MANAGEMENT • PURCHASING • ORDER OPTIMIZING • QUANTITY OPTIMIZING AND ALLOWED LOGISTICS UNITS OF MEASURE • UNIT OF MEASURE GROUPS.

Rounding Profile

The ROUNDING PROFILE can be entered that determines how the material quantity is rounded to optimize the order. The rounding profile reviews and rounds the quantity depending on the threshold value in the profile.

The ROUNDING PROFILE is configured in the IMG via the navigation path, IMG • MATERIALS MANAGEMENT • PURCHASING • ORDER OPTIMIZING • QUANTITY OPTIMIZING AND ALLOWED LOGISTICS UNITS OF MEASURE • UNIT OF MEASURE ROUNDING RULES.

6.3.5 Service Data

The SERVICE DATA section describes a number of fields related to retail companies and load building.

Price Marking Agreement

The vendor and customer enter into a price marking agreement. The vendor will apply price labels to the materials prior to shipping to the customer.

Rack-Jobbing Agreement

Retail companies use this field. If the indicator is set, then the vendor will be responsible for stock planning/replenishment and for filling the shelves at the retail outlet.

Order Entry by Vendor

When this indicator is set, the vendor is responsible for entering the PO. The order can be created in the background as a result of an EDI order confirmation received from the vendor.

Vendor Service Level

This field is used for automatic PO-based load building. If the service level drops below the desired value, SAP will attempt to order an entire load of goods for this vendor.

6.3.6 Partner Functions

The PARTNER FUNCTIONS screen shown in Figure 6.11 allows the purchasing user to define the relationships between the vendor and the company. A vendor can vary in size from a sole proprietor to the largest multinational company. To best describe the vendor's various operations, partner functionality can be described. The partner functions are used for both customers and vendors.

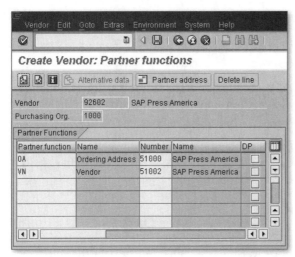

Figure 6.11   Partner Functions for the Vendor Master, Using Transaction MK01

Table 6.2 provides a selection of the available vendor partner codes.

Partner Code	Description
AZ	Alternative Payment Recipient
CA	Contract Address
CP	Contact Person
ER	Employee Responsible
GS	Goods Supplier
OA	Ordering Address
PI	Invoice Presented By
VN	Vendor

Table 6.2   List of Partner Functions

Basically, the PARTNER FUNCTION allows the purchasing department to determine what function the vendor performs within the larger vendor organization. For example, a multinational auto-parts manufacturer may supply material to your company, so you have created a vendor number (VN) for them. However, the address to which you send the POs may be a separate address in a separate division of the manufacturer's business. Therefore, you would create a vendor number for the ordering address (OA), and that record is entered into the PARTNER FUNCTION screen for the VN VENDOR.

Further, there may be a separate contact address (CA) for a vendor that supplies the invoices (PI), and an alternative payee (AZ). All of these can be created and entered into the PARTNER FUNCTIONS screen of the VN partner.

The partner functions are assigned to the vendor account groups. For example, the vendor account group 0001 may have different partner functions from the vendor account group LIEF.

The partner function can be defined in configuration via the navigation path, IMG • MATERIALS MANAGEMENT • PURCHASING • VENDOR MASTER • VENDOR HIERARCHY • DEFINE PARTNER DETERMINATION.

6.4   Business Examples – Vendor Master Data

This chapter shows that the Vendor Master is a collection of data that describes the vendor's relationship with the company. Just as the Material Master record isn't complete until all relevant departments have entered their data, the Vendor Master isn't complete until both the accounting and purchasing departments have entered their information.

6.4.1   General Data

When vendor information is loaded in SAP ERP, there are a number of areas that need to be entered that are equally important. The general data reflects information such as name, address, tax data, and bank details. Specific accounting data, such as payment transactions and dunning, can be entered separately. The third area of the Vendor Master is the purchasing data where incoterms and partner information are entered.

When a company decides to load the Vendor Master into SAP, there are a number of ways this can be done. If a company has a small number of vendors, the information can be manually loaded into SAP. It's normal for SAP to require more data than legacy systems, and there is usually a team to review the existing data and add to it where necessary. For companies with large numbers of suppliers, the task to load these into SAP will usually be automated, and new vendor data is added where necessary.

If companies load their vendors into SAP without first performing some kind of vendor rationalization, they can end up loading a lot of inaccurate and out-of-date information.

Example

A multi-national chemical company reviewed its vendor files on a number of legacy systems and found that a large percentage of the data was inconsistent and inaccurate. To reduce the amount of inaccurate data loaded on to the new SAP ERP system, the company decided to run pilot projects in the United States and Germany to find out more about the supplier data. In the United States, the project team found that there were a number of problems with the data, including multiple duplicate vendor records for the same supplier, inaccurate addresses, inaccurate fax numbers, vendors that no longer were in business, vendors that no longer supplied products to the company, and inaccuracies with pricing and contracts.

In the United States, the pilot found only 12% of records to contain no inaccuracies, while in Germany the percentage was slightly higher at 17%. Based on this information, the company created project teams in each of the countries that were part of the first SAP ERP phase to rationalize the Vendor Master records and correct inaccuracies.

6.4.2   Purchasing Data

The Vendor Master record has a number of fields that are specifically concerned with purchasing. These include condition data such as order currency and incoterms, and control data, such as the indicators for goods receipt invoice verification, ERS, and subsequent settlement.

Example

Most vendors offer some kind of discount as an incentive to their customers. The incentives usually include discounts for larger purchases, but as suppliers are having a more difficult time with bank financing, more vendors are offering their customers a discount for paying their invoices before the date determined in the payment terms. This discount may only reflect a 1% or 2% discount, but on larger purchases, this can be significant. Of course, companies have to weigh the advantages of paying early against the ability to pay early. In some instances, paying early is not always possible.

Another incentive offered by vendors is the subsequent settlement, which allows a one-time rebate or periodic settlement if certain conditions are met, such as a certain volume of materials purchased or amount spent.

A metal fabrication company agreed with its supplier of stainless steel coils that if the company spent more than $40,000 on 0.105-inch stainless steel coils per month, the vendor would rebate 3% of the total monthly spend.

This agreement is annotated in the Vendor Master, and the system updates the relevant values and calculates the conditions at the end of the month to determine the rebate.

6.5   Summary

This chapter thoroughly discussed the Vendor Master file. There are different ways to enter vendor data, and both the purchasing department and the accounting department play a role in this important task. Having the correct vendor information entered is important when material needs to be ordered quickly and correctly. Any errors in the Vendor Master file can be costly if material cannot be sourced in a timely fashion and shipments are delayed to customers. This chapter has provided all of the tools you need to work with the purchasing department in understanding their needs when SAP is implemented.

Chapter 7 examines the purchasing information data as it relates to the specific information that can be available for a vendor and a material. Contracts with vendors may have special provisions for certain materials, for example, in the number of delivery days or pricing conditions.

The documented relationship between the vendor and the material is important for the purchasing department. To reduce the length of the procurement process, the purchase order can be generated from the information in the purchasing information record, reducing manual data input.

7 Purchasing Information Data

The information found on the purchasing information record is the specific data that the vendor and the customer have negotiated in a verbal or written agreement. The information supplied by the vendor or from the contract is entered into the purchasing information record. A normal purchase information record is between a vendor and customer for a specific material. However, the vendor can supply a service that is defined by a material group rather than a specific material, and this information can be entered into a purchasing information record.

This chapter will help you as a consultant understand the data that is entered into a purchase information record. You will learn about the different types of records and how they are used by purchasing departments.

7.1 Purchasing General Data

Following are the four distinct purchasing information records:

- Standard
- Contracting
- Pipeline
- Consignment

Figure 7.1 shows the initial data entry screen for the creation of a purchasing information record. The screen shows the four types of information records that can be created.

7.1.1 Create a Purchasing Information Record

Transaction ME11 is used to create a purchasing information record. The navigation path is SAP MENU • LOGISTICS • MATERIALS MANAGEMENT • MASTER DATA • INFO RECORD • CREATE.

At the initial purchasing information screen, as shown in Figure 7.1, the purchasing user can decide what data to enter to create certain types of records.

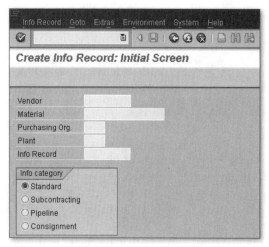

Figure 7.1 Initial Screen for Creating a Purchasing Information Record

Standard Purchasing Information Record

The STANDARD type of purchasing information record contains the information supplied by the vendor for a specific material, service, or group of materials or services.

Subcontracting Purchasing Information Record

The SUBCONTRACTING purchasing information record can be used when the order is a subcontracting order. In manufacturing plants, the material being produced may require some outside service, such as enameling or partial assembly. The work is performed by a subcontractor, and the price that subcontractor charges for the work is included in a subcontracting purchasing information record.

Pipeline Purchasing Information Record

Pipeline materials, such as electricity, water, and oil, are supplied by utility vendors and used by the customer through pipeline withdrawals. The PIPELINE purchasing information record reflects the information for this vendor/material combination.

Consignment Purchasing Information Record

When a vendor supplies material to be stored at a customer's site for customer withdrawal, the purchasing department can create a CONSIGNMENT purchasing information record for that material.

7.1.2 Create a Purchasing Information Record with Material Number

The purchasing information record can be created for a specific material by entering the supplying VENDOR. The record can be created with or without a purchasing organization. If no PURCHASING ORG. is entered, then the purchasing information record will only be created with general data, as shown in Figure 7.2. If a PURCHASING ORG. is entered with the MATERIAL and VENDOR, then the purchasing data screen will be available for the purchasing user to enter specific data that relates to that purchasing organization.

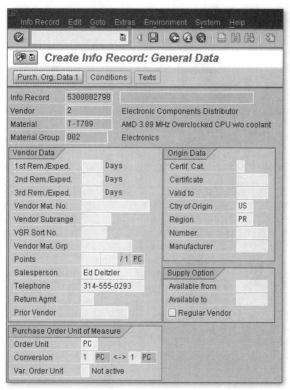

Figure 7.2 General Data Screen for a Standard Material/Vendor Purchasing Information Record

7.1.3 Create a Purchasing Information Record without a Material Number

Just entering a VENDOR in the initial data screen can create a purchasing information record. This purchasing information record will be valid for the vendor and a MATERIAL GROUP, which is a mandatory entry on the GENERAL DATA screen, as shown in Figure 7.3. It is also mandatory to enter a description for the purchasing information record that describes the material group entered in the purchasing information record. This is not required if a material is entered because the material has a description attached. This description allows the purchasing user to describe the service that the vendor will provide for the materials in the entered material group. This type of record can be created with or without a purchasing organization. If no purchasing organization is entered, then the purchasing information record will only be created with general data.

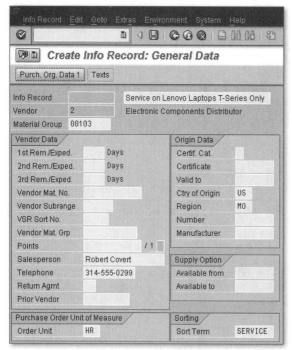

Figure 7.3 General Data Screen for a Material Group/Vendor Purchasing Information Record

7.1.4 General Data Screen

The GENERAL DATA screen is valid for either a material/vendor purchasing information record or for a material group/vendor purchasing information record. Figure 7.3

shows that for a material group/vendor record, the information record must be given a valid description. Figure 7.3 also shows that only the ORDER UNIT is shown and not the other unit of measure fields (as in Figure 7.2) because the materials in the material group may have varying ordering units of measure.

Reminder Fields

The reminder fields, 1ST REM./EXPED, 2ND REM./EXPED, and 3RD REM./EXPED, contain the number of days that urging letters or emails can be sent to the vendor for this material. Negative numbers indicate the message is prior to the delivery date; positive numbers indicate the message is after the date.

Vendor Sub-Range (VSR)

The VENDOR SUB-RANGE (VSR) can be used to subdivide the vendor's products into different ranges. For example, the vendor could be an office products company and the subranges could be computer media, paper products, ink products, and so on.

Vendor Sub-Range (VSR) Sort Number

The VSR SORT NO. allows the VSR s to have different values, which are used to create a sort sequence. When a PO is created, it uses the VSR sort number from the purchasing information records to sequence the materials in the PO. For example, if computer media has a sort number of 40, and the sort number for ink products is 24, then the ink products are sequenced before the computer media in the PO.

Points

The points system can be used where the purchasing department has negotiated with a vendor a subsequent settlement or rebate arrangement. The POINTS field in the purchasing information record allows the purchasing user to enter the number of points that are recorded each time a certain value of the material is ordered. The numbers of points is recorded for the amount ordered rather than the total value ordered.

At the end of the rebate period, the number of points accumulated determines the value of the rebate from the vendor.

Return Agreement

The RETURN AGMT field determines what arrangement the client has with the vendor for the return of the material. The RETURN AGMT field can be configured so that unique return agreements can be defined. The return agreement is usually used for retail implementations and can be configured via the navigation path, IMG •

LOGISTICS – GENERAL • MATERIAL MASTER • RETAIL-SPECIFIC SETTINGS • SETTINGS FOR KEY FIELDS • RETURN AGREEMENT.

In the next section, the discussion moves on to more specific data required by the purchasing organization.

7.2 Purchasing Organization Data

After the general information has been entered, the next screen is for the purchasing organization data.

The data fields in Figure 7.4 are also found in the Vendor Master and the Material Master. However, by entering the information in the purchasing information record, it will be specific to the vendor/material and will be used in purchasing documents.

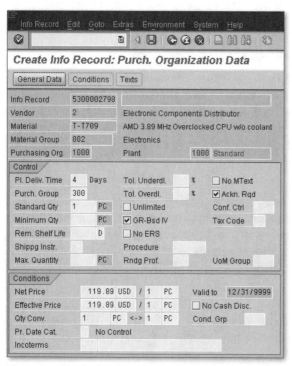

Figure 7.4 Purchasing Organization Screen for the Purchase Information Record

Depending on the agreement between the vendor and the client, the purchasing department will enter information on the tolerances, delivery time, quantities, and net price.

7.2.1 Conditions

The purchasing information record contains data that defines the conditions for the material/vendor. The CONDITION screen is shown in Figure 7.5. The screen shows that from the date 08/06/2010, the Gross Price, indicated by condition type (CNTY) PB00 for MATERIAL T-T709 from VENDOR 2 was 119.89 USD per piece.

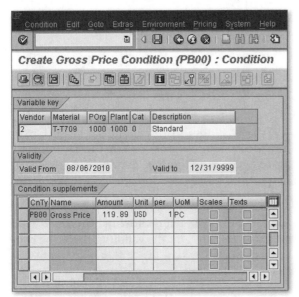

Pricing conditions in the PIR.

Figure 7.5 Condition Screen for Purchasing Information Record

Validity

The conditions that can be entered for the purchasing information record are valid for a certain time period. For instance, if the agreement with the vendor is valid for three months, then the VALID to date should reflect that. If the information is for future agreements, the validity dates can be entered to reflect this.

Price Calculation Schema

In purchasing, the condition types are used in pricing. A condition type can represent a price, tax, transportation cost, discount, and so on. The condition types can be grouped together to form a pricing procedure, sometimes called a price calculation schema. The pricing procedure can be defined in the IMG using the navigation path, IMG • MATERIALS MANAGEMENT • PURCHASING • CONDITIONS • DEFINE PRICE DETERMINATION PROCESS • DEFINE CALCULATION SCHEMA.

The calculation schema is created to produce a step-by-step procedure for a particular event. For example, in a pricing procedure, the first step is the condition type for a gross price, then a discount condition type, followed by a tax condition type, and so on.

Condition Type

The condition type is simply a function that tells the system what type of calculation to perform, for example, fixed amount, percentage, and so on.

User-defined condition types can be created in the IMG. The navigation path is IMG • MATERIALS MANAGEMENT • PURCHASING • CONDITIONS • DEFINE PRICE DETERMINATION PROCESS • DEFINE CONDITION TYPES.

The screen shown in Figure 7.6 requires that the condition type (CONDIT TYPE.) must be assigned to a condition class. Examples of the condition class (COND. CLASS) are discounts, prices, taxes, expenses, and so on. It is also mandatory for a calculation type (CALCULAT.TYPE) to be assigned to the condition type. The calculation type identifies the condition type as a percentage, quantity, formula, point, fixed amount, and so on.

The entry screen is where the purchasing user can define how the condition type can be updated, either manually or automatically, and the validity date of the condition type.

The SCALES fields allow the purchasing user to enter information on the condition type if it is valid for scaling. Scaling is when a discount from a vendor is not a blanket 4% but is different depending on the amount ordered. A vendor can give discounts for a specific material that increase the more the client purchases. For example, if the PO is for a quantity of up to 30 units, the vendor would give the client a 1% discount; from 31 to 60, the discount is 2% discount; from 61 to 120, the discount is 4%; and over 121, the discount is 6%.

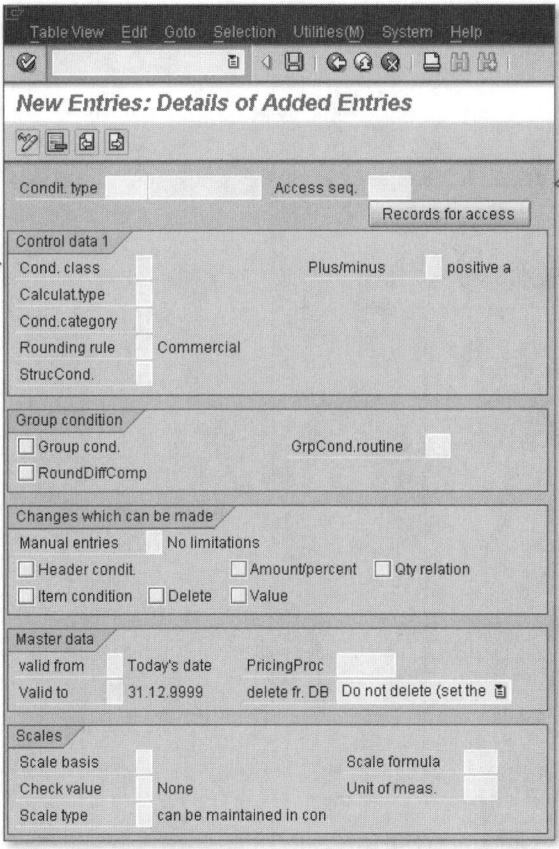

Figure 7.6 Condition Type Create Screen

Access Sequence

For each condition type, there is an access sequence that allows the condition type to access the condition tables in the correct sequence. The access sequence can be configured using the navigation path, IMG • MATERIALS MANAGEMENT • PURCHASING • CONDITIONS • DEFINE PRICE DETERMINATION PROCESS • DEFINE ACCESS SEQUENCE.

Condition Tables

The access sequence defines the sequence to read the condition tables. A number of fields are selected and records are created to assign values to those fields in the condition table. A condition table can be created in the IMG using the navigation path, IMG • MATERIALS MANAGEMENT • PURCHASING • CONDITIONS • DEFINE PRICE

DETERMINATION PROCESS • DEFINE CONDITION TABLES. Figure 7.7 shows the interaction of a condition table and access sequence.

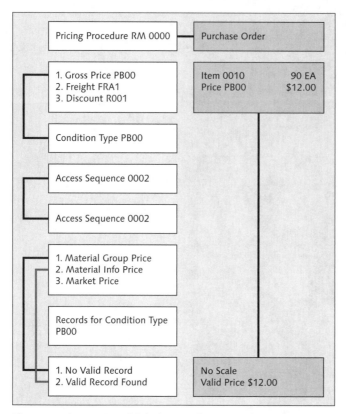

Figure 7.7 Interaction of Calculation Schema, Condition Type, Access Sequence, and Condition Table

7.2.2 Text Screen

Texts fields can be used to enter specific information regarding the particular purchasing information record. The relevance of the text fields can be determined in configuration. For each of the purchasing documents, RFQ, PO, contract, and so on, the texts defined in master records can be prioritized.

Figure 7.8 shows the two available text fields: INFO RECORD NOTE and PURCHASE ORDER TEXT.

The screen displays 5 text lines of 40 characters. However, selecting the MORE TEXT indicator displays a freeform text input screen similar to a normal word processing program. The user can include additional text here if significant information needs to be included in the purchasing information record.

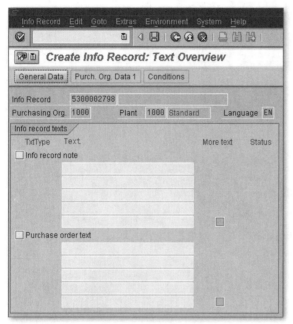

Figure 7.8 Text Input Screen for Purchasing Information Record

To the far right of the text, the Status field is displayed when text has been entered. (In this example, the Status field is not shown.) This field shows how the text can be used:

▶ Allow the text to be used as is, with only changes to the original text allowed.

▶ Allow the text to be used, and allow any changes to the text to be reflected in the original text, but adopt the modified text.

▶ Allow the text to be displayed but not printed or changed.

The texts entered on a purchasing information record should be relevant to a PO line item. In configuration, the user can define the priority against other text fields. This transaction can be accessed using the navigation path, IMG • Materials Management • Purchasing • Messages • Text for Messages • Define Texts for Purchase Order.

The configuration for the PO texts can be further subdivided into header, line item, supplement, and headings. The purchasing information record text is most relevant to the document item, which is shown in Figure 7.9.

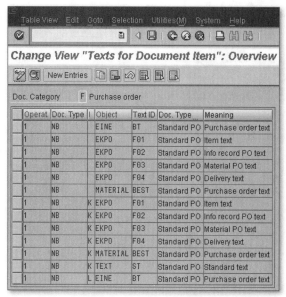

Figure 7.9 Texts Relevant for Purchase Order Line Item

The configuration screen shows the following:

▶ Document type (DOC. TYPE), which in this case is NB for standard PO

▶ OBJECT TYPE, EKPO for purchasing document item texts, and so on

▶ TEXT ID, which is relevant to the particular object

New entries can be made to this list to allow new texts or to modify the existing text sequence.

7.2.3 Statistical Data

Within the purchasing information record, statistical information is recorded and can be reviewed. The statistical screens can be accessed from within the general screen by selecting EXTRAS • STATISTICS.

The STATISTICAL DATA screens shown in Figure 7.10 can be controlled to allow a comparison between two different time periods. The statistical data reflects information on the following:

▶ Order quantity and invoice value

▶ Number of purchasing documents

▶ Delivery time information

- Delivery reliability information
- Quantity reliability information

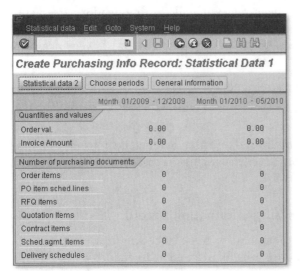

Figure 7.10 Statistical Data for the Purchasing Information Record

7.3 Business Examples – Purchasing Information Data

When the purchasing department signs an agreement with a vendor, the details of that agreement can be entered into the purchasing information record. In most cases, this will be in the form of purchasing a specific material from a specific vendor; however, a purchasing information record can also be used to record the details of a service that a vendor will perform.

7.3.1 Standard Purchasing Information Record

The majority of purchasing information records that you'll work with will be in this form. A vendor will agree to sell a material to a company at a certain price with certain conditions on delivery time and tolerances. This information is entered into the standard purchasing information record.

Example

A Puerto Rican manufacturer of specialty chemicals had implemented SAP ERP as part of a wider implementation by a U.S. company that recently acquired the manufacturer. The implementation included a migration of data from a previous standalone ERP system, and no serious problems had been encountered. The company's relationship with its small number of local suppliers was based on years of purchasing, and contract renewals were always brief and without many changes. The company's new owners had been reviewing all existing vendor agreements and had found that the prices and conditions were not in line with the market. The company was asked to go back to its vendors and negotiate lower prices and better incentives.

Although the vendors were reluctant to reduce prices, most offered some kind of incentive, such as a reduction in price for a larger minimum order quantity, better payment terms, or tiered pricing.

The company entered information from the revised agreements into the purchasing information records, by either directly changing the price and minimum quantity or by entering pricing scales.

7.3.2 Subcontracting Purchasing Information Record

During the production process, there may be an instance where an item requires work to be carried out on it that has to be performed at a vendor's location. This could be a manufacturing process such as enameling, heat treatment, or painting. Alternatively, the process could be after manufacture such as specialty packaging. Whatever the process, the agreement with the vendor is not based on a material but on a process. This agreement can be entered into SAP on a purchasing information record that is specific to subcontracting.

Example

A British manufacturer of upholstery fabric had implemented SAP ERP a number of years ago, and no changes had been made in some time because the company's processes had remained the same. After negotiations with a vendor of cardboard inserts, the vendor approached the upholstery manufacturer to see if the company would be interested in subcontracting its packaging process. The upholstery manufacturer had always purchased the polyethylene plastic rolls and packaged each roll of fabric at its own facility. The cardboard insert vendor had been approached by another upholstery company to take over the packaging of their fabric, so the vendor had spare capacity to perform the same operation for the British upholstery manufacturer.

After some analysis of current costs and transportation time to the vendor facility, the company found that by subcontracting this work, the company could save several thousand pounds a month. The two companies signed an agreement, and the completed rolls of fabric were sent to the vendor, where they were wrapped and sent back to the factory or directly to the customer. A number of subcontracting purchasing information records were entered in the company's SAP ERP system to reflect the contract details for the different types of fabric rolls produced.

7.4 Summary

This chapter has discussed the functionality of the purchasing information record. The purchasing information record contains specific data that is relevant for the purchasing department as it describes the relationship between a vendor and the material that the purchasing department procures. However, it is important to understand that the information may vary by purchasing organization. When purchasing departments negotiate with vendors, the information from the final contract is entered into the purchasing information records. This data drives the purchasing of materials and services within a business. Accurate data reduces unnecessary delays in receiving material, which in turn reduces production problems and improves overall customer satisfaction. Accurate purchasing data, stored in records such as the purchasing information record, can help reduce purchasing costs for a company.

Chapter 8 will examine the Batch Management functionality that is used to describe a quantity of the same material. The chapter will help you understand the transaction used to create, change, and delete a batch record in SAP. The chapter will also discuss the important topic of batch determination, how a specific batch is selected, and how that integrates with WM and SD.

Batch Management is an important part of a company's capability to produce, store, and sell material. The batch defines a quantity of material by characteristics unique to that batch. Those characteristics determine how the material in that batch is used, sold, or moved.

8   Batch Management Data

Certain material can be defined in SAP as being batch managed. A batch is a quantity of material that represents a homogeneous unit that has unique specifications. The batch of material may refer to a quantity of chemical that is produced in one process or a quantity of bottles of water that were filled on a certain filling line from a specific tank. There are many ways in which a batch can be defined. In SAP, the batch is used to identify units of material as they move through the system. The batch can have specific characteristics that enable it to be identified and used within the Material Management (MM) functionality. This chapter describes the processes in creating and changing a batch and the process of batch determination. The first section gives an overview of the batch and how it is used in industry.

8.1   Batch Management Overview

The definition of a batch differs among companies, industries, and countries. For example, in the pharmaceutical industry, strict guidelines and regulations determine what a batch is. These regulations on batches and batch control include the ANSI/ISA-88 standard and the Food and Drug Administration (FDA) 21 CFR Part 11 specifications in the United States.

8.1.1   Batch Definition

Although there is no one exact definition of a batch, the following definition from ExxonMobil Aviation Lubricants may help:

A batch is the specific quantity of a material produced in a single manufacturing process, i.e., under the same conditions, thus featuring identical properties. Each batch of material is given a batch number. Each batch of a material is tested with regard to relevant characteristics to ensure it meets the values or within the range for those characteristics.

A second definition of a batch is from the Marathon Oil Company, which significantly differs from other definitions:

A batch is a shipment of a single product that is handled through the pipeline without mixing with preceding or following shipments.

This third definition of a batch is from the Hawaiian Coffee Association:

A batch refers to a quantity of coffee coming to the roaster. Quantities of the same coffee arriving at different times would be viewed as separate batches. Changes from batch to batch — even of the same variety of bean — must be detected by the roaster if he is to produce coffees that are consistently the same.

Whatever the definition, the fact is that the batch has to be identified by a batch record. This can be as simple as identifying bags of coffee beans as they arrive at the plant, or as complex as identifying a batch by numerous qualifying characteristics to ensure quality and safety.

A batch of material can either be purchased from a vendor or produced internally. The need to manage materials by batch has been discussed; however, in SAP, the material must be identified as one that is batch-relevant. The Batch-Management indicator is found in the Material Master record on the Purchasing view, Sales/Plant view, Storage/Plant view, Warehouse view, and the Work Scheduling view.

The indicator for the material can be changed from "batch managed" to "non-batch managed" only if there has been no stock for the current period and the previous period. This is to allow for any previous period material posting.

8.1.2   Pharmaceutical Industry

The identification of a batch record is especially important for the pharmaceutical industry due to the regulations set down by the FDA in the United States and other regulatory bodies across the world, such as the Drugs Controller General of India (DCGI), Bundesgesundheitsamt (BGA) in Germany, Health Canada, and the Medicines and Healthcare Products Regulatory Agency (MHRA) in the United Kingdom.

These regulatory bodies are primarily interested in public safety. The regulations such as FDA 21 CFR Part 11 in the United States are aimed at improving the efficiency of quality control and the quality assurance process. Each batch produced has to be quality tested, with the results stored electronically against the batch number.

Product Recall

The batch number also can be used as the tracking device for companies in case of subsequent errors or contamination. Manufacturers publish product recalls every day, but for the pharmaceutical industry, product recalls can save lives.

A pharmaceutical company can voluntarily recall a product. If the company finds that a result from a test on a batch was incorrect and that puts the batch out of tolerance, then the product made from that batch could be hazardous.

The errors could go all of the way back to the vendor, if any of the material was purchased. If a vendor informs the company that a batch of purchased material was out of tolerance, then this batch must be traced through the production process to find all finished goods batches that may contain the faulty batch.

In the United States, the FDA has the power to request that a company initiate a recall when it believes that a drug violates the Food, Drug and Cosmetic Act (FDCA). A recall will be requested when the FDA concludes the following:

▶ A drug that has been distributed presents a risk of illness or injury or gross consumer deception.

▶ The manufacturer or distributor has not recalled the drug.

▶ FDA action is necessary to protect the public health.

In a recall, the manufacturer informs the retailer, wholesaler, or even the consumer concerning how to identify the batch number on the product and which batch numbers are part of the recall.

The next section describes the Batch Master record in detail and how a batch record is created in SAP.

8.2 Batch Master Record

The batch record for a material contains the information relevant to that specific batch. This section describes how a batch is created, changed, and deleted.

8.2.1 Creating a Batch

The batch record can be created manually through the SAP menu using Transaction MSC1N. The screen shows how fields such as the PRODUCTION DATE, SHELF LIFE EXP. DATE, and BATCH STATUS are entered for the batch. The navigation path, is SAP MENU • LOGISTICS • MATERIALS MANAGEMENT • MATERIAL MASTER • BATCH • CREATE. Figure 8.1 shows the CREATE BATCH screen.

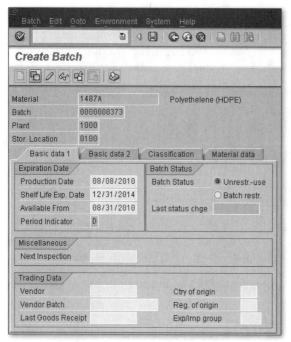

Figure 8.1 Initial Batch Creation Screen

The BATCH number can be internally or externally assigned, and the configuration paths are described in detail in Chapter 3, Master Data in Materials Management.

Production Date

The date when the batch was produced can be entered into this field. In some industries, this field is also used as the date the material was tested or retested. If a material is found to be still in tolerance after the shelf-life date has expired, the material can be retested, and the date of the retest is entered into this field, in addition to a new SHELF LIFE EXP. DATE. Check with your clients to see how they need to use this field.

Shelf-Life Expiration Date

This field is the date on which the shelf life of this batch will expire. The shelf life of a product can vary between plants. This date can be used in the sales process, as customers may have set a requirement on the acceptable number of days of shelf life remaining. Some companies use this field to indicate the date on which a batch needs to be retested.

Available From

This field indicates when the batch will be available. For example, if a material needs to remain in the quality inspection process for a certain amount of days after testing, then the quality department can enter a date to inform other departments of when the batch is expected to be available.

Batch Status

The BATCH STATUS indicator allows the batch to be classified as having restricted or unrestricted use. If the unrestricted indicator is set, then the batch has no restriction placed on its use. If the restricted use indicator is set, the batch is treated like blocked stock in planning but can be selected by batch determination if the search includes restricted-use batches.

The BATCH STATUS can be set to "restricted" from "unrestricted" by changing the indicator in the batch record. A material document will be posted that shows the movement of stock between the two statuses.

Next Inspection

This date field allows the quality department to enter the date of the next quality inspection of the batch, if applicable to this material.

Vendor Batch

If the material is purchased, then the batch number assigned by the vendor can be added to the batch record. It is important to any product recall procedure that the vendor batch number is noted. The VENDOR BATCH field allows a 15-character string to be entered.

In Figure 8.2, the SHORT TEXT field allows the user to enter a specific text for the batch record. Clicking on the icon next to the SHORT TEXT field can create a longer text item, if required.

The other fields on the screen are six date fields: DATE 1, DATE 2, and so on. These fields do not have any standard functionality. The six date fields can be used for whatever purpose is defined by the client. For example, these fields could contain the dates on which the material was inspected by the quality department.

Figure 8.2 Second Batch Entry Screen

Class

Figure 8.3 shows the third screen for the batch creation transaction. The CLASSIFICATION screen allows the user to classify this batch by using a specific CLASS selected from the CLASS TYPE 23. When the class is created, it must be assigned to a class type. The class type for batch objects is 23.

Characteristics

The class has been created using a number of characteristics. The values for this batch are assigned to the characteristics. The values of the characteristics allow users to complete classification searches to find objects, in this case, batches, given certain characteristic values. The values also can be used as part of the batch determination functionality to select batches that have characteristic values within the determination search parameters. For example, a customer may require a batch of Acetone with a specific viscosity of 0.315 cP to 0.319 cP at 20 °C. If the viscosity is a characteristic that is entered for this material batch, then the customer will be able to purchase a batch that has the specific requirements that the customer needs.

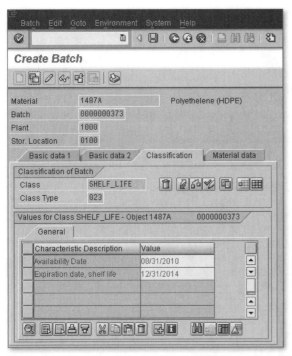

Figure 8.3 Data Entry into the Classification Screen for a Batch

Release Status

After the values have been entered against the characteristics, the user has the option to change the status of the classification.

The default for the status is RELEASED; however, the user has the option to set the status as INCOMPLETE or LOCKED. The INCOMPLETE status can be used when not all characteristic values are known at the time of data entry. A LOCKED status may be required by the user if the batch characteristics are incorrect or if the batch is to be held back because of the batch results being outside of tolerances. Figure 8.4 shows the status options available to the user.

Linked Documents

The last input screen for the batch record is the DOCUMENTS screen, shown in Figure 8.5. This allows the user to link documents that relate to the batch. These can be as simple as a quality testing document that has to be followed for testing each batch or an engineering drawing for the specifications.

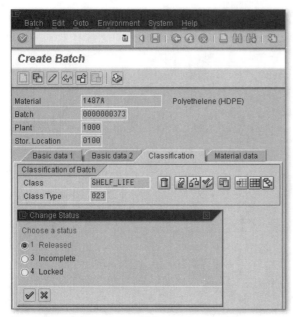

Figure 8.4 Release Status of the Batch Record

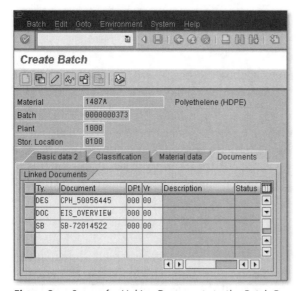

Figure 8.5 Screen for Linking Documents to the Batch Record

To allow a document to be linked to a batch, a configuration step must be completed.

Use Transaction ODOC or the navigation path, IMG • Logistics - General • Batch Management • Batch Master • Activate Document Management for Batches.

The configuration in Transaction ODOC is simply switching on the field to allow document management for batches. The options are active and inactive.

Document Type

Linked documents must be defined in the Document Management System (DMS). The document type (Ty.) field allows the purchasing user to specify a document. This Document for the batch will be of a certain category. The categories are defined in the DMS. Depending on the industry of the client, the number of document types can vary.

Document types can include recipes, specifications, quality inspection work lists, or engineering drawings, among other items.

Document

After the document type has been selected, the user can choose the relevant Document via the matchcode, using the document type as a key. The document identification is created in the DMS.

Document Part

The two other fields that can be entered by the user include the document part (DPt) and the version (Vr). The document part allows the user to enter a section or part of the document that is relevant to the batch. For example, if the batch falls under a quality testing protocol that in total is 140 pages long, the relevant text for the batch may be a certain part or section. If this is the case, that information can be entered on this screen.

Version

Documents are continually revised and updated. For a batch record, it is important that the correct version of the document be identified in this section. An incorrect version number may allow incorrect quality testing or inspection.

8.2.2   Changing a Batch

After the batch has been created, there may be an occasion where the batch record needs to be amended, either to modify a characteristic or to add a new linked document. To change a batch record, use Transaction MSC2N or SAP Menu • Logistics • Materials Management • Material Master • Batch • Change.

The user can make changes to the batch record, but these changes are recorded and are available to review. The CHANGE BATCH screen has an extra tab in the change mode. This tab accesses a screen to view all changes made to the batch record.

The CHANGES screen, shown in Figure 8.6, shows the changes made to the batch record. The information recorded includes the user who created and changed the record, as well as the fields that have been changed, including their values. This information is important to some companies because a strict audit record is needed to show compliance with federal or local regulations. In the pharmaceutical industry, companies manufacturing items that are to be consumed are under strict regulations from the FDA. Companies should at all time ensure that their record keeping is compliant with FDA regulations.

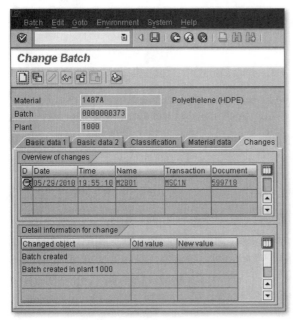

Figure 8.6 Changes to the Batch Record

8.2.3 Deleting a Batch

There is no specific transaction for deleting a batch, but you can delete a batch through the change Transaction MSC2N.

Figure 8.7 shows the initial screen of the change batch transaction, which has a field named BATCH DELETION FLAG that can be set if the batch is to be deleted. However, setting the deletion flag does not immediately delete the batch. The indicator allows the batch to be processed by an archiving program that will determine whether the batch can be deleted. If the batch cannot be deleted, the deletion flag will remain until either the archiving program determines that the batch can be deleted or until the deletion flag is removed.

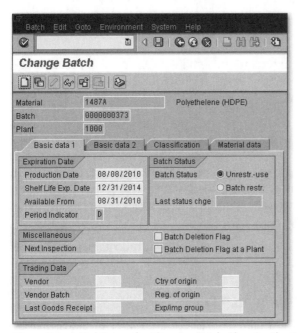

Figure 8.7 Initial Screen for Changing Batch, Showing the Batch Deletion Flag

The archiving process is unique to each company, so the deletion of a batch depends on how frequently information is archived. The BASIS team will be able to explain the archiving process for your particular client.

New for ECC 6.0

Documentary Batch Record

In some industries, such as consumer products or automotive suppliers, there are legal requirements to store where-used data of materials used for production and delivered to customers. Enabling recall actions becomes a mandatory and critical issue for these industries. The recording of data could be achieved by managing all relevant materials in batches, but this method has a negative impact on data volume. When turning on Batch Management, entering a batch number becomes obligatory for all goods movements. Then all inventory postings must be executed on batch level, and labor costs for Inventory Management will increase.

Documentary batch processing can be achieved in the following way:

▶ Documentary batches can be entered during goods movements.

▶ In a production order, entering documentary batches will only be possible at backflush.

▶ In WM, entering documentary batches must be enabled during transport order confirmation.

This section has described the transactions that you will use to create, change, and delete a batch record. The next section examines how the batch records are used to perform batch determination.

8.3   Batch Determination

The batch determination process is not unique to MM. The process is important in SD, PP, and WM as well. Batch determination uses strategy types, search strategies, and search procedures for a batch to be identified in the relevant area.

The batch determination process uses the same type of selection protocol as described in pricing conditions, that is, the use of condition tables and access sequences.

8.3.1   Batch Determination Condition Tables

The batch determination condition table consists of a number of fields that are selected and records that are created to assign values to those fields. A condition table can be created for each of the four areas that use batch determination.

The condition tables can be created in the IMG using the navigation path, IMG • Logistics - General • Batch Management • Batch Determination and Batch Check • Condition Tables.

There are five options for condition table creation:

▶ Inventory Management (Transaction OMA1)

▶ Process Order (Transaction OPLB)

▶ Production Order (Transaction OPLB)

▶ Sales and Distribution (Transaction V/C7)

▶ Warehouse Management (Transaction OMK4)

8.3.2 Batch Determination Access Sequences

For each batch strategy type, there is a batch determination access sequence. This allows the batch strategy type to access the condition tables in the correct sequence. The access sequences for the five areas, shown in the previous section, can be configured using the navigation path, IMG • Logistics - General • Batch Management • Batch Determination and Batch Check • Access Sequences.

Note that these access sequences are cross-client. Any changes in one client will affect all clients.

8.3.3 Batch Strategy Types

The batch strategy type is the specification that tells the system what type of criteria to use during the batch determination process. A batch strategy can be defined in the five areas already mentioned. In MM, a batch strategy type can be defined for different movement types.

The batch strategy type can be configured using the navigation path, IMG • Logistics - General • Batch Management • Batch Determination and Batch Check • Strategy Types • Define Inventory Management Strategy Types.

Figure 8.8 shows the available batch strategy types for MM. Strategy types ME01 and ME02 are predefined in the system and should not be modified. The other strategy types shown on this screen are user-created.

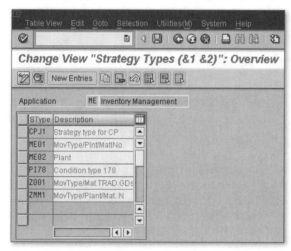

Figure 8.8 Initial Screen When Creating a New Strategy Type for MM

Figure 8.9 shows the fields that have been created for batch strategy type ZMM1. When creating a new strategy type, enter the new strategy type into the CONDIT. TYPE field. The field is defined as four characters. To indicate a user-created strategy type, it should commence with the letter Z.

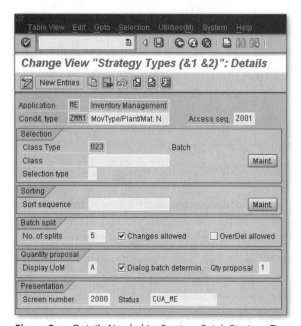

Figure 8.9 Details Needed to Create a Batch Strategy Type

The batch strategy type has to be assigned to one access sequence. The access sequence must already have been configured.

In the SELECTION fields, there is an option to define the values of certain characteristics within a class. The values can be maintained by clicking on the MAINT. button.

Also note the following:

▸ The SELECTION TYPE field allows the user to determine how the batches are selected at the commencement of the batch selection. If the SELECTION TYPE is left blank, then the system will display the batches that meet the selection criteria.

▸ The SORT SEQUENCE field allows the user to choose a sort that will define how the batches are sorted if they are selected. The SORT SEQUENCE can be maintained on this screen if desired.

▶ The BATCH SPLIT section contains the NO. OF SPLITS field that defines the number of batch splits that are allowed during the batch determination.

8.3.4 Batch Search Procedure

The batch search procedure defines how the search is defined. The batch search procedure can be configured using the navigation path, IMG • LOGISTICS - GENERAL • BATCH MANAGEMENT • BATCH DETERMINATION AND BATCH CHECK • BATCH SEARCH PROCEDURE DEFINITION • DEFINE INVENTORY MANAGEMENT SEARCH PROCEDURE.

The SAP system is supplied with one batch search procedure, ME0001, as shown in Figure 8.10. All user-defined search procedures should begin with a Z. After the name of the batch search procedure has been determined, the sequence of strategy types can be configured. To enter the strategy types, click on CONTROL DATA.

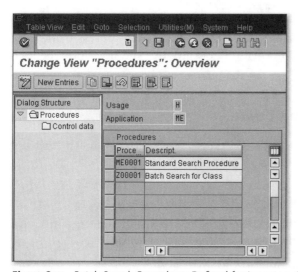

Figure 8.10 Batch Search Procedures Defined for Inventory Management

The batch search procedure is created to produce a step-by-step schema for a particular batch determination search. In Figure 8.11, the batch search procedure Z00001 is defined to search for batches according to search type ZMM1 and then search type Z001. The batch search procedure can be configured to include other strategy types.

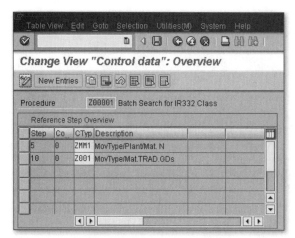

Figure 8.11 Strategy Types for Batch Search Procedure Z00001

This section described in detail how the batch determination process works. The next section looks at the Batch Information Cockpit (BIC) and how it can be used to analyze and monitor batches.

8.4 Batch Information Cockpit

The Batch Information Cockpit (BIC) is a transaction that combines views and analyses of batch information in a single location.

8.4.1 Batch Information Cockpit Overview

BIC allows the user to select batches, display all of the information regarding the batch, access follow-up transactions, and use the batch worklists.

BIC is accessed using Transaction BMBC or via the navigation path, SAP MENU • LOGISTICS • CENTRAL FUNCTIONS • BATCH MANAGEMENT • BATCH INFORMATION COCKPIT.

In Figure 8.12, BIC has been run, and 14 batches have been selected. The materials are shown, and the matches can be displayed by highlighting the material. The information regarding the batch is then displayed in a main screen. The tabs represent the number of different screens with information on this batch.

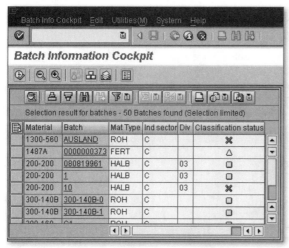

Figure 8.12 Central Area of BIC

You can view the selections of a particular user group, defined in configuration, by selecting UTILITIES • USER SETTINGS.

You can select a user group that has been configured in the IMG. The user group view allows different departments to use BIC to see batch information relevant to their departments.

8.4.2   BIC Standard Configuration

The SAP system is delivered with a predefined configuration for the selection and layout of BIC. Using Transaction OBIC_DIS, the configuration of the BIC layout can be displayed but not changed. To get to the transaction, select IMG • LOGISTICS - GENERAL • BATCH MANAGEMENT • BATCH INFORMATION COCKPIT • DISPLAY SAP STANDARD SELECTION.

The SAP standard selection is shown in Figure 8.13. The SELECTION field shows the value, for example, MATERIAL is 110, and the ACTIVE TAB TITLE shows whether the tab is active. Fields of each of the tabs can be selected and displayed as shown in Figure 8.14.

Figure 8.14 shows the fields that are associated with the SELECTION, in this case 110. The SELECTION field shows the fields to appear on the tab, for example, MATNR, WERKS, MTART, and so on.

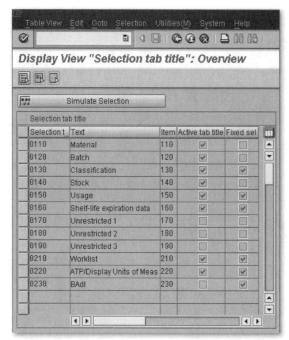

Figure 8.13 SAP Standard Selection for the BIC

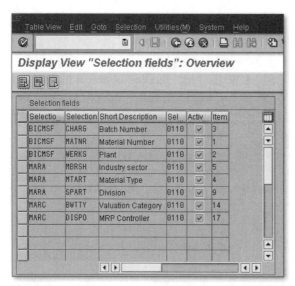

Figure 8.14 Fields Associated with Tabs from the SAP Standard Selection

8.4.3 BIC User-Defined Configuration

If the standard SAP configuration does not address all of the clients' requirements, the user can modify BIC. Some clients have found that the standard view of BIC is not suitable for all departments that need information on batches. Therefore, the user-defined BIC can be modified so that different user groups can have their own view of BIC. The user group specific selection can be found using Transaction OBIC or via the navigation path, IMG • LOGISTICS - GENERAL • BATCH MANAGEMENT • BATCH INFORMATION COCKPIT • DEFINE USER GROUP SPECIFIC SELECTION.

After the user group has been defined, the attributes to BIC for that group can be created. In Figure 8.15, the USER GROUP can be highlighted to access the SELECTION TAB TITLE table field screen, shown in Figure 8.16. The selection tab titles make up the structure that defines which fields are viewed in BIC.

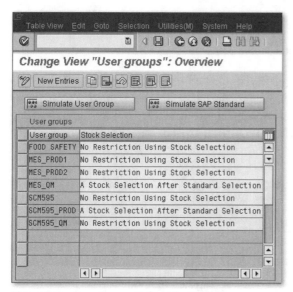

Figure 8.15 User Groups Defined for the BIC

The SELECTION TAB TITLE table field screen shown in Figure 8.16 allows the user to define what tabs will be available to the specific user group and in what order they appear. In this example, the USER GROUP MES_PROD1 has been configured to add an item to the SELECTION screen 120, with the TEXT of BATCH.

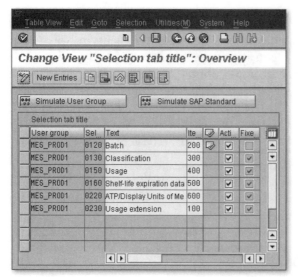

Figure 8.16 Selection Tab Fields Selected for the User Group

After the tabs have been selected for the specific user group, in this example MES_PROD1, the individual fields can be selected. In this case, the fields for SELECTION screen 120 are added, as shown in Figure 8.17. The added fields include LVORM, VFDAT, and HSDAT. The structure of the tab and the placement of the fields depend on the requirements of the user group.

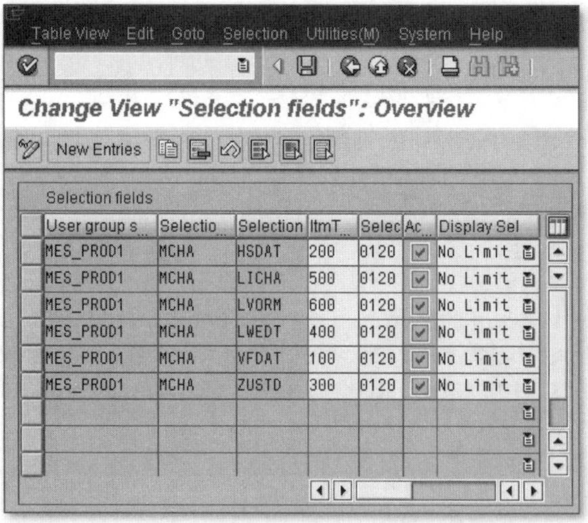

Figure 8.17 Fields Selected for One Tab Specific to One User Group

This section has described the functionality of BIC. As a consultant, you should spend time understanding how BIC works and how it can be configured for your clients' requirements.

8.5 Business Examples – Batch Management Data

When we talk about a batch of something, we each have our own definition of what that means. In SAP, the batch is used to identify units of material as they move through the SAP system. The batch can have specific characteristics that enable it to be identified and used within the various functions.

8.5.1 Batch Management Record

The batch management record for a material contains the specific information that is relevant to that batch. In configuration the level at which the batch is unique is set. Batch numbers can be at one of three levels within an SAP implementation.

Firstly the batch can be unique to the client level, so each batch number is unique for a material for all companies and plants across the client.

Secondly, if the batch configuration is set to the plant level, then the batch number is unique for a material at a plant and the data in the batch record does not transfer if the batch of material is moved to another plant.

Lastly, if the batch configuration is set to a material level then the batch number is unique, but for all plants where the material is used, so when a batch of material is moved from plant to plant the batch data is also transferred.

Example

An Austrian beverage maker had purchased a number of smaller manufacturers over a 10-year period across Europe. Each was left to run independently and operate its own legacy computer system. When it was decided to move operations out of Estonia and Latvia to manufacturing sites in Germany, the company decided to migrate the company as a whole over to a single SAP ERP system. As part of that initial project, a product rationalization team reviewed the products manufactured by the different plants and how these would be represented in the future SAP system. Part of the team's mandate was to review batch numbering and make a recommendation.

The batch-numbering schemas across the legacy systems were similar but did not uniquely identify where the batch was manufactured. Because some vendors were being supplied with product from up to three plants, the team recommended using a batch number that showed the plant where the beverage was made. The decision then had to be made whether the batch number was unique to a material across the enterprise, just to a plant, or just to the material. Because the plant would be part of the new batch number, the client level for batch numbering was considered to be unnecessary. The final decision was to make the batch unique either for a material or a plant. Ultimately, the company decided to have the batch level set to the material level because sometimes batches were moved between plants, and this would make the transfer of batches easier for warehouse staff.

8.5.2 Batch Determination

Batch determination uses strategy types, search strategies, and search procedures for a batch to be identified in the relevant area. The batch determination process uses the same type of selection protocol as described in pricing conditions, that is, the use of condition tables and access sequences. Although batch determination can be used in WM, production, process orders, and Inventory Management, the selection of batches is very important to the sales staff when finding suitable material for customers.

Example

A Swiss manufacturer of specialty additives had implemented SAP ERP as part of an enterprise-wide migration a number of years ago. The manufacturer offered a limited number of standard products, and the majority of its business was in the manufacture of custom additives that were commissioned by customers. Over time, the R&D team, along with marketing, concluded that these custom requests were narrowing to the point where the company could market a few products and produce those with a variety of specifications that would fall within the tolerances demanded by these custom requests. Each batch of product was tested for a variety of chemical and physical properties. The results of the tests were entered into a number of characteristics that were allocated to the batch. The batch-determination process in the sales function could find specific batches based on customer requirements.

Customers had the ability to call and place orders, which has since been replaced by an online ordering system, to see if a batch of product was available. If a customer found a batch that was within the required tolerances, then the product could be shipped immediately, thus saving days or weeks for the customer.

8.6 Summary

Batch Management is important to a growing number of industries. It has developed from just an identification of a group of items to a process that allows companies to perform product recalls, select and sell by batch characteristics, and identify expiring stock. As the drive for a competitive advantage continues, companies will further investigate how batch information can lower production time and hasten material to the customer.

Chapter 9 is important for all MM consultants because it examines the processes around the Material Master record. The chapter will review the creation of a Material Master record, including how it is changed and deleted, and how records can be loaded.

Creating a Material Master record depends on many different departments. Each layer of information is important in its own right, but the material record is not complete until all of the relevant data has been entered.

9 Material Master Record

Creating a Material Master record allows all of the information relevant to a specific material to be entered into a large number of tables. There is not one Material Master file but a number of tables containing information, which when combined, reflect all of the information for that material.

Many tables are updated when information is entered into the Material Master transaction. The Material Master transaction is structured so that there are entry screens for different functional information items, such as Purchasing, Sales, or Accounting, but there is also an organizational dimension to data entry. The material information can be entered at each level of the organization, for example, at the levels of plant, storage location, or sales organization.

Detailed information on the Material Master file was provided in Chapter 3, Master Data in Materials Management. In this chapter, we will discuss how Material Master records are loaded, created, modified, and deleted.

9.1 Creating a Material Master Record

The standard transaction for creating a Material Master record is MM01. Other transactions can be used to create a Material Master. If the material type of the material to be created is known, then the material can be created using a transaction specific to that material type. For example, if a Material Master record for a finished product is to be created, then the material user can use Transaction MMF1 to create a Material Master record.

9.1.1 Create a Material Master Record Through a Schedule

If the Material Master record for an item has been decided upon but is not ready to be released until a specific date, then the material can be created via a schedule. This functionality is part of the Engineering Change Management component (LO-ECH).

To create a material based on a schedule, use Transaction MM11 or the navigation path, SAP MENU • LOGISTICS • MATERIALS MANAGEMENT • MATERIAL MASTER • MATERIAL • CREATE (GENERAL) • SCHEDULE.

The entry of this record, shown in Figure 9.1, is different from a normal Material Master creation because it requires a date to be entered for the creation of the material and, if applicable, an engineering CHANGE NUMBER. The change number would be created by the engineering department to reflect a change in a specification that requires, in this case, a new material number to be created.

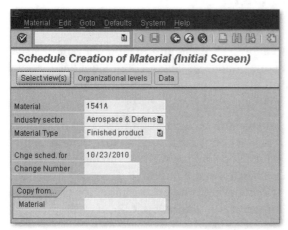

Figure 9.1 Entry Screen for Creating a Material Master Record with a Scheduled Release

9.2 Changing a Material Master Record

Material Master records are changed to allow revised data to be entered, such as changing the purchasing group on the purchasing screen, or revising the MRP controller on the MRP screen. Changes to master records are important to ensure they are as accurate as possible.

9.2.1 Change a Material Master Record - Immediately

A change to a material may be a simple correction, such as a correction to a net weight or a revision to the material due to a production change that will change the material completely. Some companies allow changes to certain fields but not other fields, whereas some companies have committees that review changes that have been requested and allow or deny them. In addition, certain industries, such as the regulated pharmaceuticals industry, require strict audit of any change made on the Material Master.

The Material Master change transaction is the tool to perform the change, but check with your client to make sure there are no policies in place regarding Material Master changes.

The most common way a Material Master is changed is via Transaction MM02 or the navigation path, SAP MENU • LOGISTICS • MATERIALS MANAGEMENT • MATERIAL MASTER • MATERIAL • CHANGE • IMMEDIATELY.

The initial screen for MM02 allows the entry of the MATERIAL number and, if applicable, engineering CHANGE NUMBER. After a material number has been entered, you may choose to select the particular area that is of relevance.

Subsequent to the MATERIAL field or fields being changed, the material is saved. The system then logs the change made and the user who initiated the change.

To find out about the changes made to a material, the information can be located in the Material Master change Transaction MM02. In the basic data screen, as shown in Figure 9.2, the DISPLAY CHANGES option can be selected from the header menu. After this has been selected, a list of all of the changes made to the material is shown in Figure 9.3.

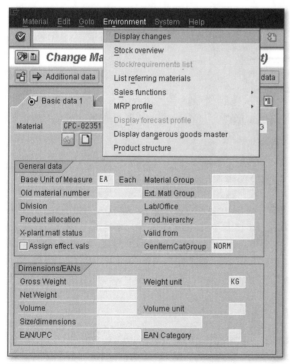

Figure 9.2 Menu Path for Finding the Log of Changes Made to a Material Master Record

Figure 9.3 shows the DATE and TIME transaction that was changed (TCODE), and the user name of the person who made the change (NAME). The SELECTED field allows a change to be selected and reviewed in more detail. In this example, the change made by users 82201, 82221, and 82661 are selected, and the change is shown in more detail in Figure 9.4.

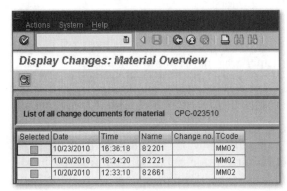

Figure 9.3 Material Change Display Showing Detail Change Information

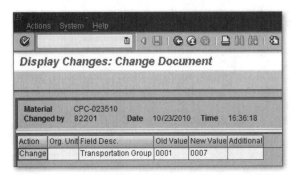

Figure 9.4 Details of Single Change Made to Material

Figure 9.4 shows the change made by user 82201. The MATERIAL number is displayed, CPC-023510. The ACTION field tells you it was a CHANGE. The FIELD DESC. tells you that the TRANSPORTATION GROUP was changed. The OLD VALUE and NEW VALUE fields inform you that the value was changed from a value of 0001 to a value of 0007.

9.2.2 Change a Material Master Record – Schedule

If the material is not scheduled to be changed until a certain date, then the material change can be set ahead of time and the date-activation Transaction MM13 can be used to put the change into effect at the right time. The transaction for this process is MM12 and can be found via the navigation path, SAP MENU • LOGISTICS • MATERIALS MANAGEMENT • MATERIAL MASTER • MATERIAL • CHANGE • SCHEDULE.

The change can also be driven by an engineering change, and the user can enter that CHANGE NUMBER into the scheduling screen, as shown in Figure 9.5.

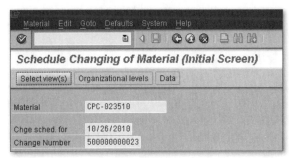

Figure 9.5 Initial Screen Allowing the User to Schedule a Material Change

9.2.3 Change a Material Master Record – Activate

This transaction allows the material user to release changes made to a material or a group of materials based on when the changes were made. For example, if a group of materials was changed because it received a new MRP controller number, then this transaction allows the material user to release the scheduled changes up to a certain date. Users can run this activation in test mode so that the actual changes do not take place as shown in Figure 9.6.

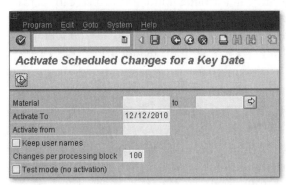

Figure 9.6 Activation Transaction for Scheduled Changes Made Through Transaction MM12

Transaction MM13 can be found via the navigation path, SAP MENU • LOGISTICS • MATERIALS MANAGEMENT • MATERIAL MASTER • MATERIAL • CHANGE • ACTIVATE.

Activate To

This field should contain the key date needed to include all scheduled changes as shown in Figure 9.6. For example, if the field contains the date 12/12/2010, then all changes up to that date will be included. If the date field is blank, then the system assumes that today's date should be used.

Activate From

This date is used to define the first date from which to include changes. For example, the system will include all scheduled changes made to the material from that date to the date entered in the ACTIVATE To field. If this field is blank, the system assumes that the field content should be copied from the ACTIVATE To field, and the activation will only be for that one day.

Keep User Names

This indicator allows the material user to decide what information is copied to the change document. If the indicator is set, then names of the user who made the scheduled changes will be copied across. If the indicator is not set, only the name of the person who ran the activation transaction will be copied across. Confer with your client concerning the requirements of any audit trail that may be required.

Changes Per Processing Block

This field allows the material user to enter a value up to 100, which can increase the efficiency of the transaction at runtime. If there is a major change that requires more processing power, then this field can be changed to a higher number. However, if the KEEP USER NAMES indicator is set, then this field must be set to 1.

Test Mode

This indicator allows the material user to run the transaction in test mode, which does not activate any of the scheduled changes.

This section described the ways in which values on the Material Master can be changed. The change mechanism should be reviewed with your client to determine if any policy is in place regarding Material Master changes. The next section examines the deletion of a Material Master record. This is something not all companies want to consider, so it is important to discuss this in advance with your client.

9.3   Material Master Deletion

Material Master deletion is a process that should be secure and require multiple checks prior to any action. Companies vary in their adoption of Material Master deletion. Some companies will never, under any circumstance, delete a material even if they have stopped using them or producing them. Returns, repairs, and other needs can cause a material to have a life in the system long after its relevance in production has ended. Other companies will have a strict procedure that allows for the deletion of material if a material has been obsolete for a period of time or a material has not been used in any transaction for a period. Other companies will regularly remove material if informed by vendors that the material is no longer available for purchase and no inventory remains in SAP. The policies and procedures of companies will vary, so confer with your client as to their particular requirements for material deletion.

The path to deleting a material starts with Transaction MM06 or MM16 for scheduling a deletion. This transaction is to flag a material for deletion.

9.3.1   Flag for Deletion – Immediately

This transaction allows a company to flag a material for deletion if it decides that the material will never be used in the system again. This transaction does not delete the material but flags the Material Master for deletion.

Transaction MM06 can be accessed through the navigation path, SAP MENU • LOGISTICS • MATERIALS MANAGEMENT • MATERIAL MASTER • MATERIAL • FLAG FOR DELETION • IMMEDIATELY.

The screen shown in Figure 9.7 shows the data that can be entered in the transaction, including the MATERIAL number, PLANT, STOR. LOCATION, VALUATION TYPE, SALES ORG., and so on. The transaction provides the option to delete the material at different levels. Entering just the material number will flag the material throughout the system. Entering a PLANT or a SALES ORG. or a WAREHOUSE NO. will flag the material to be deleted at that same level, that is, sales organization or warehouse level.

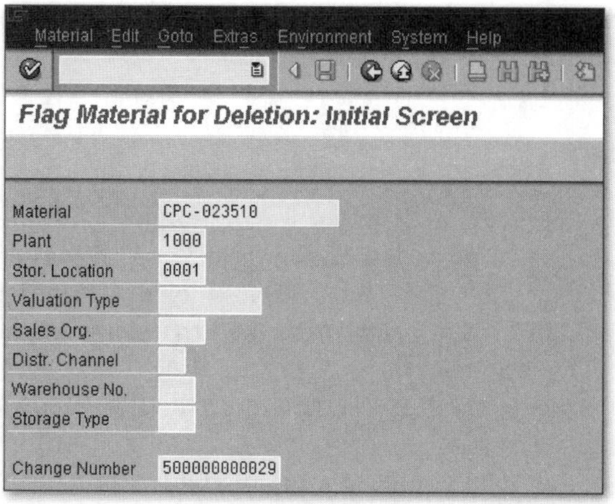

Figure 9.7 Flag for Deletion Screen

9.3.2 Flag for Deletion – Schedule

The difference between this transaction, shown here in Figure 9.8, and the immediate transaction is that the material user has to enter a date for scheduling the flag-for-deletion date, not the actual deletion date.

Transaction MM16 can be accessed through the navigation path, SAP Menu • Logistics • Materials Management • Material Master • Material • Flag for Deletion • Schedule.

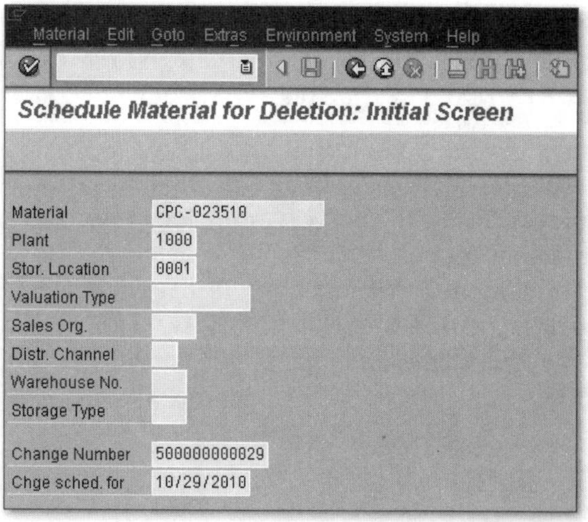

Figure 9.8 Scheduling the Flag for Deletion Transaction

9.3.3   Flag for Deletion – Proposal List

Within Transaction MM06, there is an option to flag materials for deletion via a proposal list. Choosing EXTRAS • PROPOSAL LIST opens the PROPOSED DELETION list dialog box with materials that the system has proposed to be flagged for deletion as shown in Figure 9.9. These materials have no stock in the system.

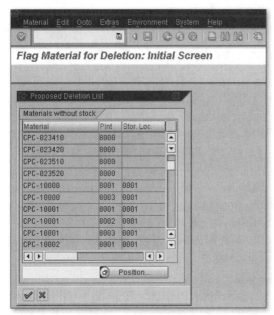

Figure 9.9 Proposal List for Materials That Can Be Flagged for Deletion

9.3.4   Material Master Archiving

The Material Master archiving program will delete the materials that have been flagged for deletion and that are suitable for deletion. The transaction for the archiving process is MM71 and can be found using the navigation path, SAP MENU • LOGISTICS • MATERIALS MANAGEMENT • MATERIAL MASTER • OTHER • ARCHIVING • ARCHIVE/DELETE.

Figure 9.10 shows the archiving transaction with the ability to enter a variant, which is useful when deciding what to archive.

> **Note**
>
> Companies often delay setting procedures for archiving materials until after the implementation of MM. As an SAP consultant, it is good practice to inform clients about their long-term archiving needs. Many clients will run archiving as part of their monthly or semi-yearly routines.

Figure 9.10 Screen for Archiving and Deleting Material Master Records

9.3.5 Remove a Material-Deletion Flag

During the deletion process, a mistake may have been made, or an investigation may find that a material is still used. If that is the case, you can remove the deletion flag after it has been entered but before the archiving program has been run. Using Transaction MM06, enter the material number of the material that has the deletion flag required to be removed. On the initial screen, enter any specific relevant plant or sales organization. The subsequent screen will highlight where the deletion flags are set. By deleting those indicators, the flagged for deletion status is removed.

This section has explained how the Material Master record can be deleted in the system. However, be sure to review and abide by each company's policies and procedures on deleting materials. The next section reviews how Material Master records are loaded into the SAP ERP system.

9.4 Loading Material Master Records

Loading materials from a legacy system may be the only time the Material Master records are loaded; however, with the number of company mergers and acquisitions increasing, you may find that Material Master loading is more frequent.

9.4.1 Loading Material Master Records via Direct Input

When working on a new implementation for a company, you may be asked about loading Material Master records. If the implementation involves reengineering, the client may have a project to rationalize and cleanse its Material Master records from the legacy systems. To construct suitable Material Master records based on legacy records, the client needs a process for adding to the Material Master record the necessary details that are not available from the legacy item master. This may include collecting information from other legacy systems or manual collection and entry.

After the Material Master information has been collated in a repository outside of the SAP system, you can load that information into the new SAP system using a load program.

Before any materials are loaded into SAP, it is good practice to clean out any spurious material records. You can use the program RMMMDE00, run from Transaction SE38, to delete all materials from the client and ensure a clean environment for the material data load.

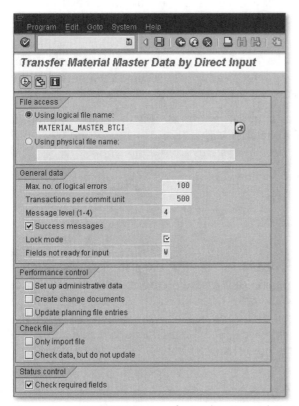

Figure 9.11 RMDATIND Program for Loading Material Master Records

Using the material load program RMDATIND, through Transaction SE38, the client can load items into SAP and into new Material Master records. This is shown in Figure 9.11, where the file containing the material data is entered; in this example, it is called MATERIAL_MASTER_BTCI. The GENERAL DATA section includes technical parameters such as the MAX. NO. OF LOGICAL ERRORS before the program terminates and allowing SUCCESS MESSAGES to be displayed for successful records.

Another program, RMDATGEN, can generate test data for the initial load program. You can run it from Transaction SE38.

9.4.2 Distribution of Material Master Records via ALE

Material Master records can be moved from one system to another via Application Link Enabling (ALE), a middleware solution in SAP's Business Framework Architecture (BFA). ALE can integrate data and processes between SAP systems and non-SAP systems. Messages between the systems are distributed by IDocs. An IDoc comprises a header, data segments, and a status record.

During a transfer of data, the outbound system creates an IDoc containing the data to be transferred, and this is transferred to the target system. In the target system, the IDoc starts inbound processing. The data is processed and then posted in the application, in this case, the Material Master creation transaction.

An ALE environment that moves material records as described can be found in clients that control the creation of Material Master records centrally and then push the new materials out to their other SAP systems around the world.

The next section discusses the production version, which is important for the production staff and planning department.

9.5   Production Versions

A production version can be assigned to a material at the plant level. It describes the types of production techniques that can be used on the material. This is important in manufacturing companies because the production information has to be correct for the version being produced. Modifications to a design can cause significant changes in the production process, and the production version allows the production department to use the most accurate version of the Material Master.

9.5.1   Production Version Overview

The material can have any number of production versions assigned to it. The production version can only be assigned to materials purchased externally and materials that are produced in-house.

9.5.2 Creating a Production Version

The production version can be entered against a material via the Material Master creation Transaction MM01 or change Transaction MM02. The production version can only be entered at the plant level, so the material must be used in at least one plant. These production versions refer to versions of the material that are valid. In Figure 9.12, only one production version is still valid after November 30th, 2009. Customers will still be buying a valid production version as long as the validity date of the version is in the range defined.

The PRODUCTION VERSION OVERVIEW dialog box can be reached through the MRP, WORK SCHEDULING, or COSTING screens. Figure 9.12 shows the PRODUCTION VERSION OVERVIEW dialog box via the MRP screen. The various fields in the PRODUCTION VERSION OVERVIEW dialog box are described next.

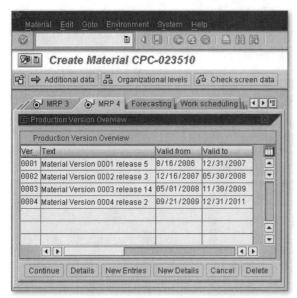

Figure 9.12 Entry Screen for the Material Production Versions

Version

This is the production version key field, which determines what production techniques are applicable for the material. The version number can be changed if the material is altered, even in the smallest way. For example, in the manufacture of a cast flange, an alteration of the cast to include a ridge on the underside would create a version change. If the depth of that ridge were increased, this would cause a further version change.

Version Text

This 40-character field is a description for the production version. Most companies probably have a specific method of describing the version. For example, the description may be prepared so that the first 20 characters are for the description of the change, the next 10 are for the version number, and the last 10 are for the release number. Check with your company to see if the version text is freeform or has specific meaning built in.

Valid To/Valid From

These date fields allow the production user to determine the date range for which the production version is valid. The version may only be valid for a certain period due to a new material that supersedes this one or because versions are always changed every so many years. Specific company policies on versions will explain any validity issues that may arise.

After these fields are entered, then the production version details can be added on the next screen, as shown in Figure 9.13.

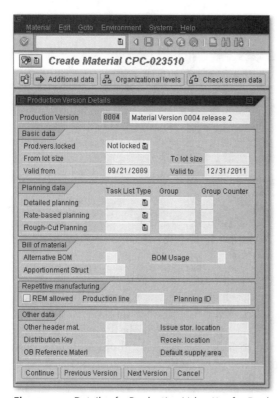

Figure 9.13 Details of a Production Value Key for Production Planning

Basic Data

The initial field in the Basic data section is the Prod.vers.locked field that specifies whether the production version is locked or not locked. If it is not locked, then the version is available for use. The next two fields relate to the minimum and maximum lot sizes applicable for this particular production version. The Basic data section also includes the validity dates.

Planning Data

Three planning areas can be defined in the production version:

▸ Detailed planning: This is used in capacity planning for short-term planning of individual capacities. It uses exact times and dates and is based on a routing.

▸ Rate-based planning: Rate-based planning takes place using rate routings.

▸ Rough-Cut planning: This is the process of converting the master production schedule into requirements for key resources, including labor and machines.

For each of these planning types, a Task List Type, a task list Group, and a task Group Counter can be selected. By entering a value for these, a particular task is being identified for the production version, and thus a particular task is identified for the material.

Bill of Material Data

The bill of material (BOM) data that can be entered for the production version includes an Alternative BOM, a BOM Usage key, and an Apportionment Struct.

An apportionment structure determines how the costs are distributed regarding co-products. The system uses the apportionment structure to create a settlement rule that distributes the costs from the order header to the order items, that is, the co-products.

Repetitive Manufacturing Data

In addition to the repetitive-manufacturing indicator (REM allowed), the other fields are Production line and Planning ID. The Production line is identified for repetitive manufacturing, which is important when working with capacity planning. The Planning ID is used to group together production versions, which can be selected from the drop-down list.

Other Production-Version Data

The last group of fields includes the Receiv. location, the Default supply area, and the Issue stor. location.

9.5.3 Production Versions – Mass Processing

There is a transaction that allows a different approach to entering production versions. A mass-processing approach allows the production user to change production versions collectively, thus saving time. Transaction C223 can be used to enter the information on production version via the Production Planning menu. The production department uses this transaction when entering large numbers of production versions for a plant.

The navigation path of Transaction C223 is SAP Menu • Logistics • Production • Master Data • Production Versions.

This section reviewed the functionality of production versions of the material. The next section examines the material revision levels.

9.6 Revision Levels

A revision level identifies a certain change status of a material and is related to the change status of an engineering change record. The revision level can be assigned to a material within the Material Master record.

9.6.1 Revision Level Overview

The revision level can be entered into the Material Master from the MRP screens. There is an icon below the Plant field that opens a dialog box as shown in Figure 9.14. The dialog box requires the production user to enter an engineering Change Number and a Revision Level number.

The engineering change document must relate to the particular material being changed; otherwise, the revision level cannot be entered.

When the production user enters a Revision Level number, the system will check to ensure that the revision number has not been used before and that it follows the sequence. The revision level functionality is configurable.

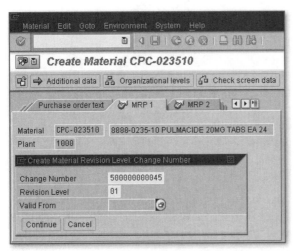

Figure 9.14 Dialog Box for Revision Number Within Material Master Change Record (MM02)

9.6.2 Revision Level Configuration

Before any configuration is performed on revision levels, a configuration step needs to be performed in the Engineering Change Management (ECM) area. Transaction OS54 is the setup transaction for the control data, which needs to be configured to make revision levels active. The navigation path is IMG • Logistics - General • Engineering Change Management • Set Up Control Data.

The key configuration for the Material Master is in Transaction OS55. This creates the sequence for the revision levels for materials. The navigation path is IMG • Logistics - General • Engineering Change Management • Revision Levels • Define Revision Levels for Materials.

9.7 Business Examples – Material Master Record

Entering a Material Master record is structured so that there are entry screens for different functional information items, such as Purchasing, Sales, or Accounting, but there is also an organizational dimension to data entry. The material information can be entered at each level of the organization, for example, at the levels of plant, storage location, or sales organization. In addition, the entry can be made immediately or scheduled for a time in the future.

9.7.1 Creating and Changing a Material Master Record

A material can be created or changed with immediate effect or be scheduled for a time in the future. Each company will have policies in place that relate to the creation or modification of a Material Master record. A change to a material may be a simple correction, such as a correction to a net weight that can be performed immediately. Alternatively, there could be a revision to the material due to a production change that will change the material completely and may require a number of quality checks before being released for use.

Example

An elevator parts manufacturer had been making changes to its Material Master records and scheduling the change to be released each Saturday evening, just after the second shift left. The scheduled changes contained all changes performed during the week, whether the change was to correct a spelling mistake or to add a new material. The process had been operating without incident for several months, with minor issues when bill of lading (BOL) documents had been printed with incorrect data and manual BOLs had to be written.

However, during one week, 70 new items were added and scheduled to be released to production on Saturday. Before the items were released to production, the company received a number of requests from customers to purchase the items. The sales staff could not enter sales orders for the items, and this affected customer service. The subsequent week, a similar event happened as another 20 items were scheduled for release, and a number of sales orders could not be processed.

The company realized that the once-a-week update for the Material Master was not working for the sales department, and a team was set up to quickly find a solution that still gave the company a chance to review changes but allow potential sales. The recommendation was to give a 24-hour review period on all new materials or changes. This gave a sufficient time for review by each relevant department and allowed sales to take orders for the new materials.

9.7.2 Material Master Deletion

The process of deleting a Material Master should require a high level of authorization and be thoroughly documented. Some companies will never delete a material even if they have stopped using it in production or indeed stopped the manufacture of the item. After the item has been discontinued, sometimes the item will need to be repaired, and this could be many years later. Therefore, a material may be required to be in the system long after its use has ended.

Example

A manufacturer of automotive spare parts implemented its SAP system in an accelerated fashion after some initial delays at the beginning of the project. To save time at the end of the project, the company abandoned the rationalization of materials and vendors, and loaded all of the legacy item master and vendor files. Subsequently, 60,000 materials and 7,000 vendors were loaded without review. The company proposed that the rationalization of the data would occur after the system was stable.

After the second month-end closing, the rationalization project recommenced. After four weeks, the team identified more than 9,000 materials and 1,200 vendors that they believed should be deleted.

As the materials had been loaded on to SAP ERP, the data governance group was responsible for the deletion of materials from the system and their process required sign-off from the different department heads responsible for data on the Material Master, including Accounting, Sales, Purchasing, Quality, Logistics, and Manufacturing.

Given the fact that the rationalization project identified 9,000 materials, the data governance group informed the company's board that based on their figure of deleting approximately 100 materials per week, this process would take close to 2 years just for the materials. The board decided to make an exception for the materials loaded in error, and they didn't require the data governance board to review these materials if no processing on the material had been performed since the initial load.

9.7.3 Version Control

A production version can be assigned to a material. This is important for manufacturing companies because the production information has to be accurate for the version that is being currently manufactured. In the production process, there may be different ways to perform certain processes, and the information in the version of Material Master should reflect the correct method for the material.

Modifications to a design can cause significant changes in the production process, and the production version allows the production department to use the most accurate version of the Material Master.

Example

An Austrian beverage manufacturer has a wide range of items that are sold across Europe. Some of the items require country-specific variations, which are accommodated using a different material number. After a change to the packaging for one of its beverages sold in Germany, Austria, and Switzerland, a distribution company in Germany informed the manufacturer that the packaging change was not acceptable for German customers and a change was required or a return to the previous packaging. The company decided to revert to the old packaging for shipments to Germany, while it worked to find a compromise. The company was then in the position of manufacturing two versions of the same material for a period of time.

9.8 Summary

In this chapter, material creation, modification, and deletion were discussed. The Material Master is a highly complex master file with hundreds of links to transactions in SAP ERP. Errors made in the Material Master can have serious effects on other functionalities, such as SD, PP, QM, and so on. The number of users who have access to the Material Master file should be limited. Any change should be carefully considered before you make it and should be audited after it is made.

Chapter 10 describes the functionality of the Vendor Master file, including creating, changing, and deleting vendor records, as well as one-time vendors and Vendor Sub-Range (VSR) functionality.

The accounting or purchasing departments can create the Vendor Master record. The record contains all of the relevant data that helps the purchasing department choose vendors based on negotiated price and performance, while the financial data aids the accounting department with invoicing and payables.

10   Vendor Master Record

In previous chapters, we have discussed the relevant data found in the Vendor Master. In this chapter, we will discuss the mechanics of the Vendor Master records and the less common elements that are important in vendor management, such as one-time vendors and Vendor Sub-Ranges (VSRs). This chapter will help you advise your clients on the vendor functionality.

10.1   Creating the Vendor Master Record

Chapter 3, Master Data in Materials Management, described how the Vendor Master could be created using one of three transaction codes:

- **XK01**: Create Vendor Centrally
- **FK01**: Create Vendor via Accounting
- **MK01**: Create Vendor via Purchasing

From the Vendor menu within MM, the purchasing user can create the Vendor Master either centrally or through purchasing. The purchasing department doesn't usually know all of the issues pertaining to the accounting side of the vendor relationship, so the different transaction codes make vendor creation easier for the departmental users.

The purchasing department uses Transaction MK01 to create a vendor with just the relevant purchasing information, as shown in Figure 10.1. This transaction can be found using the navigation path, SAP MENU • LOGISTICS • MATERIALS MANAGEMENT • PURCHASING • MASTER DATA • VENDOR • PURCHASING • CREATE.

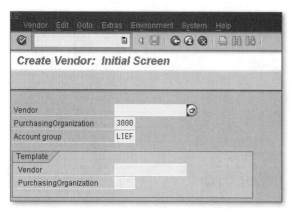

Figure 10.1 Initial Data Entry Screen for Transaction MK01

The purchasing user can enter the vendor number if the VENDOR number field has been defined as allowing external number ranges. This depends on the configuration for the account group. Otherwise, the vendor number is generated by the system, depending on the number range assigned.

Vendor number ranges are defined in the accounting area of configuration. A number range can be defined between some specific numbers, such as 9000 and 99990000, which can be assigned to an account group.

The vendor number ranges can be defined using Transaction XKN1 or by following the navigation path, IMG • FINANCIAL ACCOUNTING • ACCOUNTS RECEIVABLE AND ACCOUNTS PAYABLE • VENDOR ACCOUNTS • MASTER DATA • PREPARATIONS FOR CREATING VENDOR MASTER DATA • CREATE NUMBER RANGES FOR VENDOR ACCOUNTS.

In Figure 10.2, you can see that the number range is defined by a two-character code; in this case, the options are 01, 02, 03, 04, 06, and XX. The purchasing user can enter the code and then define the number range. This cannot overlap with existing number ranges. You can then define the number range as external by highlighting the EXT field. If the number range is not defined as external, it defaults to internal. The user can define the current number of the Vendor Master if the internally assigned numbers need to start at a certain point.

After the number range has been defined, it can be assigned to an account group or many account groups. The account groups are shown in Figure 10.3 and defined for the vendor in the Accounting configuration using the navigation path, IMG • FINANCIAL ACCOUNTING • ACCOUNTS RECEIVABLE AND ACCOUNTS PAYABLE • VENDOR ACCOUNTS • MASTER DATA • PREPARATIONS FOR CREATING VENDOR MASTER DATA • DEFINE ACCOUNT GROUPS WITH SCREEN LAYOUTS.

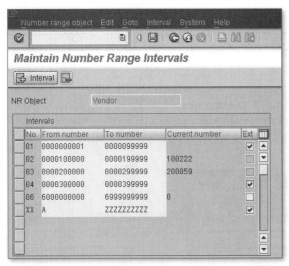

Figure 10.2 Transaction XKN1 Allowing Users to Create Number Ranges for the Vendor Master File

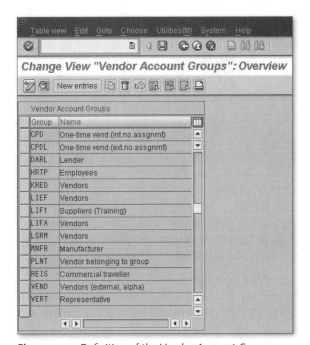

Figure 10.3 Definition of the Vendor Account Groups

The vendor account group is a way of grouping vendors that have the same number range and have the same attributes entered. The account group is defined to allow certain fields to be seen and entered on the Vendor Master.

The assignment of the vendor number range to the vendor account group can be seen in Figure 10.4 and configured using the navigation path, IMG • FINANCIAL ACCOUNTING • ACCOUNTS RECEIVABLE AND ACCOUNTS PAYABLE • VENDOR ACCOUNTS • MASTER DATA • PREPARATIONS FOR CREATING VENDOR MASTER DATA • ASSIGN NUMBER RANGES TO VENDOR ACCOUNT GROUPS.

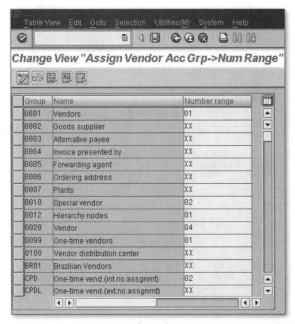

Figure 10.4 Assignment of Number Ranges to Account Groups

The Vendor Master record is especially relevant to a purchasing organization. When creating the vendor, the purchasing user is determining the data associated with that vendor that is relevant only to the single purchasing organization.

A vendor often deals with many purchasing departments of a single company, and the negotiations between the vendor and the company are limited to a specific geographical area, which may relate to a single purchasing organization. For example, if a global telecommunications company negotiates rates and discounts with a company, the terms may be different for the company's Indian locations than for the Mexican locations or the locations in China. Therefore, when entering the Vendor Master record for this telecommunications company, the differences between purchasing organizations may be significant.

On the entry screen of Transaction MK01, it is possible to use another vendor/ purchasing organization as a template for the new vendor. This is useful when entering the same vendor for a number of purchasing organizations because it saves having to make unnecessary entries. This will also reduce the level of data-entry errors.

10.2 Changing the Vendor Master Record

A Vendor Master record can be changed in two ways, either with a current change or a planned change. You'll learn what each of these entails next.

10.2.1 Change Vendor Master Record - Current

This functionality is the normal way a record is changed. The purchasing user will want the change in the record to take effect immediately.

The transaction to change the current Vendor Master record is MK02 and can be found using navigation path, SAP MENU • LOGISTICS • MATERIALS MANAGEMENT • PURCHASING • MASTER DATA • VENDOR • PURCHASING • CHANGE. The transaction screen is shown in Figure 10.5.

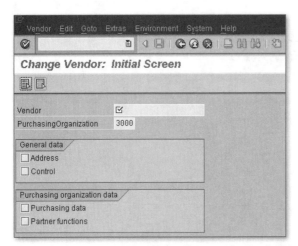

Figure 10.5 Transaction MK02 for Changing the Vendor Master Record with Immediate Effect

The purchasing user has the option of selecting the relevant area that needs to be modified from the GENERAL or PURCHASING screens. The user cannot change the accounting data for this vendor via this transaction code. To change the accounting data for the vendor, the user must use Transaction FK02 or use the navigation path, SAP MENU • ACCOUNTING • FINANCIAL ACCOUNTING • ACCOUNTS PAYABLE • MASTER RECORDS • CHANGE (CURRENT).

10.2.2 Change Vendor Master Record - Planned

This transaction can be used when the purchasing user wants to have a Vendor Master record changed at a specific future date. For example, when a new area code is created in the United States or Canada, a large number of companies have to inform all of their clients of the phone number change that will occur on a specific day. In Ontario, Canada, a new area code 249 will overlay the area code 705 on January 31st, 2011.

The Transaction to change the current Vendor Master record is MK12 and can be found using the navigation path, SAP MENU • LOGISTICS • MATERIALS MANAGEMENT • PURCHASING • MASTER DATA • VENDOR • PURCHASING • CHANGE (PLANNED).

With Transaction MK12, the purchasing user can enter a date on which the changes entered for this record will become valid. Figure 10.6 shows that the CHANGE PLANNED FOR field is a date field. As with Transaction MK02, you only have the option of selecting the relevant area that needs to be modified from the GENERAL or PURCHASING screens.

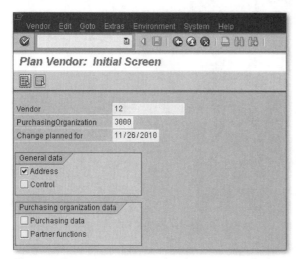

Figure 10.6 Transaction MK12 for Changing a Vendor Master at a Future Date

10.2.3 Display Planned Changes to Vendor Master Records

After the planned changes have been specified for the Vendor Master records, you can view all of the planned changes. Transaction MK14, shown in Figure 10.7, allows the purchasing user to enter a range of variables, such as VENDOR, PURCH. ORGANIZATION, VENDOR SUBRANGE, PLANT, and so on to view the planned changes made to vendors. The resulting report shows the vendors that have planned changes pending and the changes that have been made.

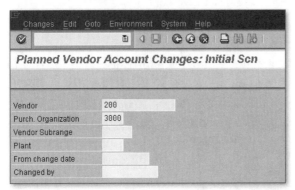

Figure 10.7 Transaction MK14 and the Selection Fields for Viewing Vendor Master Changes

Transaction MK14 can be found using the navigation path, SAP MENU • LOGISTICS • MATERIALS MANAGEMENT • PURCHASING • MASTER DATA • VENDOR • PURCHASING • PLANNED CHANGES.

10.2.4 Activate Planned Changes

The planned changes to the Vendor Master can be activated using Transaction MKH3 or using the navigation path, SAP MENU • LOGISTICS • MATERIALS MAN-AGEMENT • PURCHASING • MASTER DATA • VENDOR • ACTIVATE PLANNED CHANGES • ACTIVATION ONLINE.

As Figure 10.8 illustrates, the purchasing user can enter a single vendor or a range of vendors. The KEY DATE FOR ACTIVATION field is the final date on which changes can be activated. The field defaults to the current date.

Transaction MKH4 allows the purchasing user to create a session to perform the activation of the Vendor Master changes. This should be used for large mass changes of vendor information, where system performance may be an issue, and online activation is not practical.

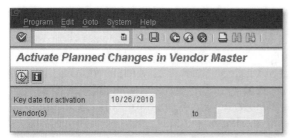

Figure 10.8   Screen for Activating Planned Changes for the Vendor Masters

10.2.5   Change Vendor Account Group

Transaction XK07 can change the account group a vendor is assigned to. This is a difficult transaction to use and should be offered to the client with a strong warning.

Figure 10.9 shows Transaction XK07 that allows the account group of the vendor to be changed. However, the Vendor Master number must be compatible with the number range of the New account group.

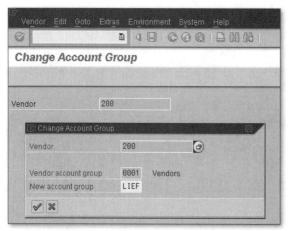

Figure 10.9   Changing the Account Group for the Vendor Master Record

The change of vendor account group can be found via the navigation path, SAP Menu • Logistics • Materials Management • Purchasing • Master Data • Vendor • Central • Account Group Change.

10.3 Deleting Vendor Master Record

The decision to delete a Vendor Master record needs to be made carefully, and all concerned parties, including accounting and purchasing, must be involved. Deletions to the vendor file tend to be less contentious than deletions on the Material Master file, but they still require careful examination. Companies will generally review records in their Vendor Master file regularly to ensure that the records are accurate, and no duplicates have been created. Duplicate vendor records are most often deleted.

10.3.1 Flag a Vendor Master Record for Deletion

A Vendor Master record can be flagged for deletion using the purchasing Transaction MK06. This can be reached through the navigation path, SAP MENU • LOGISTICS • MATERIALS MANAGEMENT • PURCHASING • MASTER DATA • VENDOR • PURCHASING • FLAG FOR DELETION.

On the initial data-entry screen, the purchasing user can enter the vendor number and the purchasing organization. Figure 10.10 shows the next screen where the user can determine how the deletion should proceed.

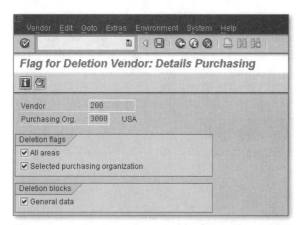

Figure 10.10 Flag-For-Deletion Fields of Transaction MK06

The two indictors in Figure 10.10 allow the purchasing user to determine what should and should not be deleted.

Deletion Flags

If the ALL AREAS indicator is set, then all of the information in the Vendor Master will be deleted. ALL AREAS means all of the data from each purchasing organization will be deleted. This indicator is used when duplicates are found and need to be purged from the system.

Using the SELECTED PURCHASING ORGANIZATION flag will just delete the vendor data for selected purchasing organizations. This type of data is usually deleted because the vendor is not authorized to sell to a certain purchasing organization or cannot sell to a certain organization for strategic or competitive reasons.

Deletion Blocks – General Data

Setting this indicator prevents the information in the general data area from being deleted. This block will ensure that at least the general data for the vendor is not deleted, although the purchasing organization data for the vendor is deleted.

10.3.2 Deleting Vendor Records via Archiving

After a Vendor Master record has been flagged for deletion, the actual deletion can take place by running the archiving program in the Financial Accounting functionality.

Transaction F58A allows the financial users to run an archiving program for Vendor Master data. The transaction as shown in Figure 10.11 can be found using the navigation path, SAP MENU • ACCOUNTING • FINANCIAL ACCOUNTING • ACCOUNTS PAYABLE • PERIODIC PROCESSING • ARCHIVING • VENDORS.

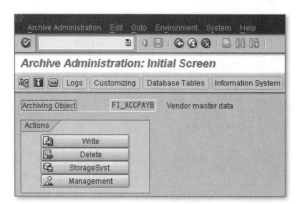

Figure 10.11 Archiving Transaction F58A for the Vendor Master Records

10.4   Display Vendor Master Record

Vendor records are often reviewed by the purchasing department, and the Vendor Master records can be displayed using a number of transactions, which are shown in this section.

10.4.1   Display Vendor Master Record – Current

The vendor record is normally displayed via Transaction MK03 or via the navigation path, SAP MENU • LOGISTICS • MATERIALS MANAGEMENT • PURCHASING • MASTER DATA • VENDOR • PURCHASING • DISPLAY (CURRENT).

10.4.2   Display Vendor Master Record – Per Key Date

The Vendor Master record can also be displayed by how it will be defined at a future date, as shown in Figure 10.12. If many changes are to be made to a Vendor Master record, users may want to view the Vendor Master record at a certain date in the future. This can be performed with Transaction MK19 or via the navigation path, SAP MENU • LOGISTICS • MATERIALS MANAGEMENT • PURCHASING • MASTER DATA • VENDOR • PURCHASING • DISPLAY (PER KEY DATE).

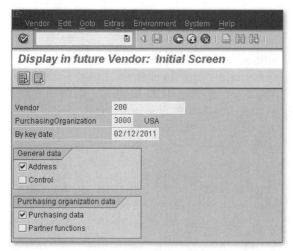

Figure 10.12   Selection Screen for Displaying Vendor Master at a Future Date

10.4.3 Display Vendors – Purchasing List

Transaction MKVZ allows the purchasing user to display the vendors for a given selection criteria. As Figure 10.13 shows, the selection can be made by VENDOR, PURCHASING ORGANIZATION, SEARCH TERM, and ACCOUNT GROUP.

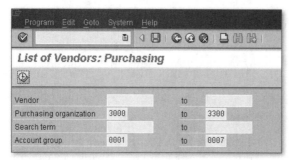

Figure 10.13   Selection Screen in Transaction MKVZ for a Particular List of Vendors

Transaction MKVZ can also be located by using the navigation path, SAP MENU • LOGISTICS • MATERIALS MANAGEMENT • PURCHASING • MASTER DATA • VENDOR • LIST DISPLAY • PURCHASING LIST.

10.5   Blocking Vendors

Vendors can be blocked for a variety of reasons that the client may determine. Often a vendor is blocked due to poor adherence to delivery dates, unsatisfactory material quality, or outside market events. The client has the option to block a Vendor Master account, which can stop any future POs from being placed with the vendor until the Vendor Master record has been unblocked.

10.5.1   Block a Vendor – Purchasing

The Vendor Master record can be set to blocked status by using Transaction MK05. This can be found using the navigation path, SAP MENU • LOGISTICS • MATERIALS MANAGEMENT • PURCHASING • MASTER DATA • VENDOR • PURCHASING • BLOCK.

Transaction MK05 is used for blocking vendors via purchasing. The initial screen of the transaction allows the purchasing user to enter the vendor number and the purchasing organization.

The second screen, shown in Figure 10.14, shows the fields that are relevant to block the vendor. The first indicator is for the user to determine whether the block should be for the vendor in ALL PURCHASING ORGANIZATIONS or just the SELECTED PURCHASING ORGANIZATION entered.

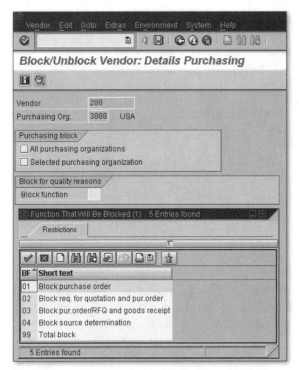

Figure 10.14 Fields Applicable for Blocking a Vendor

The other field on this screen allows the purchasing user to enter a BLOCK FUNCTION code that describes how the vendor block is to be used. The block function code is defined in configuration.

The delivery-block function is defined in the IMG using navigation path, IMG • QUALITY MANAGEMENT • QM IN LOGISTICS • QM IN PROCUREMENT • DEFINE DELIVERY BLOCK.

Each delivery block can be configured to block the vendor from being valid for some part of purchasing functionality. As Figure 10.15 shows, the purchasing block can be for any single option or combination of the following options:

► Request for quotation
► Source determination

- Purchase order
- Goods receipt

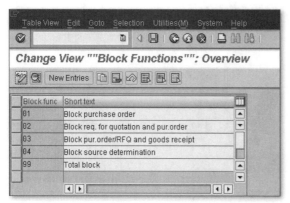

Figure 10.15 Configured Delivery Blocks and Associated Text

10.6 One-Time Vendor

A one-time vendor record, as shown in Figure 10.16, can be used for a vendor that is used once or very rarely. An example of this is where a material is needed in an emergency, and the normal vendor for that material cannot supply the item in the requested time. In this instance, a local vendor or an unapproved vendor may be used for this one-off purchase. Such a record can be used for a number of vendors because this reduces the amount of data entry and data maintenance.

Clients also use one-time vendor records for travel, expense reimbursement, and vendors that cannot accept the client's POs.

A one-time vendor record can be created in the same way as any normal vendor, using Transaction MK01. The difference is that a one-time vendor uses a special account group. In the example in Figure 10.16, the account group for one-time vendors is 0099. One-time vendor records do not usually contain any significant data or any bank and financial information.

Many clients have policies in place that ensure that Vendor Master records are not created for one-time or limited-use vendors. Some of these policies include establishing a limit on the number of transactions per year and restricting the yearly spending on these vendors. For example, if a vendor has more than four transactions a year or the total annual spending with a vendor is more than $4,000, then it cannot be called a one-time vendor; a Vendor Master record must be maintained for that vendor.

Figure 10.16 Account Groups, Including One-Time Vendor Account Groups, in Transaction MK01

10.7 Vendor Sub-Range Functionality

The Vendor Sub-Range (VSR) can be used to subdivide the vendor's products into different ranges. For example, the vendor could be an office-products company, and the subranges could be computer media, paper products, and ink products.

The VSR can be entered into the purchasing information record of a particular vendor/material combination. The allocation of a material to a certain VSR allows the vendor to see the items sorted on its PO in subrange order.

Configuration is required to allow VSRs to be used. Transaction OMSG allows the user to edit the vendor account groups. The indicator can be highlighted to allow VSRs to be relevant for that vendor account group.

Figure 10.17 shows Transaction OMSG, which can be reached via the navigation path, IMG • LOGISTICS - GENERAL • BUSINESS PARTNER • VENDOR • CONTROL • DEFINE ACCOUNT GROUPS AND FIELD SELECTION.

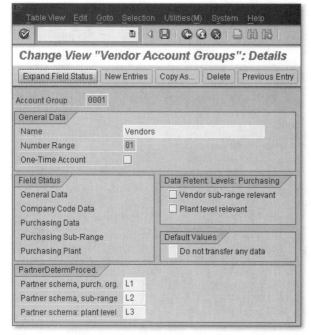

Figure 10.17 Detailed Data for the Vendor Account Group

10.8 Business Examples – Vendor Master

Entering a Vendor Master record requires general data to be supplemented with accounting-specific data and purchasing-specific data. The Vendor Master record is especially relevant to a purchasing organization. When creating the vendor, the purchasing user is entering data associated with the vendor that is relevant only to the single purchasing organization.

The addition or changes to a Vendor Master can be made immediately or planned for release in the future.

10.8.1 Creating and Changing a Vendor Master Record

A vendor record can be created or changed with immediate effect or be scheduled for release at a future date. Each company will have policies in place that relate to the creation or modification of a vendor record. A change to a vendor record may be a simple correction, such as a correction to a fax number or email address that can be performed immediately. Alternatively, there could be a revision to the vendor due to details from a new contract agreement that will change the vendor and may require a full review before being released for use.

Example

A U.S.-based manufacturer of automotive parts had been using its SAP ERP system for just over a year when the company hired a consulting company to perform an evaluation of the system with recommendations for improvement. The evaluation found a number of areas that the consulting company felt could be improved. One of these areas was the way master data was entered into the system. In particular, the report suggested that the way vendor data was entered could lead to potential problems.

After the SAP ERP system was implemented, the company didn't create a formal policy of how vendors were added. The procedure was that if a new vendor was needed, the person needing the vendor completed a form, and someone from the purchasing department entered the information. The consulting company felt this could be problematic as it failed on a number of levels. No one checked the data on the form supplied to the purchasing department, so it could contain errors. There was no formal requirement for the data to be checked to see if the vendor was already in the system either, which allowed duplicate vendor records to exist. The consulting company also felt that there should be some review by the purchasing and accounting departments so they could check the data and reject the new vendor if applicable.

Lastly, the consulting company found that the company had developed the use of one-time vendors, which they believed would have significantly reduced the number of new vendor requests.

10.8.2 Vendor Master Deletion

The process of deleting a vendor record should require a high level of authorization and be thoroughly documented. Some companies will never delete a vendor even if they have stopped using the vendor for any purchases for a number of years. After the vendor has not been active for some time, an occasion may arise where an item will need to be purchased for a repair, and this will require a vendor to be reactivated.

Example

A German automotive parts manufacturer had been using SAP ERP for more than a decade and had never deleted or archived any materials or vendors. The company's auditors recommended a review of the Vendor Master file to delete duplicated records. In addition, they proposed that a process be put in place to decide on when vendors should be deleted.

The company assembled a team to identify the duplicate vendor records, and more than 100 duplicates were found. These records were removed from the system after senior management approved the deletion.

The second recommendation by the auditors, to create a process for vendor deletion, required the data governance group to develop a step-by-step procedure for vendors that had not been active for 24 months. The procedure required both the accounting and purchasing departments to approve the deletion.

10.8.3 One Time Vendor

A one-time vendor record can be used for a vendor that is used only once or very rarely. An example of this is where a material is needed in an emergency, and the normal vendor for that material cannot supply the item in the requested time. A one-time vendor number can be used because this reduces the amount of data entry and data maintenance. Sometimes companies use one-time vendor records for expense reimbursement and for vendors that cannot accept POs.

Example

A Canadian university using SAP ERP developed a policy on the use of one-time vendors. Usually a PO would be made with a vendor from an approved list of suppliers that was established and maintained by the university's procurement services department. However, the university decided that if procurement services anticipated a vendor that needed to be paid would not be used more than once during the fiscal year, it could be treated as a one-time vendor. The policy did enforce a $5,000 limit for a one-time vendor; otherwise, the vendor had to be on the approved list of suppliers.

10.9   Summary

This chapter has examined the functionality of the Vendor Master file. The Vendor Master file contains important information for the purchasing department and the accounting department. The Vendor Master file is important for allowing the purchasing users to provide material to production at the lowest cost, at the right quantity and quality, and at the correct time. The accounting department uses the Vendor Master file to pay the vendors in the correct fashion at the agreed-upon time. The Vendor Master file is important in MM and requires adequate security to minimize the number of users who can create and modify vendor records.

Chapter 11 will examine the Purchasing functionality in SAP ERP. The chapter will focus on purchasing steps from the initial purchase requisition, through request for quotation (RFQ), the quotation sent by the vendor, and then the final PO. Other topics covered include source lists, purchasing conditions, and vendor evaluation.

Purchasing departments have come a long way from a few people doing business with paper requisitions and vendor card files and working to get the best deal with long-term local vendors. Technology has brought the purchasing department into the front line of cost-efficiency. Purchasing departments now have tools and procedures that allow them to negotiate larger savings, better quality, and more secure supply.

11   Purchasing Overview

Every company that operates a business has to purchase materials: raw materials, office supplies, services, and other items. The science of purchasing has become part of today's efficient business operation. The purchasing department can research and negotiate significant savings for a company through policies and technology.

Today's purchasing department has a plethora of information from associations, purchasing think tanks, and specialist purchasing consultants. Companies can introduce best practices along with specialized technology to ensure that the information is available to the purchasing professional for negotiating and managing contracts.

11.1   Purchase Requisition

The purchase requisition is the procedure by which general users or departments can request the purchases of goods or services that require processing by the purchasing department. Companies can allow certain authorized users to enter purchase requisitions directly into the SAP ERP system, but in situations involving a particular dollar value or type of goods and services, the company may request another method of informing the purchasing department of the purchasing requisition, such as fax or email. An example of a purchase requisition is shown in Figure 11.1.

Many companies have implemented an Internet frontend to purchase requisition-ing, and authorized users can go to a URL and enter the material or services they need instead of having direct access to SAP ERP.

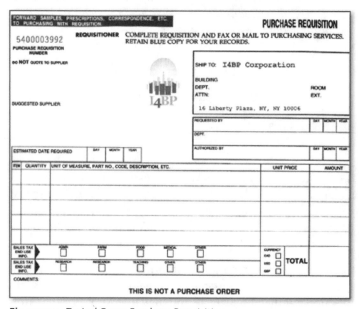

Figure 11.1 Typical Paper Purchase Requisition

After the purchase requisition has been created, it can be converted to a PO or can be used as the basis for a request for quotation (RFQ), which is described next.

11.2 Request for Quotation

After the purchasing department has received and processed the purchase requisitions, there may be an item that requires the purchasing department to offer a request for quotation (RFQ), as shown in Figure 11.2. Following are some of the reasons this might occur:

▶ Material is not previously used at the company.

▶ Previous material now has no identified vendor.

▶ New vendor is required due to termination of contract, such as quality issues.

▶ New vendor is required due to bankruptcy of vendor.

▶ New vendor is required due to government regulations.

▶ New vendor is required due to logistical issues.

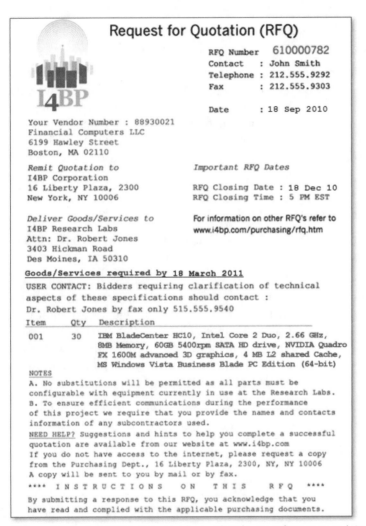

Figure 11.2 Typical RFQ Sent to Vendors with Relevant Information and Conditions

When selecting the vendors that will be invited to submit quotations, the purchasing department will use a number of inputs:

▶ Vendor suggestions from the requisitioner, especially for a new material

▶ Research on vendors, using professional associations and buying groups

▶ Trusted vendors with whom the company has contracts

In the traditional work of purchasing prior to advancements in information technology, many companies would do carry-out RFQs by selecting prospective vendors, physically sending out RFQ documents and packages of information, and receiving data and prices back. They could then review these documents and select a vendor after some period of time. However, this process meant that much of the vendor evaluation was performed after the RFQ was produced, sent, and received back.

Today, the RFQ can be sent to vendors via mail, fax, or electronically via email or EDI. The EDI transaction set for sending the RFQ to a vendor is 840.

With today's level of company spending, the purchasing department has to evaluate the vendors' volume capabilities, on-time performance, quality performance, and understanding of the company's business, long before the RFQ is sent.

For their part, vendors are becoming more aware of companies' needs to reduce purchasing cost and are preparing for RFQs in a more strategic way. A lot of vendors are using technology to calculate the threshold of what a purchasing department is willing to pay based on their quality and logistical factors. Vendors know that being the lowest bidder is not necessarily going to win the bid, but they also know that being a low bidder for RFQs is important.

The RFQ is sent to vendors, and those vendors who decide to bid will send back a quotation, described in the next section.

11.3 Quotation

The vendor sends a quotation to the purchasing department that offered the RFQ. The response from the vendor should follow the stipulations set down in the RFQ. Should the vendor fail to follow the instructions in the RFQ, the customer can disqualify the quotation from the vendor. Many vendors fail to read and understand RFQs before submitting quotes. An example of a quotation sent by a vendor is shown in Figure 11.3.

The vendor can send the quotation by EDI using Transaction set 843.

The purchasing department compares the quotations sent back by the bidders, or vendors, and then chooses one. The other quotations are rejected. The vendor that supplied the winning bid will then be offered a PO, which is described in the next section.

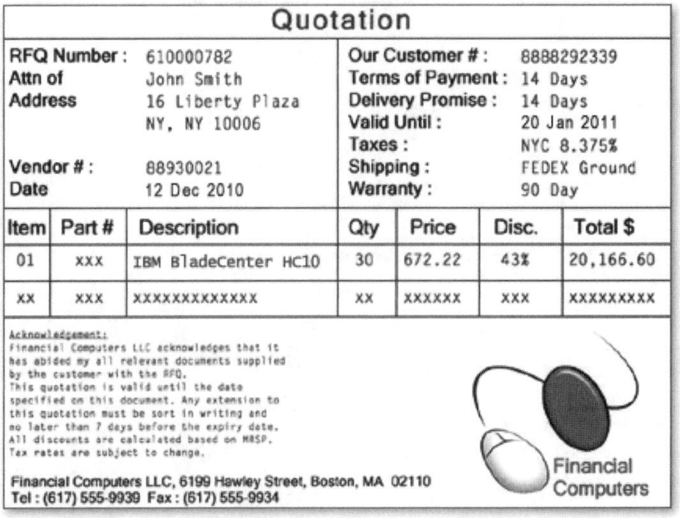

Quotation

RFQ Number :	610000782	Our Customer # :	8888292339
Attn of	John Smith	Terms of Payment :	14 Days
Address	16 Liberty Plaza	Delivery Promise :	14 Days
	NY, NY 10006	Valid Until :	20 Jan 2011
		Taxes :	NYC 8.375%
Vendor # :	88930021	Shipping :	FEDEX Ground
Date	12 Dec 2010	Warranty :	90 Day

Item	Part #	Description	Qty	Price	Disc.	Total $
01	xxx	IBM BladeCenter HC10	30	672.22	43%	20,166.60
xx	xxx	xxxxxxxxxxxxx	xx	xxxxxx	xxx	xxxxxxxxx

Acknowledgement:
Financial Computers LLC acknowledges that it has abided my all relevant documents supplied by the customer with the RFQ.
This quotation is valid until the date specified on this document. Any extension to this quotation must be sort in writing and no later than 7 days before the expiry date.
All discounts are calculated based on MRSP.
Tax rates are subject to change.

Financial Computers LLC, 6199 Hawley Street, Boston, MA 02110
Tel : (617) 555-9939 Fax : (617) 555-9934

Financial Computers

Figure 11.3 Typical Quotation in Response to the RFQ

11.4 Purchase Order

A purchase order (PO), as shown in Figure 11.4, is a commercial document issued by a purchasing department (the buyer) to a vendor (the seller), indicating the materials, quantities, and negotiated prices for materials or services that the seller will provide to the buyer.

The PO will usually contain the following:

- Purchase order number
- Date of the purchase order
- Billing address of the buyer
- Ship-to address of the buyer
- Special terms or instructions

- ► List of items with quantities
- ► Negotiated price of each item

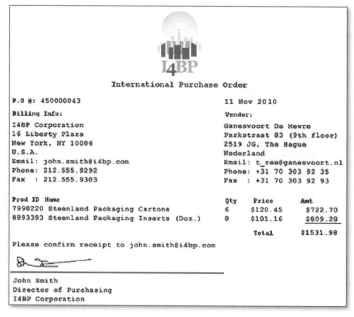

Figure 11.4 Example of a Typical Purchase Order

Companies use POs for many reasons. They allow purchasing departments to clearly communicate their intentions to vendors, and they protect vendors in the event that there is any dispute over the items, quantities, or price. The PO is also a component of the three-way match, that is, matching a PO to a goods-receipt document and a vendor's invoice.

POs can be printed and sent to a vendor or faxed to a vendor. With EDI technology, the PO can be sent electronically and be directly uploaded into the vendor's sales system. The transaction set for this EDI PO is 850. If a change is made to the PO, the document can be sent to the vendor using EDI transaction set 860.

A vendor can be assigned when the PO is created via a source list or via a process called source determination. Both of these are discussed in the next section.

EDI
Trans. #o.

List of Vendors for a material.

11.5 Source List and Source Determination

For a purchasing decision to be made, a buyer will look at the source list, which contains contracted or certified vendors for a particular material.

material/ vendor/ plant combination.

11.5.1 Single Source

Many companies are trying to implement single sourcing for their materials. A single source for a material means that for each material that is purchased, there is only one vendor. Many companies spend a great deal of effort in negotiating single-source contracts to reduce the cost of items they purchase.

For example, a purchasing department may have purchased desks from three different office supply companies: OfficeMax, Office Depot, and Staples. But with single sourcing, the purchasing department negotiated a lower price with one supplier of desks, OfficeMax, and will only use that vendor for a specified period. Single sourcing can cut cost substantially if companies also give vendors the chance to single-source a range of products, but it can leave the buyer in a problematic situation if there is a disruption in that source.

Many purchasing departments are asked by requisitioners to single-source a particular item. The purchasing department will ask the requisitioner to justify this in a document called a Sole Source Justification, often used by government and state authorities.

Compatibility

The requisitioner may have a valid reason to purchase a particular material, which was purchased previously, if no other vendor can supply the requisitioner with a compatible material. For example, a request for information (RFI) project may have found that no other vendors can supply the material in question.

If the requisitioner needs to produce a Sole Source Justification, then it is important to describe what equipment is involved and explain why there is no solution except to purchase from the vendor who originally supplied the product. In many research situations, the identical materials are needed to replicate experiments, and materials from an alternative vendor may not be acceptable for verifying results. For example, in quality inspection labs, tests that use certain chemicals may require the purchase of the chemical from the same vendor that has been used for all previous tests. This may be in violation of the purchasing department's sourcing policy, but the lab would provide a Sole Source Justification to use the same vendor as previously used.

The purchasing department will usually require some verification that an extensive search has been made, and the parts cannot be located at a lower price from a wholesaler or an alternative source. The larger the unit price of the material, the more investigation is required. If the cost is large enough, then the purchasing department may suggest using the RFQ process to ensure that the correct procedures have been followed.

Economic Justification

Requisitioners can use economic justification to suggest a single source for a material. Opting for the lowest price is not always the most economical way of purchasing a material. Other factors, such as performance and the cost of incidentals, should be taken into account.

A common example of this is the PC printer market. The prices of printers have been falling substantially in the past few years, but to create the cheaper printer, the manufacturers have produced printers that can cost less than the inkjet or toner refill. When looking at the cheapest printer in economic terms, the requisitioner needs to look at the number of prints per refill, the cost of the machines, and the cost of the refill. Therefore, the requisitioner can submit the Sole Supplier Justification based on the economic justification.

11.5.2 Multi-Source

Purchasing departments commonly use more than one vendor as a supplier of a material. Although best practices lean toward single sourcing with a trusted vendor, many companies do not want to risk a failure in the supply of material and thus will have more than one vendor qualified to supply it.

In SAP ERP, each vendor can be entered into the source list for a certain material for a particular plant and/or purchasing organization. The maintenance of the source list in SAP ERP can be accessed using Transaction ME01 or via the navigation path, SAP MENU • LOGISTICS • MATERIALS MANAGEMENT • PURCHASING • MASTER DATA • SOURCE LIST • MAINTAIN.

Figure 11.5 shows the initial screen of ME01. The purchasing user has to enter the material and the plant where the source list is being maintained. Different plants may have different vendors for the same material, due to logistical issues or the cost of transportation. Other reasons may include the fact that the vendor has different regional outlets with different vendor numbers. The screen in Figure 11.5 shows the fields that are relevant to maintaining the source list, and they are described in the following sections.

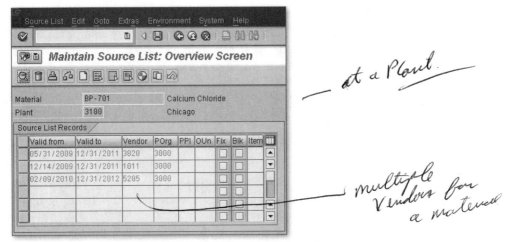

at a Plant.

multiple vendors for a material

Figure 11.5 Maintenance Screen for the Source List of a Material

Valid To/Valid From

These fields allow the purchasing user to give a validity range showing when the vendor will be allowed to be a source for the specified material at the specified plant.

Agreement/Item

These fields can be completed if there is an outline agreement between the vendor and the company. This outline agreement can be either a contract or a scheduling agreement. The ITEM field relates to the item number on the outline agreement.

Fixed Source

The FIX indicator should be set if this vendor is the preferred source of supply for the material at this plant. The system uses this indicator to select the fixed source in the source-determination process.

Blocked Source

The BLK indicator can be set if the vendor is blocked from supplying the material for a specified time, based on the validity period. The blocked-source indicator does not allow any PO to be created with this material/vendor/plant combination.

> **Note**
>
> The blocked and fixed indicators cannot both be set. Only one of the indicators can be set, or neither.

MRP Field

The source list can be used in the MRP process to determine the vendor for requisitions and instigating schedule lines from scheduling agreements. The indicator in this screen allows the planning department to determine how this source vendor influences MRP:

- If no indicator is set for this field, the vendor is not taken into account in source determination within MRP.
- If the indicator is set to 1, this vendor is taken into account as the source for purchase requisitions generated in MRP.
- If the indicator is 2, then this vendor is identified as the source for the scheduling agreement, and delivery schedule lines can be created if a scheduling agreement is in place.

11.5.3 Generate a Source List

Transaction ME05 allows the purchasing user to generate a source list for a single material or for a range of materials, rather than manually creating the lists. Use the navigation path, SAP MENU • LOGISTICS • MATERIALS MANAGEMENT • PURCHASING • MASTER DATA • SOURCE LIST • FOLLOW-ON FUNCTIONS • GENERATE.

The selection screen in Figure 11.6 allows the generation of a source list based on the selection of a MATERIAL range and a PLANT range. This is useful if no source lists have been created because a mass-maintenance program is a fast way to generate the lists.

There is a selection to include, exclude, or only allow outline agreements. Most clients will include all material or vendor scenarios in an initial source-list creation.

The other selection fields are similar to those that can be created in Transaction ME01, including validity dates and MRP relevance. There is also an option to delete all existing source list records or allow them to remain. Finally, there is a TEST RUN indicator to allow the purchasing user to run the program without actually creating the source lists. We advise running this program with the indicator set to a TEST RUN because changes in the selection parameters are often required.

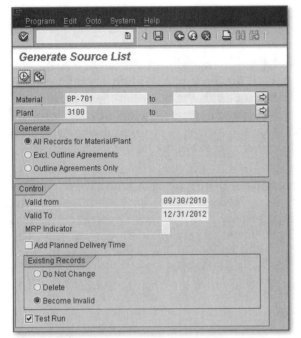

Figure 11.6 Selection Screen for Generating a Source List for a Material or Range of Materials

oTheR souRces oS vendor/ material combinaSion

11.5.4 Source Determination

Source determination allows the buyer to find the most suitable source of supply for a purchasing need, based on various sourcing information. This information does not necessarily have to come directly from the source list. There are other areas where sourcing information is found.   *-- SouRce LiST*

Outline agreements can offer the buyer information about current contracts in place with regard to the vendor/material combination. An agreement such as a quota arrangement can influence sourcing because it informs buyers of the level of commitment the vendors have contracted to for a given time period. *· Outline agreents <*

Other source-determination information can be found from the purchasing information record and plant information.   *- PIR.*

The system includes a source-determination procedure for determining the best source of supply for the buyer's need. The order of relevance for source determination is as follows:

▶ **Quota arrangement:** If the system finds a quota arrangement for the material that is valid for the date needed, then the system will determine that vendor as the source of supply.

▶ **Source list:** If there are no valid quota arrangements, then the system will review the entries on the source list for the required material/plant combination. If there is a single source or a source that is flagged as the preferred vendor, then the system will offer this vendor as the determined source. However, if there are a number of vendors on the source list that are valid by date selection, then the system will stop and offer the selection to the purchaser. A vendor can then be selected from the list.

▶ **Outline agreement and info records:** If there is no valid source list or no valid source-list line items, the system will review the contracts, outline agreements, and info records for the required material. The system will check all information records for the material for all purchasing organizations but will only offer a source if the supply region specified by the vendor is applicable to the relevant plant. After the system has reviewed all documents and info records, a selection will be available to the buyer, providing that the system has determined any valid vendors.

11.6 Conditions in Purchasing

Condition procedures are more commonly associated with the Sales and Distribution functionality; however, the same condition processes are also used in Purchasing.

11.6.1 Condition Processing

The condition procedure in Purchasing is used to calculate the purchase price by processing all relevant pricing factors. By using the defined conditions, the purchasing process arrives at a determined price for purchasing transactions, such as POs.

As already discussed in previous chapters, condition processing is made up of four distinct areas: calculation schemas, condition types, access sequences, and condition tables.

Condition Types

Condition types represent pricing dynamics in the system. The system allows condition types for absolute and percentage discounts, freight costs, duty, and taxes. With the condition type, the buyer can see how the price is calculated in the purchasing document.

Examples of Condition Types

- **PB00**: Gross Price
- **RB00**: Absolute Discount
- **ZB00**: Absolute Surcharge
- **FRB1**: Absolute Freight Cost
- **ZOA1**: Percentage Duty
- **SKTO**: Cash Discount
- **NAVS**: Nondeductible Input Tax

11.6.2 Pricing Conditions

Pricing conditions allow the purchasing department user to enter the details of the pricing agreements negotiated with the vendor into the system. These contractual agreements can include discounts, surcharges, agreed freight costs, and other pricing arrangements. The buyer can enter any of these conditions in purchasing documents such as quotations, outline agreements, and purchasing information records. These conditions are then used in POs to determine prices.

Time-Dependent Conditions

This type of condition is mostly used for scheduling agreements and quotations. Time-dependent conditions allow the purchasing department user to introduce limits and scales into the condition record. A pricing scale is based on quantity, so it can determine that the more the buyer orders of a particular product, the lower the price. The purchasing user can also create condition records with graduated scales.

A pricing scale can be created using the following criteria: quantity, value, gross or net weight, and volume. The purchasing department user can create a rate for each level of the scale. For example, if a buyer orders up to 100 units, the price may be $10.00 per unit; and if the buyer orders between 101 units and 150 units, the price may fall to $9.45. Above 151 units, the price may fall again to $9.12 per unit. The price will apply to all units purchased.

In a graduated pricing scale, the price of the unit changes at a certain level as described previously, but the price of the unit is not applicable to all of the units sold. For example, using the regular pricing scale, a purchase of 155 units would mean the total cost would be 155 multiplied by the unit cost of $9.12, which is equal to $1,413.60. Using a graduated price scale, the calculation for 155 units would be 100 units at $10.00, 50 units at $9.45, and 5 units at $9.12, for a total of $1,518.10.

Time-dependent conditions are always used in purchasing information records and contracts.

Time-Independent Conditions

Time-independent conditions do not include any pricing scales or validity periods. POs contains only time-independent conditions. Quotations and scheduling agreements can include both types of conditions.

11.6.3 Taxes

The tax information can be calculated during the price-determination process using tax conditions. The tax rate is coded into the tax field in the purchase-order item. The tax calculations are determined by the tax conditions described in the PO.

11.6.4 Delivery Costs

The delivery costs can be determined via conditions in the PO. The planned delivery costs are entered in the PO for each order item. These costs have been negotiated with the vendor or the freight company. The planned delivery costs usually include the actual freight charges, any relevant duty payments, a quality-dependent cost, and a volume cost.

This section looked at the use of conditions in purchasing to determine such things as pricing. The next section examines the use of vendor evaluation in determining the source of supply in purchasing documents.

11.7   Vendor Evaluation

Vendor evaluation is an important part of the function of the purchasing department. Selecting vendors to supply material or services can now be a formalized procedure requiring significant information gathering and analysis. Purchasing departments generally have written policies that determine a set of criteria for selecting vendors initially and then for selecting from a list of suitable vendors for a purchase document, as seen in Figure 11.7. The process of evaluating vendors will vary from company to company and will depend largely on the specific industry of the company and company policy.

Vendor evaluation in SAP ERP is a configurable scoring system that allows the purchasing department to design the evaluation to align with the company's policies and procedures.

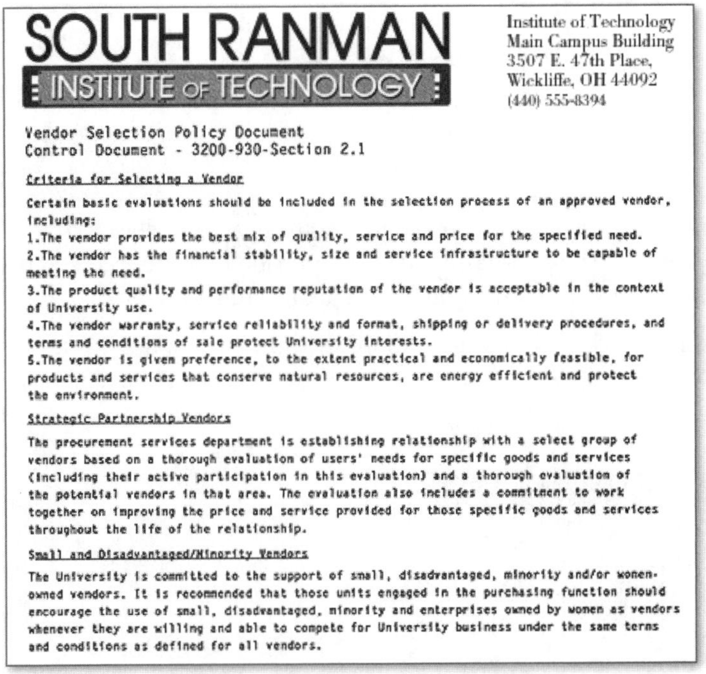

SOUTH RANMAN
INSTITUTE of TECHNOLOGY

Institute of Technology
Main Campus Building
3507 E. 47th Place,
Wickliffe, OH 44092
(440) 555-8394

Vendor Selection Policy Document
Control Document - 3200-930-Section 2.1

Criteria for Selecting a Vendor

Certain basic evaluations should be included in the selection process of an approved vendor, including:

1. The vendor provides the best mix of quality, service and price for the specified need.
2. The vendor has the financial stability, size and service infrastructure to be capable of meeting the need.
3. The product quality and performance reputation of the vendor is acceptable in the context of University use.
4. The vendor warranty, service reliability and format, shipping or delivery procedures, and terms and conditions of sale protect University interests.
5. The vendor is given preference, to the extent practical and economically feasible, for products and services that conserve natural resources, are energy efficient and protect the environment.

Strategic Partnership Vendors

The procurement services department is establishing relationship with a select group of vendors based on a thorough evaluation of users' needs for specific goods and services (including their active participation in this evaluation) and a thorough evaluation of the potential vendors in that area. The evaluation also includes a commitment to work together on improving the price and service provided for those specific goods and services throughout the life of the relationship.

Small and Disadvantaged/Minority Vendors

The University is committed to the support of small, disadvantaged, minority and/or women-owned vendors. It is recommended that those units engaged in the purchasing function should encourage the use of small, disadvantaged, minority and enterprises owned by women as vendors whenever they are willing and able to compete for University business under the same terms and conditions as defined for all vendors.

Figure 11.7 Vendor Selection Document from a University Purchasing Department

11.7.1 Vendor Evaluation Overview

The vendor-evaluation function can be configured to replicate some or all aspects of a company's written procedures on vendor selection. The functionality is based on criteria that can be objective or subjective. The objective criteria are calculated with the data from the purchasing transactions. The subjective criteria are not calculated values but rather are entered by the purchasing department. To determine what level of importance is attributed to each criterion, a weighting key is used. The weighting key can be defined as equal weighting or unequal weighting.

11.7.2 Vendor Evaluation Criteria

The evaluation criteria include the main criteria and subcriteria. Each of these can be configured for vendor evaluation.

Main Criteria

In the standard SAP system, there are a number of predefined criteria as listed here. Four of the main criteria relate to the procurement of material, whereas the fifth is used for vendors supplying services.

- ▶ Price
- ▶ Quality
- ▶ Delivery
- ▶ Service and Support
- ▶ External Service

Although the system has the five main criteria defined, the evaluator does not need to include all of the criteria. The purchasing user can include new criteria, and up to 99 main criteria are permitted by the vendor evaluation functionality.

The main criteria can be defined in configuration, as shown in Figure 11.8. The navigation path is IMG • MATERIALS MANAGEMENT • PURCHASING • VENDOR EVALUATION • DEFINE CRITERIA.

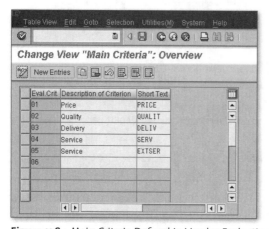

Figure 11.8 Main Criteria Defined in Vendor Evaluation

Subcriteria

Within the main criteria, there are smaller elements called subcriteria. There can be up to 20 subcriteria for each of the defined main criteria. The combined scores for subcriteria produce the overall score for each main criterion. The standard SAP ERP system includes the following:

- ▶ Subcriteria for Price includes Price Level, Price History.
- ▶ Subcriteria for Quality includes Goods Receipt, Quality Audit, Complaints.
- ▶ Subcriteria for Delivery includes Confirmation Date, Compliance, On-time Delivery, Quantity.

The subcriteria, shown in Figure 11.9, can be configured for each of the main criteria. To add new subcriteria, enter the description and the scoring method. The scoring method can be automatic, semi-automatic, or manual. The defined scoring methods are shown in Figure 11.10. These include a number of automatically determined scoring methods, such as from purchasing statistics, quality statistics, and delivery confirmations.

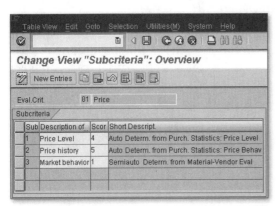

Figure 11.9 Subcriteria for the Price Main Criteria

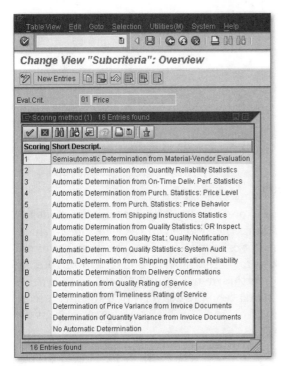

Figure 11.10 Scoring Methods Available for Subcriteria

11.7.3   Vendor Evaluation Weighting

In the vendor-evaluation configuration steps, the weighting of the criteria can be defined for each valid purchasing organization. The configuration can be found using the navigation path, IMG • Materials Management • Purchasing • Vendor Evaluation • Maintain Purchasing Organization Data.

Figure 11.11 shows that the weighting for purchasing organization 3000 is equal for all of the main criteria, 25% for each. In this case, the purchasing department has determined that no special weighting is required for one of the main criteria. If there were a change in policy to recognize price as being more important than the other criteria, then the weighting would be different; that is, it would be unequal weighting.

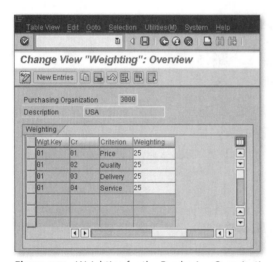

Figure 11.11   Weighting for the Purchasing Organization 3000

11.7.4   Points Scoring for Criteria

In the configuration for the purchasing organization, the user can also configure the points given for levels of evaluation. The system can calculate any variances that the vendor may have — in price, for example — and the purchasing user can determine how many points to award for certain variance ranges from 100% to plus or minus a certain total variance. As shown in Figure 11.12, the on-time delivery gives a point score of 100, a 1% variance in the delivery drops the point score to 90, a 20% variance drops the points score to 60, and a 99.9% variance drops the points score all of the way down to 0.

The points awarded are reduced, as the variance gets further away from a perfect score, that is, a zero variance. A graphical representation is shown in Figure 11.13 for points awarded to a vendor on delivery quantities.

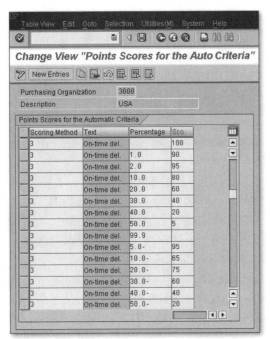

Figure 11.12 Points Score Defined for a Variance on Quantity Reliability, Automatic Criteria

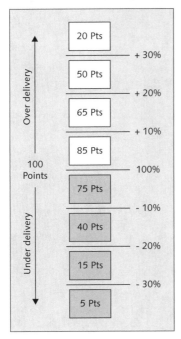

Figure 11.13 How the Point Score Varies, Based on Configuration

11.7.5 Maintain Vendor Evaluation

After the configuration is complete, the maintenance of a vendor's evaluation record can be performed. The maintenance allows the vendor to have the subjective scores entered into its evaluation. For example, the scores for price and delivery can be based on transaction data, but the scoring for quality and service can be subjective and decided upon outside of SAP ERP. The maintenance of individual vendor evaluation can be performed using Transaction ME61 or via the navigation path, SAP MENU • LOGISTICS • MATERIALS MANAGEMENT • PURCHASING • MASTER DATA • VENDOR EVALUATION • MAINTAIN.

The maintenance of a vendor's evaluation is at the purchasing organization level, which means that a vendor can be evaluated differently between purchasing organizations.

The EVALUATION DATA shows the WEIGHTING KEY and the OVERALL SCORE. There is a DELETION IND. that can be set if the record is to be deleted.

The bottom part of Figure 11.14 shows the evaluation of the main criteria. There are four main criteria for this evaluation. The PRICE, DELIVERY, and QUALITY figures are calculated scores, whereas the SERVICE score is a subjective value and must be entered. The subjective score can have a significant effect on the overall score for a vendor, and companies will generally implement a manual scoring system for the subjective or non-automatic scoring criteria. This can be as simple as a list of questions or as complex as a detailed spreadsheet.

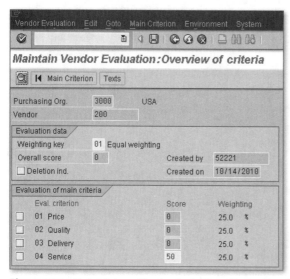

Figure 11.14 Maintaining a Vendor Evaluation, Transaction ME61

Whatever method is used, the continuity of method used to calculate the subjective score is important. Otherwise, vendors will be scored differently, and the comparison between vendors will be unsound.

11.7.6 Scoring for Automatic and Semi-Automatic Criteria

The automatic and semi-automatic criteria can be calculated via a transaction to provide the latest scores. Transaction ME63 allows the purchasing department user to enter a vendor and the relevant purchasing organization. The transaction can be found using the navigation path, SAP MENU • LOGISTICS • MATERIALS MANAGEMENT • PURCHASING • MASTER DATA • VENDOR EVALUATION • AUTOMATIC NEW EVALUATION.

The system will calculate the scores for the subcriteria defined and give an overall score for each of the objective scores, that is, the automatic and semi-automatic criteria, as shown in Figure 11.15. The automatic criteria scores are items such as PRICE, DELIVERY, and QUALITY. The semi-automatic or subjective scores are items such as SHOPFLOOR COMPLAINT, SHIPPING INSTRUCTIONS, and NOTIFICATION RELIABILITY.

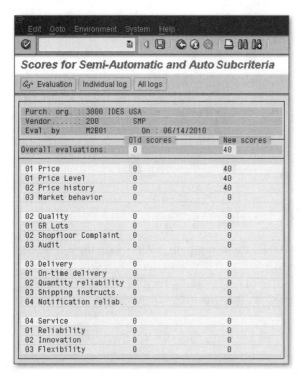

Figure 11.15 New Calculated Scores for the Vendor After Running Transaction ME63

11.7.7 Evaluation for a Material

You can perform a check on a material or a material group that will evaluate the supplying vendors and show the results. Transaction ME6B allows the purchasing user to enter a purchasing organization and the material or the material group as shown in Figure 11.16.

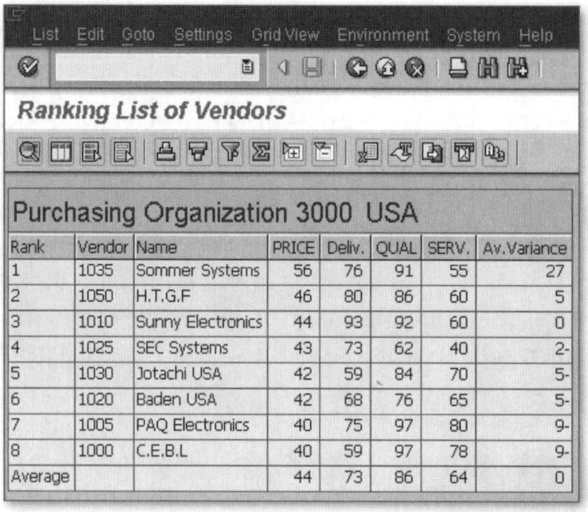

Rank	Vendor	Name	PRICE	Deliv.	QUAL	SERV.	Av.Variance
1	1035	Sommer Systems	56	76	91	55	27
2	1050	H.T.G.F	46	80	86	60	5
3	1010	Sunny Electronics	44	93	92	60	0
4	1025	SEC Systems	43	73	62	40	2-
5	1030	Jotachi USA	42	59	84	70	5-
6	1020	Baden USA	42	68	76	65	5-
7	1005	PAQ Electronics	40	75	97	80	9-
8	1000	C.E.B.L	40	59	97	78	9-
Average			44	73	86	64	0

Figure 11.16 Evaluation Results for a Material Group

The navigation path for Transaction ME6B is SAP Menu • Logistics • Materials Management • Purchasing • Master Data • Vendor Evaluation • List Displays • Evaluations per Material.

The vendor-evaluation process is frequently used by clients as they choose to either use a more subjective method of evaluating vendors or are developing single sourcing for their purchased material.

11.8 Business Examples - Purchasing

The purchasing department is a vital link in a company's supply chain. Every business has to purchase items that range from basic raw materials used in production to janitorial services that clean the facility. By making the purchase of these materials and services as efficient as possible, the company will save valuable resources and increase profitability.

11.8.1   Purchase Requisitions

The purchase requisition is the procedure by which general users or departments can request the purchases of goods or services that require processing by the purchasing department. The purchase requisition can be as simple as a list of requirements sent to the purchasing department for entry or as complex as a complete Internet system that allows users to directly enter their requirements by selecting from online vendor catalogs.

Example

A Los Angeles manufacturer of paint additives had been using an in-house developed system for its accounting, purchasing, and manufacturing processes. The purchasing function was solely based on the entry of POs and did not feature any requisitioning functionality. When the production department required raw materials, they would write the requirement in a carbonless duplicate notebook and give one copy to purchasing. All raw materials were single sourced, so the purchasing department would enter the details from the requisition into the system as a PO for the one vendor who supplied the material.

The company was purchased by a larger chemical company who had implemented SAP ERP many years previously. The company quickly migrated from its old system to SAP ERP. Initially, the company kept the same requisition process but planned to roll out the requisitioning function when the users were trained. The company decided to only allow the production manager and shift leaders to have authorization to enter purchase requisitions. After a number of months, the company introduced a comprehensive MRP process and the requirement to add purchase requisitions was minimized.

11.8.2   Source List

When a decision needs to be made about selecting a vendor for an item, the buyer can review the source list, which contains contracted or certified vendors for a particular material. The source list will show buyers the information they need to make an informed decision.

Example

An elevator parts manufacturer's auditors informed the company's purchasing department that vital information from negotiated purchasing agreements with vendors was missing from the SAP ERP system. The auditors found that vendors were being selected for POs when the agreement between the company and the vendor had expired. Although some details from the agreements had been entered into purchasing information records, the agreement dates had not.

To remedy this situation, the purchasing department reviewed their active purchasing agreements and developed source lists for materials where the expiry date of the agreement could be entered. In addition, the purchasing department introduced a procedure to more accurately enter the information from future purchasing agreements.

11.8.3 Conditions

The condition procedure in purchasing is used to calculate the purchase price by processing all relevant pricing factors. By using the defined conditions, the purchasing process arrives at a determined price for purchasing transactions. The purchasing conditions also allow vendor discounts or variable charges to be entered so that an accurate purchase price can be determined.

Example

A U.S. automotive parts distributor purchased items directly from vehicle manufacturers, parts manufacturers, or other distribution companies. During the downturn in the automotive sector in 2009, the company was approached by a number of their suppliers offering significant discounts and incentives. Many of these vendor discounts were dependent on the number of items purchased and the dollar amount of the purchase. To evaluate the overall effect of the discounts and incentives, the purchasing department introduced the various scenarios as conditions in the order. In this way, the purchasing clerk could see which vendor would give the best value for the items to be purchased.

11.8.4 Vendor Evaluation

Vendor evaluation is an important part of the purchasing decision. Selecting vendors to provide material or services can be a formalized procedure requiring information to be collected from transactions and observations. Purchasing departments usually have written policies that determine how vendors are evaluated when considering them for a purchase.

Example

A U.S. industrial tools manufacturer implemented SAP ERP after using a number of disparate PC systems for many years. One of these systems was a PC-based vendor-evaluating system that was based on data entered by the purchasing department. The data was supposed to be a record of purchasing transactions, but because no interface was ever developed from other systems, and data entry was sporadic, the system was wholly based on subjective data and viewed with some skepticism.

After the migration to SAP ERP, the PC vendor-evaluating system was not updated and was soon removed. The purchasing department decided to use the vendor-evaluation system in SAP ERP after six months of data had been established. A team was then assembled to derive a set of criteria for the evaluation, and after some trial and error, the team agreed on a percentage of subjective and objective data.

11.9 Summary

In this chapter, we discussed the purchasing functionality in SAP ERP. The purchasing of materials and services is a large part of a company's business function. Selecting vendors and obtaining the best price and service for a material are keys to producing products at a competitive price for the customer while maximizing company profits.

Chapter 12 examines the purchase requisition process. The requisition can be manually created or created by other functionality such as production. Chapter 12 discusses creating, modifying, and processing purchase requisitions.

non-stock
item

The purchase requisition is the procedural method by which users or departments can request the purchase of goods or services. The purchase requisition can be entered manually by a user or generated automatically as a result of a demand from requirements planning.

12   Purchase Requisition

A purchasing requisition is the first step in the demand for material either entered by the requisitioner or generated out of a requirements system such as MRP. The requisition contains the material or services to be procured, a required date of delivery, and a quantity. The purchase requisition does not contain a vendor. Because it is an internal company document, it is generally not printed.

This chapter describes in detail all aspects of the purchase requisition. Purchase requisitions are created indirectly by another process or directly by a user. Both of these methods are described in this chapter.

12.1   Indirectly Created Requisition

An indirectly created purchase requisition is created via other SAP functionality. The purchase requisition is created if some functionality needs to have materials or services assigned to it.

12.1.1   Purchase Requisition Created by Production Order

In a production order, two elements determine how the production order functions. The routing is a sequence of the operations that take place, and the bill of materials (BOM) is the recipe used to produce the final material.

A purchase requisition can be generated automatically when the routing in the production order involves an operation whereby the material needs to be sent out for external processing, for example, subcontracting work.

Another way a purchase requisition can be produced is when the BOM calls for a material that is a non-stock item. This may occur when a special item is required for the production order or if the material is no longer purchased by the company. For example, a company that produces furnaces may need to incorporate a special filter for furnaces that are made for customers based in California. The clean air laws in California may require a special part to be ordered and fitted during the production process. This would trigger a purchase requisition for the special part and possibly a purchase requisition for a subcontractor to fit the part.

12.1.2 Purchase Requisition Created by Plant Maintenance Order

This type of order produces purchase requisitions that are similar to the production order. The maintenance order is created for Plant Maintenance operations on a technical object, in other words, equipment, at the plant. Similar to a production order, a maintenance order has a list of operations that have to be performed. The operations give the maintenance user a step-by-step list of what needs to be performed and the materials and equipment needed for each step.

In the operation, there may be a need for a certain non-stock material, which may cause a purchase requisition to be created. The maintenance order may also have an operation that requires performance of an external operation by a subcontractor, which will also cause an indirect purchase requisition to be created.

12.1.3 Purchase Requisition Created by Project Systems

Within the Project Systems (PS) component, there are objects called networks. A network consists of a set of instructions that tell the project's user what tasks need to be performed, in what order, and by what date.

The network has two options for creating material requirements. The network can create purchase requisitions for non-stock materials and external services, similar to the production and maintenance orders. The network can also be configured to allow creation of purchase requisitions as soon as the network has been released.

12.1.4 Purchase Requisition Created by Materials Planning

The consumption-based Planning component can create purchase requisitions based on its calculations. The Planning component creates POs with quantities and delivery dates that are calculated. The planning run can also produce planned orders for in-house production, but these can be converted to purchase requisitions.

The purchase requisition is an internal purchasing suggestion that can be modified before being converted to POs. After the MRP controller has determined the accuracy of the external purchasing requirements, the controller can convert some planned orders to purchase requisitions and perhaps convert some purchase requisitions to POs. The level of interaction between the planning department and the purchasing department will determine what procedures are in place to allow the MRP controller to create purchase requisitions and POs.

12.2 Directly Created Requisition

A directly created purchase requisition is created by a requisitioner and not by other SAP functionality. The majority of non-production purchase requisitions is created this way.

12.2.1 Create a Purchase Requisition with a Material Master Record

The most common way a requisition is created is by using an item or service that has a Material Master record.

The purchase requisition can be created using Transaction ME51N via the SAP menu using the navigation path, SAP MENU • LOGISTICS • MATERIALS MANAGEMENT • PURCHASING • PURCHASE REQUISITION • CREATE.

This transaction allows the requisitioner to define what fields are viewed on the screen when entering the requisition data. Many fields can be viewed and entered. Figure 12.1 shows the MATERIAL, the SHORT TEXT description, QUANTITY, UNIT OF MEASURE, and DELIVERY DATE fields. In addition to the fields shown in Figure 12.1, the following information can be entered in the requisition line item: material group, plant, storage location, requisitioner, purchasing organization, manufacturer's part number, purchasing information record, desired vendor, and the requirement tracking number.

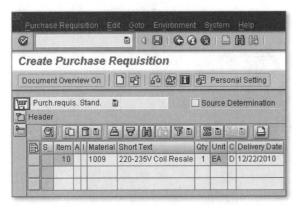

Figure 12.1 Purchase Requisition Screen for Transaction ME51N

The requisition for the materials that have a Material Master record requires the requisitioner to enter the following information:

- Material number of item or service
- Quantity to be procured

- ► Unit of measure
- ► Date of delivery of the material

The requisition process will default the information into the PURCHASE REQUISI-TION screen. Examples of this include the material group and purchasing group.

Document Type

Doc Type in Req.

The document type for a purchase requisition is important because it defines the internal and external number ranges that are used for requisitions, and it defines the valid item categories and the follow-on functions. A configuration specialist can also configure the item number interval and the screen layout. Figure 12.1 shows the document type defaulted to PURCH.REQUIS. STAND, which refers to the document type NB, as shown in Figure 12.2.

The standard SAP system is delivered with the document types NB for a standard purchase requisition and TB for a transport order. The number ranges are already in place for these document types. More document types can be created for other types of purchase requisitions that are appropriate for your client.

The transaction to configure the document type for the purchasing requisition can be found using the navigation path, IMG • MATERIALS MANAGEMENT • PURCHAS-ING • PURCHASE REQUISITION • DEFINE DOCUMENT TYPES. Figure 12.2 shows the different purchase requisitions that have been configured. The standard purchase requisition has the TYPE NB. The configuration allows the internal (NORGEINT) and external (NORGEEXT) number ranges to be defined for each requisition type.

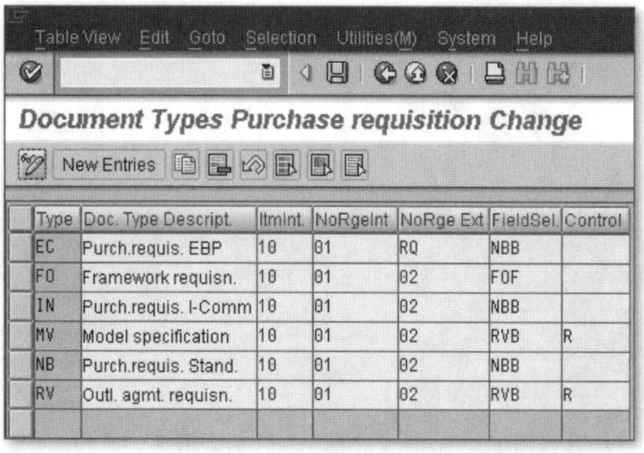

Type	Doc. Type Descript.	Itmint.	NoRgeInt	NoRge Ext	FieldSel.	Control
EC	Purch.requis. EBP	10	01	RQ	NBB	
FO	Framework requisn.	10	01	02	FOF	
IN	Purch.requis. I-Comm	10	01	02	NBB	
MV	Model specification	10	01	02	RVB	R
NB	Purch.requis. Stand.	10	01	02	NBB	
RV	Outl. agmt. requisn.	10	01	02	RVB	R

Figure 12.2 Purchase Requisition Document Types

Purchase Requisition Number

The purchase requisition number can be defined as internal or external. This is an attribute of the document type that has been configured in Figure 12.2. The internal number range (NoRgeInt) has been configured with range number 01, and the external number range (NoRgeExt) has been configured with range number 02.

Item Category

Refer to Figure 12.1 to see the item category field (I), which is another control field that allows the purchase requisition to follow the correct path, for that category of purchase requisition. The SAP system is delivered with a set of item categories:

- **Blank**: Standard
- **K**: Consignment
- **L**: Subcontracting
- **S**: Third-party
- **D**: Service
- **U**: Stock Transfer

The item category allows the display of certain fields and not others. For example, if a purchase requisition item has an item category K for consignment, then invoice receipts will not be allowed.

Account Assignment Category

Figure 12.3 shows the account assignment category field (A), which determines what type of accounting assignment data is required for purchase requisitions. Examples of account assignments are cost centers, cost objects, GL accounts, and assets.

The account assignment categories can be configured in the IMG. The user can create a new account assignment category by following the navigation path, IMG • MATERIALS MANAGEMENT • PURCHASING • ACCOUNT ASSIGNMENT • MAINTAIN ACCOUNT ASSIGNMENT CATEGORIES.

The purchasing user can create a new account assignment category and configure the fields shown in Figure 12.3. For example, some companies may not want certain fields to appear or to be changed when using particular account assignments. The configuration allows the fields, such as ASSET, BUSINESS AREA, and COST OBJECT, to be a mandatory entry (MAND.ENT.), an optional entry (OPT.ENTRY), a display-only field (DISPLAY), or HIDDEN. The accounting department would primarily be involved in creating new account assignment categories.

Required account assignment data is needed for specific account assignments, as described here:

▶ **Asset (A)**: Asset number and subnumber.

▶ **Production Order (F)**: Production order number.

▶ **Cost Center (K)**: Cost center and GL account number.

▶ **Sales Order (C)**: Sales order and GL account number.

▶ **Project (P)**: Project Number and GL account number.

▶ **Unknown (U)**: None.

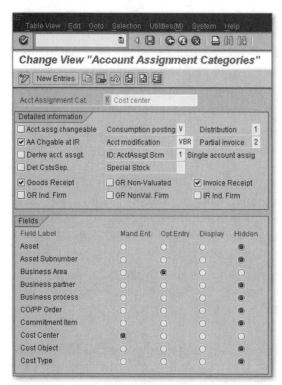

Figure 12.3 Configuration Data for the Account Assignment Category

The next four fields can be entered on the line item of the purchase requisition, as shown in Figure 12.1, but are not shown.

Plant/Storage Location

The plant and storage location fields can be entered if the location of where the material is to be "shipped to" is known. If there is one receiving dock for the whole plant, then this can be defaulted.

Purchasing Group

The purchasing group number is the number for the buyer or buyers for a material. If a purchasing group is entered at the order level, then this will be defaulted for each of the purchase requisition line items.

Requirement Tracking Number (RTN)

This is not the number of the requisition or the number for the requisitioner but a freeform field in which a tracking number can be entered. This field can be used by the person entering the RFQ to uniquely identify specific POs. For example, if purchasing agents are entering a number of POs for a project, they may want to enter a unique RTN so that the POs can be located together instead of having to know each individual PO number.

Requisitioner

This field is another freeform field that allows the purchasing user to add the requisitioner's name to search and order the purchase requisitions. For example, if one person is tasked with entering all purchase requisitions for a department, that person may enter the name of the person who wrote the requisition in the Requisitioner field.

New for SAP ERP

Requirement Prioritization

The Requirement Prioritization function can be used to control the servicing of material requisitions in the supply chain according to their urgency. Requirement Prioritization serves to determine a priority for the further processing of requirement items in the Logistics process.

The requirement urgency can be assigned at item level in purchasing and reservation documents. You can uniquely assign each requirement urgency to a requirement urgency group in customizing. The system determines the relevant requirement priority or overall priority of a material requisition from the combination of requirement urgency group and organizational priority. In the standard SAP software supplied, you define the organizational priority in customizing via plant/storage location combinations.

when no Material Master

12.2.2 Create a Purchase Requisition without a Material Master Record

When a purchase requisition is to be created without a Material Master record for the item, then the purchase requisition has to use account assignment to direct the cost to a specific account.

The account assignment categories described in the previous section allow the requisitioner to allocate the costs of the purchase to the correct accounts.

To enter a purchase requisition for an item without a Material Master record, the transaction is still the same as before: ME51N. The requisitioner can enter information on the initial screen or enter nothing and go directly to the line-item screen.

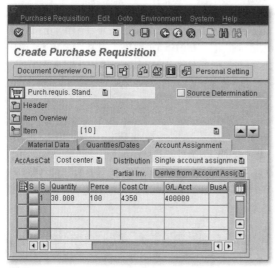

Figure 12.4 Account Assignment Information Required for a Purchase-Requisition Line Item with No Material Master Record

In the detail line-item screen, the information has to be entered because there is no Material Master record to refer to. The requisitioner must enter a short description of the following:

▶ Material
▶ Account assignment category
▶ Quantity to be supplied
▶ Unit of measure

- Delivery date
- Plant
- Purchasing group
- Material group

The information that is required to be entered will correspond to what account assignment category was entered in the line item. Figure 12.4 shows the account information that can be required.

12.3 Processing a Purchase Requisition

After the purchase requisition has been created, it can be further amended using the change process. This section also discusses the methods for displaying purchase requisitions.

12.3.1 Change a Purchase Requisition

The purchase requisition can be changed as part of the material planning process, that is, by the MRP controller or by the requisitioner prior to being processed by the purchasing department. The purchasing requisition can be changed using Transaction ME52N or via the navigation path, SAP Menu • Logistics • Materials Management • Purchasing • Purchase Requisition • Change.

12.3.2 Display a Purchase Requisition

This section shows a number of methods used to display purchase requisitions.

Purchase Requisition – Display

The purchase requisition can be displayed using Transaction ME54N or via the navigation path, SAP Menu • Logistics • Materials Management • Purchasing • Purchase Requisition • Display.

Purchase Requisition – List Display

The display purchase requisitions Transaction ME5A can be executed by the requisitioner to show a list of purchase requisitions. This transaction can be found using the navigation path, SAP Menu • Logistics • Materials Management • Purchasing • Purchase Requisition • List Displays • General.

Figure 12.5 shows the initial screen for Transaction ME5A, which allows the requisitioner to enter a wide range of selection criteria to display the valid requisitions. Some of these selection criteria are commonly used such as PURCHASE REQUISITION, MATERIAL, REQUIREMENT TRACKING NUMBER, and DELIVERY DATE.

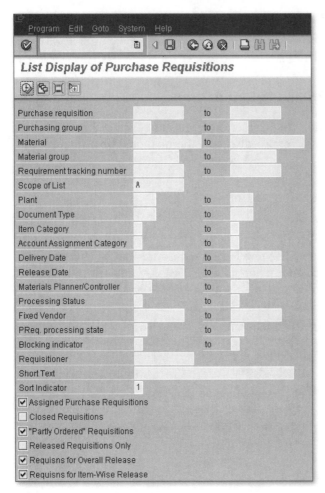

Figure 12.5 Criteria for Selecting a List of Purchase Requisitions

Purchase Requisitions by Tracking Number

Transaction MELB can be used to select purchase requisitions by the RTN. This number is not the requisitioner but a tracking number entered by the requisitioner to identify that person's particular purchase requisitions.

Figure 12.6 shows this transaction, which can be found using the navigation path, SAP MENU • LOGISTICS • MATERIALS MANAGEMENT • PURCHASING • PURCHASE REQUISITION • LIST DISPLAYS • BY ACCOUNT ASSIGNMENT • TRANSACTIONS PER TRACKING NUMBER.

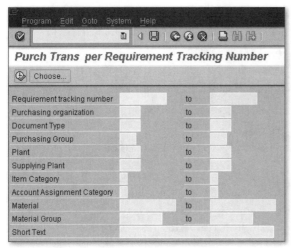

Figure 12.6 Purchase Requisition by RTN

12.3.3 Close a Purchase Requisition

A purchase requisition can be closed if an indicator is set within the item detail screen. Normally, the purchase requisition is closed when the amount requested to be ordered on the line item of the purchase requisition is equal to the amount that has been purchased via a PO.

To close a line item on a purchase requisition, the requisitioner needs to access the change-purchase-requisition Transaction ME52N. The line item that needs to be flagged for deletion must be selected, and the requisitioner should select DELETE. The DELETE indicator on the line item then will be checked as shown in Figure 12.7.

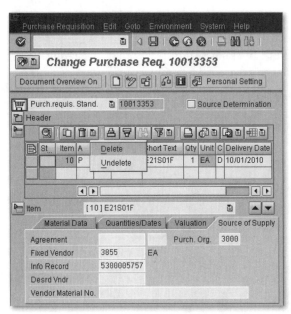

Figure 12.7 Setting the Delete Indicator for a Purchase Requisition Line Item

12.3.4 Follow-On Functions

As the purchase requisition is processed, it is possible to carry out some follow-on functions before the purchase requisition is converted to a PO.

Assign Source

Transaction ME56 allows the purchasing user to select a range of purchase requisitions to have a source assigned. The purchase requisitions can be selected via a large range of selection criteria, including material group, item category, delivery date, cost center, and so on.

The transaction can be found via the navigation path, SAP Menu • Logistics • Materials Management • Purchasing • Purchase Requisition • Follow-on Functions • Assign.

Figure 12.8 shows the initial screen allowing the entry of a large selection of variables to create a list of purchase requisitions for vendor assignment.

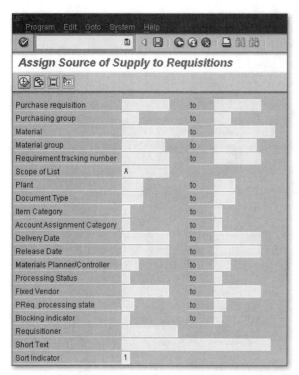

Figure 12.8 Selection Screen for Vendor Assignment to a Requisition

After the selection criteria have been entered into the initial screen of Transaction ME56, the transaction will return a number of relevant purchase requisitions based on that search criteria.

Figure 12.9 shows the purchase requisitions that were returned as a result of the selection criteria entered. You can select the purchase requisitions that will be assigned a vendor.

After the purchase requisitions are selected, you have the choice to have the vendor assigned to the purchase requisitions automatically, using the ASSIGN AUTOMATICALLY button, or you can use the function keys, Shift + F6.

You can also assign the source vendor manually using the ASSIGN MANUALLY button, or you can use the function keys, Shift + F7. When assigning the source to the purchasing requisition manually, a dialog box appears that allows you to enter the vendor, as shown in Figure 12.10.

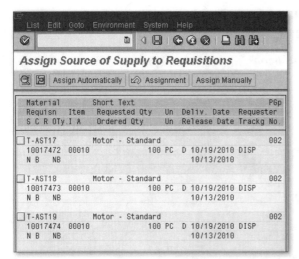

Figure 12.9 Purchase Requisitions to Be Assigned a Source of Supply

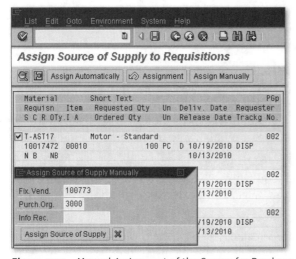

Figure 12.10 Manual Assignment of the Source for Purchase Requisitions

This section has shown how purchase requisitions can be amended and the processes used to display them. In addition, you have seen how to close a purchase requisition and how to assign a source of supply to a purchase requisition line item.

12.4   Business Examples – Purchase Requisitions

A purchasing requisition is the initial demand for an item entered into the system or generated out of a requirements system, such as MRP. The requisition will contain the material or services that are needed, as well as the required date of delivery and a quantity, but it does not contain a vendor.

12.4.1   Indirectly Created Purchase Requisition

The indirectly created purchase requisition is produced when some functionality in SAP requires material to be procured. A number of areas generate purchase requisitions, including PP, PM, and PS.

Example

A British upholstery fabric manufacturer was an established SAP user that used MRP for its production planning. As part of the MRP process, planned orders and purchase requisitions were generated. During the company's yearly review for costing analysis, the team found that a number of products had been purchased in higher numbers than previously. In a review of the purchasing documents, the team found that the POs for 12 items were higher than the requisitions that were generated as part of the MRP process. After discussions with the production manager, the team determined that at the beginning of the year, the company had been informed by one of its vendors that it was having production issues. Some of the vendor's items were not always within tolerance, so the vendor suggested the company order an extra 15% and return the product that failed quality. The production manager had routinely been changing the MRP generated purchase requisitions to reflect this constraint.

12.4.2   Directly Created Purchase Requisition

Authorized users can create purchase requisitions manually. Not all companies allow their users to enter requisitions. In general, the purchasing department reviews requisitions and then generates POs to send to the vendor.

Example

An Irish manufacturer of linen had been using an AS/400-based ERP system for accounting, manufacturing, and procurement. The system allowed POs to be entered, but there was no way to enter purchase requisitions. The requisition process consisted of a purchasing clerk calling the department heads each Monday to get a list of items they needed for the week. For office supplies, the purchasing clerk would walk around the building with a list of items available and ask employees what they needed. From that list and the requirements of the department heads, a number of POs would be processed.

A multi-national clothing company purchased the linen company and planned a migration to SAP ERP. As part of the project, the company discussed the purchase requisition process and decided to allow department heads to enter purchase requisitions directly into SAP ERP. The purchasing clerk would review the requisitions for accuracy, select the appropriate vendor, and then process the POs

12.5 Summary

This chapter examined the purchase requisition process. Most companies use a requisition process to identify where material is needed and to allow the purchasing department to review and create the optimum PO for each vendor by taking into account volume discounts and favorable terms offered by the vendor. Without the purchase requisition, purchasing decisions would be made by the end user and not by the purchasing department.

Chapter 13 follows on from the creation and processing of the purchase requisition and discusses the creation of a request for quotation (RFQ). The RFQ is not universally used and may not be part of the purchasing policy of your client. However, the RFQ is an important purchasing tool, and you should understand the processes to create it and process it.

After the purchasing department has received a purchase requisition and processed it, there may be a line item that requires the purchasing department to send out a request for quotation (RFQ) to certified vendors for that material at a particular plant.

13   Request for Quotation

In some cases, the purchasing department cannot process purchase requisition items by simply selecting a vendor or issuing a PO to a single-source vendor. In cases where the company has never used the material or when a new vendor is required due to vendor bankruptcy or decertification, the purchasing department issues an RFQ.

13.1   Creating a Request for Quotation

A request for quotation (RFQ) can be created using Transaction ME41, shown in Figure 13.1, or via the navigation path, SAP MENU • LOGISTICS • MATERIALS MANAGEMENT • PURCHASING • RFQ/QUOTATION • REQUEST FOR QUOTATION • CREATE.

13.1.1   RFQ Type

The RFQ TYPE can be defined in the configuration and allows the company to distinguish between types of RFQs that it may send out. The predefined RFQ type is AN, which does not need any configuration changes if the company has simply RFQ needs. If the company wants to distinguish between RFQs and needs to create more RFQ types, this can be carried out in the IMG.

The configuration transaction can be found using the navigation path, IMG • MATERIALS MANAGEMENT • PURCHASING • RFQ/QUOTATION • DEFINE DOCUMENT TYPES.

Figure 13.2 shows the configuration for the RFQ document type. The two-character field defines the document type, and it is necessary to enter a description and number ranges for internal and external assignment.

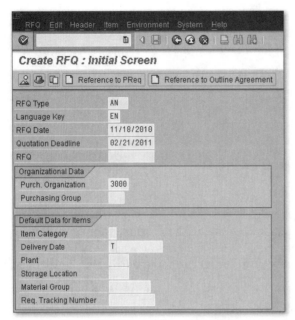

Figure 13.1 Initial Entry Screen for Transaction ME41: Create RFQ

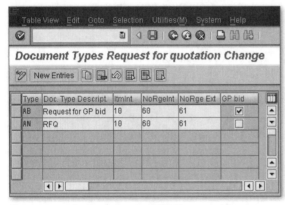

Figure 13.2 Configuration for RFQ Document Types

The other field to note is the GP BID field. This is set if the RFQ is for a global percentage (GP) bid. The standard RFQ type for the GP bid is supplied with standard SAP, which is the document type AB.

The GP bid is used by purchasing to send suppliers a price that purchasing is willing to pay for a service, rather than having the supplier send in a bid. In this case, the supplier will send back a percentage, either positive or negative, to indicate the level below or above the bid amount sent by the purchasing department that it can accept. Although uncommon, this method is less complicated than the normal RFQ procedure.

13.1.2   RFQ Date

Figure 13.1, shown previously, shows the RFQ DATE field, which is defaulted with the date of entry but can be overwritten with the appropriate date.

13.1.3   Quotation Deadline

The date entered in the QUOTATION DEADLINE field is the date by which the suppliers need to reply to the RFQ with their quotation. This field is mandatory and should be clearly identified to suppliers on the RFQ print or fax document.

13.1.4   RFQ Document Number

The document number, shown by the field RFQ in Figure 13.1, for the RFQ is determined to be either externally or internally assigned. This is defined in the configuration shown in Figure 13.2. The field should be entered if the number assignment is external.

13.1.5   Organizational Data

The PURCH. ORGANIZATION and PURCHASING GROUP should be entered for the RFQ. The PURCH. ORGANIZATION is a four-character field, and the PURCHASING GROUP is a three-character field.

13.1.6   Default Data for Items

The purchasing user can enter information that is pertinent to items that are to be included in the RFQ. The fields that can be defaulted include ITEM CATEGORY, DELIVERY DATE, PLANT, STORAGE LOCATION, MATERIAL GROUP, and REQ. TRACKING NUMBER. These fields are described in this section.

Item category

The following categories can be entered in the ITEM CATEGORY field:

- ▶ **L:** For subcontracting.
- ▶ **S:** For third party.
- ▶ **D:** For a service.
- ▶ **Blank:** For a standard item category.

Delivery Date

This is the DELIVERY DATE for the item to be delivered or service to be performed to the client by the supplier.

Plant/Storage Location

These are the client locations where the item should be delivered or the service should be performed. These are the default plant and storage locations for deliveries.

Material Group   *— use material group master. if no Material master.*

The MATERIAL GROUP can be used in lieu of a material number or service (if these are not known). The material group is assigned to each material when it is created. This configured field groups together materials of similar characteristics. For example, if material group 017789 represented HD DVD players, then this material group could be entered in the RFQ if the actual material was not known at the time, but the RFQ was for an HD DVD player.

Requirement Tracking Number (RTN)

This tracking number can be traced back to the original requisition if the RTN was entered at that level. The person entering the RFQ can use the REQ. TRACKING NUMBER field to uniquely identify specific POs.

For example, if purchasing agents were entering a number of POs for a project, they may want to enter a unique RTN so that the POs can be located together instead of having to know each individual PO number.

The header details for the RFQ can be seen in Figure 13.3 and are described next. The data entered in the initial screen are defaulted through, and further information can be added in the administrative fields.

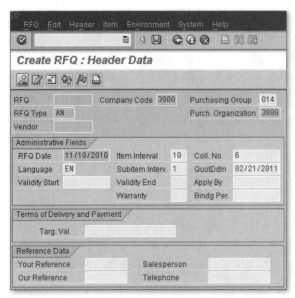

Figure 13.3 RFQ Header Details Screen

13.1.7 Collective Number

Companies that send out RFQs for a collective bid can use the collective number (COLL. NO.). For example, if a client is creating a new product, there may be dozens of new materials that it needs to use, as well as new services. To collectively identify the many RFQs, the client may use a collective number to ensure that the individual RFQs are tied to the single project. The collective number can be used to search purposes. It is easier to find RFQs that have a collective number than individually. Transaction ME4S allows the display of RFQs by collective number.

13.1.8 Validity Start/Validity End

The VALIDITY START/VALIDITY END fields are defined as the dates between which the material or services should be delivered or performed.

13.1.9 Apply By

The APPLY BY date field is different from the quotation deadline date. The application date is the date by which the suppliers need to inform the client that they will submit quotations. This date does not necessarily need to be entered, but if it is, then this date needs to be clearly identified to the prospective suppliers.

13.1.10 Binding Period

The BINDG.PER. is the period of time after the quotation deadline during which the quotation should be valid. For example, if the quotation deadline is April 1, then the client may insist upon a binding period until May 31. This allows the client to process the quotations sent by the suppliers.

13.1.11 Reference Data

The REFERENCE DATA can be added to the RFQ header that relates to the client reference and its contact information. This data can be printed on the RFQ document sent to the supplier.

13.1.12 RFQ Item Detail

The line-item details include the ITEM category, MATERIAL number, description (SHORT TEXT), RFQ QUANTITY, DELIV. DATE, and material group (MAT GRP).

Figure 13.4 shows the item detail allowing purchasing users to add the materials or services that require the creation of the RFQ.

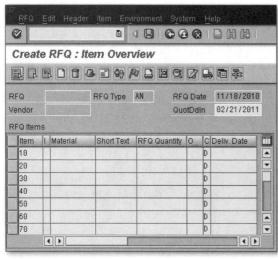

Figure 13.4 RFQ Item Detail Screen

13.1.13 RFQ Delivery Schedule

After the item detail information has been added, additional information can be entered if relevant.

To access the DELIVERY SCHEDULE screen, the purchasing user selects ITEM • DELIVERY SCHEDULE or uses the function keys `Shift` + `F5`.

For example, if the RFQ requires that the supplier deliver the material to the plant in a certain sequence on certain dates, this requirement can be entered in the DELIVERY SCHEDULE screen, shown in Figure 13.5.

In the DELIVERY SCHEDULE screen, the purchasing user can enter the date, time, and the amount required on that date. Any number of delivery schedule lines can be entered for the amount of material specified in the line item.

Figure 13.5 Delivery Schedule Screen for the RFQ Item

13.1.14 Additional Data

To enter any further data for the line item, the purchasing user can access the additional data screen by selecting ITEM • MORE FUNCTIONS • ADDITIONAL DATA or by using function keys `Ctrl` + `F1`.

Figure 13.6 shows the data that can be added here, including the planned delivery time and the reason for the order. The REASON FOR ORD. field is configurable and can be used by the purchasing department for statistical data collection.

The REASON FOR ORD. field can be defined in configuration using the navigation path, IMG • MATERIALS MANAGEMENT • PURCHASING • PURCHASE ORDER • DEFINE REASONS FOR ORDERING.

'Reason for order'

config.

349

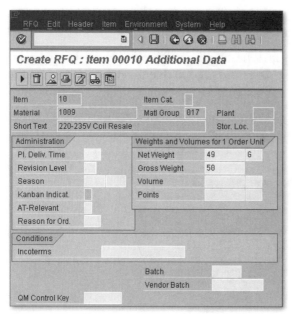

Figure 13.6 Additional Data Screen for the RFQ Line Item

Figure 13.7 shows the ordering reason codes that have been configured. The reason code (ORRSN) is a three-character field, and a short DESCRIPTION can be added that is appropriate for the client.

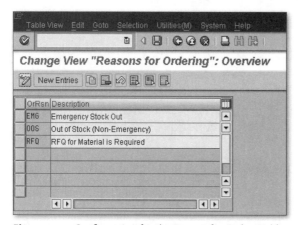

Figure 13.7 Configuration for the Reason for Order Field

*Vendor must be
selected to receive the
R FQ.*

13.1.15 Vendor Selection

After the material details have been entered with any additional data, the RFQ requires that a vendor be selected to receive the RFQ. The vendor can be selected by using the menu selection HEADER • VENDOR ADDRESS or by using the function key F7 .

The VENDOR ADDRESS screen, shown in Figure 13.8, allows the purchasing user to select a vendor for the RFQ. After the vendor is entered, you can save the RFQ. The screen is refreshed, and the RFQ number appears on the status line at the bottom of the screen.

*.... can Repeat the
scroen to send to
multiple vendors.*

Figure 13.8 Vendor Address Screen, Where Vendors Are Assigned to the RFQ

The screen shown in Figure 13.8 allows another vendor to be entered. If the RFQ is to be sent out to more than one vendor, more vendor numbers can be entered, and saving after each addition creates a number of RFQ documents for the same item details.

Now that we have examined the creation of the RFQ, the next section discusses the process to change the RFQ after creation.

13.2 Changing a Request for Quotation

RFQs can be changed using Transaction ME42 or via the navigation path, SAP Menu • Logistics • Materials Management • Purchasing • RFQ/Quotation • Request for Quotation • Change.

If the purchasing user does not know the RFQ number to be changed, then a matchcode can be selected. Figure 13.9 shows the valid matchcodes that can be used to find the RFQ. Note that in Figure 13.9, two matchcodes can be used if the relevant data was added to the RFQ:

▶ Purchasing Documents per Req Tracking Num

▶ Purchasing Documents per Collective Number

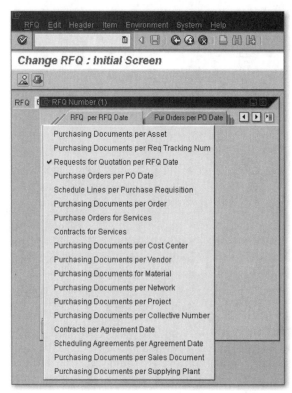

Figure 13.9 Initial RFQ Change Screen with Valid Matchcodes Available to Find an RFQ

After the correct RFQ number has been entered or selected via a matchcode, the RFQ line item detail is displayed, and certain fields become available for editing.

Figure 13.10 shows a number of fields that can be edited. These include the RFQ material quantity (RFQ QTY), the quotation deadline (QUOTDDLN), and the required delivery date (DELIV. DATE). Note that if the RFQ has already been sent to the vendor, any changes to these dates need to be communicated to the vendor associated with the RFQ.

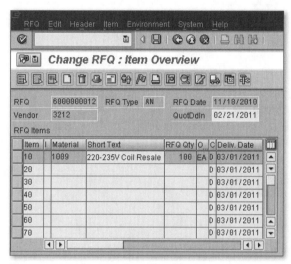

Figure 13.10 Line Item Detail for the RFQ

Figure 13.11 shows the options for the line item. If a line item has been entered incorrectly, or if the RFQ is no longer needed, the line item can be deleted in Transaction ME42. To delete the line item, first select the line item, and then set the delete indicator by choosing EDIT • DELETE or by using the function keys Shift + F2. The deletion indicator can be removed by choosing EDIT • RESET DELETION IND.

If the line item does not need to be deleted, but the status of the RFQ is in doubt, the line item can be blocked using Transaction ME42 as well. To block the line item, select it, and then set the blocking indicator by choosing EDIT • BLOCK or by using the function keys Ctrl + Shift + F2. The blocking indicator can be removed by choosing EDIT • RESET DELETION IND.

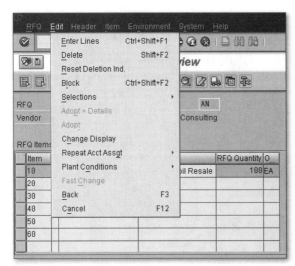

Figure 13.11 Options for the Line Item, Including Deletion and Blocking

This section has described how to change RFQs. The next section discusses the method by which the RFQ can be released.

13.3 Releasing an RFQ

After the RFQ has been completed, the document can be subject to release. The release procedure is more often associated with purchase requisitions or POs but can be relevant for RFQs, depending on your client's needs.

The release procedure for RFQs only allows the RFQ to be released at the header level and not at the line-item level. Therefore, the RFQ as a whole is released or not released.

Figure 13.12 shows the screen in ME45, which allows the purchasing user to enter information to release RFQs based on the information entered.

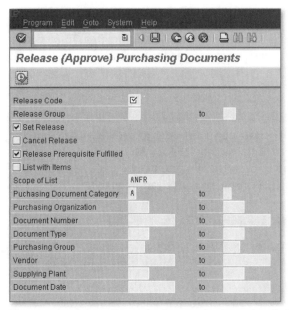

Figure 13.12 Release Screen for Request for Quotations in Transaction ME45

13.3.1 Release Code/Release Group/Release Strategy

The RELEASE CODE is the code that has been configured for a position in the company, such as manager, supervisor, and so on. The release code is associated with a release group. The RELEASE GROUP contains a number of release strategies that are defined in configuration. The release strategy is configured using classification characteristics. The characteristic can be defined to allow ranges of values for the RFQ. Below a certain value, the RFQ is not subject to release strategy; above a certain amount, it is. The release can be made using Transaction ME45.

13.3.2 Set Release/Cancel Release

These indicators can be set to allow the purchasing user to release the relevant RFQs or to cancel their release.

13.3.3 Release Prerequisite Fulfilled

This indicator, when set, allows the purchasing user to view only those RFQs that are ready to be released. If the indicator is not set, all RFQs are released, even if they have not fulfilled all of the prerequisites.

13.3.4 List with Items

If this indicator is set, then the RFQs will be shown with all line item information shown. If the indicator is not set, then only the header information for the RFQ is shown.

13.3.5 Scope of List

The SCOPE OF LIST field is a variable that shows different information based on the selected value. The default value for Transaction ME45 is ANFR, which in this case is for RFQs with a collective number. Using the function key F4 causes a scope of list selection to appear, from which a different choice can be made.

13.3.6 Purchasing Document Category

The PURCHASING DOCUMENT CATEGORY for RFQs is the single character A. Other documents are F for Purchase Orders, K for Contracts, and L for Scheduling Agreements.

13.3.7 Other Selection Criteria

A number of other selection criteria fields can further narrow down the search for RFQs to be released in Transaction ME45. These criteria include PURCHASING ORGANIZATION, PURCHASING GROUP, VENDOR, DOCUMENT NUMBER, and DOCUMENT DATE.

After the RFQ has been released for sending to a number of vendors, the RFQ has to be issued to those vendors. The next section describes the mechanisms for issuing the RFQ.

13.4 Issuing a Request for Quotation to a Vendor

After the RFQ has been entered into the system, the purchasing department has to decide either to fax or send a copy to the particular vendor. The RFQ document can be printed using Transaction ME9A or via the navigation path, SAP MENU • LOGISTICS • MATERIALS MANAGEMENT • PURCHASING • RFQ/QUOTATION • REQUEST FOR QUOTATION • MESSAGES • PRINT/TRANSMIT.

Figure 13.13 shows that the RFQ can be selected by a number of criteria. If the DOCUMENT NUMBER is not known, the document can be found by entering the VENDOR, PURCHASING ORGANIZATION, PURCHASING GROUP, or DOCUMENT DATE, which is the date the RFQ was created.

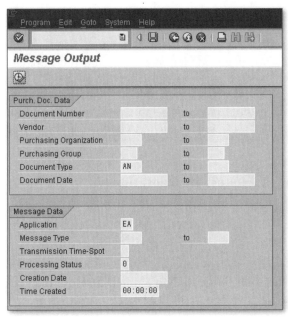

Figure 13.13 Screen for Printing or Transmitting the RFQ

After the selection criterion has been entered, and the transaction is executed, the results for the selection criteria are shown if any RFQs are found.

From the results, shown in Figure 13.14, the appropriate RFQ can be selected, and printed or transmitted. The resulting RFQ printout can be modified to reflect your client's requirement either by using ABAP, SAPscript, or a tool such as Adobe Form Designer.

PRiNToUT Tools

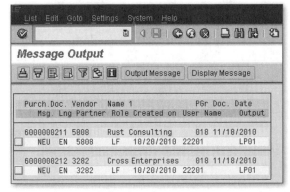

Figure 13.14 Result for the Selection Criteria Entered into Transaction ME9A

13.5   Business Examples – Request for Quotation

A purchasing department issues RFQs for a number of reasons. A material may have been requisitioned that has not been purchased before, and the purchasing department will need to find a supplier who can offer the best price and conditions. Sometimes a material has not been purchased for some time, and the last vendor who supplied the material may not be able to fulfill the request. There are also other reasons why RFQs are issued, such as vendor bankruptcy or decertification.

13.5.1   Creating and Changing a Request for Quotation

The RFQ can be created for a single item or multiple items. When a company is looking to single-source a number of materials, then the RFQ can contain a large number of products.

RFQs are frequently changed to accommodate vendors. For example, if a vendor feels that it cannot satisfactorily respond to the RFQ in a timely fashion, the vendor may request that the deadline for the RFQ response be extended.

Example

A Puerto Rican specialty chemicals manufacturer was frequently asked to develop variations of its products based on customer requirements. This required the research department to purchase items that either had not been purchased previously or not since the company had been using SAP ERP. The research department worked with the purchasing team to develop a requisition based on the chemical composition of the product required. The purchasing team reviewed vendor catalogs to identify if the product was currently available to purchase from a trusted vendor. If not, the purchasing team developed an RFQ and worked with the research department concerning when they needed the material delivered.

The purchasing team worked with a list of about 20 trusted vendors and had a secondary list of more than 100 vendors. The secondary list contained vendors who they had dealt with in the past but were not regularly used or had an issue with a previous purchase.

The purchasing team worked with the research department to decide what vendors should receive the RFQ. If no vendors were selected, then the research department reviewed other vendors to suggest to the purchasing team.

13.5.2 Releasing a Request for Quotation

The release of a RFQ can be triggered in the same way as a purchase requisition or PO. The requirements for whether an RFQ is subject to a release strategy depend on the configuration the company puts in place. The release strategy for an RFQ may depend on the dollar value or the type of material to be purchased.

Example

The manufacturer of specialty chemicals in Puerto Rico created RFQs for the research department, which were sent to a number of vendors, usually less than a dozen. However, because of the nature of the chemicals being purchased, the company decided that the final review of the RFQ should not be given to the purchasing team, but to the head of research. To ensure this occurred correctly, the company implemented an RFQ release strategy that applied to materials belonging to certain material groups. If the release strategy was triggered, then the RFQ would have to be released by the head of research.

13.6 Summary

RFQs are important for the purchasing department because they are a powerful tool with which the department can influence the vendor's price and terms and conditions in a competitive bid situation. The process examined in this chapter looked at the tools available in SAP ERP that are designed to make the RFQ process simple to use while allowing for the flexibility that is crucial for complex situations found in purchases for large projects.

Chapter 14 discusses the next process in the RFQ scenario: the vendor's reply with quotation. The chapter examines how to work with vendor quotations in detail.

After the purchasing department has received responses from the selected vendors that were sent RFQs, the quotations are entered into the system, comparisons are made, and the most appropriate vendor bid is accepted.

14 Quotation

In Chapter 13, Request for Quotation, you saw that significant purchasing department effort is involved in creating the RFQs and selecting appropriate vendors for bid submission.

After the vendors have replied to the RFQs within the bid submission deadline, the purchasing department then has to enter the bids and process them to make an informed decision on the best bid for the RFQ.

The first section of this chapter examines the functionality of entering a quotation that has been sent from the vendor in response to the RFQ.

14.1 Entering a Quotation

The quotation that has been returned by the vendor should be entered into the SAP ERP system in a timely manner due to the deadline determined within each RFQ. The quotation can be entered into the system by using Transaction ME47 or via the navigation path, SAP MENU • LOGISTICS • MATERIALS MANAGEMENT • PURCHASING • RFQ/QUOTATION • QUOTATION • MAINTAIN.

The initial screen of Transaction ME47 requires the purchasing user to enter a single RFQ number. The RFQ also can be found using matchcodes discussed in Chapter 13.

The vendor's bid details for the line items need to be entered into the screen. In Figure 14.1, the vendor has entered a bid for 225,000 USD per item on the RFQ. For each vendor quotation that is submitted, the appropriate RFQ is updated with the quotation.

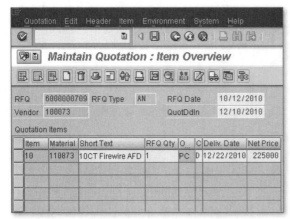

Figure 14.1 Line Item Screen for the Quotation Maintenance Transaction ME47

The price quotation can be entered as a single figure in the NET PRICE field. If there are discounts, taxes, or other conditions, these can be added into the system using the CONDITIONS screen.

Figure 14.2 shows that an entry was made in the quotation of 225,000 USD per item. In the condition record, a further entry has been made using the condition for a discount (RA00) of 4%. A further entry has been made for the freight (FRB1) to be charged by the vendor for the items to be delivered. On this CONDITIONS screen, any tax details that may be relevant for the purchase or further discounts and freight costs can be added. The actual price is then determined to be 217,400 USD.

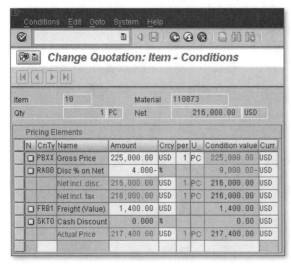

Figure 14.2 Quotation Price Entered into the Condition Screen

After the quotation has been entered, the quotations need to be compared to select the vendor who will be offered the PO. This next section examines how the quotations are compared.

14.2 Comparing Quotations

After the quotations have been entered for the RFQ's and sent to vendors, then the purchasing department reviews them and decides on a vendor for the material or service put out to bid.

One element of the quotation process is to compare the bids on a price comparison basis. This is the most basic comparison that can be made and not necessarily the deciding factor. Each purchasing department will have a procedure for selecting vendors based on RFQ/quotation responses.

14.2.1 Price Comparison Factor in Quotations

The price comparison can be found using Transaction ME49 or via the navigation path, SAP MENU • LOGISTICS • MATERIALS MANAGEMENT • PURCHASING • RFQ/QUO-TATION • QUOTATION • PRICE COMPARISON.

The price comparison can be performed between several quotations as shown in Figure 14.3, and these can be selected by a number of selection criteria, such as PURCHASING ORGANIZATION, VENDOR, MATERIAL, or COLLECTIVE RFQ number. The collective number is the most useful field when sending a number of RFQs to different vendors. The collective number can be used to easily obtain a comparison.

The other criteria in Transaction ME49 include the following comparison value criteria:

- REFERENCE QUOTATION: This is the quotation that all others are compared against. If no REFERENCE QUOTATION is entered, then the quotations are compared against each other.
- MEAN VALUE QUOTATION: If this indicator is set, then the comparisons are made against the average price of the quotations. The quotations are averaged, and the average quote is ranked at 100%. The quotes then reflect a percentage that shows whether it is above or below the average. For example, a lower-than-average quote will show a percentage below 100%; a higher than average quote will show a percentage of greater than 100%.

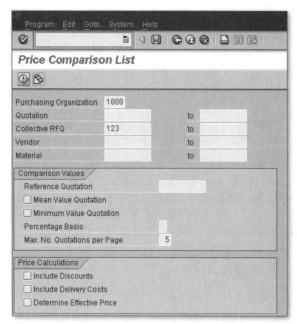

Figure 14.3 Price Comparison Selection Screen for Transaction ME49

▶ MINIMUM VALUE QUOTATION: If this indicator is set, then the comparisons are made against the lowest price quotation. This means that the first rank, or the best price quote, is a 100% rank. All other more expensive quotes will show a percentage that is calculated from the lowest bid, that is, 124%, 136%, and so on.

▶ PERCENTAGE BASIS: The PERCENTAGE BASIS allows the purchasing user to specify which value will be used as the 100% basis. This can be the mean price, the maximum price, or the minimum price. This will alter how the rank percentage is shown in the quotations.

In addition to the comparison value criteria, the following price comparison criteria indicators can be set:

▶ INCLUDE DISCOUNTS: If this indicator is set, the quotation comparison will include any price discounts that the vendor has applied. If the indicator is not set, then the discounts will not be used in the comparison.

▶ INCLUDE DELIVERY COSTS: If the indicator is set, then the delivery costs will be included in the price on the quotation and therefore used in the quotation comparison. The delivery costs can include the freight costs, duty levied, or other procurement costs such as packing, insurance, and handling.

▶ DETERMINE EFFECTIVE PRICE: This indicator is set if the cash discounts and delivery costs are used in the price comparison.

After the selection criteria have been decided on and entered, you can obtain the price comparison.

Figure 14.4 shows the price comparison for collective RFQ number 6. It shows the quotations from three vendors, or bidders, for a quantity (QTY) of MATERIAL 110873. The price comparison has been used with the MEAN VALUE QUOTATION indicator set. In other words, the average price has been set as 100%, and bids will be a lower percentage or a higher percentage.

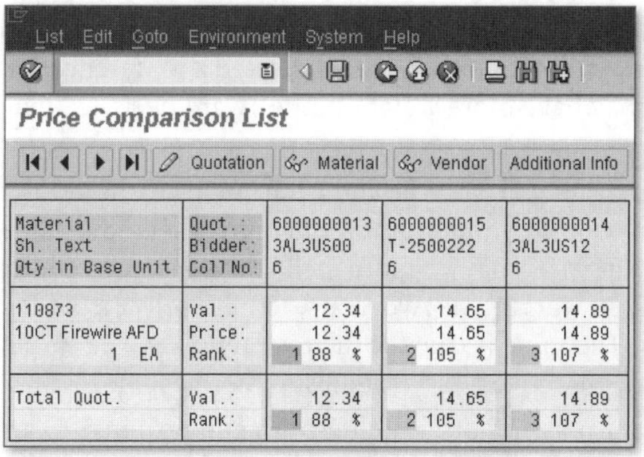

Figure 14.4 Price Comparison Between Three Quotations for a Collective RFQ Number

14.2.2 Other Qualitative Factors in Quotations

The price comparison report gives a clear indication to the purchasing department of which bidder is giving the client the best price for the material. However, this may only be one of the factors that the purchasing department takes into account. Many purchasing organizations believe that choosing vendors based only on the low-bid dollar amount often results in purchasing a lower quality of goods. Successful bids are more often awarded on a comparative evaluation of price, quality, performance capability, and other qualitative factors that will prove the most advantageous to the client.

Other qualitative factors that may be identified by a purchasing department include the following:

▶ **Previous relationship with client**: If the bidder has a successful relationship with the client, this may be taken into account in any final decision on the winner of the bid.

- **Compliance with the Equal Opportunity Act (EOA) (US):** Many clients insist that any vendor must be in compliance with EEO laws. For example, the EOA can be violated if a company discriminates by a number of factors, including age, disability, national origin, race, or religion.

- **Strategic alliances:** The client may have a number of strategic alliances with vendors or trading partners, which may weight the decision of awarding a bid. For example, a client may have put an RFQ out to vendors for a new UNIX server, and the lowest bidder by price was HP. However, if the client had a strategic relationship with IBM, the bid may be placed with IBM despite the lower bid from HP.

- **Minority and women-owned businesses (US):** Some clients may have a preference to give minority-owned or women-owned businesses certain contracts or POs. If the RFQ falls into an area where the client has indicated a preference for this type of vendor, then this may have more weight in the award decision than the price.

- **Warranty and return process:** The warranty period of an item or the return policy offered by the bidder may be very important to the purchaser. For example, if the RFQ is for PCs, the purchaser may be more inclined to accept a bidder with a higher price per unit if the warranty is two years, than to select a bidder offering a six-month warranty. The same is true for the return policy. The easier the return procedure, the more attractive a bid from a supplier becomes.

- **Creative pricing:** Often a bidder may not offer the best price in response to an RFQ but may offer a creative pricing schedule. Purchasing departments are often looking for ways of reducing cost outlay and welcome vendors who can offer the company ways of purchasing material with delayed payments or payments on performance.

This section has looked at how quotations are compared when they are received from the vendor. The next section will look at the process of rejecting the quotations from vendors that have not been selected.

14.3   Rejecting Quotations

After the purchasing department has compared the quotations from the bidders, as shown in the previous section, they will then inform the vendors whose quotations were rejected. In the system, the quotations also need to be flagged as rejected.

14.3.1 Flagging the Quotation as Rejected

The unsuccessful quotations can be flagged as rejected in the system using Transaction ME47 or via the navigation path, SAP MENU • LOGISTICS • MATERIALS MANAGEMENT • PURCHASING • RFQ/QUOTATION • QUOTATION • MAINTAIN.

The purchasing user enters the RFQ number for the quotation to be rejected, as shown in Figure 14.5. The line item should be selected and flagged with a checkmark in the rejected column, shown in Figure 14.5 as R, to reflect that the quotation has been rejected.

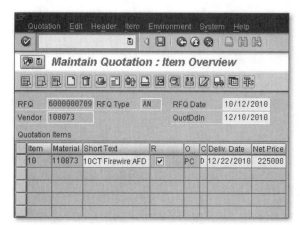

Figure 14.5 Quotation Being Flagged as Rejected

14.3.2 Printing the Quotation Rejection

If appropriate, all unsuccessful vendors in the RFQ process will be notified by the client representative, often the purchasing department, in writing. Notification is made as quickly as possible following the award of the contract, or when it has been determined that the vendor will not be asked to continue in the RFQ process.

The rejection letter can be printed from the system using Transaction ME9A or via the navigation path, SAP MENU • LOGISTICS • MATERIALS MANAGEMENT • PURCHASING • RFQ/QUOTATION • REQUEST FOR QUOTATION • MESSAGES • PRINT/TRANSMIT.

For each rejected quotation, a rejection notice can be printed based on the RFQ number, as shown in Figure 14.6. The purchasing user enters the correct MESSAGE TYPE rejection quotation, which is ABSA. The client can modify the standard rejection notice with SAPscript or tools such as Adobe Form Designer or JetForm.

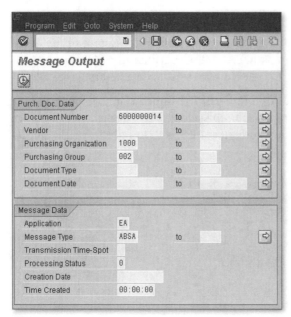

Figure 14.6 Transaction ME9A: Rejection Notes Can Be Printed Using a Message Type

14.3.3 Advising Unsuccessful Bidders

Sometimes the rejection notice is not an appropriate manner of rejecting a vendor's quotation submission. If the RFQ is for a particular project or of large monetary value, the client may decide that all of the unsuccessful vendors should be given, or may request, a debriefing session with respect to their submissions. These sessions with the client should concentrate on the strengths and weaknesses of the individual vendor's response.

The way in which quotations are rejected should be part of a greater purchasing policy that each company will adhere to. Check with the individual purchasing department for the correct method to use.

14.4   Business Examples – Quotations

After receiving an RFQ from a company, the vendor must decide whether to respond to the RFQ or decline to respond. It is not unusual for vendors to decline to respond because many suppliers don't have the resources to respond to every RFQ, especially when they have no relationship with the company sending the RFQ.

When a response is received from the vendor, it is entered into the system and compared with quotations of other vendors who replied to the RFQ. The responses are analyzed and a decision is made as to which vendor, if any, will receive the PO. The other vendors can be informed that their quotation has been declined.

14.4.1 Comparing Quotations

When the quotations from the vendors have been received, the purchasing department compares the details. Some companies will look at price as the deciding factor, but many will review other criteria from the quotations such as quality, warranty, performance capability, and other more subjective factors.

Example

An Irish manufacturer of linen uses the same vendor to supply the basic raw materials used in manufacturing for many years. However, to reduce costs, the company frequently requested quotations for office supplies, IT services, and packaging. The products in these areas were reviewed yearly and RFQs were sent to a variety of Irish and British vendors. The company sent out RFQs to no less than 10 vendors and thoroughly analyzed the vendor's quotations. The company weighed their criteria, depending on product line, and selected the top 3 vendors for each. The company then encouraged the 3 vendors to revise their quotations if they could improve their price or terms. After the second round of quotations, the company selected a vendor who then had to submit to further review and negotiation before an agreement was signed. None of the vendor's quotations in the process were rejected until after the final contract was signed with the vendor, in case a substitute vendor was required.

14.4.2 Rejecting Quotations

After the purchasing department has compared the vendor's quotations, they will issue the PO to the winning vendor and then inform the vendors whose quotations were rejected.

Example

When quotations were rejected by a manufacturer of specialty chemicals in Puerto Rico, a the purchasing department adhered to a formal process they had developed. After informing the winning vendor of the company's decision, the purchasing department prepared the rejection documents for the other vendors. The document informed each vendor of the reasons why the bid was unsuccessful. The purchasing department decided to use this method of informing vendors because they found that vendors who were given detailed information on why they were not selected were more likely to respond to future RFQs and offer better terms.

14.5 Summary

This chapter described the receiving and processing of the quotation. The quotation allows the purchasing department to review the price and terms offered by each vendor and to make the best decision for the company based on the replies given by vendors. The acceptance of a quotation and issuing of a PO will reflect that the vendor has the right to supply the material to the customer for a period of time. Purchasing departments periodically will seek quotations from other vendors to ensure that the material cannot be procured at a better price elsewhere.

In Chapter 15, the focus turns to the actual purchasing of the material and the use of the PO. There are a number of purchasing functions to discuss, including account assignment in a PO, outline purchase agreements, and contracts.

The purchase order is the document that shows the intent of the buyer to buy a certain quantity of product at a certain price from a specific vendor. In accepting a PO, the vendor agrees to supply the quantity of product to the buyer on or before the required delivery date.

create ME21N
change ME22N
Release ME29N

15   Purchase Order

A purchase order (PO) is an external document issued by a purchasing department to send to a vendor. The PO contains the required products, the quantity of the products needed, and the price agreed to by the client and the vendor. As well as the products, quantity, and price, the PO usually contains the PO number, order date, delivery address, and terms.

POs are used to communicate the request to the vendor and to give the vendor a written confirmation of the request. Depending on the legal jurisdiction involved, the PO can be considered a legal and binding document.

In some cases, the PO does not specify the specific item number but rather gives a detailed description of the item. This occurs where the material number does not exist or when the customer does not know the material number.

15.1   Create a Purchase Order

The PO can be created without any other specific purchase-related documents being created. For instance, a PO can be created from a purchase requisition. Depending on the complexity of the client's purchasing activities, the client may not want to implement purchase requisitions and may allow POs to be created directly.

15.1.1   Create a Purchase Order with Vendor Known

To create a PO without any reference to a purchase requisition but with the vendor known, you use Transaction ME21N or the traditional PO create program Transaction ME21. This is illustrated in Figure 15.1. The navigation path used to find the transaction is SAP MENU • LOGISTICS • MATERIALS MANAGEMENT • PURCHASING • PURCHASE ORDER • CREATE • VENDOR KNOWN.

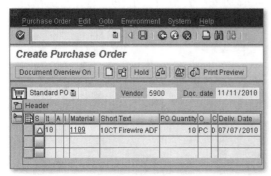

Figure 15.1 Detail Screen from Transaction ME21N

Transaction ME21N allows the entry of most of the required information in one location. The left column of the screen can be used to select POs and quickly see the purchasing information. The line detail and header detail can be seen on one screen, and these can be minimized to make the screen clearer. In Figure 15.1, the purchase line item detail is displayed, but the header detail is filtered out. The material, 1109, has been entered with a PO QUANTITY of 10 and a delivery date (DELIV. DATE) of 07/07/2010.

This sample is a standard PO, type NB, but a different order type can be selected from the drop-down menu. Figure 15.2 shows the same PO created with the traditional Transaction ME21. In Figure 15.2, 5900 has been entered as the VENDOR, the purchasing organization (PURCH. ORGANIZATION) has been entered as 1000, with the PURCHASING GROUP 014. The DELIVERY DATE has been entered as 12/21/2010.

15.1.2 Create a Purchase Order Where the Vendor Is Unknown

When a PO has to be created, and the vendor is not known, Transaction ME25 should be used, as shown in Figure 15.3. The information can be entered on the initial screen, including date required, PURCHASING GROUP, PLANT, and ITEM CATEGORY, if required. This transaction can be found using the navigation path, SAP MENU • LOGISTICS • MATERIALS MANAGEMENT • PURCHASING • PURCHASE ORDER • CREATE • VENDOR UNKNOWN.

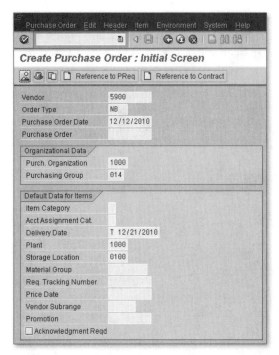

Figure 15.2 Initial Purchase Order Screen for Transaction ME21

Figure 15.3 Initial Screen for Transaction ME25

After the initial data is entered, materials on the line-item detail screen can be added. Materials and quantities for the PO can be added, as shown in Figure 15.4. In this figure, the MATERIAL, 1109, has been entered with a QTY REQUESTED of 3 and a DELIV. DATE of 12/23/2010.

Subsequent to the material being added, you can assign a source of supply, that is, a vendor. If a source list is created for the material, the PO program will review all relevant source lists and offer a list of vendors or select the vendor if there is only one source list.

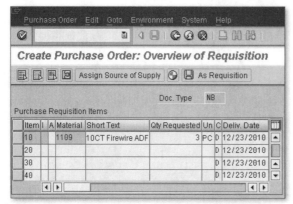

Figure 15.4 Material Added to Transaction ME25 When Vendor Is Not Known

After the vendor has been assigned, the document can be saved as a PO. Subsequent to posting, the PO number will be displayed.

The completed PO should be forwarded to the vendor by the method agreed to between the purchasing department and the vendor. If EDI is being used to transmit the PO, then EDI code 850 is used.

This section has described the elements involved in creating a PO. The next section reviews the maintenance of the PO after it has been created.

15.2 Maintaining a Purchase Order

After a PO has been created, there may be an occasion where the purchasing department needs to modify the PO. This may be due to a change of vendor, a change in the material quantity required, or removal of a line item altogether.

To change the PO, use Transaction ME22N, which can be found using the navigation path, SAP MENU • LOGISTICS • MATERIALS MANAGEMENT • PURCHASING • PURCHASE ORDER • CHANGE.

Apart from changes to a line item, a PO line can be added for another material, or a line item can be deleted.

After the PO is changed, it should be resent to the vendor. The PO should be forwarded to the vendor by whatever method is appropriate: fax, email, EDI, and so on. However, if the vendor has already delivered an amount against the PO, the purchasing department will not be able to reduce the ordered quantity below that which the vendor has already delivered.

If the vendor's invoice has been received, then any changes to the PO will not be valid.

Now that we've reviewed the maintenance of POs, the next section will examine blocking and canceling POs.

15.3 Blocking and Canceling a Purchase Order

POs are often blocked and canceled for a variety of reasons. This section describes the functionality evoked for blocking and canceling POs.

15.3.1 Block a Purchase Order Line Item

A PO may need to be blocked after it has been created. This stops any goods receipt for the relevant line item. A block may be placed on the line item for many reasons, including quality issues with the material that has already been received at the plant.

You can block a PO line item by using the PO change Transaction ME22N, as shown in Figure 15.5.

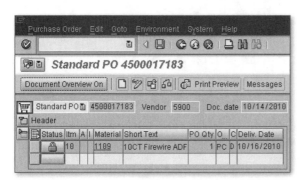

Figure 15.5 Line Item in Purchase Order Blocked by Using Transaction ME22N

15.3.2 Canceling a Purchase Order Line Item

A decision may be made to totally cancel a line item, rather than just block it. There may be issues with the vendor, or the material may no longer be required. You cancel the material by using the PO change Transaction ME22N. You can then choose the delete icon for the selected line item.

If the PO line item has already been subject to a partial goods receipt, the line item cannot be fully deleted because of the delivery. If the line item does not show any delivery, then the PO can be set to zero to cancel out the line item.

After the line item has been canceled, as shown in Figure 15.6, the purchasing department needs to inform the vendor of the change of PO. This can be performed by whatever method has been agreed upon between the purchasing department and the vendor. For EDI, use code 860.

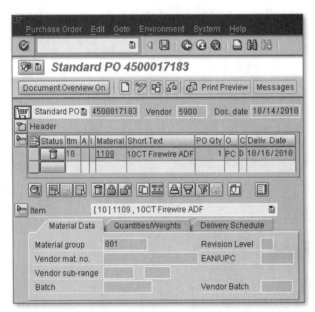

Figure 15.6 Cancellation of Line Item in Transaction ME22N

This section has discussed how to block and cancel a PO. The next section reviews how account assignments are made in a PO.

15.4 Account Assignment in a Purchase Order

A line item in a PO can be assigned to an account or a number of accounts that are charged when the invoice for the PO items is posted.

15.4.1 Account Assignment Overview

You can assign a single account code or a number of account codes to a PO. Assigning account information describes how the purchased material is being used, such as fulfilling a sales order or consumption by a cost center.

15.4.2 Account Assignment Categories

A number of account assignment categories can be used in the PO. On the initial screen of Transaction ME21, CREATE PURCHASE ORDER, the purchasing user can enter an account assignment, as shown in Figure 15.7.

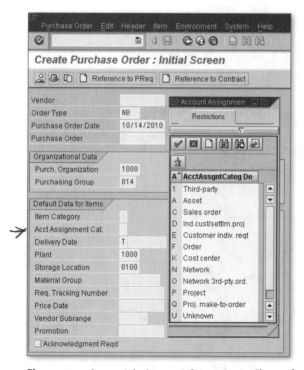

Figure 15.7 Account Assignment Categories to Choose from in Transaction ME21

The account assignment category determines what account assignment details are required for the item. So if AcctAssgntCateg K is selected, then the transaction would, depending on the specific configuration, require a GL account and cost center to be entered.

The different account assignments can be configured in the IMG. The configuration allows a new account assignment to be added and the fields modified to be required, optional, or hidden. The transaction, as shown in Figure 15.8, can be found using the navigation path, IMG • MATERIALS MANAGEMENT • PURCHASING • ACCOUNT ASSIGNMENT • MAINTAIN ACCOUNT ASSIGNMENT CATEGORIES.

After a new account assignment has been created, it has to be assigned to an item category in configuration. The transaction to complete this assignment is found via the navigation path, IMG • MATERIALS MANAGEMENT • PURCHASING • ACCOUNT ASSIGNMENT • DEFINE COMBINATION OF ITEM CATEGORY/ACCOUNT ASSIGNMENT CATEGORIES.

added to item category

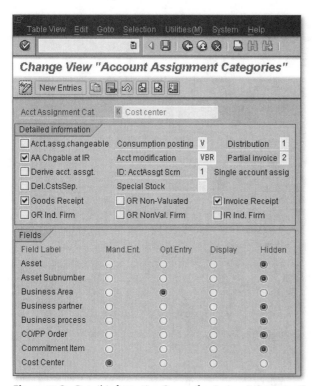

Figure 15.8 Detail Information Screen for Account Category Configuration Transaction

The purchasing user can decide which item category is relevant for the new account assignment, as shown in Figure 15.9.

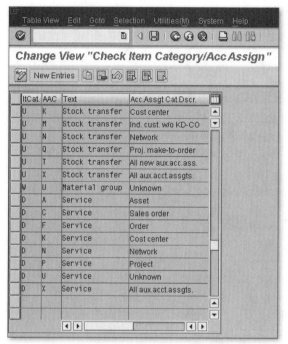

Figure 15.9 Configuration for Item Category and Account Assignment Combination

most common.

15.4.3 Single Account Assignment

Single account assignment is the most common account assignment for POs. The single account assignment simply means that one account is assigned, as can be seen in Figure 15.10.

The account assignment can be made in the PO creation Transaction ME21. After the line item has been entered into the transaction, the purchasing user can navigate to ITEM • ACCOUNT ASSIGNMENTS to access the ACCOUNT ASSIGNMENT dialog box.

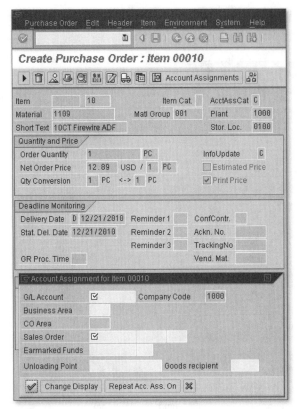

Figure 15.10 Account Assignment Dialog Box for Transaction ME21

15.4.4 Multiple Account Assignment

The multiple account assignment allows a number of accounts to be assigned to one PO line. This scenario could occur if a line item is for a material or service that is used by three laboratories, and the cost is split between the three. The user can divide the amount of the material into that used by each lab, or the user can decide to split the charge by a percentage.

To assign multiple accounts, access the multiple account screen from the ACCOUNT ASSIGNMENT dialog box as shown in Figure 15.10. The purchasing user accesses the dialog box as if entering one account and then accesses the multiple account screen by clicking on the CHANGE DISPLAY button.

After the multiple account screen is displayed as shown in Figure 15.11, the DISTRIBUTION field can be changed to 1 for quantity assignment or 2 for percentage assignment.

Any number of accounts can be added for the line item, as long as the total percentage does not exceed 100%, or the total quantity exceeds more than the quantity entered in the line item.

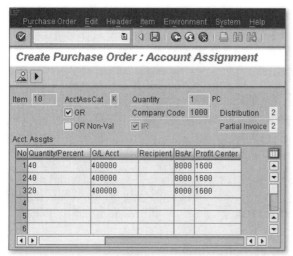

Figure 15.11 Multiple Assignment Screen in Purchase Order Transaction ME21

15.5 Outline Purchase Agreement

The outline purchase agreement is often referred to as a blanket or umbrella PO. This section reviews the functionality of the outline purchase agreement.

15.5.1 Outline Purchase Agreement Overview

An outline purchase agreement is basically a long-term agreement between the purchasing department and a vendor for materials or services for a defined period of time. The purchasing department negotiates with the vendor a set of terms and conditions that are fixed for the period of the agreement.

15.5.2 Outline Purchase Agreement Types

The two types of outline purchase agreements are contracts and scheduling agreements:

▶ A contract is an outline purchase agreement against which release orders can be issued for materials or services when the customer requires them.

381

▶ A scheduling agreement is an outline purchase agreement whereby the purchasing department has arranged to procure materials based on a schedule agreed upon between the purchasing department and the vendor. This type of outline purchase agreement is useful to customers who operate repetitive manufacturing, where production consumes the same materials each month and can plan accordingly.

15.6 Scheduling Agreement

A scheduling agreement can be created manually or can be copied with reference to purchase requisitions, quotations, and centrally agreed contracts.

15.6.1 Scheduling Agreement Overview

Before creating a scheduling agreement, the purchasing user must define the account assignment, purchasing organization, and purchasing group. A scheduling agreement can be created for subcontracting, consignment, and stock transfer.

15.6.2 Create a Scheduling Agreement Manually

Creating a scheduling agreement manually requires the purchasing user to enter the details rather than referencing a quotation, purchase requisition, or contract. Transaction ME31L is used to create the scheduling agreement. This can be found in the navigation path, SAP MENU • LOGISTICS • MATERIALS MANAGEMENT • PURCHASING • OUTLINE AGREEMENT • SCHEDULING AGREEMENT • CREATE • VENDOR KNOWN.

In Figure 15.12, there is an option to enter an AGREEMENT TYPE, which can be either LP for a scheduling agreement or LU for a stock transport scheduling agreement. There is also the opportunity to enter a scheduling agreement number (AGREEMENT) if an external number has been assigned.

Figure 15.13 shows the validity dates of the scheduling agreement and the terms of delivery that have been agreed upon between the purchasing department and the vendor. The purchasing department may have agreed on a target dollar amount for the contract, which can be entered into the scheduling agreement.

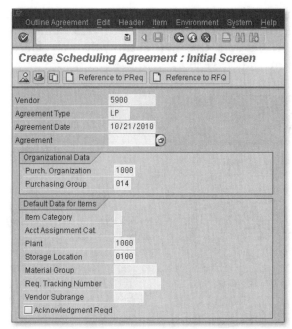

Figure 15.12 Initial Screen for Creating a Manual Scheduling Agreement

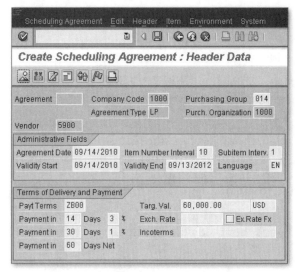

Figure 15.13 Header Data for Manual Scheduling Agreement

Subsequent to the header information being entered, the line items can be entered for the scheduling agreement. Each line item requires that a target quantity be entered, as shown in Figure 15.14. The TARG. QTY is the quantity that was agreed upon by the purchasing department and the vendor.

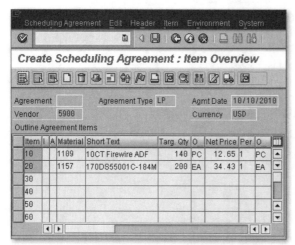

Figure 15.14 Detail Line Items for Scheduling Agreement Using Transaction ME31L

15.6.3 Create a Scheduling Agreement with Reference

If there is a purchase requisition or quotation that should reference the scheduling agreement, the document can be identified when Transaction ME31L is run.

When the transaction is run, the user can reference other documents. Figure 15.15 shows that a scheduling agreement can be created based on the details from a purchase requisition.

After choosing a purchase requisition, the details from the requisition are available to be adopted and entered into the scheduling agreement. The purchase requisition line items are shown in Figure 15.16. Users then use the ADOPT + DETAILS button to copy the details into the scheduling agreement.

After the purchase requisition lines are copied to the scheduling agreement, the user enters the agreed price and posts the scheduling agreement.

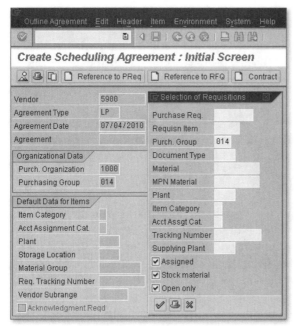

Figure 15.15 Scheduling Agreement Created with Reference to a Purchase Requisition

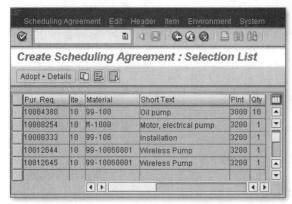

Figure 15.16 Referenced Purchase Requisition for Scheduling Agreement

The next section reviews the contract, both by quantity and value; how a contract is entered; and how releases are made against it.

15.7 Contracts

A contract is an agreement between the vendor and the customer for the vendor to supply material to the customer at an agreed price over a specified period of time.

15.7.1 Contract Overview

[handwritten: Releases are made against the contract]

Unlike the scheduling agreement, the contract is based on releases to the contract, or a blanket order, as it is often called. These contracts can be either based on a total quantity or a total value.

Quantity Contract *[handwritten: — based on quantity]*

A quantity contract allows the purchasing department to agree with the vendor on a contract for a set quantity of material or services. A typical example involves a vendor that supplies technical support for desktop computers. The vendor agrees to provide 480 hours under a yearly contract with the customer. This allows the customer to use the support service without having to create a new PO each time the services are needed. A release is made against the contract, which allows the vendor to be paid for the service provided. When all of the hours have been used, the contract has been fulfilled, and a new contract can be negotiated.

Value Contract *[handwritten: based on value]*

A value contract allows a purchasing department to cap the spending with one particular vendor. The value contract is not concerned with the quantity of material supplied by the vendor but by the total spending with the vendor for that material. The process of supply is the same as with the quantity contract because release orders are used to receive material.

However, the release orders are only valid until the total spending for the value contract reaches the total agreed to. In this way, the purchasing department can limit spending at vendors to allow other vendors to supply material.

15.7.2 Centrally Agreed Contract *[handwritten: — not just for one plant.]*

The centrally agreed contract allows a central purchasing organization to create a contract with a vendor that is not specific just to one plant. In this way, the purchasing organization can negotiate with a vendor by leveraging the whole company's spending for certain materials.

Many companies allow plants to negotiate deals with vendors independently of each other, and it often turns out that the plants have chosen the same vendor for materials but have negotiated an array of prices and terms that place some plants at a disadvantage. By creating a central contract, a central purchasing organization can combine the spending of all plants and work on obtaining the best price for the whole company. The materials and services involved can be as complex as specialized chemicals or as simple as telephone services or express-mail services. Many companies have hundreds of contracts for express-mail service that have been negotiated by local staff over a long period of time, and a central contract could achieve a tremendous cash saving if put in place.

mE 31 K

15.7.3 Creating a Contract

The contract is created in a very similar way to the scheduling agreement. The purchasing user uses Transaction ME31K to create a contract. This is found in the navigation path, SAP MENU • LOGISTICS • MATERIALS MANAGEMENT • PURCHASING • OUTLINE AGREEMENT • CONTRACT • CREATE.

The initial screen, as shown in Figure 15.17, is similar to the initial screen for creating a scheduling agreement.

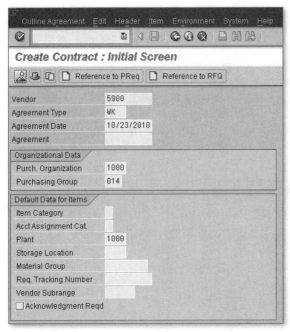

Figure 15.17 Initial Screen of Transaction ME31K

The AGREEMENT TYPE field, shown in Figure 15.17, should be entered to determine what type of contract is being created. The options are listed here:

- ▶ **WK:** Value Contract
- ▶ **MK:** Quantity Contract
- ▶ **DC:** Distributed or Centrally Agreed Contract

After the initial information has been entered, the transaction displays the header information that needs to be completed, as shown in Figure 15.18. The value contract requires a target value (Targ. Val.) to be entered for the contract.

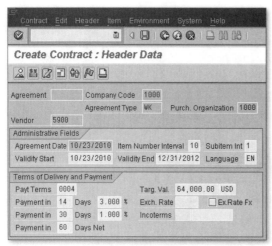

Figure 15.18 Header Information for a Value Contract Using Transaction ME31K

The line items that need to be added to the detail screen are shown in Figure 15.19. The purchasing user must add a target for the line item.

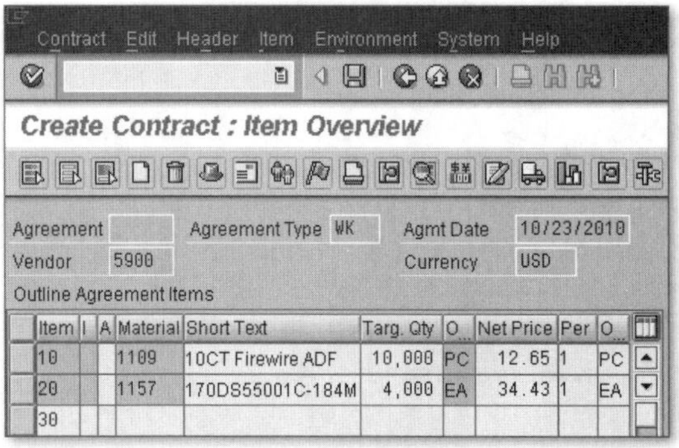

Figure 15.19 Detail Line-Item Information for a Value Contract

15.7.4 Release Order Against a Contract

ME21

After the contract is in place, material can be requested from the vendor by using a release order against the contract. This release order can be created via the CREATE PURCHASE ORDER screen in Transaction ME21. On the initial screen, as shown in Figure 15.20, the purchasing user can access the contract by selecting the REFERENCE TO CONTRACT icon.

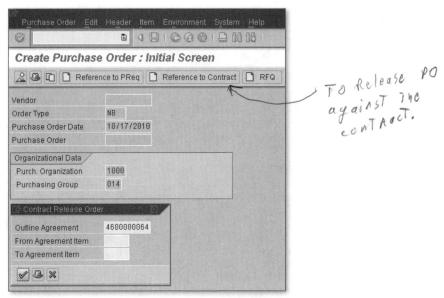

To Release PO against the contract.

Figure 15.20 Initial Screen for Creating a Release Order for a Contract

A dialog box appears where the user can enter the contract number to create a release for, as shown in Figure 15.20. Following the entry of the contract number, the detail lines are displayed, and the user enters a quantity for each line item on the release order against the contract. The line item also shows the quantity available on the contract, as shown in Figure 15.21.

After the quantities are entered for the release order, the user can click the ADOPT + DETAILS button to copy the details into the release order. The release order can then be saved.

This section reviewed the contract, both quantity and value. The next section reviews the confirmation sent by the vendor after receiving the purchasing document.

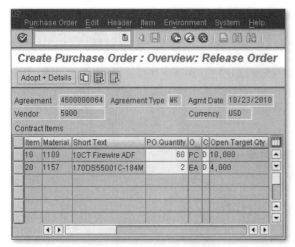

Figure 15.21 Contract Line Items Assigned to a Release Order in Transaction ME21

15.8 Vendor Confirmation

A vendor confirmation occurs when the vendor communicates to the customer regarding a PO or inbound delivery.

15.8.1 Vendor Confirmation Overview

The vendor communication to the purchaser can be in the form of a fax, email, or EDI. The communication can be for the following:

▸ Order Acknowledgement

▸ Transport Confirmation

▸ Advance Ship Notification (ASN)

▸ Inbound Delivery

The vendor confirmations are manually entered into SAP ERP. Confirmations are only loaded automatically when the confirmation is sent from the vendor using EDI.

Vendor confirmations are important to a client because they provide updated information on delivery of goods. This means that the client does not have to rely solely on the delivery dates agreed to by the vendor at the time of PO creation, or even before. This allows the planning department to adjust the production schedule based on the vendor's information.

15.8.2 Confirmation Configuration

The confirmation categories can be configured in the IMG for external or internal confirmations. External categories are defined for manual entries of vendor confirmations, whereas the internal categories are for the vendor confirmations through EDI. The EDI transaction sets for vendor acknowledgement include 855 for Purchase Order Acknowledgement and 856 for Advance Ship Notification (ASN).

External Confirmations

The external confirmation categories can be configured using a transaction found on the navigation path, IMG • MATERIALS MANAGEMENT • PURCHASING • CONFIRMATIONS • DEFINE EXTERNAL CONFIRMATION CATEGORIES.

You can also add new categories for confirmations, as shown in Figure 15.22, depending on the requirement for confirmations.

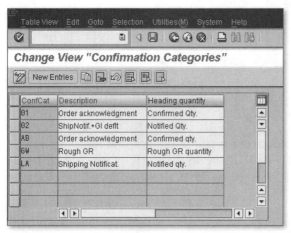

Figure 15.22 Configuration Traction for External Confirmation Categories

Internal Confirmations

Three internal confirmation categories for EDI are supplied in the standard system:

▶ **Category 1**: Used for order acknowledgments.

▶ **Category 2**: Used for Advance Shipping Notification (ASN) or inbound delivery.

▶ **Category 3**: Used for rough goods receipt.

An external confirmation category can be assigned to each internal confirmation category, as shown in Figure 15.23. This enables purchasing documents to be automatically updated with data from the relevant confirmations. The external confirmation categories can be configured using a transaction found on the navigation path, IMG • MATERIALS MANAGEMENT • PURCHASING • CONFIRMATIONS • DEFINE INTERNAL CONFIRMATION CATEGORIES.

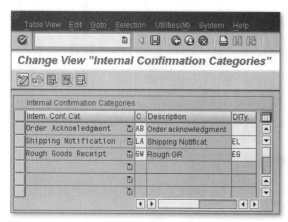

Figure 15.23 Internal Categories and Their Assignment to External Categories

15.8.3   Enter a Manual Confirmation

When a vendor has sent or faxed a confirmation, the acknowledgement can be entered manually into the PO line item. However, before the confirmation can be entered, the line item should be checked to see if a confirmation is relevant for confirmation control.

The method used to check a line item for confirmation control is to display the line item detail screen within the PO change Transaction ME22, as shown in Figure 15.24.

From the detail line-item screen, the purchasing user can enter the confirmation by choosing ITEM • CONFIRMATIONS • LIST.

The screen that appears, shown in Figure 15.25, allows confirmations to be added manually by selecting the type of confirmation; in this case, the confirmation control is AB, which represents order acknowledgement. The purchasing user then adds the information related to DELIVERY DATE, time of delivery (TIME), and QUANTITY. If the ASN is available, that also can be entered, in the field CC, using confirmation control, LA.

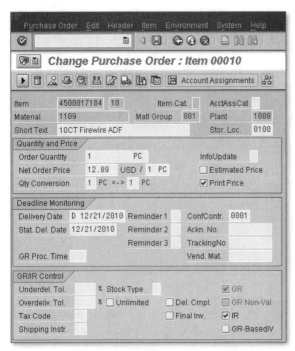

Figure 15.24 Detail Line Item for Purchase Order

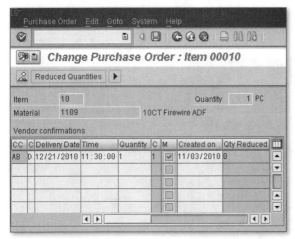

Figure 15.25 Manual Entry of Vendor Confirmation for Purchase Order Line Items

This section reviewed the confirmation that a vendor can send to acknowledge receipt of the PO. The next section reviews the messages and outputs associated with a PO.

15.9 Messages and Outputs

POs are frequently printed so that a purchaser can inform the vendor of requirements. This section reviews the messages and output associated with POs.

15.9.1 Message Overview

After a PO has been created or changed, the document must be in a format where it can be sent to the vendor by fax, mail, or EDI. The system will generate a message for each document posted.

The output message is created by the same conditions technique that is used for price determination. Subsequent to a message being produced for a PO, contract, and so on, the message is placed in the message queue that contains all messages that are still to be processed. Messages in the queue are available to be processed immediately or at a later time.

15.9.2 Message Creation

The message is created when a document is posted. The message processing can be seen within the PO from Transaction ME22 by choosing HEADER • MESSAGES.

The message that has been created can be viewed, as shown in Figure 15.26. If the message can be processed, the status is green. By selecting the PROCESSING LOG icon, the purchasing user can view any error or warning messages that may be causing the document not to be processed.

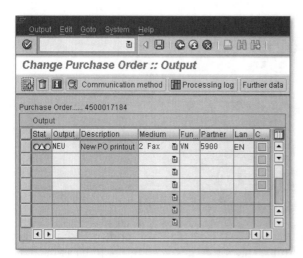

Figure 15.26 Fax Output for Purchase Order Transaction ME22

15.9.3 Message Output Definition

The output format of the message can be configured in the IMG if the standard format is not suitable. The format can be changed for the purchasing outputs, RFQ, contract, PO, and scheduling agreement.

To change the texts for a PO, the transaction can be found using the navigation path, IMG • MATERIALS MANAGEMENT • PURCHASING • MESSAGES • TEXT FOR MESSAGES • DEFINE TEXTS FOR PURCHASE ORDER.

The text can be changed for the document header and the document items for any of the different print operations, such as change, rejection of RFQ, or new PO. In Figure 15.27, the first line that can be changed is for print operation 1 for a new output of document type NB, which is a PO. The header text is F01.

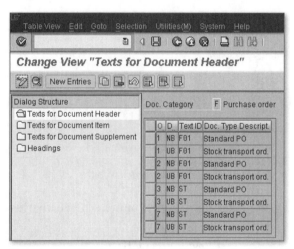

Figure 15.27 Structure of Document That Can Be Modified

15.9.4 Output Messages

Messages can be processed either by a scheduled batch job or manually. The batch job that can be run to process the output is RSNAST00, and this should be run when it is appropriate.

To process messages produced by purchasing documents, you use Transaction ME9F, which can be found via the navigation path, SAP MENU • LOGISTICS • MATERIALS MANAGEMENT • PURCHASING • PURCHASE ORDER • MESSAGES • PRINT/TRANSMIT.

As shown in Figure 15.28, this transaction allows a range of PO document numbers, purchasing organization, purchasing group, vendor, and so on, to be entered. After the selection criteria are entered, the transaction returns a number of POs that can be printed when the purchasing user selects them.

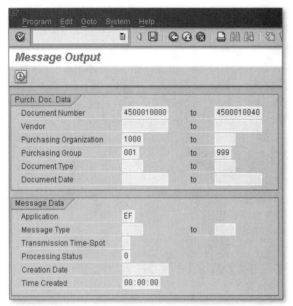

Figure 15.28 Selection Criteria for Printing Purchase Orders in Transaction ME9F

The next section examines pricing and taxes that can be found in the Purchasing functionality.

15.10 Pricing Procedures *- used during PO creation!*

Within the Purchasing functionality, pricing procedures are used during PO creation. The total value of material is based on a number of conditions that add or subtract amounts in the equation. These conditions can be discounts, surcharges, taxes, freight charges, and so on.

15.10.1 Pricing Conditions

The condition technique is used to determine purchase and valuation prices. This technique is based on conditions that are illustrated by condition types, stored in condition records and tables, found by means of access sequences, and arranged in calculation schemas.

Conditions are agreed upon with vendors regarding prices, discounts, freight charges, and so on. The system determines the net purchase price in a PO based on these pricing elements. Conditions can be maintained when a user enters a quotation, purchase information record, outline purchase agreements, and POs.

Discounts or surcharges may be percentage-based, quantity-dependent, or absolute values. A user can enter conditions that do not take effect immediately at the time of a transaction but at a later date, such as with subsequent settlement rebates.   *Discounts*

There are also differences in conditions that are valid for a certain period, known as time-dependent conditions, and conditions for which no special validity period can be defined, known as are time-independent conditions.

15.10.2 Condition Types

Individual conditions are described by means of condition types. There are condition types used for the gross price, various discounts and surcharges, freight charges, fixed costs, and so on. Each condition type can be configured in the IMG, as shown in Figure 15.29, using the navigation path, IMG • MATERIALS MANAGEMENT • PURCHASING • CONDITIONS • DEFINE PRICE DETERMINATION PROCESS • DEFINE CONDITION TYPES.

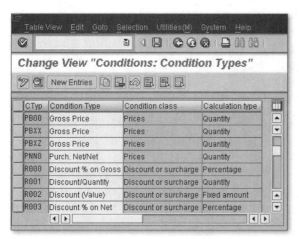

Figure 15.29 Defining Condition Types

An access sequence can be assigned to a condition type, as shown in Figure 15.30. The access sequence is a search strategy that enables a user to specify the order in which condition tables are to be searched for the appropriate entries for a condition type.

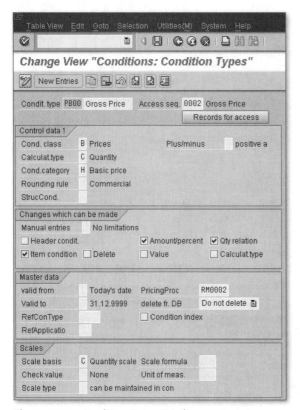

Figure 15.30 Condition Types Details

15.10.3 Condition Tables

Conditions are stored in the system as condition records, and the condition tables reference condition records. Entries in condition tables consist of a key part and a data part. The data part contains the number of a condition record. Each condition record is stored in one of the following tables:

- **KONP**: Time-dependent conditions
- **KONH**: Header conditions
- **KONM**: Quantity scales
- **KONW**: Value scales

A condition table can be created using Transaction M/03 (see Figure 15.31) or by using the navigation path, IMG • MATERIALS MANAGEMENT • PURCHASING • CONDITIONS • DEFINE PRICE DETERMINATION PROCESS • MAINTAIN CONDITION TABLE.

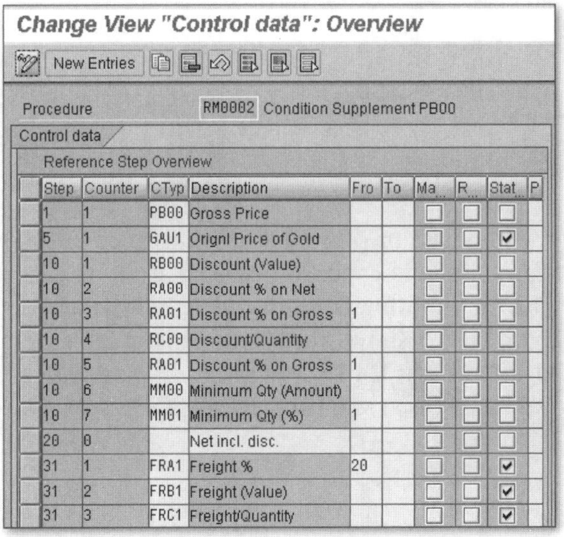
Change View "Control data": Overview

New Entries

Procedure RM0002 Condition Supplement PB00

Control data

Reference Step Overview

Step	Counter	CTyp	Description	Fro	To	Ma...	R...	Stat...	P
1	1	PB00	Gross Price			☐	☐	☐	
5	1	GAU1	Orignl Price of Gold			☐	☐	☑	
10	1	RB00	Discount (Value)			☐	☐	☐	
10	2	RA00	Discount % on Net			☐	☐	☐	
10	3	RA01	Discount % on Gross	1		☐	☐	☐	
10	4	RC00	Discount/Quantity			☐	☐	☐	
10	5	RA01	Discount % on Gross	1		☐	☐	☐	
10	6	MM00	Minimum Qty (Amount)			☐	☐	☐	
10	7	MM01	Minimum Qty (%)	1		☐	☐	☐	
20	0		Net incl. disc.			☐	☐	☐	
31	1	FRA1	Freight %	20		☐	☐	☑	
31	2	FRB1	Freight (Value)			☐	☐	☑	
31	3	FRC1	Freight/Quantity			☐	☐	☑	

Figure 15.31 Display of a Condition Table

15.10.4 Access Sequences

As mentioned previously, an access sequence can be assigned to a condition type. The access sequence is a search strategy that enables a user to specify the order in which condition tables are to be searched for relevant entries for a condition type. For example, if you are searching for a price, you can state that the system is to search first for a plant-specific price, and if one is not found, the system should then search for a price that is applicable to all plants. The order of the search is determined by the order of the condition tables in the access sequence.

Each access sequence can be configured in the IMG, as shown in Figure 15.32, using the navigation path, IMG • MATERIALS MANAGEMENT • PURCHASING • CONDITIONS • DEFINE PRICE DETERMINATION PROCESS • DEFINE ACCESS SEQUENCES.

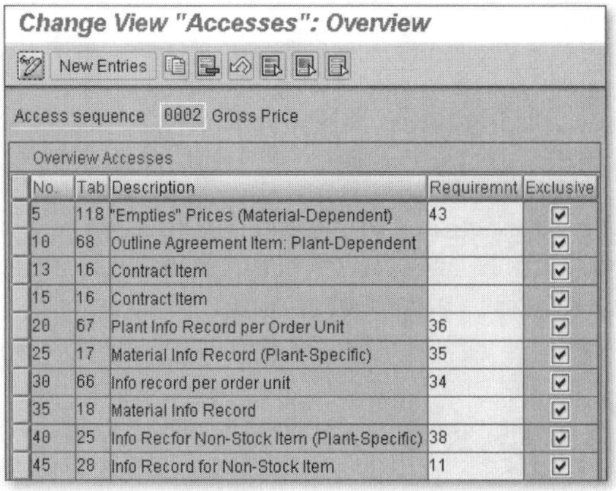

Change View "Accesses": Overview

New Entries

Access sequence 0002 Gross Price

Overview Accesses

No.	Tab	Description	Requiremnt	Exclusive
5	118	"Empties" Prices (Material-Dependent)	43	☑
10	68	Outline Agreement Item: Plant-Dependent		☑
13	16	Contract Item		☑
15	16	Contract Item		☑
20	67	Plant Info Record per Order Unit	36	☑
25	17	Material Info Record (Plant-Specific)	35	☑
30	66	Info record per order unit	34	☑
35	18	Material Info Record		☑
40	25	Info Rec for Non-Stock Item (Plant-Specific)	38	☑
45	28	Info Record for Non-Stock Item	11	☑

Figure 15.32 Display of an Access Sequence

15.10.5 Calculation Schema

The framework for determining the purchase price is known as the price calculation schema, which groups together all of the condition types that are relevant to this process. In the Sales and Distribution function, this calculation schema is known as a pricing procedure. Figure 15.33 shows the schema that can be configured in the IMG using the navigation path, IMG • MATERIALS MANAGEMENT • PURCHASING • CONDITIONS • DEFINE PRICE DETERMINATION PROCESS • DEFINE CALCULATION SCHEMA.

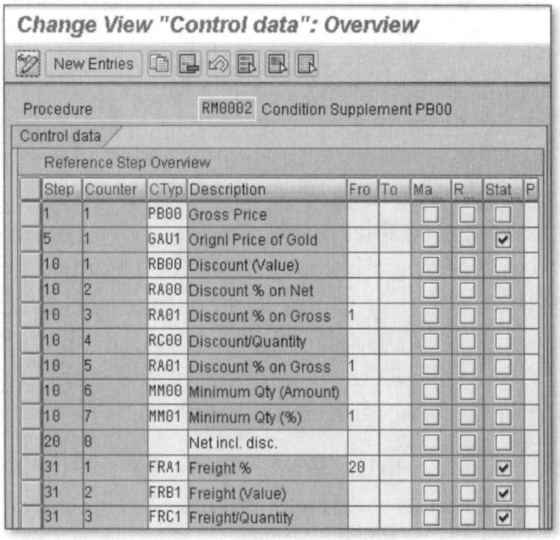

Change View "Control data": Overview

New Entries

Procedure RM0002 Condition Supplement PB00

Control data

Reference Step Overview

Step	Counter	CTyp	Description	Fro	To	Ma...	R...	Stat	P
1	1	PB00	Gross Price			☐	☐	☐	
5	1	GAU1	Orignl Price of Gold			☐	☐	☑	
10	1	RB00	Discount (Value)			☐	☐	☐	
10	2	RA00	Discount % on Net			☐	☐	☐	
10	3	RA01	Discount % on Gross	1		☐	☐	☐	
10	4	RC00	Discount/Quantity			☐	☐	☐	
10	5	RA01	Discount % on Gross	1		☐	☐	☐	
10	6	MM00	Minimum Qty (Amount)			☐	☐	☐	
10	7	MM01	Minimum Qty (%)	1		☐	☐	☐	
20	0		Net incl. disc.			☐	☐	☐	
31	1	FRA1	Freight %	20		☐	☐	☑	
31	2	FRB1	Freight (Value)			☐	☐	☑	
31	3	FRC1	Freight/Quantity			☐	☐	☑	

Figure 15.33 Display of a Calculation Schema

[handwritten margin note: conditions are contained in the Info Records.]

15.10.6 Price Determination

When a purchasing agent creates a PO, the system searches existing info records and documents for valid conditions and assumes any it finds as default values in the new document.

The price determination process is carried out in a number of steps:

1. The relevant calculation schema is determined. A calculation schema can be predefined for POs in configuration using the navigation path, IMG • MATERIALS MANAGEMENT • PURCHASING • CONDITIONS • DEFINE PRICE DETERMINATION PROCESS • DEFINE SCHEMA DETERMINATION.

2. The system searches for condition records for all condition types listed in the calculation schema that have an access sequence assigned to them.

3. The search for condition records is performed in the order specified in the access sequence.

4. The search is complete when a valid condition record is found.

15.10.7 Standard Pricing Condition Type PB00

When a purchasing clerk enters a purchasing information record manually or automatically, the gross price entered is assigned to that standard pricing condition type PB00. After a PO is created, a vendor's gross price for a material is adopted from the purchasing information record as the default value for condition type PB00. If there is no valid purchasing information record or no order price history, the system cannot suggest a price and therefore requires a purchasing clerk to manually enter a net price. If this occurs, the manually entered price is assigned to condition type PBXX.

When a PO is created, the system determines whether a condition record belonging to PB00 with valid conditions exists. If one does exist, then the condition type PBXX becomes irrelevant. The only situation where that is not the case is when the exclusion indicator (field KOMP-KZNEP) is set.

15.10.8 Calculation Schema for Condition Type PB00

For the standard condition type PB00, the calculation schema is called RM0002. This can be seen in the details of the PB00 condition type in the IMG, which can be accessed using navigation path, IMG • MATERIALS MANAGEMENT • PURCHASING • CONDITIONS • DEFINE PRICE DETERMINATION PROCESS • DEFINE CONDITION TYPES.

Condition types that are assigned to this calculation schema are discounts and surcharges, such as RA00 and RA01, or freight conditions, such as FRA1 and FRB1. The different condition types associated with the calculation schema can be seen in configuration using navigation path, IMG • Materials Management • Purchasing • Conditions • Define Price Determination Process • Define Calculation Schema.

The condition types of the values can be assigned or entered so that the actual price of a PO line item will depend on the values of these condition types. The PB00 or PBXX price is increased if there are valid condition records for freight or surcharges, but the price is reduced if valid condition records for discounts exist.

In the Purchasing functionality, there are three different prices:

▸ **Gross price**: Price excluding any possible discounts or surcharges, which is found using condition type PB00 or PBXX.

▸ **Net price**: Price taking discounts, surcharges, and possibly taxes into account.

▸ **Effective price**: Net price plus or minus delivery costs, cash discount, and various provisions for accrued costs or rebates.

The next section examines the reporting structure that is in place for purchasing.

15.11   Reporting

The Purchasing functionality in SAP ERP contains a large number of standard reports that can be run on an ad hoc basis.

15.11.1   Reporting Overview

Purchasing reports such as the archived purchasing documents (ME82), the subcontractor stick per vendor (ME20), and the monitoring confirmations program (ME2A) all can be run from the standard SAP ERP menu.

A number of companies use a large number of standard reports, SAP ERP queries, information from the Logistics Information System (LIS), and customized reports to provide them with an overall view of the Purchasing function.

Before customizing reports for a client, review the standard reports with the client to determine whether the standard reports will fit the client's purposes.

The next section reviews the release procedures that can be implemented for POs.

15.12   Release Procedures

The PO, as well as other purchasing documents, can be configured to follow a defined release path, depending on a number of factors that can be determined by the client.

15.12.1   Introduction to Release Procedures

The release procedure in SAP ERP is the process that allows documents to be held because of specific conditions and only released when they are approved or go through a series of approvals. These approvals are electronic signatures because the process is conducted within the SAP ERP system.

The release procedure is valid for purchase requisitions, POs, scheduling agreements, RFQs, contracts, and service entry sheets.

The main difference in the release procedure is between the internal and external documents. The internal document, the purchase requisition, can be released at the item level or the header level. In addition, the purchase requisition can be released with classification or without classification. However, it is important to realize that release with classification provides much more flexibility.

The external documents, such as the PO and the RFQ, can only be released at the header level and can only be released by the classification method.

15.12.2   Release with Classification for a Purchase Requisition

For the release with classification, the characteristics and appropriate classes need to be defined in the classification system. Remember that a class should be created for each purchasing document.

The configuration for releasing a purchase requisition without classification is already predefined in SAP ERP. The release with classification within the IMG must be configured.

The configuration for releasing purchase requisitions is found in the IMG using the path, IMG • MATERIALS MANAGEMENT • PURCHASING • PURCHASE REQUISITION • RELEASE PROCEDURE • PROCEDURE WITH CLASSIFICATION • SET UP PROCEDURE WITH CLASSIFICATION.

Represent Release conditions

Edit Characteristics

Each characteristic represents a release condition. Characteristics can be set up that describe the conditions that need to be satisfied for a release strategy to be assigned.

Characteristics can be created easily, using Transaction CT04, as they would be in classification. Classification is discussed in more detail in Chapter 27, Classification System.

Characteristic assigned to class

Edit Class

When the class is created, using Transaction CL02, the characteristics defined for the purchase requisition are assigned to the class. The class for the release strategy needs to be linked to class type 032, which is the class type for the release strategy.

Release Groups

The release groups, shown in Figure 15.34, are defined in standard SAP ERP. Release group 01 is defined for purchase requisitions; release group 02 is defined for POs.

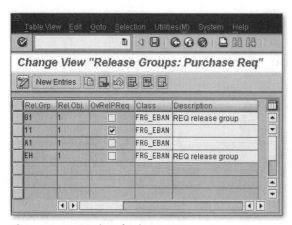

Figure 15.34 Display of Release Groups

Release Codes

The release code, shown in Figure 15.35, is a two-character field that usually represents the person responsible for the approval.

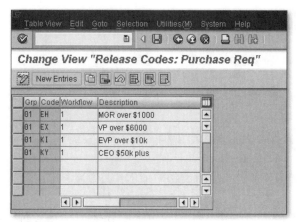

Figure 15.35 Display of Release Codes

can assign a user or a Role to the Release code.

Release Indicator

The release indicator, shown in Figure 15.36, represents the document that was released of the purchasing document.

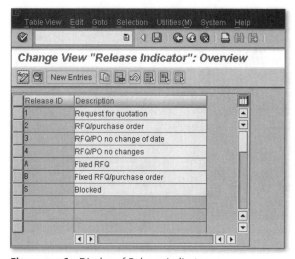

Figure 15.36 Display of Release Indicators

Release Strategy

The release strategy, as shown in Figure 15.37, defines the release codes with which a purchase document must be released and the sequence in which the release must be used.

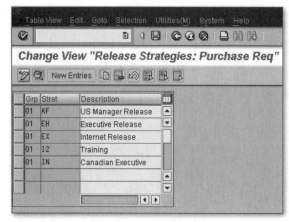

Figure 15.37 Display of Release Strategies

Workflow

Using the workflow configuration, the purchasing department can assign a user or role to a particular release code (see Figure 15.38).

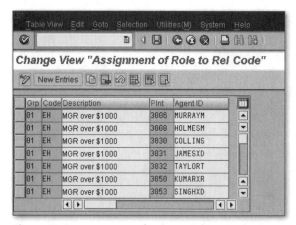

Figure 15.38 Assignment of Roles to Release Codes

In the next section, we look at some business-relevant examples involving PO functionality.

15.13   Business Examples – Purchase Orders

A PO is an external document issued by a purchasing department to send to a vendor. The PO contain details of the required products, the quantity of the products needed, and the price agreed to by the client and the vendor

15.13.1   Blocking a Purchase Order

PO line items can be blocked from processing, usually due to delivery issues, quality issues, or problems with the vendor.

Example

A U.S. based automotive parts manufacturer had been using U.S. and Canadian vendors for its basic raw materials but had recently approved vendors from Vietnam, China, and Korea. The MRP process generated purchase requisitions, which the purchasing department had begun to source with the vendors from Asia. The quality department tested the first deliveries of raw material prior to the material being moved into unrestricted stock. Although the material was within tolerances for all tests, the quality department found that the material barely passed. The quality team suggested to the manufacturing department that they allow a single batch of product into inventory so they could use it in a production order.

The manufacturing team used the single batch of the material in the next production order and monitored the process through the operations. The team asked the staff to perform a number of extra checks for each operation and report any defects to the management. The material passed each operation, but failed the last stress test. Based on the test, the manufacturing team asked the purchasing department to block all future POs from the vendor. The manufacturing team began working with the vendor to improve quality before accepting any more deliveries.

15.13.2   Outline Purchase Agreement

The outline purchase agreement is often referred to as a blanket or umbrella PO. A company creates outline purchase agreements with vendors who they regularly purchase the same item from.

Example

An Irish manufacturer of linen had a small number of local vendors before implementing SAP ERP, and due to the relationship with the vendors, the agreements were not formalized. After the SAP ERP implementation, the agreement with each vendor was established and entered into the system as necessary. Many vendors supplied material to the company, but no signed documents existed. The purchasing department spent a number of months deciding what documentation needed to exist and having that information entered in to the system. The team realized that the arrangements with many of the vendors were in fact blanket POs whereby the vendor would regularly supply material when called by someone from the purchasing team. These arrangements were formalized and entered into the system.

15.13.3 Scheduling Agreement

The scheduling agreement is a long-term purchase agreement, where the vendor delivers material based on a delivery schedule. The scheduling agreement is useful for companies who require materials based on their production schedule

Example

A Spanish manufacturer of household appliances consolidated its manufacturing facilities. As such, vendors who had been local to some sites now were considerable distances from the remaining manufacturing locations. As part of an agreement with local authorities, the company agreed to source materials for one year from these vendors despite the distances involved.

To minimize delivery costs to the vendors, the company arranged to accept items based on a scheduling agreement. This meant that instead of the vendor supplying material to the vendor at the discretion of the company, the vendor would supply material based on a once a week or once a month delivery schedule.

15.13.4 Contracts

A contract is an agreement between a company and a vendor for a predetermined quantity or predefined value. Each time a material or service is required, a PO is created that references the contract for delivery of the item. This type of PO can be referred to as a contract release order or a call off order.

Example

When an Austrian beverage company acquired a manufacturing facility from a company in Latvia, it decided not to acquire the bottling plant that made up the other half of the company. However, as part of the agreement with the Latvian company, the beverage company did agree to use the bottling plant for some of its bottling needs for a period of time.

The purchase of the manufacturing facility was dependent on the bottling plant receiving a one-year contact for 75,000 Euros. This contract covered the bottling of beverages produced at the manufacturing facility and another facility in Poland.

The contract was entered into the SAP ERP system as a value contract valid for one year. Each time the plant was used for bottling, a PO was created that referenced the existing value contract.

15.13.5 Releasing a Purchase Order

A PO can be subject to a release procedure, which means that depending on a number of factors, the PO can require release authorization from one or more users.

Example

A Dutch distributor of electronic components purchased items from vendors all over the world. Most vendors offered small batches of items and PO values were low. When a vendor from Vietnam was able to supply larger numbers of components, the purchasing department took advantage of the situation and requested larger quantities.

At that time, POs for electronic components were not covered by a release strategy because no single PO had exceeded 1000 Euros in value. The POs for the vendor in Vietnam were over 5000 Euros in value, which would have triggered a release strategy if the PO was for services or fixed assets.

The first of the delivery of components from the Vietnamese vendor arrived significantly later than promised. The quality department found that some items received did not match those ordered, and the quantities received were almost 15% lower than on the delivery note.

Based on the problems with the POs, the purchasing department proposed a release strategy for electronic components. The strategy required release authorization for POs over 1000 Euros and approval by a company board member for POs in excess of 5000 Euros.

15.14 Summary

The PO is probably the most familiar process in MM. The PO is important in that it provides material to the production process or requestor in a timely fashion, at the best available price, and with the best terms. For the MM user, and especially for a purchasing user, all aspects of creating and maintaining a PO should be studied. The MM user needs to understand links with Finance, for example, account assignments. Two areas that were discussed here, message output and release strategy, often create many issues for purchasing users. If POs cannot be printed, it can cause delays in receiving material, and understanding the process of printing purchasing output is very important. Release strategy can be complex to implement, but this depends on the client. Understanding how the release strategy is configured and how it works within the purchasing documents will help a client adopt a successful and straightforward release policy.

Chapter 16 will examine the functionality of external service management (ESM). We will discuss the key points such as the Service Master record and the Standard Service Catalog (SSC).

Companies purchase as many services as they do materials. Services can be managed and analyzed in the same way as any material. However, services have some unique aspects and require the SAP user to understand the differences to benefit from the ESM functionality.

16 External Service Management (ESM)

External service management (ESM) incorporates functionality that is relevant to the procurement and execution of services at a company. The Service Master record is the document that contains the information on a service. The service specifications are listed services that can make up a particular task or project that a company needs to procure.

Services can be planned — using a Service Master record — or unplanned, therefore not referencing a Service Master but rather referencing a monetary limit for the services performed. The service can be entered using a service entry sheet, whereby the documented hours can be approved and authorization given for payment.

The first section of this chapter describes the document that contains the basic information of a service, called the Service Master record.

16.1 Service Master Record

The Service Master record is the document that contains the basic information of the service, similar to a Material Master record.

The Service Master record can be entered using Transaction AC03, as shown in Figure 16.1 or via SAP Menu • Logistics • Materials Management • Service Master • Service • Service Master.

Figure 16.1 shows the entry of a description: "General Labor – Gardening Service." In addition, General Services is entered as the Service Category. The third entry for the Service Master record is the Base Unit of Measure of H.

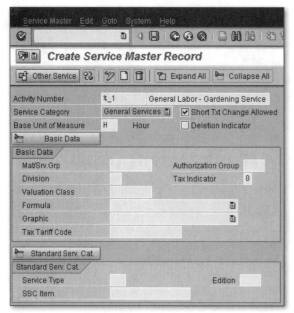

Figure 16.1 Entry Screen for Creating the Service Master Record

16.1.1 Activity Number

The Activity Number is similar to the material number, and this field can be defined for external or internal numbering. The number ranges can be defined in configuration using Transaction ACNR or via the navigation path, IMG • Materials Management • External Service Management • Service Master • Define Number Ranges.

16.1.2 Service Category

The Service category differentiates between different types of services, similar to what a material type does for materials. The service category, as shown in Figure 16.2, can be configured in the SAP IMG using the navigation path, IMG • Materials Management • External Service Management • Service Master • Define Service Category.

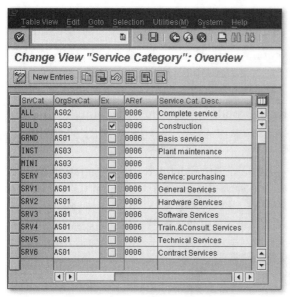

Figure 16.2   Configuration for Service Category

16.1.3   Material/Service Group

The material/service group (Mat/Srv.Grp) field allows the material group to be selected for grouping purposes. The selection is the same for the Service Master as it is for the Material Master.

16.1.4   Tax Indicator

The Tax Indicator for the Service Master allows the purchasing user to enter a "not taxed" code if the service is not taxed or a tax code for taxable service.

16.1.5   Valuation Class

The Valuation class for the Service Master is the same field that is used in the Material Master. Using the valuation class, the system can find the GL accounts that are associated with the service's financial postings.

16.1.6   Formula

The Formula field allows a defined formula to be chosen for a service that has been predefined in configuration. Depending on the service to be performed, the effort involved in performing a task may be definable by a number of variables.

For instance, there may be a formula for lawn maintenance that is variable depending on the size of the area to be maintained.

Formula can be defined in configuration using the navigation path, IMG • Materials Management • External Service Management • Formula for Quantity Determination • Define Formulas.

The formula is defined by entering a formula key and then the formula with variable names. The formula can use variables that are defined elsewhere in configuration. The formula must also have a base unit of measure.

The variables in the formula calculation must be defined in configuration also, as shown in Figures 16.3 and 16.4. The variables are defined using the navigation path, IMG • Materials Management • External Service Management • Formula for Quantity Determination • Specify Names of Formula Variables.

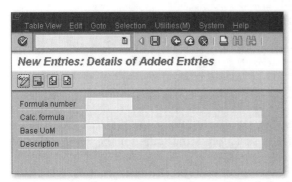

Figure 16.3 Configuration Screen to Create a Formula for Quantity Determination in the Service Master

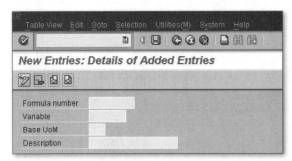

Figure 16.4 Configuration of Formula Variables for Service Master Calculation

16.1.7 Graphic

The Service Master includes a GRAPHIC field where the purchasing user can select a picture or graphic that can aid the supplier of the service. For example, the service may be to polish a finished good, and the company may have a specific way of completing the task. The graphic could be included with the PO or RFQ to ensure the service was performed correctly.

The next section discusses the Standard Service Catalog (SSC), which is a list of the service descriptions that is used to reduce the number of entries the purchasing user has to make.

16.2 Standard Service Catalog (SSC)

SSC is a record containing service descriptions that are used when the Service Master has not been created.

16.2.1 Overview

SSC is used to keep a standard list of the descriptions to eliminate the need for descriptions to be created each time a non-Service Master record is entered. This prevents a great deal of data duplication.

16.2.2 Creating a SSC Entry

The SSC entry can be created by using Transaction ML01 or by following the navigation path, SAP MENU • LOGISTICS • MATERIALS MANAGEMENT • SERVICE MASTER • STANDARD SERVICE CATALOG • CREATE.

On the initial screen for entering SSC, shown in Figure 16.5, the user can enter a SERVICE TYPE number and an EDITION, or version number. The detailed information for the service type includes a validity period, shown as a VALID FROM and VALID TO fields, and the SERVICE CATEGORY, which has been entered as SRV1.

The structure of the service type is defined where the structure can be divided into a number of meaningful sections. The maximum number of characters in the structure is 18.

For instance, in Figure 16.5, in the STRUCTURE OF SERVICE TYPE section, the SSC entry for service type 001 will have an 11-character structure made up of a 3-character string followed by four separate 2-character numeric strings. The field TxTMNo.

contains the five elements of the character, T1 through T5. Each of those has a FOR-MAT defined and a string length (LNGTH).

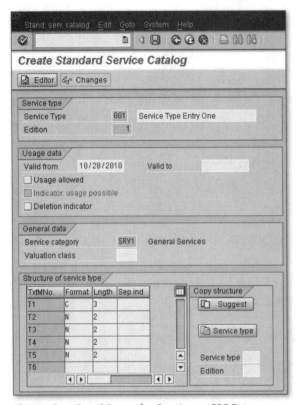

Figure 16.5 Detail Screen for Creating an SSC Entry

Figure 16.6 shows how the different elements of the structure are made up. The first four characters are the highest in the hierarchy in column T2, then the next three in column T3, and so on. The structure can be thought of as a service tree where the lowest elements of the tree are where the actual time is reported, that is, in column T5. The T5 levels show that the hours are collected for the ABAP Programming and the Documentation. In Figure 16.6, note that the unit of measure should only be added to the lowest level of the structure, T5; otherwise, an INVALID TEXT MODULE error will occur.

The next section reviews the conditions that are found in service management.

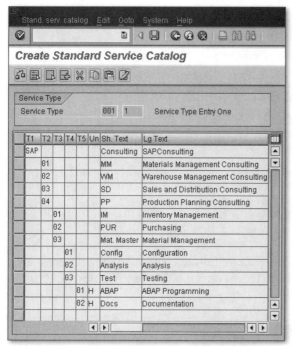

Figure 16.6 Elements of Service Type Hierarchical Structure

16.3　Conditions in ESM

Conditions are found in service management similar to those found in normal purchasing. Conditions apply to services such as discounts, surcharges, and taxes.

16.3.1　Total Price Condition

One method of entering a condition for a service is to enter a total price condition by using Transaction ML45 or via the navigation path, SAP MENU • LOGISTICS • MATERIALS MANAGEMENT • SERVICE MASTER • SERVICE • SERVICE CONDITIONS • FOR SERVICE • ADD.

This transaction allows the purchasing user to enter a condition that gives an overall estimate of the service to be performed over a certain time period.

In the example shown in Figure 16.7, the service has been given a total price condition (AMOUNT) of $50,000 for 2,000 hours (PER) of work VALID TO 11/21/2010. The total price condition can also be defined as a scale by pressing the F2 function key or by choosing GOTO • SCALES.

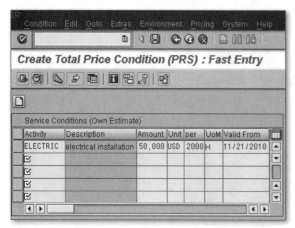

Figure 16.7 Total Price Condition for a Service for a Given Validity Period

The condition can be entered with a different value being valid for a different level of the scale as shown in Figure 16.8. The example in this figure shows the VALIDITY PERIOD as VALID TO 12/31/14.

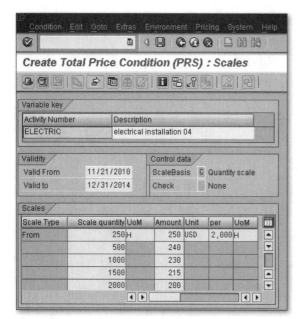

Figure 16.8 Condition Defined Using Scales for a Given Time Period

The CONTROL DATA section shows that the SCALEBASIS is set to C, which defines a quantity scale.

The SCALE TYPE shows that the scale is from one SCALE QUANTITY to another. The scale shows that from 250 hours to 500 hours, the AMOUNT is $250 per hour. From 500 hours to 1,000 hours, the amount is $240 per hour. The scaling continues until the upper limit is reached at 2,000 hours, in which any hours above that amount are charged at $200 per hour.

This section reviewed the conditions that can be applied to the Service Master record. The next section describes the actual procurement of services.

16.4   Procurement of Services

Companies purchase services in the same way that they purchase materials. A vendor supplies a service, rather than a material, and when that service has been received, an invoice is matched against the PO and a goods receipt document, which for a service could be time sheet.

16.4.1   Using a Purchase Order

Services can be purchased using the normal PO creation Transaction ME21. In addition to the entry of the VENDOR, PURCH. ORGANIZATION, PURCHASING GROUP, and DELIVERY DATE, the ITEM CATEGORY needs to be entered and set to D for services as shown in Figure 16.9.

Figure 16.10 shows the data-entry screen for the service specification. A number of items can be entered in this screen.

Overall Limit

An OVERALL LIMIT can be entered for all of the unplanned services on the PO. This limit may not be exceeded.

Expected Value

An EXPECTED VALUE of unplanned services can be entered. This value does not necessarily need to be equal to the overall limit, and the expected value can be exceeded unlike the overall limit. The expected value is the figure that is used if there is an appropriate release strategy in place.

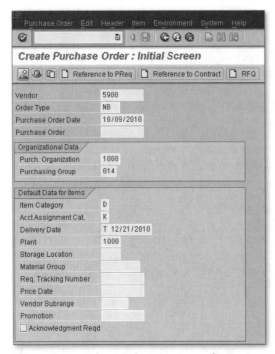

Figure 16.9 Purchase Order Entry Screen for Services

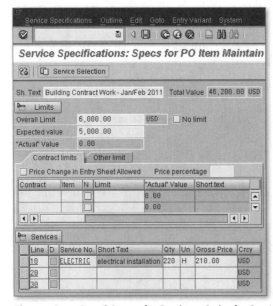

Figure 16.10 Detail Screen for Purchase Order for Services

"Actual" Value

This field is calculated by the system and is updated continually from service sheet entry or from goods receipt transactions.

Contract

The service PO can allow the purchasing user to add one or a number of purchase CONTRACTS. A limit to the services purchased against the contract can be added.

Services

Many services can be added to the PO that are required for the PO. The SERVICE NUMBER is entered with a quantity (QTY) and price per unit (UN) of measure. After the information is entered for the individual services, the PO can be completed after the header information shown in Figure 16.11 has been verified.

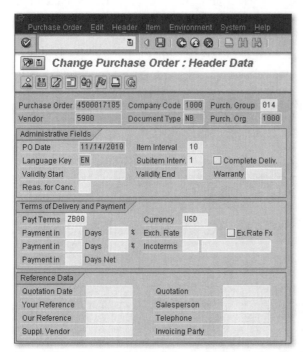

Figure 16.11 Header Information Screen for Service Purchase Order

The next section reviews the entry of services that have been performed and will require payment.

16.5 Entry of Services

When a supplier has completed a service or the service has been partially performed, the information can be entered into the SAP ERP system. The entry of this data is recorded on the service entry sheet. The information on the service entry sheet is for planned and unplanned services.

16.5.1 Service Entry Sheet

The service entry sheet is the transaction where data is entered with respect to the service that has been ordered via a PO. The service entry sheet is found using Transaction ML81N or via the path, SAP MENU • LOGISTICS • MATERIALS MANAGEMENT • SERVICE ENTRY SHEET • MAINTAIN.

The service entry sheet, shown in Figure 16.12, is based on the service in a PO, so the entry point for the transaction is the selection of a FOR PURCHASE ORDER number. After the PO number is entered, the SERVICE NO. that was entered as a line item in the PO is displayed; in this case, the service number is 3000011. The QUANTITY of the service, either partial or complete, can be added into the PO as well.

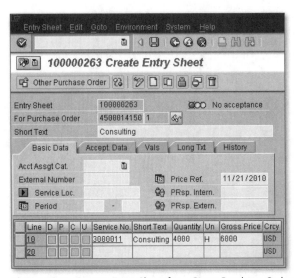

Figure 16.12 Service Entry Sheet for a Given Purchase Order

After the data has been entered, the data sheet can be accepted. Subsequent to being entered, the service-entry sheet will appear as accepted or ready for being accepted on the Transaction ML81N initial screen, shown in Figure 16.13.

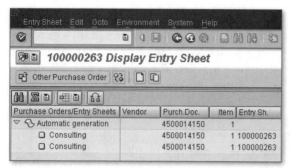

Figure 16.13 Purchase Order and One Service Entry Sheet Ready to Be Accepted

After no more service entry sheets are to be entered against the PO, the final entry indicator can be set by choosing ENTRY SHEET • SET STATUS • FINAL ENTRY.

The next section reviews the blanket PO that many companies use to purchase services.

16.6   Blanket Purchase Order
_ FoR low-Value Services.

A blanket PO is used when a client needs to purchase low-value services or materials and wants to perform this purchasing at a minimum cost. By reducing the effort needed by the purchasing department, the client can achieve some monitoring of the transaction at an economic cost.

16.6.1   Creating a Blanket Purchase Order

A blanket PO is created via the normal PO Transactions ME21 or Transaction ME21N, as shown in Figure 16.14.

Document Type

The DOCUMENT TYPE for a blanket order is FO rather than the normal document type for a PO, NB. When creating a blanket order, make sure that the correct document type is used.

Item Category

The item category for a blanket order is B for a limit order. This means that the PO will be created with a limit value and not a line item. This is not shown on the CREATE PURCHASE ORDER screen.

Validity Period

Using the blanket PO requires that the value limit be contained within a period of time. Therefore, the vendor has a limited period in which to submit invoices up to the value limit entered within the blanket order. The validity period is shown in Figure 16.14 by two fields, VALIDITY START and VALIDITY END.

Figure 16.14 Detail Information for a Blanket Purchase Order

Vendor Invoicing

The vendor will send invoices to the purchasing department with reference to the PO. The accounts payable (AP) department will process the invoices, if the invoices fall within the validity period of the blanket PO. The invoices will also only be processed if the total amount of the combined invoices from the vendor does not exceed the OVERALL LIMIT in the blanket PO, as shown in Figure 16.15. However, if there is no limit to the value amount of the invoices sent for the PO, the NO LIMIT indicator should be checked.

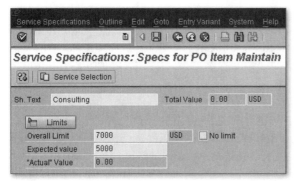

Figure 16.15   Value Limit Entry for a Blanket Purchase Order

16.7   Business Examples - External Service Management

ESM functionality is used for procurement and execution of services. The process uses the Service Master record as the repository for information about a service. The actual task that a company needs to have performed can be made up of a series of service specifications. For example, if a company needs a package for resale, the task would include specifications for removing the product from its original packaging, painting the product, repackaging the product, shrink-wrapping, and finally applying customer labeling.

16.7.1   Service Master Record

The Service Master record permits a company to enter information about a service the company requires. This can be a task that is regularly procured such as hazardous waste disposal services or less regularly required such as building painting. Service Master records are not used by every SAP ERP user, but the Service Master and the ESM functionality are useful when services are regularly purchased.

Example

A German auto parts manufacturer was a long-time user of SAP ERP but did not take advantage of ESM. The company had created Material Master records for the basic services that it procured such as IT support, janitorial, and warehouse equipment repair. The company created a PO for a specific number of hours of the service, based on the vendor's estimation. If the vendor spent more than the estimated hours, it sent an invoice for the actual hours. The company then paid the invoice.

A new head of purchasing asked for a review of service expenditure. The analysis found that for each PO for services of IT support, IT consulting, and network cabling, the vendors never invoiced an amount less than the estimate. This was not the case for other services that were procured, such as painting, plumbing, and electrical.

The purchasing team was asked to review the ESM to ascertain whether the functionality would permit the services to be accurately recorded. The conclusion was that if the services currently recorded as Material Master records were re-entered as Service Masters, the service entry function would provide the company with accurate values.

16.7.2 Procurement of Services

When a company needs to purchase a service, it is procured the same way in which materials are, with a PO. The service is performed and then recorded on a service entry, which could reflect the entries on a timesheet. When an invoice is received from the service supplier, it is matched against the PO and the service entry, which acts as the goods receipt.

Example

A Canadian university implemented SAP ERP for accounting, human resources, and some asset purchasing. The university decided to increase the number of staff using the Purchasing functionality by permitting the purchasing of services in SAP ERP. A project team was assembled to review the services the university used and which would be applicable to purchase through the system. After the review, the project team identified five potential services: external marketing, IT support, specialty printing, pest control, and snow removal. These services were not purchased on a regular schedule, and the length of the services performed would vary from one PO to the next.

16.7.3 Blanket Purchase Order

A blanket PO can be used when a company needs to procure a service on a regular basis. The purchasing department can create a single blanket PO rather than many individual POs. The benefit is that it reduces the effort on the part of the purchasing department; however, many companies prefer blanket orders to be for lower cost services.

Example

An Australian bottling company used Service Master records for approximately 20 services that were performed at the main facility. These included waste disposal, scrap metal removal, IT support, and office cleaning. The purchasing department introduced new guidelines for services, and part of the new process was the introduction of blanket POs. However, the new guidelines stated that the blanket orders could only be created for services less than $25 per hour. This meant that blanket POs could only be created for office cleaning and general waste disposal. The guidelines required timesheets to be used for the office cleaning staff and waste disposal team.

Issues arose almost immediately when the timesheets handed to the purchasing team from the office cleaning staff did not match the invoices sent by the office cleaning company. Discussions with the vendor revealed that the timesheets were completed on a weekly basis, but the invoice represented a monthly total. The purchasing department requested that the invoices be sent every two weeks and in return the invoices would be paid in 14 days rather than the agreed upon 30 days.

16.8 Summary

In this chapter, we discussed the external service management (ESM) functionality. Companies purchase services, as well as materials, and the functionality in ESM allows the purchasing department to influence how services are purchased and to monitor their consumption of those services. As more companies use SAP ERP to purchase and record service usage, purchasing personnel will be required to be fully familiar with this functionality. The topics in this chapter should help you understand more fully the procurement of services, which will help you more competently assist your client on this subject.

The next chapter examines the methods used in consumption-based planning (CBP), which is a planning method used in MM that is based on past consumption of materials.

In any company, material is consumed in the production of items, by performing a service, or by daily operations. To replenish the stock of material, the company can use consumption-based planning (CBP) to determine when future purchases need to be made.

17   Consumption-Based Planning

Consumption-based planning (CBP) is a planning method based on past consumption of a material and using the entered forecast to determine future material requirements. CBP is not calculated via independent or dependent requirements such as those found in master production scheduling. CBP is initiated either by the level of material hitting a defined reorder point or by the forecast requirements calculated using consumption values found in the Material Master record.

This chapter reviews the functionality of CBP. It is important for MM consultants to understand the touchpoints with other components, and CBP is a key integration with the PP functionality.

17.1   Master Data in CBP

This section reviews the mater data that is used in CBP. This data can be found in the Material Master record.

17.1.1   Material Master Record

Consumption figures for a material are stored in the Material Master record and are calculated for unplanned and total consumption. Either figure can be viewed and/or updated in the Material Master record.

Transaction MM02 is used to view/change the consumption values and can be found using the navigation path, SAP Menu • Logistics • Materials Management • Material Master • Change • Immediately.

The user enters the material number, clicks the organizational level icon, and then requests a view, such as MRP or Forecasting. On the detail screen, the user can click the Additional Data icon to see a number of tabs, including the Consumption tab.

The consumption figures for a material are held within the Material Master record and are updated by transaction data from Inventory Management. The data can be viewed in the format shown by the PERIOD INDICATOR; in Figure 17.1, the format is M for monthly consumption.

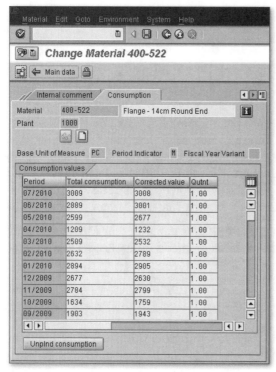

Figure 17.1 Total Consumption Figures per Month for Material Using Transaction MM02

The CONSUMPTION screen for the material is shown in Figure 17.1. All of the consumption figures for the material are displayed in chronological order. The user can view the unplanned consumption and the total consumption per time period. If the material has been entered, and consumption data are missing, the data can be added in this screen for the relevant time periods.

17.1.2   Planning Calendar

The planning calendar is used to define the period lengths for CBP at the plant level, as shown in Figure 17.2. The planning calendar is defined by using Transaction MD25 or using the navigation path, SAP MENU • LOGISTICS • MATERIALS MANAGEMENT • MRP • MASTER DATA • PLANNING CALENDAR • CREATE PERIODS.

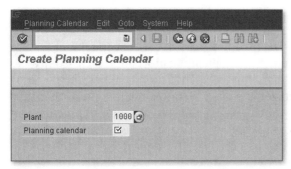

Figure 17.2 Initial Screen for Transaction MD25

The planning calendar is created for each plant. When creating a new planning calendar, you can enter a three-character code for the new calendar.

When creating the planning calendar, you can define certain variables, such as in Figure 17.3, where the calendar has been flagged to start a period as a weekday. Other options allow the first day of the period to be a workday or not a workday, previous to a non-working day, or after a non-working day. The planning calendar ascertains whether a day is a working day or a non-working day by referencing the relevant factory calendar configured in the IMG.

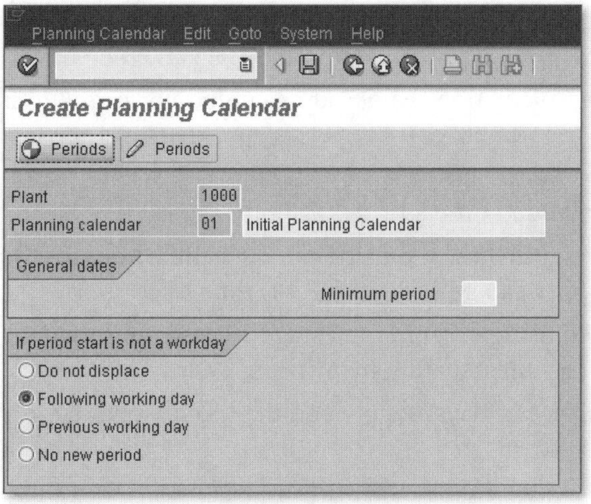

Figure 17.3 Variables for a New Planning Calendar

Now that we have discussed the data used in CBP, the next section goes into detail about the planning process at the plant and storage location level.

17.2   Planning Process

CBP procedures are simple materials planning procedures used to set and achieve targets with minimal input. Therefore, these planning procedures are used in areas without in-house production. In planning with production facilities, the planning run follows this path: Check if material should be in the planning run, check if a material requirement exists, carry out lot-sizing, calculate schedule of procurement proposal, and determine the correct proposal, such as planned order, requisition, or schedule line. This planning can be achieved at the plant or storage location level.

17.2.1   Planning at the Plant Level

The planning process normally takes place at the plant level. Planning at the storage location level can also be defined. The following processes are involved in CBP:

1. Initially, SAP ERP checks the planning file entries. The system will check whether a material has been changed, relevant to MRP, and whether this material needs to be included in the planning run.

2. SAP ERP then completes a net-requirements calculation for every material. SAP ERP checks the available warehouse stock and receipts from purchasing and production to ensure that the requirement quantity is covered. If the net requirement quantity is not covered, a procurement proposal is then created.

3. SAP ERP performs a lot-sizing calculation. Values are rounded up or down, if necessary.

4. SAP ERP performs scheduling to determine the start and finish dates of the procurement proposals, such as planned orders or requisitions.

5. SAP ERP creates planned orders, purchase requisitions, or schedule lines for the procurement proposal. A supplier can be assigned at this time also.

6. Critical situations are identified using exception messages. These are situations where the planner has to process the situation manually.

7. Finally, SAP ERP calculates the actual days' supply and the receipt days' supply of the material.

17.2.2   Planning at the Storage Location Level

The planning of material is normally performed at the plant level, with the total amounts of all storage locations taken into account. However, there are occasions when a client may not want to perform planning in that manner.

One common reason for storage-location planning is logistical. Clients with storage locations that are remote from the associated plant may want to perform planning at a lower level. In addition, storage locations that are unique — for example, locations that only contain a certain type of material relevant to plant maintenance or repairs — may want to plan these separately.

Two options are available to the client to identify some storage locations as unique for planning purposes: plan at the storage location level, or exclude the storage location from planning.

Storage Location Planning

In this scenario, the planning department needs to ensure that the reorder level for the material and the replenishment quantities are defined at the storage-location level.

For the planning to be completed at the storage-location level, the storage location MRP fields in the Material Master need to be completed. Depending on the version of SAP your client uses, these fields may appear on a different MRP screen from that in Figure 17.4.

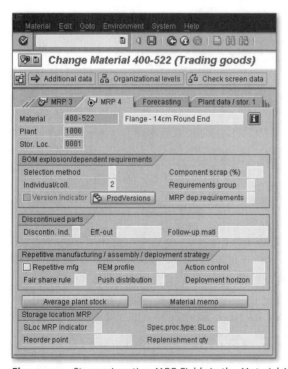

Figure 17.4 Storage Location MRP Fields in the Material Master Relevant for Storage Location Planning

The procurement proposals for the storage location that is planned separately will not be part of the plant stock levels.

Excluding Storage Location from Planning

A storage location can be excluded from planning, and the stock will not be included in the available stock totals. The storage location can be excluded from the planning process by selecting the appropriate value for the SLoc MRP INDICA-TOR for the storage location, as shown in Figure 17.5.

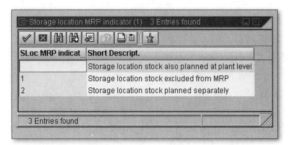

Figure 17.5 Options Available for the Storage Location MRP Indicator in the Material Master

This section described the planning process required for requirements planning. The next section examines the planning evaluation functionality of MRP and the stock/requirements list.

17.3 Planning Evaluation

Two methods are available to evaluate the planning results in CBP: the MRP list and the stock/requirements list.

17.3.1 MRP List

During the planning run, the nature of the MRP lists depends on how the creation indicators are configured. The basic MRP list contains the planning result information for the material. The MRP list is the initial working document for the MRP controller to work from. The MRP list is a static list, so changes are not reflected on the list until the next planning run.

The MRP list for an individual material can be displayed using Transaction MD05 or via the navigation path, SAP MENU • LOGISTICS • MATERIALS MANAGEMENT • MRP • MRP • EVALUATIONS • MRP LIST – MATERIAL.

In Figure 17.6, the MRP list shows that a purchase requisition has been created because the stock has fallen below the safety stock level. The error messages in the dialog box relate to the column EX on the MRP list.

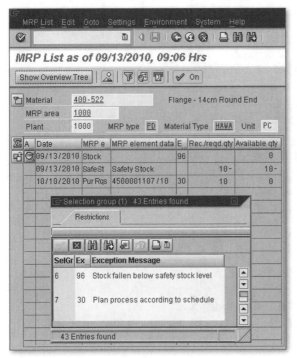

Figure 17.6 MRP List for a Material Fallen Below Its Safety Stock Level

17.3.2 Stock/Requirements List

The STOCK/REQUIREMENTS LIST screen shows the current stock and requirements situation. The stock/requirements list is dynamic, as it is updated each time it is displayed, unlike the MRP list. The stock/requirements list shown in Figure 17.7 displays two purchase requisitions that would not appear on the MRP list for the same material. The requisitions were created after the MRP list was created and will not appear until another MRP list is created via planning.

The stock/requirements list for an individual material can be displayed using Transaction MD04 or via the navigation path, SAP MENU • LOGISTICS • MATERIALS MANAGEMENT • MRP • MRP • EVALUATIONS • STOCK/REQMTS LIST.

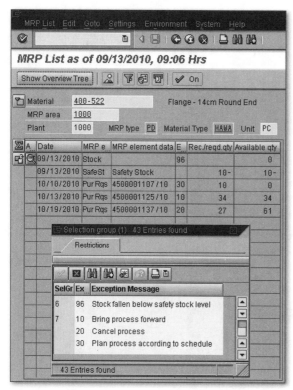

Figure 17.7 Stock/Requirements List for the Same Material, But Showing the New Purchase Requisitions

This section examined the functionality of the MRP list and the stock/requirements list. The next section reviews the procurement proposal that arises from the planning process.

17.4 Procurement Proposal

During the planning process, the system determines the requirements for the material and creates procurement proposals based on settings defined by the purchasing department. The procurement proposals created by the system specify when stock movements should be made and the quantity of stock required.

Three types of procurement proposals are used in the planning process: purchase requisitions, schedule lines, and planned orders.

17.4.1 Purchase Requisitions

The planning process determines that a purchase requisition is required for material that is procured externally. The purchase requisition can be seen on the MRP list as a line item. The planning process also determines the quantity for that PO. The MRP controller reviews the MRP list and determines whether the purchase requisition is appropriate before passing it on to the purchasing department. The purchase requisition is an internal planning element that can be changed or deleted if necessary.

17.4.2 Schedule Lines

A schedule line is the result of the planning process when the material is procured externally, and the material has a source and a scheduling agreement in place. The schedule line is unlike the purchase requisition, which involves a fixed agreement and, therefore, cannot be changed. This makes it much more flexible than the purchase requisition.

17.4.3 Planned Orders

The planned order is a result of the planning process for materials that are produced internally. Like the purchase requisition, the planned order is an internal planning element that can be changed or deleted if deemed necessary. The planned order can be converted to a production or a process order, depending on the production methods of the client. If the material is procured externally as well as produced in house, the planned order can be converted to a purchase requisition. The MRP controller can use Transaction MD14 to convert an individual planned order or use the navigation path, SAP MENU • LOGISTICS • MATERIALS MANAGEMENT • MRP • MRP • PLANNED ORDER • CONVERT TO PURCHASE REQUISITION • INDIVIDUAL CONVERSION.

17.5 Business Examples – Consumption-Based Planning

CBP is based on a company's past consumption and the forecast of future consumption. The planning is triggered when the stock level for a material drops below the reorder point. CBP is a simple planning tool that is particularly suitable for companies that do not have wide variations in raw material consumption.

17.5.1 Planning Process

CBP can be performed at the plant or storage location level. During the planning run, the system performs a number of steps — it checks planning file for changes, carries out a net requirements calculation, performs the lot-sizing calculation, carries out the scheduling to determine start and end dates, and finally creates planned orders or purchase requisitions.

Example

A Florida-based industrial tools manufacturer implemented SAP ERP five years ago for the Accounting, Human Resources, and Inventory Management functions. The company was considering expanding the use of SAP ERP to the purchasing and production areas. A team from the production department was assembled to review the finished goods and determine what would be the best method to use for planning the components that are used. The team's analysis of the products found that they could implement MRP, which would require BOMs to be developed for all finished goods. The BOMs were available on a PC system, but these had not been updated in a number of years and, accuracy was a major concern.

The team believed that using CBP would be acceptable for the majority of raw materials. This required the consumption data to be entered into SAP ERP from the existing PC-based manufacturing software.

To pilot the project, the consumption data for five products was entered into SAP ERP, and the team simulated changes in the inventory balances. This triggered the planning process for the raw materials, and the resulting requirements were deemed to be satisfactory for the project to be extended to other raw materials.

17.5.2 Planning Evaluation

Two methods are available to evaluate the planning results in CBP: the MRP list and the stock/requirements list. The one big difference is that the stock/requirements list updates after every transaction whereas the MRP list updates only after each MRP run. This means that between MRP runs, the MRP list will not change.

Example

The Florida-based industrial tools manufacturer decided to extend the use of its SAP ERP system to the Production Planning function after the successful pilot project. The company decided to use CBP for the components that were used in the company's top-selling products, which covered approximately 400 components. The consumption data was loaded into SAP ERP from the company's legacy PC-based manufacturing system, and a two-week parallel run was planned. After the data was loaded, the MRP process was run on a nightly basis, and the results were compared against the values from the PC-based system. The conclusion was that the requirements generated from the MRP list were accurate when compared with the legacy system. The production staff believed that SAP ERP gave them an advantage because they could manipulate the purchase requisition prior to it being handed off to the purchasing department. This feature meant they had a level of control that they did not have previously.

17.6 Summary

This chapter described the basics of CBP. This type of planning is found in the vast majority of manufacturers today. This functionality shows the integration between the Production Planning functionality and the Purchasing functionality. It is important to understand how purchasing is involved in planning and what responsibilities the purchasing department has to provide timely action to ensure that material is available for production.

It is important to understand CBP because it is part of the MM functionality. If a company does not have an in-house production facility, the CBP can be used to drive planning.

Chapter 18 further develops the theme of planning with an examination of the functionality of material requirements planning (MRP).

Material requirements planning (MRP) has to meet three objectives simultaneously: first, to ensure that material is available for production and delivery to customers; second, to maintain the lowest possible level of inventory; and third, to plan manufacturing activities, delivery schedules, and purchasing.

18 Material Requirements Planning

Manufacturing companies face the problem that their customers requires finished goods available in less time than it takes to produce them. To achieve this, manufacturing companies need to adopt a planning strategy, and this is found in material requirements planning (MRP).

Companies need to control the quantities of materials they purchase, plan which materials are to be produced and in what quantities, and ensure that they are able to meet current and future customer demand, at the lowest possible cost.

MRP was first developed in the early 1960s and has been modified and improved to the level found today in SAP ERP and in the methodology adopted by organizations such as the American Production and Inventory Control Society (APICS).

There are three procedures within MRP:

▶ Reorder-point planning

3 Procedures.

▶ Forecast-based planning

▶ Time-phased planning

Let's examine these in detail now.

18.1 Reorder-Point Planning

The basic premise behind reorder-point planning is that procurement is triggered when the sum of the stock in the plant, plus the firmed receipts, falls below the reorder point.

18.1.1   Manual Reorder-Point Planning

In manual reorder-point planning, the planner manually enters the REORDER POINT and the SAFETY STOCK in the individual Material Master record, Transaction MM01. Other key fields that are entered onto the MRP screen on the Material Master include MRP CONTROLLER and the MRP TYPE as shown in Figure 18.1.

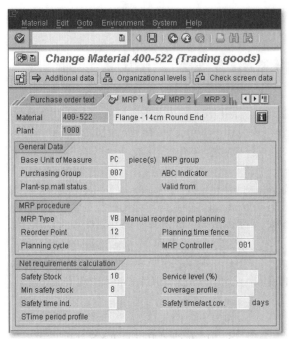

Figure 18.1   Material with MRP Type VB for Manual Reorder-Point Planning

18.1.2   Automatic Reorder-Point Planning

In automatic reorder-point planning, the system calculates the reorder level and the safety stock level. To do this, the system uses past consumption data of the material to forecast future requirements of the material. The system then uses these forecast values to calculate the reorder level and the safety stock level. Figure 18.2 shows a material with the MRP type that facilitates automatic reorder-point planning.

This section described the functionality of reorder-point planning. The next section reviews the functionality of the forecast-based planning scenario.

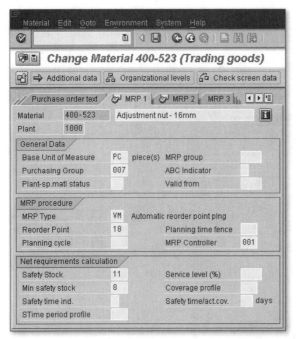

Figure 18.2 Material with MRP Type VM for Automatic Reorder-Point Planning Based on Consumption

18.2 Forecast-Based Planning

Like reorder-point planning, forecast-based planning relies on the historical material consumption. Similar to reorder-point planning, forecast-based planning uses the historical values, whereas the forecasting program determines the forecast values and future requirements. The forecast values are used in MRP as the forecast requirements.

The forecast-based planning procedure, MRP TYPE VV shown in Figure 18.3, can be described in three phases:

▶ The system takes the forecast it has produced and makes sure that every future period forecast is covered by the available stock, planned purchases, or planned production. If the forecast is greater than the total of the available stock, planned purchases, or planned production, then the system will generate a procurement proposal (purchase requisition or planned order).

[handwritten: system will generate a PR, or planned Order]

▶ The procurement proposals are checked against the lot-size procedures in the Material Master, and forecasts are combined or not, depending on the lot size required for purchasing/production.

▶ On each of the procurement proposals, the system defines the date on which the proposal must be converted into a production/process order or a PO.

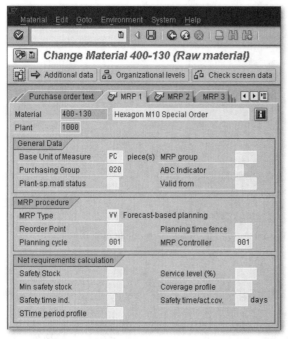

Figure 18.3 Material with MRP Type VV for Forecast-Based Planning

This section described the functionality of forecast-based planning. The next section reviews the functionality of time-phased planning.

18.3 Time-Phased Planning

The premise of time-phased planning is that the date of the planned requirement should coincide with a known date, such as the date when the supplier delivers. If delivery from a vendor is always on the same day, then this can be used in the planning of a material. This planning procedure requires that the material forecasting be completed for the material, which can be done within the Material

Master record. Figure 18.4 shows the forecast amounts that are calculated within the Material Master.

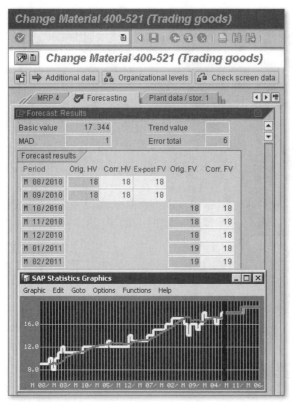

Figure 18.4 Material Forecast Calculated Within the Material Master Transaction MM02 and the Forecast Graphic Tool

To run the time-phased planning procedure, the MRP type needs to be entered as R1, as shown in Figure 18.5. The user enters the PLANNING CYCLE, and sets the LOT SIZE LOT-FOR-LOT ORDER QUANTITY.

During the planning run, the system takes into account the scheduled delivery dates. The system calculates against the forecast requirements and determines whether the forecast can be covered by the total of the available stock, planned purchases, or planned production. Again, if there is a shortfall based on the scheduled deliveries, then a procurement proposal is generated. Because lot-for-lot sizing is used, the procurement proposal covers the shortage.

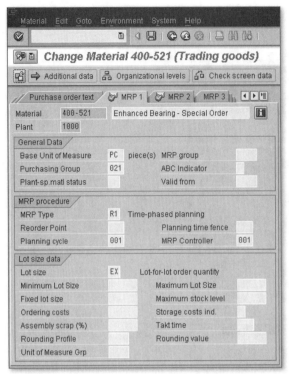

Figure 18.5 Prerequisites for Time-Phased Planning in the Material Master Record

18.4 Business Examples – Material Requirements Planning

Companies use MRP to control the quantities of materials they purchase, plan which and how many materials are to be produced, and ensure that they are able to meet current and future customer demand. MRP can be run using reorder-point, forecast-based, or time-phased planning

18.4.1 Reorder Point Planning

Reorder-point planning uses the material's reorder level as the trigger to procure additional material to be delivered to the plant. The process calculates the material stock level as the sum of the stock in the plant plus any confirmed receipts. If this figure falls below the reorder level, which is found on the material master record, then during an MRP run, the system will trigger a purchase requisition or planned order to be created.

Example

An Ohio-based saw blades manufacturer sold its products to tool manufacturers and home improvement stores. The company's products required few raw materials, and sales showed only minor fluctuations. When its parent company implemented SAP ERP, the manufacturer migrated from its simple in-house software packages. The company used a small subset of SAP ERP transactions, including procurement and accounting, but not production.

The management encouraged the department heads to use as much of the SAP ERP functionality as possible if it reduced effort and costs. One area that the production team thought may help was to begin running MRP for raw materials, not based on consumption or forecast, but by simple reorder levels. The company had a small number of raw materials, and the lead time from vendors had always been long but fairly static over a number of years. The production department believed they could save significant effort if they ran MRP and let the system generate requisitions based on the reorder level of the raw materials. After some modification of reorder levels and the number of times MRP was run each week, the company did achieve a stable position where reorder-point planning was generating requisitions for the purchasing department.

18.4.2 Forecast-Based Planning

Forecast-based planning uses the historical and the forecasted consumption of the material to determine whether additional stock is needed. The system takes the forecast and ensures that every future period forecast is covered by available stock, planned purchases, or planned production. If the forecast is greater than the sum total of the available stock, planned purchases, or planned production, then the system will generate a purchase requisition or planned order.

Example

An Austrian beverage company had been aware that certain products sold in greater volumes at certain times of the year. The sales department led the production plan because they believed they knew what customers wanted, even if the sales figures did not accurately reflect this.

The production facilities in Austria and Germany worked with one production plan and produced items based on the sales forecast. However, after two years of inaccurate forecasting, the warehouses at the production facilities were holding a large volume of product that was quickly coming to the end of its shelf life. The production team was being told by the sales team and their forecast to continue to make the same product that was sitting in the warehouse. The company's management realized that modifications needed to be made to relieve the situation.

The production team asked for permission to plan a number of products using forecast-based planning. This would take into account the past consumption and more accurately predict the requirements.

The team used five finished goods as their test, and the overall requirements showed a significant reduction. The sales management disputed the results because they believed that knowledge of consumer behavior had been excluded. The company's management asked that the production team work with the sales department to understand their needs but to continue to expand the use of forecast-based planning at the facilities.

18.4.3 Time-Phased Planning

Time-phased planning is the procedure where the materials are planned in a specific time interval. For example, if a vendor always delivers its products on the third Monday of each month, then it is sensible to plan the material according to the same specific time interval.

Example

An Irish linen manufacturer had been operating without forecasting or planning since implementing SAP ERP. The production staff believed they knew that the capacity of the manufacturing facility was fairly static, and based on years of experience, they could determine the raw material requirements.

This changed when the company began to receive large orders from the United States, and the facility was unable to cope with the demand. In the past, the company had just given customers a delivery date that was far into the future, but management wanted to try to fill these orders and proposed to use a third party to help with manufacturing. The third-party manufacturer was a former competitor that had moved away from linen production but still had manufacturing capacity to help fulfill the orders from abroad. The facility was a few miles away, and the raw material could be trucked over.

The production staff realized that they could not accurately determine the raw material requirements of the two facilities and were forced into looking at the MRP procedures in SAP ERP. Because the factories were located in rural Ireland, the ability to get raw material to the sites quickly was extremely difficult, and vendors were unlikely to accommodate changes to their schedule. The decision was made to adopt the time-phased procedure for the majority of materials because the company could always rely on specific dates on when the vendors would deliver. Other raw material that was delivered by post or package carrier would use the regular reorder-point planning.

18.5 Summary

This chapter described the three main objectives for MRP. MM users should understand the basics of production planning because there are many touch-points between MM and PP. Terms such as reorder points, MRP types, lot sizes, and forecast models should be familiar to those who work alongside production personnel.

MRP is an integration area with PP. It is important to understand the mechanism of the planning function because it drives a number of scenarios in MM, especially the procurement proposals.

Chapter 19 examines the functionality of forecasting in SAP ERP. Despite being part of the MM functionality, forecasting can be extremely complex, depending on the industry. As an MM consultant, you will be expected to understand the functionality of forecasting.

Business decisions are based on forecasts. Decisions of material require-ments are based on forecasts of future conditions. Forecasts are needed continually, and, over time, the impact of the forecast on actual results is measured, the initial forecasts are updated, and decisions are modified.

19 Forecasting

Forecasting is a prediction of what will occur in the future and, therefore, is an uncertain process. Because of the uncertainty, the accuracy of a forecast is as impor-tant as the outcome predicted by the forecast. This chapter focuses on the key fore-casting functions that are available in SAP ERP, including the forecast models, the parameters in forecasting, and the forecasting options.

19.1 Forecast Models

Forecast modeling has been devised to aid in forecasting particular events. The forecast model is designed around factors that the client believes are important in influencing the future use of a material. The client also uses past performance of a material to determine future use. Both of these methods should produce an accurate forecast.

A number of forecast models are available in the Forecasting functionality within SAP ERP, as shown in Figure 19.1.

19.1.1 Constant Model

The constant model assumes that the use of material is constant. This is not to say that the use of material is the same each month, but that the variation in material usage fluctuates little, and a constant mean value is calculated. This forecast model would apply to electricity consumption in an office, for example. Although sum-mer months would raise electricity consumption due to increased air conditioning use, the consumption would not vary a great deal from the mean value.

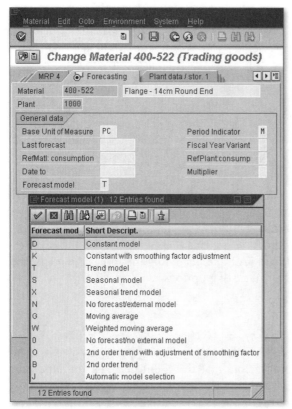

Figure 19.1 Forecast Models Accessed When Adding Forecast Information to a Material Master Record

19.1.2   Trend Model

The trend model is used when there is an identifiable increase or decrease of material over a period of time. The trend may include areas of movement away from the trend, but the overall movement follows the trend. For example, a downward trend over time may represent the use of printer cartridges for top-selling printers that become obsolete over a short period of time, perhaps only 12 to 18 months. As the purchase and use of the printer becomes less, the cartridges used in that printer will slow also.

19.1.3   Seasonal Model

The seasonal model affects many businesses due to the weather, holidays, or vacations. The seasonal model is defined as a pattern that repeats for each period.

For example, the annual seasonal pattern has a cycle that is 12 periods long, if the periods are months. A seasonal model may be applicable to a company that makes patio furniture, which experiences a greater demand in the months of May through September, and this pattern is repeated each year.

19.1.4 Seasonal Trend Model

The seasonal trend model is similar to the seasonal model, except that instead of the same pattern occurring each period, the pattern is moving further away from the mean value, either positive or negative. For example, California sparkling wine manufacturers can see a positive seasonal trend. They have a seasonal pattern in demand for their products, and for them, the seasonal pattern has a positive trend, as sales have continued to rise. A negative seasonal trend can be shown in beer manufacturers who have a seasonal market, but the overall trend continues to be negative as sales slow each year.

This section examined a number of forecast models that are used in the majority of companies. The next section reviews the parameters that are entered into the Material Master record.

19.2 Forecast Parameters

The parameters on the Forecast screen in the Material Master record can be predefined using a forecast profile. The forecast profile allows the user to create a default that copies the parameter values directly into the Material Master record.

19.2.1 Create Forecast Profile

The forecast profile for the forecast parameters can be created using Transaction MP80 or via the navigation path, SAP MENU • LOGISTICS • MATERIALS MANAGEMENT • MATERIAL MASTER • PROFILE • FORECAST PROFILE • CREATE.

In the initial screen of Transaction MP80, shown in Figure 19.2, the user can select which parameters to enter values for. In addition, the user can determine whether the value is defaulted into the Material Master or the parameter is write-protected and cannot be changed in the Material Master.

The fields shown in Figure 19.3 for the FORECAST PROFILE CREATE: DATA SCREEN are described in the following section.

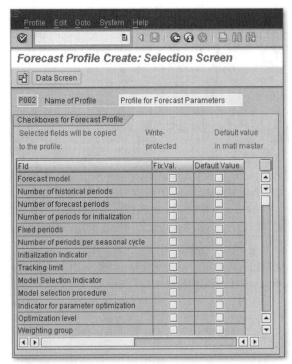

Figure 19.2 Selection Screen for Transaction MP80 for Creating a Forecast Profile

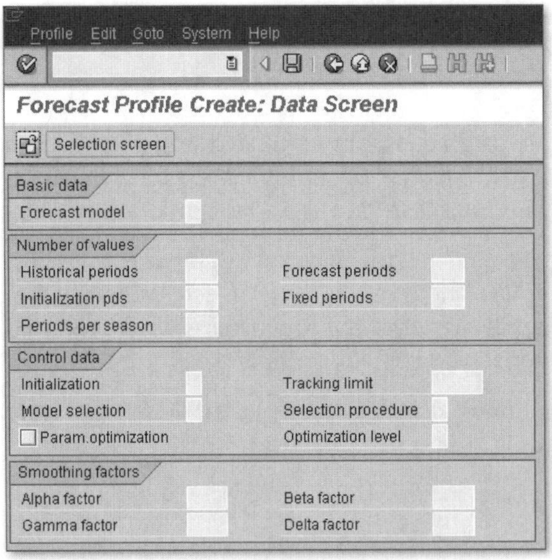

Figure 19.3 Detail Screen for Transaction MP80

Forecast Model

The FORECAST MODEL field has been discussed in Section 19.1, Forecast Models. The selection for the forecast model can be made from the following choices:

► N: No forecast model or external model.
► J: Automatic model selection.
► D: Constant model.
► K: Constant with smoothing factor adjustment.
► T: Trend model.
► S: Seasonal model.
► X: Seasonal trend model.
► G: Moving average model.
► W: Weighted moving average model.
► B: Second order trend model.
► O: Second order trend with smoothing factor adjustment.

Historical Periods

The number of HISTORICAL PERIODS entered into this field is used to calculate the forecast. If this field is left blank, no periods will be used in the profile.

Forecast Periods

The number entered in this field is the number of periods over which the forecast will be calculated.

Number of Periods for Initialization

This number is for the historical values that the user wants to be used for the forecast initialization. If the field is blank, no historical values are used to initialize the forecast.

Fixed Periods

The FIXED PERIODS field is used to avoid fluctuations in the forecast calculation or because production can no longer react to changed planning figures. The forecast will be fixed for the number of periods entered in this field.

Number of Periods per Seasonal Cycle

If your client uses a seasonal forecast model, then the PERIODS PER SEASON field can be used to define the number of periods that make up a season for this material.

Initialization Indicator

If the forecast needs to be initialized, the INITIALIZATION indicator can be set to allow the system to initialize the forecast. It also allows manual initialization.

Tracking Limit

The TRACKING LIMIT is the value that specifies the amount by which the forecast value may deviate from the actual value. This figure can be entered to three decimal places.

Model Selection

This field is only active if there is no value entered for the FORECAST MODEL. This allows the system to select a model automatically. To aid the system in choosing a forecast model, the MODEL SELECTION field can be set to one of the following three indicators:

► T: Examine for a trend.

► S: Examine for seasonal fluctuations.

► A: Examine for a trend and seasonal fluctuations.

Selection Procedure

The SELECTION PROCEDURE field is used when the system is selecting a forecast model. There are two selection procedures to select from:

► Procedure 1 performs a significance test to find the best seasonal or trend pattern.

► Procedure 2 carries out the forecast for all models and then selects the model with the smallest mean absolute deviation.

Indicator for Parameter Optimization

If the indicator for PARAM.OPTIMIZATION is set, then the system will use the smoothing factors for the given forecast model. If the indicator is not set, then the smoothing factors are not used, and the forecast will have greater variances from the mean value.

Optimization Level

This indicator can be set to fine, middle, or rough. The finer the optimization level, the more accurate the forecast, but this comes at the expense of processing time.

Smoothing Factors

Some form of random variation is found in a collection of data taken over time, that is, in consumption of material over a given period. There are methods for reducing or canceling the effect due to random variation. A common technique used in forecasting is smoothing. This technique clarifies the underlying trend, seasonal, and cyclic elements.

Four smoothing factors can be used in the forecast profile:

▶ ALPHA FACTOR: The smoothing factor for the basic value.

▶ BETA FACTOR: The smoothing factor for the trend value.

▶ GAMMA FACTOR: The smoothing factor for the seasonal index.

▶ DELTA FACTOR: The smoothing factor for the mean absolute deviation.

This section examined the parameters that are entered in the Material Master for forecasting. The next section discusses the forecast options, including the manual and automatic forecast model selections.

19.3 Forecast Options

The forecast model selection can be made manually, or the system can automatically select the forecast model using option J in the FORECAST MODEL field in the Material Master record.

19.3.1 Manual Forecast Model Selection

The forecast model selection is often determined manually because companies have been developing forecast models for many years. Large companies have departments of analysts working on historical data to fine-tune forecasts. Given this wealth of analysis, your client may want to manually determine the forecast model.

19.3.2 Automatic Forecast Model Selection

If your clients have not developed forecast models in the past, they may want to allow the SAP ERP system to analyze the historical data and determine an appropriate forecast model to use. After the model has been selected, the client can use this as a starting point and make modifications in the future.

To set the system to automatically determine a forecast model for the material, the user must complete two fields in the FORECASTING screen of the Material Master, as shown in Figure 19.4.

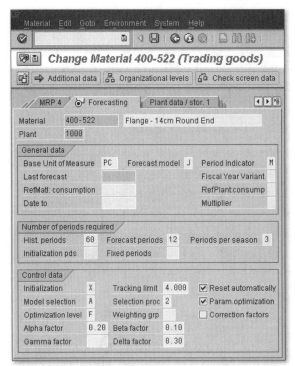

Figure 19.4 Settings for Automatic Forecast Model Selection in the Material Master

Forecast Model

Earlier in this chapter, we established that to prompt the system to automatically select the model, the option J has to be selected in the FORECAST MODEL field.

The system has two selection procedures, described in the next sections, which can help the system select a forecast model.

Selection Procedure 1

If you choose SELECTION PROC 1 in the CONTROL DATA section of Figure 19.4, the system carries out checks to see if a trend or seasonal pattern exists in the historical data. The system checks for a trend pattern by completing a regression analysis on the data and then checks for a trend. To check for a seasonal pattern, the system dismisses any trend pattern and then carries out an autocorrelation test.

Selection Procedure 2

If you choose SELECTION PROC 2, the system performs a more detailed analysis of the data at different levels of the smoothing factors to determine the most appropriate model based on the lowest mean absolute deviation.

If neither of these procedures finds an appropriate forecast model to use, the system will propose a constant forecast model. This model may not be suitable for your clients, so be sure your client is aware of this. The constant forecast model continues to forecast amounts that are the same over time. This forecast model is used for materials where consumption does not vary from period to period. Not many industries have materials with a non-varying forecast. Some companies do produce the same amount of material month to month; for example, Morgan Motor Company in England produces the same amount of cars each month, but this is due to physical and economic limitations rather than a constant level forecast.

19.4 Business Examples – Forecasting

Forecasting is important for some companies where sales rely more on future prediction than past consumption. A number of forecast models are available in the SAP ERP system, such as constant, trend, and seasonal models, as well as models for moving average values and weighted moving average values. A company can have the system determine a model or can have one assigned manually.

19.4.1 Forecast Models

A number of models can be used for forecasting material usage. The constant model assumes that the use of material is constant. The trend model is used when there is an identifiable increase or decrease of material over a period of time. The seasonal model affects many businesses due to the weather, holidays, or vacations. The seasonal trend model is similar to the seasonal model, except the pattern is moving further away from the mean value (i.e., increasing or decreasing).

By making the appropriate settings for the Material Master, you can estimate consumption figures for materials that are smoothed, removing random elements from the data.

Example – Constant Model

Constant forecasting models are used by companies that manufacturer items that are in the mature phase of the product lifecycle. For example, a company that manufactures traditional two-slice toasters can assume that demand for that type of toaster is fairly constant. Demand may vary slightly at Christmas, but not to such a level where it becomes a trend. If the manufacturer makes a radically new design, then the forecasting model is unlikely to be constant. As such, that company is likely to use the constant model in the forecasting data of the applicable Material Master records.

Example – Trend Model

When a company is considering using the trend forecasting model, it knows that the demand will follow a pattern based on other items the company has manufactured from examples in the industry.

An Austrian beverage company used statistical forecasting to estimate the demand and calculate raw material usage. When the company marketed one of its beverages using a sweepstakes type competition, the company changed the design of the can and the packaging. As such, the company needed to forecast the quantities of these items over the period of the sweepstakes promotion. If the company failed to order enough special cans or promotional packaging, the company would not see the level of sales desired. However, if the company ordered too many cans, then the promotional product would still be on the supermarket shelves long after the promotion ended. To help the company forecast the requirements, a trend forecast model was used. The company had run dozens of successful promotions and felt confident that it could obtain the correct requirements based on the trend model.

Example – Seasonal Model

The seasonal forecast model is the easiest for companies to understand because many businesses have times of the year where sales rise and times when sales fall. Some companies believe that their products are seasonal, but when they perform the analysis, they find that it is not the case.

A multi-national beverages company owned several boutique vodka manufacturers in Japan, Europe, and the United States. The company decided to keep the companies autonomous to continue the uniqueness of each brand. The company did require that new acquisitions moved to their SAP ERP platform to improve global purchasing and accounting.

The company constantly reviewed sales for these companies and analyzed their forecasted projections. Corporate management did notice that the U.S. manufacturers forecasted for markedly increased sales at Christmas time, but the European businesses did not. The manufacturers in the United States and Europe were asked to explain their holiday forecasts and to show how they derived their figures. The U.S. manufacturers both cited the upcoming holiday season as a time when sales would spike and that sales followed a seasonal trend. They showed that during December, the sales would show a 5% to 9% increase, although the percentage in the past three years had been closer to 5%.

The European manufacturers showed the company very similar figures, but indicated that they did not see a real seasonal trend to their sales. They showed that sales increased up to 6% between November 15 and January 15, but sales during the rest of the year showed fluctuations of 3% to 5% also.

The U.S. manufacturers were rigid in their belief that their sales followed a seasonal pattern, and they manufactured product based on that theory. However, when the results were analyzed, they found that they could follow a more constant forecast model instead of unnecessarily increasing production to fulfill inflated sales demands.

Example – Seasonal Trend Model

A manufacturer of plastic garden furniture had used statistical forecasting for the majority of its products. The company identified the seasonal forecasting model as the most appropriate because sales were high from May to August and significantly low between November and March. Based on the seasonal trend forecasting, the company had been successful in matching supply to sales demand. Over a period of years, the company became aware that sales for certain items were lower than in previous years. Although the seasonal element for demand was there, the trend was markedly downward. The company reviewed its product line and found that approximately 15% of its products followed this same trend. These items were competing against newer and cheaper products that competitors were importing.

The company decided to introduce a new range of products but decided against halting production of the older range as it continued to be profitable, despite lower demand. The company understood that it needed to make changes to its statistical forecasting and as such applied the seasonal trend forecasting model to a number of items that were trending downward.

19.5 Summary

This chapter discussed the forecasting methods available in SAP ERP. Forecasting is important to companies because it can determine how much material they produce, how much material they will need, and when to market the product based on forecasts. However, for a forecast to be close to being accurate, the forecast must be run with complete and verified data. The forecast model is used in companies that can produce a forecast for their materials. Some companies spend a great deal of time creating forecasts to aid in calculating the production requirements in the future. Food and beverage companies regularly use forecasting to determine how much product is made to ensure that an overproduction or underproduction does not occur. As an MM consultant, you must understand the way forecasting functionality works in the component and how it integrates with other functionalities, such as PP and SD.

Chapter 20 introduces the Inventory Management functionality, including goods issue, goods receipt, physical inventory, returns, stock transfers, and reservations.

The processes supported by the Inventory Management functionality in SAP ERP allow a company to meet customer needs for the availability of material, while maximizing the company's profits and minimizing its costs.

20 Inventory Management Overview

Management is under constant pressure to reduce the time between customer order and customer delivery. A customer will use order-to-delivery time as a factor in deciding on a vendor. Therefore, companies must use effective Inventory Management processes to reduce this time to a minimum. Companies are reengineering the order-to-delivery process. Improvements can be made by performing the following:

- Improving the EDI process with customers and vendors
- Increasing the single sourcing of materials
- Increasing the level of just-in-time (JIT) inventory
- Reducing dependence on long-term forecasts for stocking levels
- Using real-time reports and inventory figures

Inventory Management within SAP ERP gives the client an effective set of processes for all types of goods movement within the plant. Streamlining plant processes can help companies compress order-to-delivery time, decrease costs, reduce inventory, and improve customer service.

20.1 Goods Movements

The Inventory Management processes within SAP ERP are, in essence, movements inside the plant that can create a change in stock levels within the storage locations designated to that plant. The movement of stock is inbound from a vendor, outbound to a customer, a stock transfer between plants, or an internal transfer within a plant.

For every goods movement, the SAP ERP system can create two types of documents: a material document and an accounting document. The SAP ERP system follows the accounting principle that for every material movement, there is a corresponding document that provides details of that movement. In addition, an accounting document is produced that describes the financial aspects of the goods movement. However, the accounting document is only relevant if the material is valuated.

20.1.1 Stock Overview

The inventory in the plant is managed by quantity or value. The inventory movements are entered in real time, and a snapshot can be taken at any given moment to inform the inventory user of any material status. This snapshot, as shown in Figure 20.1, is called the Stock Overview, Transaction MMBE, and can be found using the navigation path, SAP MENU • LOGISTICS • MATERIALS MANAGEMENT • INVENTORY MANAGEMENT • ENVIRONMENT • STOCK • STOCK OVERVIEW.

The stock overview gives the material stock balance across the company, plant, storage location, and batch as shown in Figure 20.1.

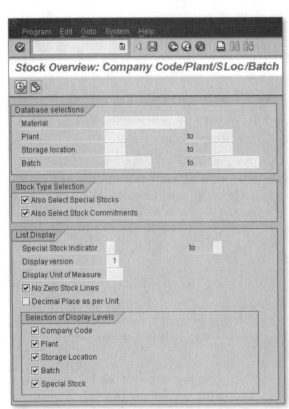

Figure 20.1 Selection Screen for the Stock Overview Transaction MMBE

m BO3

20.1.2 Material Document

The material document is produced for each movement and is an audit of the details of the material movement. The material document contains the date of the material movement, the material number, the quantity of the material moved, the location of the movement, the batch number if applicable, and the movement type.

The material document number is displayed subsequent to a material movement. Figure 20.2 shows the material document for the goods receipt of material 400-523. The material document is the audit document showing the movement of the material. The document can be checked to review the details of the movement.

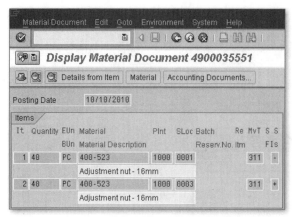

Figure 20.2 Material Document Detail Using Transaction MB03

View the material document by using Transaction MB03 or using the navigation path, SAP Menu • Logistics • Materials Management • Inventory Management • Material Document • Display.

Changes cannot be made to the material document after it has been posted. If an error was made on the material movement, the material document cannot be changed to alter the material movement. If an error was made, then the material movement has to be reversed, and the movement correctly entered. This produces a material document for the reversal and then a new material document for the correct movement.

20.1.3 Movement Types

The movement type is a three-character field, used to describe the type of material movement that needs to be performed. The movement type is used for all type of movements: receipts, issues, transfers, reversals.

The SAP ERP system is delivered with predefined movement types between 100 and 899. Movement types 900 and higher can be used for customized movement types.

A movement type can be created with Transaction OMJJ or via the navigation path, IMG • MATERIALS MANAGEMENT • INVENTORY MANAGEMENT AND PHYSICAL INVENTORY • MOVEMENT TYPES • COPY, CHANGE MOVEMENT TYPES.

The user can create a new movement type by copying an existing movement type and modifying the field contents.

The new movement type number is entered, and the field details from the existing movement type are copied across, as shown in Figure 20.3. The inventory user can then change the contents of the new movement type to create the desired effect of the new movement type.

OMJJ Creating a new movement Type

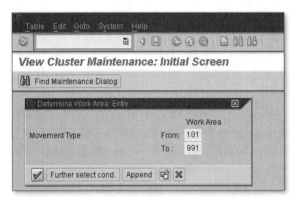

Figure 20.3 New Movement Type Creation by Copying from Existing Movement Type Using Transaction OMJJ

Existing movement types can be modified to restrict or allow certain functionality. For example, certain movement types may require certain reasons, which requires configuration of the CONTROL REASON field as shown in Figure 20.4. The CONTROL REASON field is defaulted as optional, but this can be configured as a requirement for any movement type.

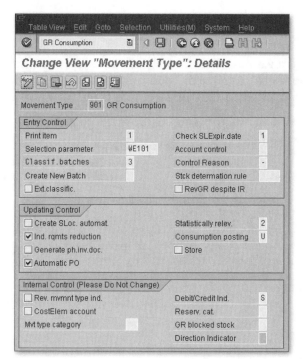

Figure 20.4 Field Contents of the New Movement Type That Can Be Configured

Overall, the movement type is a key to the Inventory Management process because it controls the updating of the stock quantity, determines what fields are displayed and required for entry, and also updates the correct account information.

This section described the goods movements in SAP ERP and some of the supporting functionality such as stock overview and material documents. The next section focuses on the movement of material by goods issue.

20.2 Goods Issue

A goods issue is a movement of material that causes a reduction of stock, that is, the amount of stock in the warehouse is reduced, triggered by one of the following:

- Shipment to a customer
- Withdrawal of stock for a production order
- Return of material

▸ Material required for sampling

▸ Material scraping

The movement types identify the various goods issues. Many scenarios can be called goods issues, such as goods issue to scrap or goods issue to sampling, and these and others are discussed more fully in Chapter 21, Goods Issue.

The other movement of materials opposite to a goods issue is the goods receipt, which is examined in the next section.

20.3   Goods Receipt

The goods receipt process allows the receipt of material from a vendor or from the in-house production process. In addition, SAP ERP allows other types of goods receipt, including initial stock creation. A goods receipt is an increase in stock that is triggered by one of the following:

▸ Receipt from a production order

▸ Receipt from a PO

▸ Initial entry of Inventory

▸ Other triggers

There are a number of different goods receipts, including a goods receipt for a PO and a goods receipt from a production order. These and other goods receipts are discussed more fully in Chapter 22, Goods Receipt.

The next section examines how a business counts the material in its plant.

20.4   Physical Inventory

Physical inventory is a process where a company stops all goods movement transactions and physically counts inventory. A physical inventory may be required by financial accounting rules or local tax regulations to determine an accurate value on the inventory. Other reasons for a physical inventory may include the need to establish inventory levels so materials can be restocked.

Cycle counting is a type of physical inventory. Cycle counts have the advantage that they are less disruptive to operations, provide an ongoing measure of inventory accuracy, and can be configured to focus on higher value materials or materials with frequent movement. Physical inventory is becoming a very important topic for companies as they work to keep their inventory count as current and accurate as possible. The many important steps in performing a physical inventory are discussed more fully in Chapter 23, Physical Inventory.

The next section discusses the subject of returns. These are not just materials to be returned to the vendor but also items such as returnable packaging.

20.5   Returns

The returns process often varies among companies. Each plant can have a different policy and procedure for creating and processing returns.

20.5.1   Introduction to Returns

[handwritten: See Reverse Logistics Book.]

The process of returning material is sometimes referred to as reverse logistics. These cover activities related to returning materials, pallets, and containers. Companies also return material to vendors for disposal or recycling. Returns to a vendor may also be related to a product recall notice.

Before any material can be returned to the vendor, the agreement between the customer and vendor with regards to returns should be examined. The agreement is either part of an overall agreement between the two companies or specifically for the individual material or group of materials. *[handwritten: Returns clause on returns]*

The returns clause usually determines the valid reasons that allow material to be returned to the vendor. These include an obvious material defect, incorrect material received, an overdelivery of material, and returnable packaging material. The process may involve the customer obtaining a Return Material Authorization (RMA) number from the supplier, which allows the vendor and customer to successfully track the return. *[handwritten: RMA from Vendor]*

Material to be returned to the vendor does not need to be in a special status. Material returns can be from stock in quality inspection, blocked stock, goods-receipt blocked stock, or even unrestricted stock.

20.5.2   Creating a Return

[handwritten: Same Transaction mIGO as for receipt.]

The returns process is the reverse of the goods receipt process. A return delivery is created by Transaction MIGO_GR, which is the same transaction for the goods receipt of materials. The transaction can be found using the navigation path, SAP MENU • LOGISTICS • MATERIALS MANAGEMENT • INVENTORY MANAGEMENT • GOODS MOVEMENT • GOODS RECEIPT • FOR PURCHASE ORDER • GOOD RECEIPT FOR PURCHASE ORDER. *[handwritten: mov Type 122]*

The return delivery, shown in Figure 20.5, obtains the information from the material document created from the original goods receipt for the PO.

The information from the material document shows the VENDOR, the vendor's DELIVERY NOTE number, and the item details. The line item details show the MOVEMENT TYPE for the return delivery, which is 122, and the material status, either UNRESTRICTED USE, QUALITY INSPECTION, or BLOCKED STOCK. The inventory user can alter the quantity of the material to be returned and also can enter a reason for the return, if this is configured.

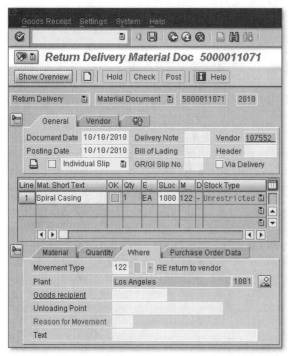

Figure 20.5 Return-Material Document Created via Transaction MIGO_GR

20.5.3 Configuring Reason for Movement

The reason for the return can be entered into the return process on the line-item level. The reason can only be added if it is configured for that movement type, in this case, movement type 122.

Transaction OMBS is used to create and change the reason for movement and can be accessed via the navigation path, IMG • Materials Management • Inventory Management and Physical Inventory • Movement Types • Record Reason for Goods Movements.

The transaction allows a number of reasons to be added for goods movement for each movement type.

The inventory user can add in a number of reasons for return of goods, and the Reason field can be used to monitor returns to vendors, as shown in Figure 20.6. This allows the purchasing department to identify issues with vendors or particular materials.

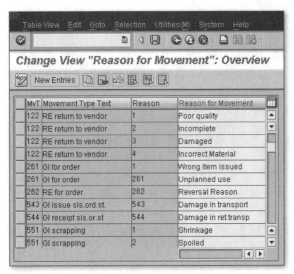

Figure 20.6 Transaction OMBS Where the User Can Configure Reasons for Goods Movements

The reason for movement (Reas) field can be configured to be suppressed, optional, or mandatory as shown in Figure 20.7. This can be carried out in same configuration Transaction OMBS. There are three options to choose from for each movement type. The inventory user can use a plus sign to represent that the field is mandatory and a minus sign to indicate that the field is suppressed. A blank field indicates that a reason is optional.

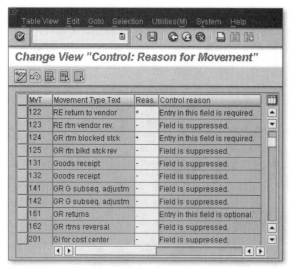

Figure 20.7 Control of the Reason for Movement Field in Transaction OMBS

20.5.4 Material Documents

After the reason for movement has been chosen, and the return is posted, the SAP ERP system will produce a material document to provide a trail of what happened.

The material document shows the material, quantity, and the original PO for the material, as shown in Figure 20.8. The material document can be identified as a return to a vendor because the movement type 122 is shown at the line item. The material document can be found using Transaction MB03.

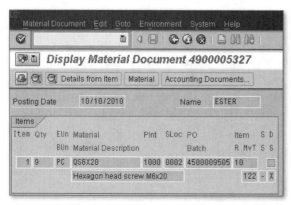

Figure 20.8 The Material Document for the Return to Vendor

The material documents relevant for goods receipt and return delivery can be seen by selecting the relevant line item and selecting ENVIRONMENT • MATERIAL DOCUMENT FOR MATERIAL as shown in Figure 20.9.

Figure 20.9 Path to the Material Documents from Inside Transaction MB03

— from here can go to mB51 to see Transaction for material/vendor combination.

This function transfers the process into Transaction MB51 with the material and vendor information carried over from the material documents. The detail screen of Transaction MB51 shows all material documents relevant for the material/vendor combination.

In this case, shown in Figure 20.10, there are five material documents, shown under the heading MAT. DOC.: Three are goods receipts, 5000001922, 5000001909, and 5000001900, for the amounts four, three, and three units, shown by movement type 101; and two are returns to vendor, 4900005328 and 4900005320, shown by movement type 122 also for amounts both of three units. The latter are shown as minus figures because they are reducing the inventory.

The returns process can be complex and require policies that vary from company to company and even site to site within a company. The next section reviews the functionality of the material reservation, including manual reservations and the link between reservations and MRP.

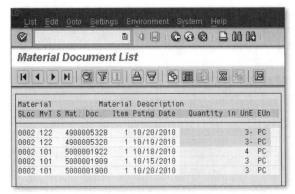

Figure 20.10 Material Documents Relevant for a Particular Material and Vendor Combination

20.6 Reservations

A reservation is a request to hold material in the plant or storage location for movement to a process before that process begins. For example, if material is needed for a production order, then a reservation can be created for that material so that it is allocated for production.

20.6.1 Introduction to Reservations

Automatic reservations can be created by a process such as a projector a production order that creates a reservation for the material without manual intervention. Automatic reservations can also be created at the storage-location level when stock levels fall below the specified amount, and a reservation for a stock transfer can be created.

After a reservation has been created, the reserved amount can be viewed using the stock overview Transaction MMBE. This shows the reserved quantity for the material. However, the unrestricted stock total will not be reduced by the reserved stock amount. The reserved stock is still part of the unrestricted stock.

The reservation is treated differently within MRP. The reservation of material lowers the MRP available stock in the stock-requirements list. Therefore, it is important to realize the effect the reservation has on different parts of the system.

MB21 - manual reservation.

20.6.2 Creating a Manual Reservation

A manual reservation can be created using Transaction MB21 or via the navigation path, SAP MENU • LOGISTICS • MATERIALS MANAGEMENT • INVENTORY MANAGEMENT • RESERVATION • CREATE.

The reservation is a planned movement, so the date of the reservation cannot be in the past. Before creating a reservation, the movement type should be determined because after the reservation is created; the movement type cannot be changed. However, the reservation can be deleted and reentered if the movement type was initially entered incorrectly.

The reservation line item has detailed information on the item that the reservation is created for, as shown in Figure 20.11.

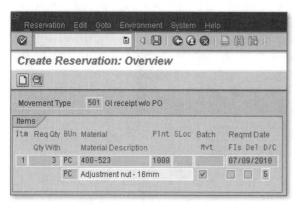

Figure 20.11 Detail Line for a Reservation Created Using Transaction MB21 for Movement Type 501

Movement Type

There are a number of movement types to choose from:

▶ **Consumption**: Such as consumption by a cost center, network, or sales order.

▶ **Transfer posting**: Such as plant to plant or storage location to storage location.

▶ **Goods receipts**: Such as from production, by-product, or without PO.

Requirements Date

REQMT DATE in Figure 20.11 is the date of the planned movement. This cannot be a date in the past and should be as accurate as possible, as this date is relevant to MRP.

Requirements Quantity

Enter a quantity that is the most accurate at the time the reservation is made in the Req Qty field. This quantity can be fixed by setting an indicator on the item detail screen.

Movement Indicator

The movement indicator (Mvt) is defaulted to be always on, allowing a goods movement to take place for the entered reservation. However, if the inventory user does not want to allow the goods movement to take place until a future period, this indicator can be unchecked, thus disallowing any goods movement.

FI Indicator

The Final Issue, or FIs, indicator is automatically set when there has been a goods movement or a number of goods movements that have fulfilled the reservation. If the inventory user decides that after a partial goods movement the reservation cannot or should not be completed, the user can set the FIs indicator.

Deletion Indicator

The deletion indicator (Del) is used when the inventory user has decided that the reservation line item is incorrect or no longer needed.

Debit/Credit Indicator

The D/C indicator shows whether the line item is a credit or debit. An H indicates a credit; an S indicates a debit.

20.6.3 MRP and Reservations

The reservation is relevant to MRP, and when MRP is run, the reservation appears on the MRP list for that material.

Transaction MD05 can be used to view the MRP list for a material. The transaction can also be found using the navigation path, SAP Menu • Logistics • Materials Management • Material Requirements Planning • MRP • Evaluations • MRP List – Material.

The line items in Figure 20.12 show the manual reservations with their DATE of expected delivery as available quantity (AVAILABLE QTY) on that date. The other line items refer to future POs that need to be placed.

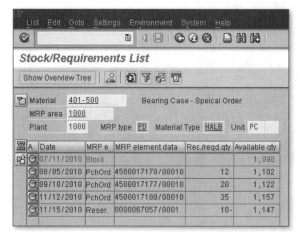

— M DO5
— M RP list —

Figure 20.12 MRP List for a Material, Which Includes the Manual Reservations

20.6.4 Reservations Management Program

M BVR

The reservations that are created need to be managed to control old and unnecessary reservations. You use Transaction MBVR for this, which can be accessed via the navigation path, SAP MENU • LOGISTICS • MATERIALS MANAGEMENT • INVENTORY MANAGEMENT • RESERVATION • ADMINISTER.

The reservation-management program allows the inventory user to set the deletion indicator on the reservation file based on user-entered selection criteria, as shown in Figure 20.13.

The main reason this management program is needed is that many goods movements do not reference the reservation that was made for that movement. In such cases, the material has already been received or consumed, but the reservation remains in the system until the management program cleans up these unnecessary reservations.

To manage Reservations
possibly remove old items etc.

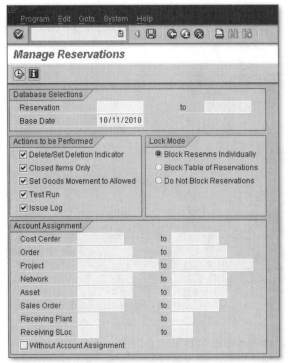

Figure 20.13 Selection Screen for the Reservation-Management Program, Transaction MBVR

The management program sets the deletion indicator for the following two scenarios:

▶ The final indicator (FIs) has been set on the reservation indicating that the reservation has been satisfied.

▶ The requirement date of the reservation is prior to a date calculated by the system. The system calculates the date using the base date entered in Transaction MBVR, minus a set number of retention days. The usual number of the retention days set for this transaction is 30. However, this can be changed to the customer's needs in configuration.

To change the number of retention days for the reservation-management program, changes need to be made in configuration. Transaction OMBN allows the user to change the retention days for the calculation, as shown in Figure 20.14. This transaction can be found via the navigation path, IMG • MATERIALS MANAGEMENT • INVENTORY MANAGEMENT AND PHYSICAL INVENTORY • RESERVATION • DEFINE DEFAULT VALUES.

The inventory user can change a number of defaults for the reservation based on the plant.

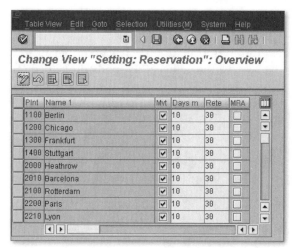

Figure 20.14 Configuration Transaction OMBN That Allows the User to Change the Reservation Default Values

Movement Indicator

If the movement indicator (MVT) is set, this specifies that goods movement is allowed for the reservation item. If the indicator is not set, then this indicator needs to be set manually in each reservation line item before a goods movement can take place.

Days for Movement Default Value

The DAYS field is used when the movement indicator (MVT) is not set in configuration. The reservation-management program uses this value to set the indicator in the reservation line item, if it has not already manually been set.

If the requirement date of a reservation item is farther in the future than the number of days configured in this field, the goods movement indicator (MVT) is not set, and no goods movements are allowed for that item.

Retention Period in Days

The inventory user can enter a value for the retention period (RETE), which is the number of days that the reservation item resides in the system before being deleted by the reservation-management program.

If the required date of a reservation item is older than the current date minus the number of retention days, the reservation-management program sets the deletion indicator (DEL) in the reservation item.

MRA Indicator

If this indicator is set, the storage location information is created automatically, based on the information from the reservation, when the goods movement is made.

20.7   Stock Transfers

A stock transfer can occur physically, for example, by moving material from one storage location to another, or logically, for example, by moving stock from quality inspection status to unrestricted.

20.7.1   Stock Transfer and Transfer Posting

The term *stock transfer* normally refers to a physical move, whereas transfer posting usually describes the logical move. A stock transfer occurs in three distinct ways:

▸ Storage location to storage location
▸ Plant to plant
▸ Company code to company code

A stock transfer can be performed by either a one-step procedure or a two-step procedure.

Transferring stock, either from storage location to storage location, or plant to plant, can be performed either using Transaction MB1B, which was available in previous releases of SAP, or using Transaction MIGO_TR.

[handwritten note: MB1B or MIGO-TR]

20.7.2   Transfer Between Storage Locations Using Transaction MB1B

Movement of material between storage locations in a plant arises because of normal everyday operations. Material is moved due to storage limitations, future needs, reclassification of stock, and so on. The movement of material between storage locations does not create a financial record because the material is valuated the same within a plant. The movement can be carried out by either a one-step or two-step procedure.

[handwritten note: → no FI posting because stays valuated within the plant.]

One-Step Procedure

This is a straightforward procedure where the material is moved in one step between storage locations. The stock levels in the different storage locations are changed in relation to the amount entered in the transaction.

The user can perform the one-step storage location to storage location transfer using Transaction MB1B, which is found via the navigation path, SAP MENU • LOGISTICS • MATERIALS MANAGEMENT • INVENTORY MANAGEMENT • GOODS MOVEMENT • TRANSFER POSTING.

The MOVEMENT TYPE entered on the initial screen, shown in Figure 20.15, is 311, which is the movement type for a one-step move between storage locations. However, if the material to be moved is a special stock, then the SPECIAL STOCK indicator needs to be entered as well as the MOVEMENT TYPE.

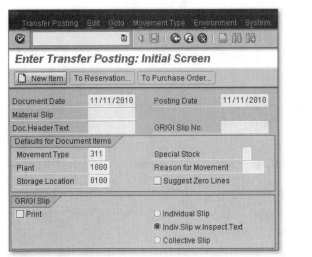

Figure 20.15 Initial Screen for One-Step Stock Movement Between Storage Locations: Transaction MB1B

Subsequent to a 311 movement, there is the possibility of reversing this movement by using the reverse movement type 312. This should be used if an error has been made.

On the item detail screen for Transaction MB1B, shown in Figure 20.16, the receiving storage location (RCVG SLOC) and the MATERIAL to move should be entered with the relevant QUANTITY and BATCH number, if applicable.

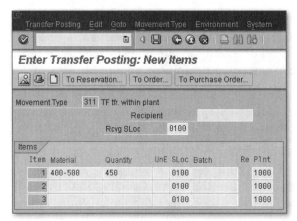

Figure 20.16 Line Item for the One-Step Move of Stock Between Storage Locations, Transaction MB1B

*maTeRial in TRansiT
for a Time beTween
sToRage locoTions.*

Two-Step Procedure

*moul.
Type
313
out*

The two-step transfer between storage locations is used where the materials are actually in transit, that is, not stored in a physical or logical location. This situation occurs in the plant where material must be moved out of a storage location, but where it is not possible to store the material in the receiving storage location until a later time. However, the only material that can be moved using the two-step procedure is unrestricted stock.

*only
unResTRicTed
sTock*

The two-step procedure uses the same transaction as a one-step transfer: Transaction MB1B. In this case, there are two movements to be made, a stock removal and a stock placement. The first movement is with movement type 313, which removes the material from one storage location, and then the second movement is with movement type 315, which places the material into the receiving storage location.

*movuT
Type
315
un*

Because the movement of material between storage locations is not instant, as with the one-step procedure, the materials are in different stock statuses as the movement progresses. The movement type 313 produces the following:

▸ Originating storage location unrestricted stock level is reduced.

▸ Receiving storage location stock in transit stock level is increased. *sToRage in
locaT
in TRansiT*

▸ Plant unrestricted stock level is reduced.

▸ Plant unrestricted stock in transit stock level is increased.

The movement type 315 produces the following:

▸ Receiving storage location stock in transit stock level is reduced.

▸ Receiving storage location unrestricted stock level is increased.

▶ Plant unrestricted stock level is increased.

▶ Plant unrestricted stock in transit stock level is reduced. — *has a Financial Impact.*

20.7.3 Transfer Between Plants Using Transaction MB1B

Movement of material between plants occurs when material is moved to replenish stock levels, to deliver material from a production site to a distribution center, or to move obsolete or slow-moving stock, among other reasons.

Movements between plants can use a one-step or two-step procedure as with storage locations, but there is a financial element in this transaction. Transaction MB1B can be used for the plant-to-plant transfer of material.

mvt type 301

One-Step Procedure

The one-step plant-to-plant transfer is similar to the one-step storage location transfer with the movement type 301 used for plant transfers. In this case, the receiving plant and storage location are required by the transaction.

In the one-step transfer shown in Figure 20.17, the stock is reduced in the supplying plant and increased at the receiving plant simultaneously. Both material and accounting documents are produced by the system.

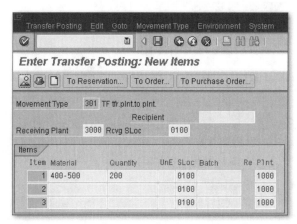

Figure 20.17 Detail Item Line for the One-Step Plant-to-Plant Transfer Using Transaction MB1B

Two-Step Procedure

For the two-step procedure, the material is removed from the supplying plant and placed in the receiving plant. In the same method as with storage locations, this

303 out 305 in

requires two movement types, 303 to remove the material from the supplying plant and 305 to place that material into the receiving plant.

When the movement type 303 is posted, the stock is reduced at the supplying plant and placed in the receiving plant's stock in transit. After the material is received and placed into stock at the receiving plant using movement type 305, the material moves from stock in transit to unrestricted stock.

20.7.4 Transfer Between Storage Locations Using MIGO_TR

could us mI GO as an option

The storage location to storage location transfer can also be executed by using Transaction MIGO_TR. This transaction can be found via the navigation path, SAP Menu • Logistics • Materials Management • Inventory Management • Goods Movement • Transfer Posting (MIGO).

my type 311

Figure 20.18 shows the transaction screen for MIGO_TR showing the material movement type 311. This is selected from a drop-down option for the field, TF tfr within plant. In this case, the one-step procedure was chosen with no special stock. The information regarding the transfer posting, the material, the quantity, and locations involved in the move are available in the tabs shown in Figure 20.18.

Figure 20.18 Transfer of Material Between Storage Locations Using Transaction MIGO_TR

20.7.5 Transfer Between Plants Using MIGO_TR

The plant-to-plant material transfer can also be executed by using Transaction MIGO_TR. This transaction can be found via the navigation path, SAP MENU • LOGISTICS • MATERIALS MANAGEMENT • INVENTORY MANAGEMENT • GOODS MOVEMENT • TRANSFER POSTING (MIGO).

Figure 20.19 shows the transfer of material between plants 3300 and 3350 using Transaction MIGO_TR. The information is displayed in a number of tabs, such as TRANSFER POSTING, MATERIAL, QUANTITY, and WHERE.

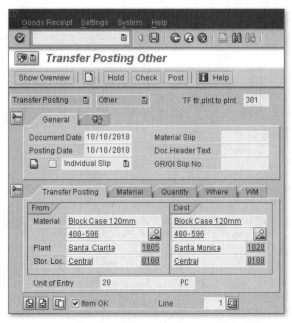

Figure 20.19 Transfer of Material Between Plants Using Transaction MIGO_TR

20.7.6 Transfer Between Company Codes

The company code transfer is functionally the same as a plant-to-plant transfer. Material is moved between different plants. The differences are that the plants belong to different company codes. Additional account documents are produced for either a one-step or two-step procedure.

An accounting document is created for each of the plant movements. In addition, an accounting document is created for the stock posting in the company clearing accounts.

Stock transfers are common in companies where material often has to be moved from a manufacturing plant to a central distribution warehouse and then to smaller regional sites. The frequency is then increased when it is the company policy to move material from site to site when necessary.

20.8   Business Examples – Inventory Management

Inventory Management offers the user a number of processes for the variety of goods movements that are required within the plant. By efficiently using these processes, companies can compress order-to-delivery time, decrease costs, reduce inventory, and improve customer service.

20.8.1   Physical Inventory

When a business performs a physical inventory, it is counting material that is located at a location, whether that is a physical plant, a third-party warehouse, or a customer's site. A physical inventory does not have to involve every material but can refer to a subset of the company's current stock.

Example

An Austrian beverage company owned and operated a bottling plant in Poland. The staff at the Polish plant performed a count of items in the warehouse each Friday after second shift for years before being purchased by new owners and before SAP ERP was implemented. The count would show minor discrepancies but nothing significant. After the plant was acquired, it stocked more brands than before and some that had never been sold in Poland.

Immediately, the Friday inventory count began to show some larger than normal discrepancies. The variations were found in three of the new brands that were stocked. The items were recounted several times, and each time, the error was an over-count of approximately 30%.

The error was quickly found by the warehouse shift manager who understood the issue with the new products. The counter had been counting the boxes in the warehouse and assuming the box contained 12 bottles. In fact, the three products were sold in boxes of 9, not 12, so the count would always be off by a third. After the counter recounted with correct calculation, the physical inventory was correct.

20.8.2 Returns

The returns process covers the activities that are related to returning materials, pallets, and containers to a supplier. Companies can also return material to vendors for disposal or recycling or the return may be related to a supplier's product recall notice.

Example

A Mexican automotive parts distributor received inbound deliveries on wooden pallets. The pallets were either sent back to the supplier when the next delivery arrived or used in the warehouse. One of the company's largest suppliers changed the way in which they moved items and switched from wooden to plastic pallets that contained RFID chips. The supplier requested that the pallets be returned either immediately to them or at the latest when the next delivery arrived.

The parts distributor understood the requirement, but on occasion, the company was short of pallets and used the supplier's pallets in the warehouse. The accounting department received an invoice for pallet rental from the supplier for pallets that had not been returned in the specified time frame.

The accounting department informed the warehouse that the new agreement required the warehouse to return the supplier's pallets when the next delivery arrived. To ensure that this process occurred, the warehouse created return deliveries for the pallets, based on the goods receipt for the inbound delivery. In this way, the warehouse would collect the pallets in the returns area so that they were ready for the supplier's vehicle when it next arrived.

20.8.3 Reservations

A reservation is a request to hold material for movement to a process before that process begins. For example, if material is needed for a production order, then a reservation can be created for the material to be held and allocated for that production order.

Example

A Spanish manufacturer of household appliances had a number of locations across Spain. Due to a downturn in consumer spending, the company decided to consolidate manufacturing and administration in a central facility. Three manufacturing facilities and a parts store, which also housed the company's administration, were closed. The new warehouse supplied items for both the parts business and the manufacturing department. Previously neither business had access to each other's inventory on SAP ERP. But now in a single location, the issue was that neither business owned the inventory, and problems arose when inventory was low. The manufacturing department staged material in storage locations in the production area a day before they were needed. However, the material was still showing as available to the parts department, and the parts department would sell the parts if a customer needed them.

This caused two issues: First, if the part was sold and removed from the production area, the manufacturing process stopped. Second, if the part was sold but subsequently used in production before the parts department removed it, the customer had to be informed that the part could not be delivered. Either way, the management did not like the situation and insisted that the manufacturing department use reservations to indicate that the material was to be used and not to be sold. As a concession, however, the parts department was able to sell the reserved part if the manufacturing department agreed and could change their production schedule with minimum time and cost.

20.9 Summary

This chapter introduced the Inventory Management functionality. Traditional goods movements, such as issues and receipts, will be discussed in detail in later chapters. However, it is important for the MM user to understand returns, reservations, and stock transfers. Returns are a part of everyday life at most companies. Often, material is delivered that cannot be used by the client. Knowing your client's return process is important when decisions are being made concerning the material. In addition to returns, reservations can be very important to a manufacturing company, so you must understand how and when your client uses reservations. Stock transfers occur regularly, and the decision of whether to use one-step or two-step transfers should be made early in an implementation.

In Chapter 21, goods issue is discussed with an emphasis on how it is used in production and for other production-related operations.

A goods issue decreases the stock levels and makes a financial posting to reduce the value of the stock. This occurs when the materials are issued. A goods issue process results in material and accounting documents being created in SAP ERP.

21 Goods Issue

The goods issues for material movements include issues to production orders, sampling, scrapping, and internal goods issues. For all of these goods issues, financial and material documents are created.

You will encounter many goods issue scenarios when working with MM. If working in the manufacturing industry, the most common may be the goods issue to a production order. Other important goods issue scenarios include the goods issue to scrap and the goods issues for sampling processes. The mechanisms of these goods issues are discussed in this chapter.

21.1 Goods Issue to a Production Order

The production order requires materials that are identified in the bill of materials (BOM) to complete production of finished goods. The MRP process plans the order and ensures the correct materials are available, and the MM process supplies material to the order through a goods issue. Apart from the planned issue of material to a production order, the material can be issued to a production order by an unplanned issue and also by a process known as backflushing.

21.1.1 Planned Goods Issue Using MB1A

When a production order is planned, the system produces a reservation for the material. The goods issue to the production order references a reservation if applicable.

A goods issue can be created using Transaction MB1A, which is found in the navigation path, SAP MENU • LOGISTICS • MATERIALS MANAGEMENT • INVENTORY MANAGEMENT • GOODS MOVEMENT • GOODS ISSUE.

The goods issue initial screen, shown in Figure 21.1, requires that the inventory user enter a MOVEMENT TYPE. For goods issue of materials to a production order, the 261 MOVEMENT TYPE is used.

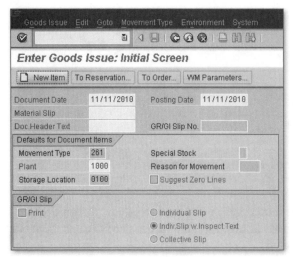

Figure 21.1 Initial Screen for Goods Issue Transaction MB1A

The goods issue to a production order requires the inventory user to enter the production order number as well as the material number and quantity.

After all of the line items have been entered for the goods issue, as shown in Figure 21.2, the transaction can be posted, producing a material and an accounting document. In Figure 21.2, one line ITEM has been entered for material 110-000203, for a QUANTITY of 4.

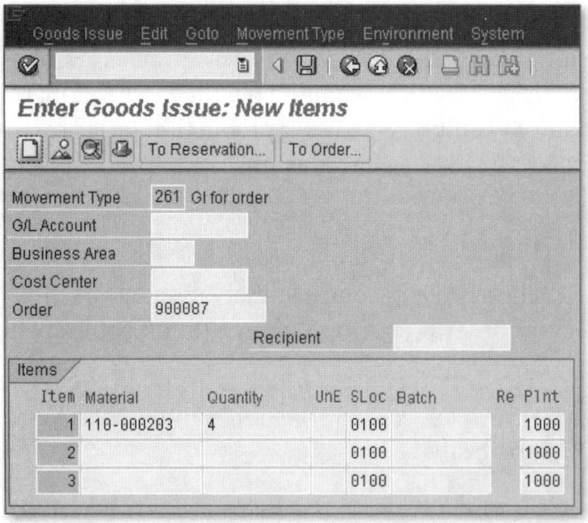

Figure 21.2 Detail Line Item Screen for Goods Issue Transaction MB1A

21.1.2 Planned Goods Issue Using Transaction MIGO_GI

In SAP ERP, a goods issue can be created using either Transaction MB1A or Transaction MIGO_GI. The previous section showed the planned goods issue using Transaction MB1A; this section shows the same goods issue using Transaction MIGO_GI.

The transaction can be found using the navigation path, SAP Menu • Logistics • Materials Management • Inventory Management • Goods Movement • Goods Issue (MIGO).

The initial screen for the MIGO_GI goods issue transaction, shown in Figure 21.3, requires that the correct type of goods issue be executed. For goods issue of materials to a production order, Goods Issue and Order are entered; the transaction will default to the correct movement type, in this case, 261, which is shown in the GI for order field.

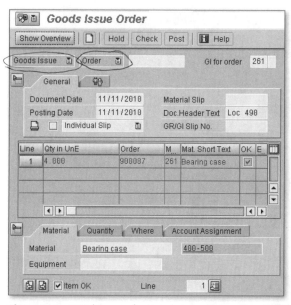

Figure 21.3 Initial Screen for Goods Issue Transaction MIGO_GI

After the order number is entered, the transaction adopts the materials from the production order, in this case, the material is 400-500, and the quantity expected is 4. At this point, the quantity can be changed for the goods issue.

On the Transaction MIGO screen, further materials can be added to the goods issue if unplanned material is required for the production order.

21.1.3 Unplanned Goods Issue Using Transaction MB1A

It often becomes necessary to issue additional material to a production order that is unplanned. For example, if a production order requires 100 kilograms of raw plastic pellets, goods issued 100 kilograms, and then the production supervisor asked the inventory department for an additional 40 kilograms to be issued to that production order, that would be an unplanned issue. There are many reasons why this would occur, including damage to the original material issued or problems with the production process. In such cases, additional material needs to be issued on an unplanned basis.

If the inventory user has information on the production order and the material needed, the goods issue can be created with reference to the BOM.

The inventory user can enter the header information as usual for the goods issue, but after the relevant movement type is entered, that is, 261, the inventory user selects Goods Issue • Create with Reference • To BOM.

After the information is entered for the BOM as shown in Figure 21.4, the inventory user can adopt the information from the BOM for the goods issue. The materials from the BOM will be pulled into the goods issue screen.

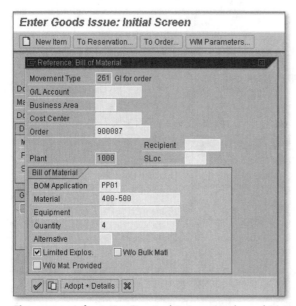

Figure 21.4 Information Required to Issue Unplanned Material to BOM

21.1.4   Backflushing

Backflushing is a process that occurs after production has taken place. Materials used in the production order are not consumed in the system until the production is posted against the operation in the routing. The backflushing procedure then processes the production order using the sum of the finished products and scrap quantity to recalculate the materials required. The inventory user then issues all of the materials as one transaction, as the user would have done initially in a normal goods issue to a production order.

At this time, the user can change individual material quantities and add individual scrap quantities to detail lines. As an example, we can look at the production order from Section 21.1.3, Unplanned Goods Issue Using Transaction MB1A, which requires 100 kilograms of raw plastic pellets. If the production order had not issued the 100 kilograms, but instead it was backflushed, then the backflush would have one issue of 140 kilograms and an added scrap line item of 40 kilograms.

Backflushing occurs when either the material, production work center or routing has been flagged as relevant for backflushing, and this designation is copied to the production order, shown in Figure 21.5. The material can be flagged for backflushing by setting an indicator on the Material Master record. The BACKFLUSH indicator can be found in the MRP area of the Material Master record.

Figure 21.5   Backflush Indicator on the Material Master Record

Backflushing can be very useful to production operations because it provides significant benefits over the normal goods issue procedure for certain production situations:

- If a production process has a long operation time, such as days or weeks, then it may not be beneficial to the company to move material out of stock and issue to a production order, given that the material will not be recorded as consumed for a long period of time. With backflushing, this material will remain in stock until the operation is complete.

- When a production operation involves a lot of scrap material, a complicated issuing process may ensue in which the inventory user will not know exactly how much material to issue. It is simpler to use backflushing to calculate the used material on the basis of finished product plus scrap quantity.

- Bulk materials make exact issuing very difficult, and backflushing simplifies the issuing process. It is easier to allow the system to backflush the correct quantity after the operation.

The goods issue to a production order is the process most familiar to those working in MM, however, other goods issues scenarios need to be understood. The next section looks at the goods issue to scrap.

21.2 Goods Issue to Scrap

Scrap material can be defined in any way that a company decides. A material that is scrap for one company may not be scrap for another. The most useful general definition is that a material can be defined as scrap when it is no longer of any use or value to a company. Scrap material can be any of the following:

- **Material that has exceeded its expiry date**: Some materials in the warehouse may be configured to have an expiry date, such as foodstuffs and chemicals. If material expires, it may have to be scrapped if it cannot be reworked.

- **Material that is no longer in tolerance with respect to quality**: Some chemicals may require retesting periodically because their characteristics may change over time. For example, if an ethenol-type material is tested and found to have a viscosity of 1.049 cP, and the tolerance limits are between 1.065 and 1.083 cP, then the material is out of tolerance and may be scrapped.

- **Material that is unusable due to the production process**: Some materials may not have expiry dates or quality tolerances but still may not be suitable for production. For example, if plastic beads to be used in the production of white plastic items have discolored, they may no longer be suitable and need to be scrapped.

▶ **Material that is damaged in the warehouse**: Material can easily be damaged as it moves around the warehouse. Damage by forklift often occurs as does damage to material by environmental factors, such as water damage or sunlight damage.

Material that has been identified as scrap material needs to be removed from stock, and the value of the stock needs to be reduced. To perform the scrapping of material, the inventory user can perform a goods issue with the relevant movement type for scrapping.

Material to be scrapped can be either in unrestricted stock, quality inspection stock, or blocked stock. Depending on the company and the scrapping procedure it uses, the material can be located in any of the three areas.

21.2.1 Goods Issue to Scrap Using Transaction MB1A

Transaction MB1A can be used for the goods issue with Movement Type 551, as shown in Figure 21.6. The scrapping of material reduces the inventory by the quantity entered in Transaction MB1A. The transaction also has an accounting element that posts the value of the stock to a scrapping account and posts any scrapping costs to a cost center that is entered in the scrapping transaction.

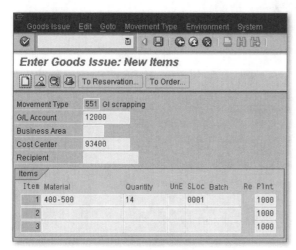

Figure 21.6 Line Item to Be Scrapped and Relevant Cost Center for Scrapping Costs

In many companies, the inventory user has to enter a reason for movement, and the configuration has been set to allow for this. Scrapping material can be very costly, and companies are always trying to reduce the level of scrap and find ways to stop scrapping material if at all possible.

21.2.2 Goods Issue to Scrap Using Transaction MIGO_GI

Transaction MB1A can be used for the goods issue with movement type 551, as shown in Figure 21.7, with the description GI SCRAPPING. The COST CENTER for the scrapping costs can be entered for the line item.

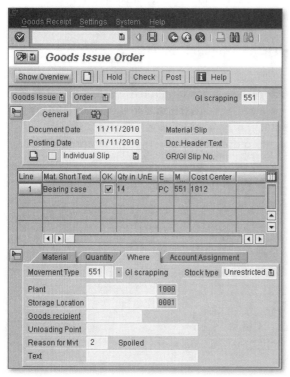

Figure 21.7 Item to Be Scrapped Using Transaction MIGO_GI

Goods issue to scrap is found in manufacturing plants; especially where material used in the production process is susceptible to damage or can easily go out of tolerance. The next section discusses another goods issue process: performing goods issue for sampling.

21.3   Goods Issue for Sampling

Companies take samples of material in conjunction with testing for quality. Chemical materials can be safe to use within a range of certain tolerances. If the material changes its chemical makeup over time, for example, the company needs to know that information. To monitor the material, the company instructs the quality department to test samples of the material in stock. In the majority of cases, a sample of the material is tested.

21.3.1   Goods Issue for Sampling Using Transaction MB1A

To test a sample, it must be removed from stock. A goods issue is performed to issue some material for sampling. The sample can be taken from material in unrestricted, quality, or blocked stock. This section shows the goods issue using Transaction MB1A.

Sending material for sampling reduces the inventory by the quantity entered in Transaction MB1A, as shown in Figure 21.8. The transaction has an accounting element — shown by means of the G/L Account and Cost Center — which posts the value of the stock to a sampling account. The element posts any costs involved in sampling, such as external testing labs or procedures, to a cost center that is entered in the sample transaction.

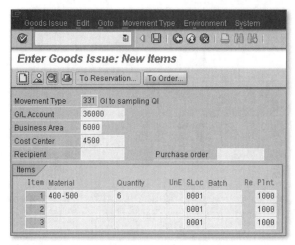

Figure 21.8   Line Item to Be Issued as Sample Using Transaction MB1A

21.3.2 Goods Issue for Sampling Using Transaction MIGO_GI

Transaction MIGO_GI can also be used to goods issue material for sampling. Figure 21.9 shows the goods issue to sampling using Transaction MIGO_GI. In this example, the material and a quantity of 60 pieces have been entered to be issued to sampling.

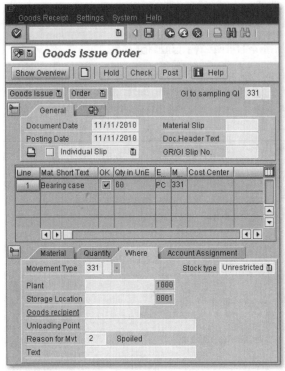

Figure 21.9 Goods Issue of Material to Sampling Using Transaction MIGO_GI

21.4 Goods Issue Posting

When a goods issue is posted, for example, to a production order, the system produces accounting and material documents, updates tables, and triggers events in other components. This section shows the events that occur when a posting is made: creating material and accounting documents, printing the goods issue slip, changing stock levels, and changing the G/L account.

21.4.1 Material Document

The material document is the audit document that describes the movements of the material entered in the goods issue. The material document is created during the posting of the goods issue and can be displayed using Transaction MB03.

21.4.2 Accounting Document

The accounting document is created in parallel with the material document during the posting of the goods issue. The accounting document describes the financial movements associated with the material issue, and it can be accessed from the material document Transaction MB03.

21.4.3 Goods Issue Slip

The goods issue slip is a printed document that can be used by the warehouse to find the material and provide a physical record that the material has been picked for goods issue. The goods issue slip can be described as an IM version of a WM picking ticket.

There are three goods issue slip printed versions that can be selected in Transaction MB1A:

▶ **Individual slip**: An individual goods issue slip is printed for each of the material document items.

▶ **Individual slip with inspection text**: One goods issue slip is printed per material document item but will include any quality inspection text that is contained in the Material Master record.

▶ **Collective slip**: This goods issue slip contains all of the items.

The goods issue slip has three printed versions defined within SAP ERP: WA01, WA02, and WA03. These can be modified to include the information relevant for the issuing procedure of each company.

21.4.4 Stock Changes

When a goods issue is posted, the relevant stock levels will change. The stock level will be reduced for a goods issue and increased for a goods issue reversal.

21.4.5 General Ledger Account Changes

As part of the goods issue process, the accounting software posts updates to the GL material accounts. When the goods issue posts, the material is valuated at the current price, whether the material is valuated at a standard price or at a moving average price. Therefore, the goods issue process reduces the total value and the total quantity in relation to the price, but the price of the material does not change as a result.

This section discussed the posting of goods issue, but in the next section, we cover how to deal with the situation when changes need to be made and a goods issue reversal has to be executed.

21.5 Goods Issue Reversal

When material is issued to a production order, it is issued because it will be part of the BOM for the item that is being produced. The BOM is a list of materials with quantities that go into producing the finished item. Items on the BOM are goods issued to the production order.

In some industries, the exact issued amount will be consumed in production, for example, in assembly operations. In other industries, such as chemicals, the exact amount of the end product is variable and therefore so is the amount of material consumed. If there is a goods issue to the production order for 500 kilograms of a material, and only 300 kilograms were consumed, the remaining 200 kilograms can be returned to stock. The inventory user issues the material back to stock by performing a goods issue reversal.

The reversal can be entered with reference to the material document, created on the initial goods issue.

21.5.1 Goods Issue Reversal with Reference to a Material Document

This section examines how to make a good issue reversal by canceling a material document. Figure 21.10 shows the cancellation of MATERIAL DOCUMENT 4900035551. By canceling the material document, there is no requirement for a movement type to be entered. This goods issue reversal method uses Transaction MIGO_GI. The material document is entered, and the CANCELLATION option should be selected.

After the material document has been entered, the detail section is displayed, and the details of the material to be reversed are displayed with reference to the material document.

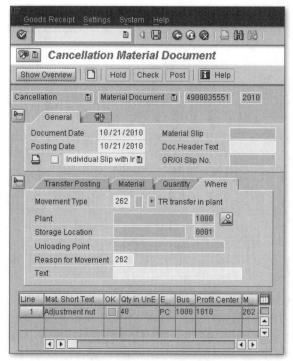

Figure 21.10 Goods Issue Reversal with Reference to a Material Document

The goods issue reversal is an important transaction that may be required if mistakes are made. Some companies have strict policies on use of reversal movement types, such as a goods issue reversal, so make sure that you follow the client's policy.

21.6 Business Examples – Goods Issue

The goods issues for material movements include issues to production orders, sampling, scrapping, and internal goods issues. For each of these goods movements, a material and an accounting document are created.

The goods issues that most consultants find themselves reviewing are goods issue to a production order, goods issue to scrap, and goods issue for sampling processes.

21.6.1 Goods Issue to Scrap

When material cannot be used in the manufacturing process, due to quality issues, or if finished goods have exceeded their best before date, a company can decide to scrap the material. The definition of scrap material will vary between companies and industries. In general, scrap material is defined as such when it is no longer of any use or value to a company.

Example

An Ohio-based saw blades manufacturer sold its products to tool manufacturers and home improvement stores. The company used coils of steel to fabricate the saw blades, and each blade was pressed from the steel using the minimum amount of waste possible. Even using the most complex fabrication machinery, there was a very small percentage of scrap that could not be avoided.

However, on occasion, due to slight differences in the steel coils, the blades would not pass the quality checks of the company's customers who had very specific requirements. When this happened, the shipment was returned to the manufacturer, and the sales department contacted other customers and home improvement stores to find a buyer. Often the large DIY stores would take the product, and the company suffered only a small loss.

When a buyer was not found, however, the logistics management analyzed how much it would cost to store the unwanted items and calculated how long the company wanted to store them until a buyer was found. The sales staff was given that information, but if the shipment was not sold, it had to be scrapped and written off. Fortunately, the contract with the steel vendor stated that the vendor would take scrapped shipment and give a percentage discount on the next order.

21.6.2 Goods Issue to Sampling

To test a material for quality, a sample is used and has to be removed from stock. A goods issue is performed to issue a quantity of material for sampling. This sample of materials can be taken from unrestricted, quality, or blocked stock.

Example

A Spanish manufacturer of household appliances consolidated manufacturing and administration in a central facility. Three manufacturing facilities and a parts store, which also housed the company's administration, were closed. As a result, some suppliers who had been local to the manufacturing plants were no longer used, and vendors closer to the new site were found. The parts supplied by the new vendors were tested to check that they were within tolerances prior to any agreements being signed. However, management decided the quality department should check the items sent by the new vendors for the first 10 deliveries.

The inbound deliveries from the new vendors were receipted directly into quality inspection so that the quality department could check them. Because the tests performed by the quality department could damage the parts so they could no longer be used for production, a quantity of material is goods issued for sampling. If the tested parts were not damaged by the testing process, the parts were returned to inventory by reversing the goods issue.

21.6.3 Backflushing

Backflushing is a process whereby materials used in production are not consumed until the production order is posted. The backflushing procedure recalculates the materials that were required using the sum of the finished products and any scrap quantity. The Inventory Management user will goods issues the materials as one transaction.

Example

The Ohio-based saw blades manufacturer uses large coils of steel to produce its saw blades. The amount of steel varies depending on the size of the saw blade being produced. Although the amount of steel is known, it is not possible to measure off the steel before the production of the blades. Therefore, the production staff accurately measures the amount of steel used after the end of the production, enters this into the production order, and then posts the order. The amount of steel used is then backflushed, removing the correct amount from inventory.

21.7 Summary

Goods issue to production orders occur every day in a manufacturing plant, and PP elements such as backflushing should be understood by the MM user.

The MM user should also closely examine the issuing material to scrap process. This process writes value from the company books; therefore, any movement of this kind requires a detailed procedure with checks at several levels. Issuing material to scrap is a simple transaction to perform in SAP ERP, but the ramifications of the transaction can have a large financial effect.

Chapter 22 examines the processes that make up the goods receipt function. The chapter describes the necessary steps for successful goods receipt processing.

A goods receipt transaction is used to receive material from a purchase order or an in-house production order. The goods receipt process can be simple or complex depending on the nature of the material being received.

22 Goods Receipt

Goods receipts are mainly used for receipt of stock from an external vendor via a PO or receipt of material from in-house production via a production order. Goods receipts are also used as the movement that initially creates inventory in the system and enters materials that were received without a PO. A goods receipt is important to a company because it moves the material into stock, updating the stock levels and allowing production to occur.

Every company has its own procedures for the receipt of material, and these procedures must be considered when using the goods receipt functionality in SAP ERP. If the material is received into stock, either unrestricted or quality, the value of the material is posted to the plant accounts, which means that the company has spent money to have that material in the plant. Minimizing the length of time that materials spend in the goods receipt process saves the company money.

This chapter will familiarize you with the goods receipt process and help you configure the steps required for successful goods receipt processing.

22.1 Goods Receipt for a Purchase Order

A goods receipt is a company's formal acceptance that materials were received from a vendor against a PO. After the material is received, and the transaction is completed, the value of the material is posted to the GL.

22.1.1 Goods Receipt with a Known Purchase Order Number

The goods receipt transaction is accessed through Transaction MIGO. The transaction can be used whether the PO is known or unknown. The transaction can be accessed via the navigation path, SAP MENU • LOGISTICS • MATERIALS MANAGEMENT • INVENTORY MANAGEMENT • GOODS RECEIPT • FOR PURCHASE ORDER • PO NUMBER KNOWN.

In the initial entry screen for Transaction MIGO, as shown in Figure 22.1, the PURCHASE ORDER number, is entered if known. The information from the PO will be transposed to the goods receipt MIGO transaction, where the PO details can be checked and amended if necessary.

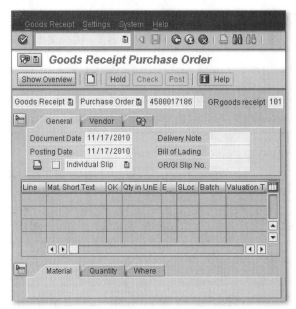

Figure 22.1 Initial Entry Screen for the MIGO Transaction When the Purchase Order Number Is Known

After the PO information has been transposed to the MIGO transaction, changes can be made to the delivery quantity if needed, as shown in the QTY IN UNE field in Figure 22.2. If the DELIVERY NOTE from the VENDOR shows an amount different from that on the PO, then this can be entered into the goods receipt along with the actual amount delivered.

After all of the relevant information for the goods receipt has been entered, the goods receipt can be posted.

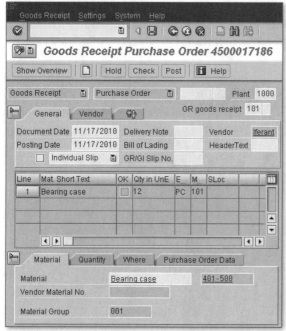

Figure 22.2 Detail Screen for the Goods Receipt with Information from the Purchase Order Displayed

↗ many companies don't accept w/o a PO #.

22.1.2   Goods Receipt with an Unknown Purchase Order Number

On rare occasions, material arrives from a vendor with no PO on the documents from the vendor, and no suitable PO number can be found in SAP ERP. This may be due to a delay in entering the PO in SAP ERP or because of an error by the vendor in which the material was never ordered. In any case, the company needs a procedure for handling these instances.

Some companies will not accept material without a PO on the documents or for which no suitable PO can be found in SAP ERP. In this case, the material is refused, and the delivery is not accepted. Other companies will accept delivery of the materials and keep the material in quality or blocked stock until the situation is resolved. In this case, the material needs to be received using the correct movement type in SAP ERP.

The goods receipt for receiving material without a PO number uses the same goods receipt Transaction MIGO. The information required for this transaction is minimal because there are no details available from a relevant PO. The material and quantity information should be entered as well as storage location information.

After all relevant information has been entered, most importantly the material number and quantity, the goods receipt can be posted, as shown in Figure 22.3. The material will be part of the plant stock unless it is receipted into goods receipt blocked stock.

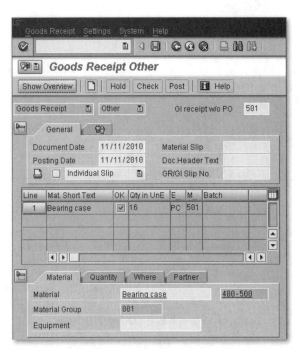

plant stock or blocked stock.

Figure 22.3 Goods Receipt Transaction for Receiving Material Without a Purchase Order

22.1.3 Goods Receipt Posting

After the goods receipt has been posted, a series of events are triggered. These are described in this section.

Material Document

The material document is the audit that describes the movements of the material entered in the goods receipt. The material document is created during the posting of the goods receipt and can be displayed using Transaction MB03.

Accounting Document

The accounting document is created in parallel with the material document during the posting of the goods receipt. The accounting document describes the financial movements associated with the material receipt and can be accessed from the material document Transaction MB03.

Goods Receipt Note

The goods receipt note is a printed document that the warehouse uses to store the material in the correct location.

Three goods receipt note printed versions can be selected in Transaction MIGO:

- **Individual GRN**: An individual goods receipt note is printed for each of the material document items.
- **Individual GRN with inspection text**: One goods receipt note is printed per material document item but will include any quality-inspection text that is contained in the Material Master record.
- **Collective slip**: One goods receipt note is printed containing all of the items.

The goods receipt note has three printed versions defined within SAP ERP: WE01, WE02, and WE03. These can be modified to include the information relevant for the issuing procedure of each company.

Stock Changes

When a goods receipt is posted, the relevant stock levels change. The stock level will be increased for a goods receipt and decreased for a goods receipt reversal. A goods receipt reversal may occur if the material was found to be defective or failed quality inspection. If this occurs, the inventory control department may decide to reverse the goods receipt so the material will be deducted from the plant stock level.

New for SAP ERP

Within the Inventory Management function, two new movement types are available in SAP ERP:

107: Goods receipt to valuated GR blocked stock.

109: Goods receipt from valuated GR blocked stock.

This section described in detail how material arriving at the plant is received using the goods receipt process for a PO. The next section examines the goods receipt process for production orders.

— once goods have been manufactured — To put into inventory.

22.2 Goods Receipt for a Production Order

If yours is a manufacturing company, then you will need to perform goods receipts for production orders to receive the finished goods into stock for use or sale.

The production order quantity can be receipted into stock by using the goods receipt transaction for orders, Transaction MIGO_GO, or via the navigation path, SAP MENU • LOGISTICS • MATERIALS MANAGEMENT • INVENTORY MANAGEMENT • GOODS RECEIPT • GR FOR ORDER.

MiGO-GO

The transaction requires the entry of the appropriate production order number in the ORDER number field. The production order number is usually found on the documents supplied from the production facility, as shown in Figure 22.4.

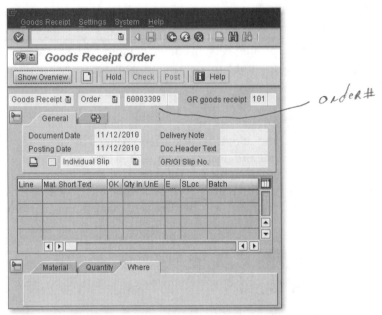

— order #

Figure 22.4 Initial Screen for a Goods Receipt from a Production Order

After the production order is entered, the material information is transposed to the goods receipt. The quantity of the finished material can be entered into the goods receipt if it varies from that on the production order.

After the goods receipt is posted, the production order is determined to be fully delivered or partially delivered, providing that a partial quantity was delivered to the warehouse, as shown in Figure 22.5. In this figure, the amount receipted is equal to the production order, which was for 18 units. The delivery completed indicator ("DEL.COMPLETED" IND.) is set to automatic when the delivery quantity is equal to the production order quantity.

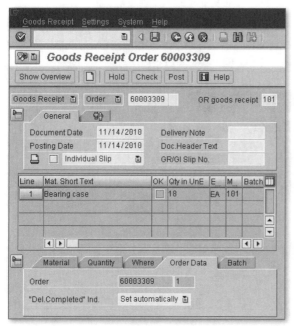

Figure 22.5 Detail Screen for the Goods Receipt with Information Displayed from the Production Order

This section discussed the goods receipt for a production order. In the next section, the focus moves from goods receipt to how inventory is initially entered into the SAP ERP system.

22.3 Initial Entry of Inventory

When a new SAP ERP system is brought into production, a number of tasks need to be completed to make the transition from the legacy system to the new SAP ERP system as seamless as possible. When replacing a legacy inventory system, the inventory on hand in the warehouse must be entered into the SAP ERP system to reflect the current situation.

22.3.1 Initial Inventory Load

To enter the inventory balances, primarily at the initial go-live of an SAP ERP system, the goods receipt process uses specific movement types, depending on the status of the material.

The initial load of inventory uses Transaction MB1C, as shown in Figure 22.6. This can be found using the navigation path, SAP MENU • LOGISTICS • MATERIALS MANAGEMENT • INVENTORY MANAGEMENT • GOODS RECEIPT • OTHER.

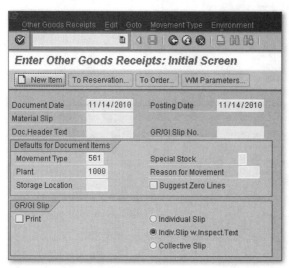

Figure 22.6 Loading Initial Inventory into SAP ERP Using a Goods Receipt

The transaction requires the user to enter a MOVEMENT TYPE. Three movement types can be used for initial inventory loads:

- **561**: Goods receipt for initial entry of stock balances into unrestricted.
- **563**: Goods receipt for initial entry of stock balances into quality inspection.
- **565P**: Goods receipt for initial entry of stock balances into blocked stock.

Figure 22.7 shows a detailed goods receipt for an inventory load using Transaction MB1C and MOVEMENT TYPE 563, which represents the initial load of material balances into quality inspection. If the material will be placed in quality inspection, then the 561 movement type is used if it is unrestricted stock; if the stock will be placed in blocked stock, then the 565 movement type is used.

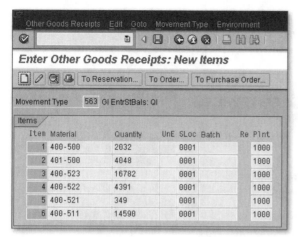

Figure 22.7 Detail Screen for the Initial Inventory Load Goods Receipt

This section explained how material is initially entered into the SAP ERP system. The following section describes other less familiar goods receipt processes that you may encounter as a MM consultant.

22.4 Other Goods Receipts

In some scenarios, the material cannot be receipted by one of the normal procedures. These scenarios include the following:

▶ Goods with no production order

▶ Goods from production that are by-products

▶ Goods that are free goods

In these cases, the goods receipt is treated slightly differently. It is the company's decision whether and how these goods receipts take place. If the company decides that no goods receipt will take place without a PO, then goods that arrive without a PO number are rejected and not received. However, most companies need material that arrives without appropriate documentation at times, and there should be procedures in place to deal with these anomalies.

22.4.1 Goods Receipt Without a Production Order

If your company or client has not implemented PP, then the goods receipt of finished goods from production cannot reference a production order. In this case, the material needs to be receipted into stock using a miscellaneous goods receipt.

The goods receipt of finished goods without production orders uses the same transaction as the initial load of inventory, MB1C, as shown in Figure 22.8. The difference in this case is that the movement type used is not 561 but can be 521, 523, or 525.

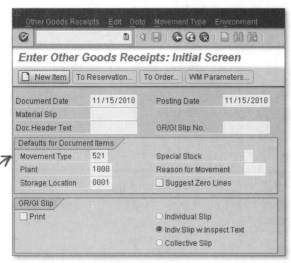

Figure 22.8 Initial Screen for the Goods Receipt Without a Production Order

A goods receipt without a production order requires that one of three movement types is entered:

- **521**: Goods receipt for finished goods without a production order into unrestricted stock.
- **523**: Goods receipt for finished goods without a production order into quality inspection stock.
- **525**: Goods receipt for finished goods without a production order into blocked stock.

This can be found using the navigation path, SAP MENU • LOGISTICS • MATERIALS MANAGEMENT • INVENTORY MANAGEMENT • GOODS RECEIPT • OTHER.

22.4.2 Goods Receipt of By-Products

A by-product is a secondary or incidental product created by the manufacturing process or from a chemical reaction in a manufacturing operation. It is not the primary finished product being manufactured. In many cases, the by-product can be captured, receipted into stock, and either used again in part of the manufacturing process or sold as a finished good.

An example of the by-product scenario is the creation of lanolin from the processing of wool into textiles. The wool is processed into cloth, and a by-product of that process is lanolin, also known as wool wax. Lanolin is sold as a finished good for skin ointments and waterproofing and also as a raw material for the production of shoe polish. The by-product can be received into stock using Transaction MB1C. Movement type 531 is used for receiving by-products.

22.4.3 Goods Receipt for Free Goods

Occasionally, a delivery from a vendor contains goods for which payment is not required. These free goods may be promotional items or sample products. Although the materials are free of charge, their quantities and value will be posted to the GL.

The purchasing department can create a PO for a zero value for free-of-charge goods if the delivery from the vendor is planned. If a PO is entered into the system, then the goods receipt can be referenced to that PO.

If no PO was created, then the goods receipt can be performed using Transaction MB1C with the MOVEMENT TYPE 511 as shown in Figure 22.9.

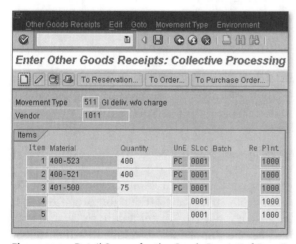

Figure 22.9 Detail Screen for the Goods Receipt of Free Goods

22.4.4 Goods Receipt for Returnable Transport Packaging (RTP)

Packaging material can be very expensive for the vendor to produce, and, as a result, the vendor may require that it be returned for reuse. The returnable transport packaging (RTP) may be as simple as a drum or tote but can be specific to an item and be costly to produce.

In these instances, the packaging can be receipted into inventory using the good receipt Transaction MB1C and the MOVEMENT TYPE 511, with a SPECIAL STOCK indicator, M (see Figure 22.10).

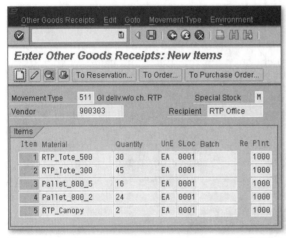

Figure 22.10 Detail Screen for the Goods Receipt of RTP

This section has dealt with a number of goods receipt processes that are not as common as receipts for POs or production orders. However, it is important to understand how these less common receipts are processed.

22.5 Business Examples – Goods Receipts

Goods receipts are used for receipt of stock from an external vendor via a PO or receipt of material from in-house production via a production order. A goods receipt is an important process because it moves the material into stock, updating the stock levels, so customer orders can be shipped and production can occur.

22.5.1 Goods Receipt for a Purchase Order

A goods receipt is a company's formal acceptance that materials were received from a vendor against a PO. Subsequent to the goods receipt being posted, the value of the material, if the material is valuated, is posted to the GL.

Example

An elevator parts manufacturer developed a goods receipt procedure for receiving raw materials used in the manufacturing process. Because the parts manufactured had to pass strict quality control, the company employed a goods receiving procedure that was equally as stringent. The receiving staff visually examined each delivery of raw material for damages to the packaging, and if they believed that the item was damaged, it was rejected before any other tests were made. If the packaging was found to be satisfactory, the raw material was received into a blocked stock area where more physical and chemical tests were performed. If the quality department approved the items, then the goods receipt was processed and received into inventory.

The process ensured that only materials meeting the company's specifications were received, but the lengthy process only verified the results given to them by the vendor. The length of the process was a problem on occasion due to material being needed for production orders that were about to commence. The production department became concerned that a lot of money was being wasted verifying data supplied by vendors who they had been working with for up to 15 years. In addition, the added time in processing the goods receipt was causing problems.

The supply chain management team looked at the concerns of the production department as well as the purchasing and quality teams who were equally concerned that items could be received that were not of sufficient quality.

The management worked with the most trusted vendors and proposed a revised procedure. Some vendors would allow testing of the parts at their facilities on a regular basis, which would allow their items to be expedited through the goods receipt process. This meant the production department received their items in a timely fashion for production orders, while the warehouse and quality departments spent less time and resources on receiving material that had already been tested.

22.5.2 Goods Receipt Without a Purchase Order

Occasionally, material will arrive at a plant, and the PO is not known because it does not appear on the documents from the vendor, and no suitable PO number can be found in SAP ERP. This may be due to a delay in entering the PO in SAP

ERP, or it can be because of an error by the vendor in which the material was never ordered. Some companies will not accept the items into inventory without a PO number, so they are either returned or are placed in a holding area until a PO number is found.

Example

When an Austrian beverage company acquired a small manufacturer in Poland, the acquired company was operating on a number of disparate systems, which were connected by batch-run interfaces. Before the Polish facility migrated to SAP ERP, the company frequently received items into the plant from suppliers without a valid PO due to a number of factors such as the item had not been set up in the item master or the changes to the vendor file were waiting for a batch update. The staff was aware of these issues, and items were received into stock due to a lack of space to hold these incoming deliveries without valid paperwork.

After the migration to its parent company's SAP ERP system, the warehouse staff was informed that they should always have a PO available due to the real-time nature of the data. Nevertheless, the staff still on occasion received deliveries directly into stock without a PO. This practice was immediately halted when it was found that one vendor frequently sent deliveries with quantities greater than the order quantity with a shorter shelf life and with no order documents.

After this situation was found, the company instituted a zero-tolerance policy where no delivery was accepted without a PO.

22.5.3 Goods Receipt for Returnable Transport Packaging (RTP)

With the advances in packaging technology, companies are making use of some very special material to package their products. Some of this packaging is so unique and expensive that the transport packaging must be returned. The returnable transport packaging (RTP) may be as simple as a drum or tote but can be specific to an item and be costly to produce.

Example

When items were received at a Mexican distributor of automotive parts, the packaging was discarded. Within the last year, a number of the company's vendors have informed the distributor that the packaging should be stored and then returned to the vendor. Some of these vendors have moved from disposal packaging materials to recyclable and reusable packaging that is initially more expensive but can be reused many times.

The parts distributor then had to create new Material Master records on its SAP ERP system for more than 20 different types of packaging. When a goods receipt is processed for items and the returnable packaging, the packaging items are brought into the warehouse and then returned to the vendor when the next shipment arrives. The issue for the parts distributor is that this packaging can take up valuable warehouse space, and they have tried to develop other ways of storing it, such as in empty trailers and in unused parking areas.

22.6 Summary

This chapter discussed the goods receipt process that occurs in a normal manufacturing company. It is important to receive the material to keep the production line operational and to avoid stockouts. As companies move to JIT operation, goods receipt must be achieved in a timely fashion to keep operations flowing. Understanding the processes of a goods receipt for a PO or a production order is important to you as a MM consultant because these are fundamental steps in the movement of materials. Other less common goods receipts are often found at plant sites and should be understood to successfully advise your client.

Chapter 23 examines the physical inventory functionality. The regular counting of inventory, either by physical inventory or by cycle counting, has become a key element in helping companies ensure their inventory records are accurate and current.

Regular physical inventories in the plant, combined with improvements in inventory accuracy, are important goals for companies. Physical inventories can be customized to produce faster and more accurate results, lowering inventory costs and improving customer service levels.

23   Physical Inventory

Performing a physical inventory entails counting what is currently in stock in the plant or storage location, comparing that count to what the SAP ERP inventory system says is in stock, and making any necessary adjustments to get the counts to match the physical warehouse counts.

Some companies perform a full physical inventory only once a year, which is the traditional method. However, many companies need more accurate information more frequently. Many companies with fast-moving stock will perform cycle counting, which means that selected parts of the warehouse or specific products are counted, usually on a more frequent basis.

Physical inventory in SAP ERP covers all aspects of counting material at the plant. This includes the yearly inventory, cycle counting, continuous inventory, and inventory sampling.

Physical inventory can be performed on stock that is held in unrestricted, quality inspection, or blocked status. Physical inventory also can be performed on the company's own stock and special stocks, such as returnable packaging and consignment stock at customer locations.

The initial section of this chapter discusses the preparatory steps required prior to the actual physical inventory process.

23.1   Physical Inventory Preparation

Before the physical inventory can begin, a series of operations needs to be performed to prepare for the count.

In complex plants, companies may have to develop count procedures that use different approaches to counting, such as one method for finished goods and another for raw materials. Deciding what to count is very important because counting the wrong materials negates any count that takes place.

Companies should weigh the effects of inventory inaccuracies to determine which materials or warehouse sections are more critical than others. Small variances in the stock levels of certain materials may have little or no affect on operations, whereas small inaccuracies in the inventory of critical materials may shut down production. Inventory inaccuracies in finished goods will have a negative effect on customer service if deliveries are delayed or cancelled due to lack of inventory.

The steps involved in preparing for the actual physical count are described in the following subsections. The first step is to prepare for the physical count.

23.1.1 Preparations for a Physical Inventory Count

The following procedures should be followed to complete the physical inventory process:

1. Process and post all transactions that will affect inventory counts: goods receipts, inventory adjustments, transfer postings, and sales orders that have been filled and shipped. These steps should be followed to keep the inventory transaction history sequenced properly.
2. Put away all of the materials that are being counted in the warehouse.
3. Segregate from the rest of the warehouse the material stock that has been used to fill sales orders but that has not physically left the warehouse.
4. Stop all stock movements within the warehouse.
5. Stop all transactions in the warehouse.

Run a Stock On-Hand report for the items you are going to count. Transaction MB52 will show you the material in unrestricted, quality inspection, and block quantities for each storage location. This is a record of the inventory status before you start the physical inventory count.

23.1.2 Creating the Physical Inventory Count Document

You create the physical inventory count sheets by using Transaction MI01 or the navigation path, SAP MENU • LOGISTICS • MATERIALS MANAGEMENT • PHYSICAL INVENTORY • PHYSICAL INVENTORY DOCUMENT • CREATE.

Posting Block

You can set the posting block on the physical inventory count document when you create it, as shown in Figure 23.1. Because there is often a delay between a material movement and the posting of the movement, there can be a discrepancy between the physical warehouse stock and the book inventory. To ensure that there is no discrepancy during the physical inventory count, you should set the POSTING BLOCK indicator on the initial screen of the count document. The posting block is automatically removed when the counting results are posted for the physical inventory document.

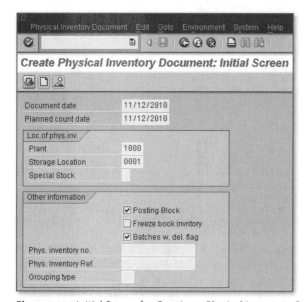

Figure 23.1　Initial Screen for Creating a Physical Inventory Count Document

Freeze Book Inventory

If the inventory count has not been completed, the book inventory balance can be frozen in the physical inventory document with the FREEZE BOOK INVNTORY indicator. This is to prevent the book inventory balance from being updated by any goods movements, which could lead to incorrect inventory differences.

Include Deleted Batches

The BATCHES W. DEL. FLAG option allows the count document to include batches of a material that have been flagged for deletion. To ensure these batches are included in the count, the indicator must be set on the initial entry screen.

The material to be counted is added line by line for the count document as shown in Figure 23.2. The line items will not show a quantity of current stock.

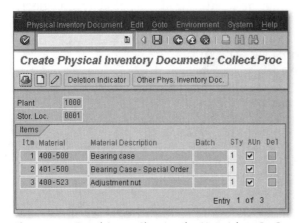

Figure 23.2 Detail Screen Showing the Materials to Be Counted

23.1.3 Printing the Physical Inventory Count Document

After the physical inventory documents have been entered, the count documents can be printed out for the actual physical count. The count documents can be printed using Transaction MI21, which can be accessed through the navigation path, SAP MENU • LOGISTICS • MATERIALS MANAGEMENT • PHYSICAL INVENTORY • PHYSICAL INVENTORY DOCUMENT • PRINT.

The selection can be entered to decide which count documents should be printed; for example, Figure 23.3 shows the selection by PLANNED COUNT DATE, PLANT, STORAGE LOCATION, or PHYSICAL INVENTORY DOCUMENT numbers. After the selection has been determined, the count documents can be printed.

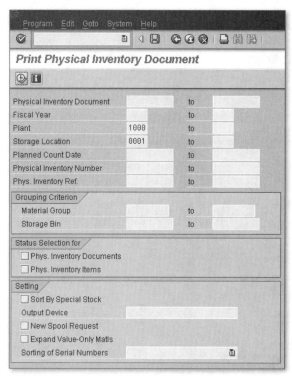

Figure 23.3 Selection Screen for Transaction MI21

Figure 23.4 is an example of a printed physical inventory count sheet. The physical count document is given to the person who will count the materials in the physical area of the plant described on the document. Figure 23.4 shows that the material to be counted is in plant 1000, storage location 0001. The line items on the count document show the materials to be counted, and the person performing the count will write the amount they counted on the document.

The next section examines how the completed count documents are entered into the system and what happens if a recount is required.

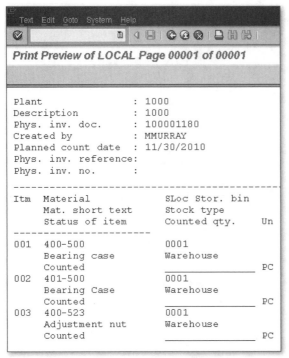

Figure 23.4 Example of a Printed Physical Inventory Count Sheet

23.2 Counting and Recounts

After the physical inventory count sheets are printed, they can be distributed to the personnel allocated for the counting process, and the count can begin.

With more emphasis on accuracy of material counts, many companies now only use highly trained employees to count materials accurately. Companies with the high inventory accuracy believe that giving employees direct responsibility for counting inventory and resolving discrepancies will significantly improve the physical inventory process.

23.2.1 Entering the Count

After the count has been completed, the physical count needs to be entered into the SAP ERP system. The count quantities from the count sheets are transferred to their respective physical inventory documents. The inventory user accesses Transaction MI04 or uses the navigation path, SAP Menu • Logistics • Materials Management • Physical Inventory • Inventory Count • Enter.

The inventory user transfers the quantity from the inventory count sheet into the line item in Transaction MI04, shown in Figure 23.5. After all of the inventory count has been entered, the transaction is posted. The posting releases the posting block if one had been placed on the physical inventory document. The count can be posted and the physical count completed at that point.

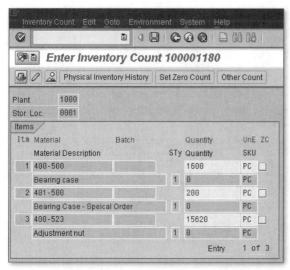

Figure 23.5   Entry of Count Results Using Transaction MI04

If the inventory user made an error when entering the count document, using Transaction MI05 can change the physical count. The inventory user needs to know the physical count document to perform this transaction. After the changes are made, the count can be posted if the inventory user or the supervisor is satisfied.

23.2.2   Difference List

The count can be compared against the book inventory by using Transaction MI20. The transaction allows the inventory user to enter a material and the physical inventory document. The transaction can be accessed via the navigation path, SAP MENU • LOGISTICS • MATERIALS MANAGEMENT • PHYSICAL INVENTORY • DIFFERENCE • DIFFERENCE LIST.

After the selection information, PLANT and PHYSICAL INVENTORY DOCUMENT number in the example shown in Figure 23.6, has been entered, the report can be executed. The resulting report shows the materials relevant to the selection.

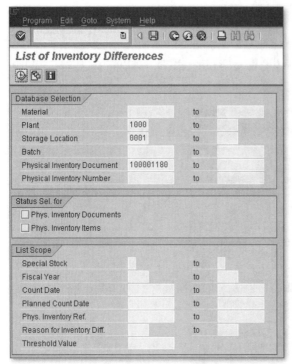

Figure 23.6 Selection Screen for the Differences List for Physical Inventory Documents

The report, shown in Figure 23.7, identifies the book quantity (Book QTY), the counted quantity (QTY COUNTED), and the difference (DIFF QTY), if any. After the differences have been identified, the count can be repeated to check the differences, or the differences can be posted when approved by management.

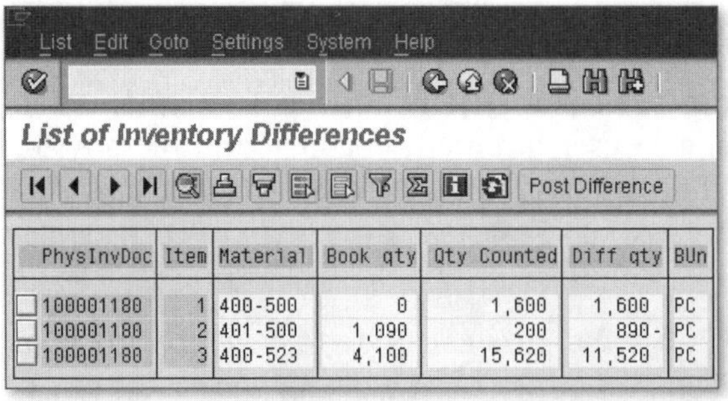

PhysInvDoc	Item	Material	Book qty	Qty Counted	Diff qty	BUn
☐ 100001180	1	400-500	0	1,600	1,600	PC
☐ 100001180	2	401-500	1,090	200	890-	PC
☐ 100001180	3	400-523	4,100	15,620	11,520	PC

Figure 23.7 Difference List for the Physical Inventory Document Entered in Transaction MI20

23.2.3 Missing Material

Management must decide how to resolve inventory differences. The physical inventory procedures within SAP ERP show where the material discrepancies occur, but management must decide how to find the missing material. Many companies have designed an auditing process to aid the physical inventory process in investigating the discrepancies. In many instances, an adjustment is made to the book quantity of the missing product, and then an offsetting adjustment is made days later when the material is found. In this case, the changes cause additional work, disrupt the production schedule, and may lead to excess inventory of this material.

Some companies have created a variance location to move the lost and found material to and from, as a way of showing the variances without creating adjustments. A variance location must be closely monitored, and there must be an ongoing procedure for finding the material discrepancies.

23.2.4 Recounts

If management does not accept the discrepancy, or the discrepancy is above a certain tolerance, then those materials need to be recounted. The recount allows the users to recount the material in the location on the physical inventory document. The recount Transaction MI11 can be found via the navigation path, SAP Menu • Logistics • Materials Management • Physical Inventory • Physical Inventory Document • Recount.

The recount transaction allows the inventory user to enter the physical count document number and view the detail lines. The detail information, displayed in Figure 23.8, shows the materials relevant to the count document as well as the physical count quantity and the difference from the book quantity.

After the recount document has been printed, the recount can be performed. When the recount is complete, the material quantities can be entered into Transaction MI04. At this point, the count can be posted within Transaction MI04, or the count can be posted through Transaction MI07.

The next section reviews the processes involved subsequent to the recount process and discusses the posting of the count document.

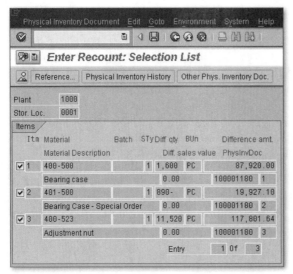

Figure 23.8 Item Detail from the Recount Document

23.3 Physical Inventory Posting

The count and recount process results in a document that has a final inventory figure for each counted material. This figure is the best and most accurate total produced by visually counting the material in the plant. After the supervisor organizing the count approves the document, the count document can be posted in the SAP ERP system.

23.3.1 Posting the Count Document

After the count has been entered, the document can be posted using Transaction MI07, which can be found using the navigation path, SAP MENU • LOGISTICS • MATERIALS MANAGEMENT • PHYSICAL INVENTORY • DIFFERENCE • POST.

The physical document number has to be entered along with the posting date and threshold value. This is an optional field that holds the maximum amount to which inventory differences are allowed for the inventory document.

The detail lines of the count document, shown in Figure 23.9, identify the difference quantity (DIFF QTY) and the difference value (DIFF. SALES VALUE). For example, in Figure 23.9, line item 1 shows that MATERIAL 400-500 has been counted, and the quantity counted is 600 pieces greater than the book quantity. The difference in value is also shown; in this case, it is $900. The inventory user can post the differences unless the difference value totals more than the threshold value, assuming the threshold value was entered.

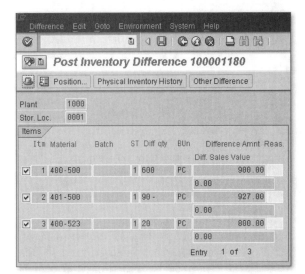

Figure 23.9 Detail Lines for Recount Document Before Posting in Transaction MI07

For each line item on the count document, the user posts the difference and a reason code to clearly show why the count does not correspond with the book quantity. The reason codes can be configured for each movement type required. The internal movement type used for posting inventory differences is 701. The configuration can be found using Transaction OMBS or using the navigation path, IMG • MATERIALS MANAGEMENT • INVENTORY MANAGEMENT AND PHYSICAL INVENTORY • PHYSICAL INVENTORY • RECORD REASON FOR GOODS MOVEMENT.

Figure 23.10 shows the configuration for the REASON FOR MOVEMENT used for identifying differences that are posted in the physical inventory documents. In Figure 23.10, there are a number of common reasons that have been configured for movement type 701, including INCORRECT BARCODE, INCORRECT RFID, INCORRECT LABELING, and so on.

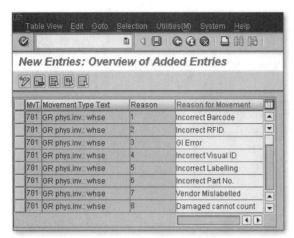

Figure 23.10 Configuration of Reason Codes for Physical Inventory Goods Movements

23.3.2 Posting a Count Without a Document

If a count is made without a physical count document, the count can be entered directly into a transaction and then be immediately posted, as shown in Figure 23.11. In this screen, the required basic information has been entered to post a count's COUNT DATE, PLANT, and STORAGE LOCATION. Transaction MI10 can be accessed though the navigation path, SAP MENU • LOGISTICS • MATERIALS MANAGEMENT • PHYSICAL INVENTORY • DIFFERENCE • ENTER W/O DOCUMENT REFERENCE.

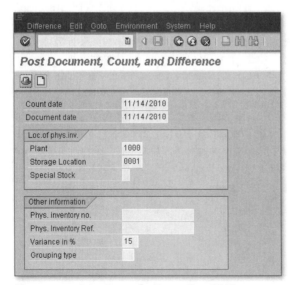

Figure 23.11 Entry Screen for Transaction MI10

The inventory user can add individual line items that have been counted and enter the amount for each line item. If a variance percentage was entered on the initial screen, then the user will be warned if the amount entered is greater than the allowed variance.

After the material line items are entered, as shown in Figure 23.12, the document can be posted, and the values from the document will become the book quantity for those materials. The stock quantities for the materials can be checked using Transactions MMBE or MB53.

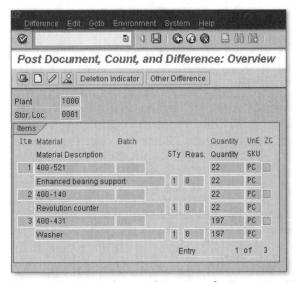

Figure 23.12 Counted Material Line Items for Transaction MI10

23.3.3 Accounting of Inventory Differences

When the inventory differences are posted, the total stock is automatically adjusted to the counted quantity on the document. When the document is posted, the differences will correspond to either a goods receipt or goods issue.

If the counted quantity is smaller than the book inventory, the stock account is credited with the value of the inventory difference. The accounting entry is posted to the expense from physical inventory account.

Subsequently, if the counted quantity is greater than the inventory balance, the stock account is debited with the value of the inventory difference. The accounting entry is posted to the income from physical inventory account.

This section discussed posting the physical count document that is used in the count of material in the warehouse. However, as described previously, there are instances in which a physical count can be entered without a count document. Check with the organizer of the physical counts at your client to see what the policies are for physical counts and whether counts without documentation can be posted.

23.4 Business Examples – Physical Inventory

Physical inventory in SAP ERP covers all aspects of counting material at the plant, including the yearly inventory, cycle counting, continuous inventory, and inventory sampling.

23.4.1 Physical Inventory Preparation

Before any physical inventory count can begin, preparation needs to be completed, including processing any transactions that will affect the count, putting away all materials that are in holding areas, identifying the items to be counted, and educating the counters.

Example

A U.S. industrial tools manufacturer implemented SAP ERP after using a number of disparate PC systems for many years. In its legacy system, the physical inventory was taken each weekend for the company's main warehouse and once a month for material stored in offsite third-party warehouses.

With the advent of its SAP ERP implementation, the company initially continued weekly physical inventories but found that inventory accuracy was significantly higher than previously. With more accurate data, the company decided to perform counts at the weekend for items that had inaccuracies during the week. The weekend count now only represented 10 to 20 items having to be counted. The count was performed for the items, but the count produced conflicting results. Some of the counted materials showed a count total equal to the book total, while others were significantly different; some variations were greater than the issues during the week.

The warehouse management decided to postpone any more weekend counts until the issue was resolved. The ensuing investigation of the count process found that the preparation work before the count was causing the inaccuracies. The team had asked the warehouse second shift to print off the count documents so that the counters could start early on Saturday morning. Because of this, the count documents were printed before all movements in the warehouse were completed. Some material was moved in the warehouse late Friday night, but the confirmation of the warehouse transfer orders would not be processed until Monday morning. This caused material to physically be in the correct bin, but the system did not reflect this. The count documents therefore did not show the correct physical total in the bin, and the count was never accurate. After this issue was identified, management asked that all transfer orders be processed before the count documents were printed. This change in the preparation allowed a more successful count to take place.

23.4.2 Physical Inventory Posting

The count and recount process creates a document that includes final inventory totals for the counted materials. These represent the most accurate figures produced by visually counting the material in the plant. After the document has been approved, it can be posted and the inventory totals updated.

Example

A British electronic components distributor implemented SAP ERP after using a number of AS/400 programs designed in-house specifically for the company's processes. The company had more than 10,000 unique items, and most were small and difficult to count. The physical inventory process had always been a challenge for the company, and obtaining an accurate total for low-value items was a costly exercise. After the SAP ERP implementation, the company decided to make changes to its counting process. Previously, the company spent a great deal of time ensuring that the items were properly counted and that inventory was accurate. However, this process took days to complete, and the monetary value of large inventory accuracies was relatively small.

With the SAP ERP physical inventory, the company's system integrators suggested that they allow some tolerances when performing physical inventory. The consultants proposed choosing 20 items to count and allow a £20 tolerance in value, which equated to a difference of more than 500 for some items.

The count of the 20 test items showed that although every item had a count difference, the greatest variation was less than £8, or 120 items. Based on that test, the counts for each of the 20 items could be posted. After the company understood the small variances made little monetary difference to its inventory, the company introduced the policy for all items that were valued less than £25, which was over 80% of the items the company stocked.

23.5 Summary

This chapter explained the aspects of performing a physical inventory in the traditional manner, with count sheets and recounts, and the less conventional manner of entering counts directly into the system without count sheets. Physical inventory is an important part of Inventory Management despite being a simple process to follow. The writing off and on of material affects the following other areas:

▶ **Production**: Is there enough stock for production orders?

▶ **Sales**: Is there enough stock for customers sales orders?

▶ **Accounting**: Will the total stock value go up or down?

If the physical inventory is not accurate, and errors are made, then others are affected. Therefore, it is important to investigate all potential count differences to ensure that the count is accurate, and the difference is not just due to a counting error.

The next chapter discusses Invoice Verification, which produces a number of touchpoints with the Financial Accounting component.

Invoice Verification is the procedure through which vendors will be paid for the material that they deliver to the customer. The procedure can involve a three-way matching process among the customer's purchase order, the goods-received note, and the vendor's invoice.

24 Invoice Verification

Invoice Verification is part of the accounts payable (AP) process where vendors are paid for materials or services that they have provided to their customer. The verification of the invoice is important to both the vendor and the customer because it ensures that the quantities and the pricing are all correct and that neither party has made an error. The standard method of Invoice Verification is the three-way match. This chapter describes this process and a process called Evaluated Receipt Settlement (ERS), which is a two-way match between the PO and the delivery note, whereby the vendor is paid without an invoice being sent to the customer. The first section of this chapter discusses the traditional verification of the invoice using a three-way match.

24.1 Standard Three-Way Match

This method uses the PO supplied to the vendor, the goods receipt or delivery note supplied by the vendor, and the invoice sent to the customer from the vendor. In a successful three-way match, the quantity and price of the three documents will match, and the payment to the vendor will be sent via check or bank transfer at a date agreed to by both parties.

24.1.1 Entering an Invoice

The receipt of an invoice at the AP department triggers the Invoice Verification process. The invoice can either be in the form of a fax, hard copy, or through EDI. The invoice can be entered into the system using Transaction MIRO or by following the navigation path, SAP MENU • LOGISTICS • MATERIALS MANAGEMENT • LOGISTICS INVOICE VERIFICATION • DOCUMENT ENTRY • ENTER INVOICE. The initial entry screen for Transaction MIRO is shown in Figure 24.1. The key entry fields for this screen are the POSTING DATE, the AMOUNT, and the TAX AMOUNT. The TAX

AMOUNT field is important when dealing with taxable items. Often errors in the invoice process can be related to taxes.

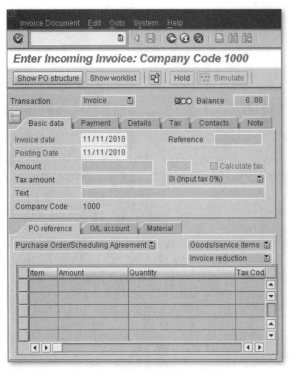

Figure 24.1 Entry Screen for Transaction MIRO

The invoice entry screen requires the user to enter the details from the incoming invoice. The completed Transaction MIRO screen is shown in Figure 24.2. The PO number has been entered for the invoice, which shows the total amount, as well as the quantity of material ordered and delivered.

Invoice Date

The user needs to enter the date of the invoice. Do not enter the INVOICE DATE as a future date. The POSTING DATE is defaulted to the current date but can be changed as necessary.

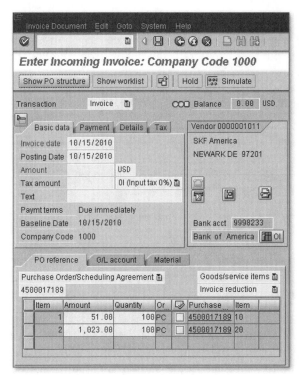

Figure 24.2 MIRO Transaction with Relevant Purchase Order Details Displayed

Amount

The user enters the AMOUNT of the invoice as displayed on the vendor's invoice. The user should also enter the currency of the invoice as stated on the invoice. Invoices produced by international vendors may be in their local currencies rather than the currency entered in the PO.

Calculate Tax

This indicator should be set if the user wants the tax to be calculated automatically when the invoice is posted. If the vendor has entered the tax information on the invoice, then this field should not be set, and the tax details should be entered from the invoice into the TAX AMOUNT fields.

Purchase Order Number

The match can only take place when the PO number is entered into Transaction MIRO. After the purchase order number is entered, the details from the PO are displayed in the PO REFERENCE tab.

New for SAP ERP

Invoice Verification has a new report called display list of invoice documents (RMMR1MDI), which does just that. As an addition to the existing program invoice overview, Transaction MIR6, there are extended selection criteria and display options. For example, on the initial screen, you can make selections by one-time customers, invoice gross amount, and entry date. In the output list, the report shows both posted and held invoices.

24.1.2 Simulate Posting

After the details have been transferred from the PO to the invoice, and the user believes that the invoice can be posted, the user can test the posting of the invoice by simulating the posting. The user simulates the document by accessing the header menu and selecting INVOICE DOCUMENT • SIMULATE DOCUMENT.

The simulation is a trial posting. Even if the invoice can be posted, the simulation will not actually post the invoice. If the simulation process cannot post the invoices, messages will be posted to a message log, as shown in Figure 24.3. The message log shows errors and warnings. In this case, the errors are due to tax codes, amount inconsistencies, and the tax jurisdiction. The messages indicate to the user what issues are preventing the posting.

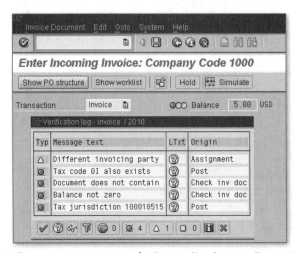

Figure 24.3 Message Log for Posting Simulation in Transaction MIRO

24.1.3   Invoice Posting

After the message log has been cleared, there is nothing to prevent the invoice items from being posted. When the posting is complete, the information is passed through to the payment process in Financial Accounting in SAP ERP Financials. The payment process updates GL accounts relevant to the posted document.

The payment process is defined by a number of payment rules that can be defined in master records for the customer and vendor as well as configuration in the payment program.

New for SAP ERP

Prepayment of Vendors

In SAP ERP, it is now possible to prepay vendors within the Invoice Verification function. This can be used to prepay highly favored vendors. The function enables payment after issue of the invoice and full exploitation of the date of required payment and existing cash discounts, by posting the vendor liabilities, taxes, and cash discounts in Financial Accounting in advance. The system executes the payment of the invoice regardless of the relevant goods receipt and the outcome of the Invoice Verification check.

When the system posts invoices, it continues to execute the standard checks. If the system has already posted the prepayment document, you can only make restricted changes to the header fields of the invoice.

Upon prepayment, the system debits this account and then settles the account again after executing the check.

To execute the payment program, you use Transaction F110 in the Financial Accounting component via the navigation path, SAP MENU • ACCOUNTING • FINANCIAL ACCOUNTING • ACCOUNTS PAYABLE • PERIODIC PROCESSING • PAYMENTS.

To schedule the payment's processing, you use the Schedule Manager via Transaction SCMA. The Schedule Manager can run a number of periodic tasks that are executed on a regular basis, for example, daily, weekly, or monthly. Most companies process invoices on a daily or weekly basis.

New for SAP ERP

A new report (RMMR1MDC) is available within Invoice Verification, with which you can automatically settle planned delivery costs. To invoke the report, use Transaction MRDC or the navigation path, SAP MENU • LOGISTICS • MATERIALS MANAGEMENT • LOGISTICS INVOICE VERIFICATION • AUTOMATIC SETTLEMENT • AUTOMATIC DELIVERY COST SETTLEMENT.

Most companies will still use the traditional three-way match to process invoices and pay vendors. However, as more efficiencies are being sought in the supply chain in an effort to reduce costs, other techniques are being introduced. The next section discusses the use of one of those processes, Evaluated Receipt Settlement (ERS).

24.2 Evaluated Receipt Settlement

Evaluated Receipt Settlement (ERS) is the process whereby the goods receipt and the PO are matched and posted without any invoice, in other words, a two-way match. The vendor does not send an invoice for materials that are defined for evaluated settlement. This process is not standard for most companies because the evaluated-receipt process requires a significant level of cooperation and trust between customer and vendor. However, this method is of particular benefit to companies that purchase materials between different parts of the organization. The evaluated-receipt process reduces the need for sending and matching invoices between departments.

24.2.1 Benefits of ERS

The benefits of ERS include the following:

- No quantity or price variances with invoices
- Purchasing process completed sooner
- Vendors paid on receipt of goods at customer
- Favorable material prices from vendor

The ERS indicator can be found on the Vendor Master record, Transaction MK02 or MK03, as shown in Figure 24.4. The ERS indicator on the vendor file is passed through to the PO by way of the purchase information record or the vendor file. It is possible to remove the ERS indicator in the PO if normal Invoice Verification is required.

Figure 24.4 shows there are two indicators for evaluated receipt settlement. The first, AutoEvalGRSetmt Del., is used when evaluated receipts are to be used for normal deliveries from a vendor. The second, AutoEvalGRSetmt Ret, should be set when the evaluated receipt process is also valid for returns from the vendor.

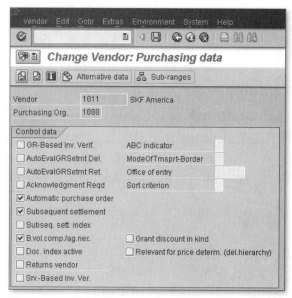

Figure 24.4 ERS Indicator on the Vendor Master Record

24.2.2 Running the Evaluated Receipt Settlement

The ERS process can be run on a schedule or on an ad-hoc basis. The ERS Transaction MRRL can be found by the navigation path, SAP Menu • Logistics • Materials Management • Logistics Invoice Verification • Automatic Settlement • Evaluated Receipt Settlement.

The selection screen, as shown in Figure 24.5, allows the user to restrict the program to a certain Plant, Vendor, or date range. After the selection has been made, the program can be executed. In Figure 24.5, the selection has been made to restrict processing to one particular vendor, 1011, and perform a test run, by checking the Test Run indicator.

The next section examines how to deal with document parking, which refers to invoices that are not ready to be posted in the system.

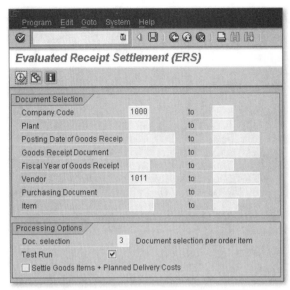

Figure 24.5 Selection Screen for Transaction MRRL

24.3 Document Parking

Document parking allows the user to enter the invoice but not to post it. The invoice document can be defined as parked. The invoice should be parked if the invoice is not ready for posting. This can happen for a number of reasons such as if the invoice needs changes to ensure successful posting, or if the balance of the invoice is other than zero.

24.3.1 Benefits of Document Parking

The main reason that documents are parked and not simply placed on hold is that the invoice in a parked status can be modified, whereas the invoice that is just held remains in its current state.

24.3.2 Parking an Invoice

The invoice can be parked using Transaction MIR7, which can be found using the navigation path, SAP MENU • LOGISTICS • MATERIALS MANAGEMENT • LOGISTICS INVOICE VERIFICATION • DOCUMENT ENTRY • PARK INVOICE.

The transaction is similar to Transaction MIRO for entering an invoice. The main difference is that when you are parking an invoice, the document does not need to be correct or to balance to zero because the invoice is not going to be posted. The document is parked and can be modified as needed.

If, after entering the information into Transaction MIR7, the user decides that the invoice does not need to be parked or that all of the information needed to post the invoice is now entered, the invoice can be posted. The user can select INVOICE DOCUMENT • SAVE AS COMPLETED or use the function keys, ⌘ Ctrl ⌘ + ⌘ F8 ⌘.

If when entering an invoice into Transaction MIRO, the user decides that the information is not sufficient for posting the invoice, the user can park the invoice and not post it. This can be performed in Transaction MIRO by selecting EDIT • SWITCH TO DOCUMENT PARKING.

The next section discusses the principle of variances. This is an important topic that you as a consultant will need to address with your client's AP department.

24.4 Variances

The AP department of any company will want the invoice matching to be exact with no variances. However, in the real world, variances do occur. When there is a variance, among the PO, goods receipt, and invoice, the system can allow a variance tolerance to be configured.

24.4.1 Variances Overview

An invoice has a variance if there are items, such as quantity or value, that are different between the invoice and the other documents. There are four types of variances associated with invoices:

▶ **Quantity variance**: Differences in the quantity delivered and the invoice quantity.

▶ **Price variance**: Price differences between the PO and the invoice.

▶ **Quantity and price variance**: Differences in price and quantity.

▶ **Order price quantity variance**: Price per ordered quantity is different, that is, $3 per Kg in the PO but $3.25 per Kg in the invoice.

Variances occur when the invoice is entered, and the matching process finds one of these four scenarios.

24.4.2 Tolerance Limits

The invoice can be posted if the variance is within the stated tolerance limits. The tolerance limit can be an absolute limit or a percentage limit. If the user does not want to block an invoice on the basis of a particular variance, the tolerance limit indicator should be set to DO NOT CHECK.

The different types of tolerances are called tolerance keys, and these are predefined in SAP ERP. Each tolerance key describes a variance between the invoice and the goods receipt or PO. The tolerance limits are assigned to each tolerance key. Each tolerance key can be defined for each separate plant. The tolerance limits can vary for each plant for the same tolerance key.

The tolerance keys defined in the SAP ERP system are given here:

Tolerance key assigned to plant.

– can also have Vendor specific Tolerance limits

- ▶ **AN**: Amount for item without order reference
- ▶ **AP**: Amount for item with order reference
- ▶ **BD**: Form small differences automatically
- ▶ **BR**: Percentage order price quantity unit variance (invoice receipt before goods receipt)
- ▶ **BW**: Percentage order price quantity unit variance (goods receipt before invoice receipt)
- ▶ **DQ**: Exceed amount: quantity variance
- ▶ **DW**: Quantity variance when goods receipt quantity equals zero
- ▶ **KW**: Variance from condition value
- ▶ **LA**: Amount of blanket purchase order
- ▶ **LD**: Blanket purchase order time limit is exceeded
- ▶ **PP**: Price variance
- ▶ **PS**: Price variance of the estimated price
- ▶ **ST**: Date variance
- ▶ **VP**: Moving average price variance

The configuration to define the tolerance limits can be found in Transaction OMR6 or by using the navigation path, IMG • MATERIALS MANAGEMENT • LOGISTICS INVOICE VERIFICATION • INVOICE BLOCK • SET TOLERANCE LIMITS.

Figure 24.6 shows the tolerance limit keys (TLKY) for each company code (COCD) that is defined in Transaction OMR6. After the tolerance key is established, the tolerance limits can be entered. In Figure 24.7, the tolerances for company code 6000 show that the LOWER LIMIT for the tolerance has an ABSOLUTE variance allowed of 20 pesos, and a maximum PERCENTAGE tolerance of 10%. On the UPPER LIMIT, the tolerances are the same. This means that if an invoice is entered of 3000 pesos, and the PO is for 2900 pesos, the absolute variance is triggered because the variance is 100 pesos above the 20-peso tolerance.

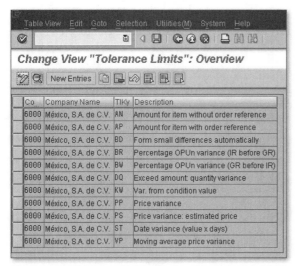

Figure 24.6 Tolerance Limit Keys for Company Code 6000

Figure 24.7 shows the details for each COMPANY CODE/TOLERANCE KEY. These are found by selecting GOTO • DETAILS.

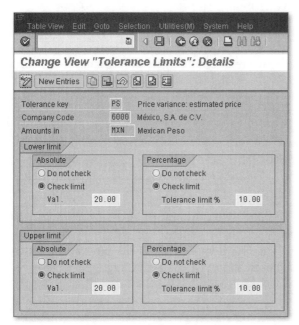

Figure 24.7 Tolerance Details for a Tolerance Key in Transaction OMR6

Figure 24.7 shows the upper and lower tolerances that can be configured for both a price value, in the specified currency, and a percentage value. The user does have the option to set the Do not check indicator, which will not check the invoice for this type of variance.

If a variance is found, the AP department can then block an invoice from being paid. The next section discusses how to block invoices in SAP ERP.

24.5 Blocking Invoices

When the invoice has been blocked, the invoice amount cannot be paid to the vendor.

24.5.1 Blocking Invoices

There are a number of ways in which an invoice can be blocked:

▶ Manual block

▶ Stochastic or random block

▶ Block due to amount of an invoice item

▶ Block due to variance of an invoice item

After an invoice is blocked, all of the individual line items are blocked. This is problematic when there are many line items, and only one item is causing a variance. It is then up to the finance department to investigate the variance to unblock the invoice for payment.

24.5.2 Manual Block

The user can set the manual block during the entry of the invoice in Transaction MIRO. The manual block (Pmnt Block) field can be found on the Payment screen of the document header, shown in Figure 24.8. Once set, the whole invoice is blocked for payment.

You can also set the manual block indicator in the appropriate line item, as shown in Figure 24.9. This will not just block that line item but will block the whole invoice from payment. Note that the line item will show the blocked indicator (Man Blk), but the manual block field will not be changed until after posting.

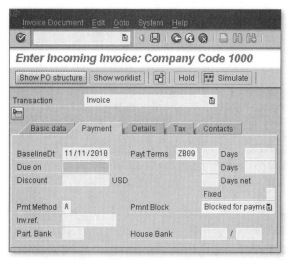

Figure 24.8 Manual Block Field of Invoice Header in Transaction MIRO

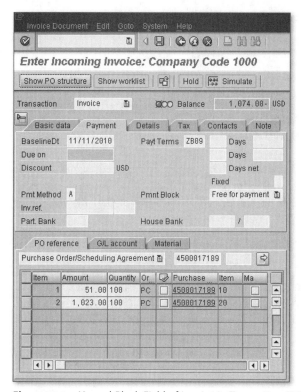

Figure 24.9 Manual Block Field of Invoice in Transaction MIRO

24.5.3 Stochastic or Random Block

The stochastic or random block allows the company to check invoices at random or above a threshold value defined in configuration. Setting the stochastic block is a two-step process in configuration. First, the stochastic block has to be activated at the plant level. Second, a threshold can be set for each plant, as well as a percentage that represents the degree of possibility of the invoice being checked.

The configuration for the activation of the stochastic block is shown in Figure 24.10. The configuration transaction can be found using the navigation path, IMG • Materials Management • Logistics Invoice Verification • Invoice Block • Stochastic Block • Activate Stochastic Block.

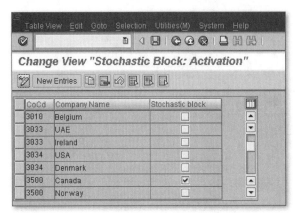

Figure 24.10 Activation of Stochastic Block at Plant Level in Configuration

When the threshold value and probability are being configured, users have to realize how the stochastic block works. If the total value of the invoice is larger or the same as the configured threshold value, the probability of that invoice being blocked is configured.

However, if the total value of the invoice is smaller than the threshold amount, the probability that the invoice will be blocked is calculated proportionally to the percentage configured.

Therefore, if the user configures the Threshold value for company code (CoCd) 3034 to be $6,000 USD and configures the Percentage to be 50.00, each invoice entered over $6,000 USD would have a 50% probability of being blocked, as shown in Figure 24.11. If an invoice of $3,000 USD were entered, then this would have a 25% change of being blocked because it is half the value of the THRESHOLD VALUE. If the users require the degree of probability to be the same for all invoices, the THRESHOLD VALUE should be configured to zero.

Figure 24.11 shows the configuration for the threshold values of the stochastic block, which can be found using the navigation path, IMG • MATERIALS MANAGEMENT • LOGISTICS INVOICE VERIFICATION • INVOICE BLOCK • STOCHASTIC BLOCK • SET STOCHASTIC BLOCK.

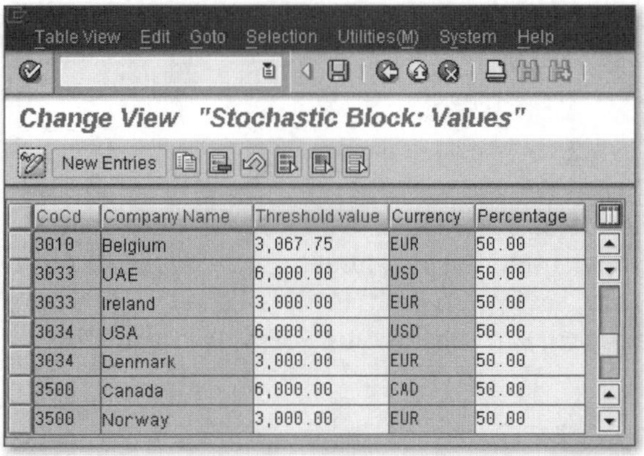

CoCd	Company Name	Threshold value	Currency	Percentage
3010	Belgium	3,067.75	EUR	50.00
3033	UAE	6,000.00	USD	50.00
3033	Ireland	3,000.00	EUR	50.00
3034	USA	6,000.00	USD	50.00
3034	Denmark	3,000.00	EUR	50.00
3500	Canada	6,000.00	CAD	50.00
3500	Norway	3,000.00	EUR	50.00

Figure 24.11 Threshold Value and Percentage Probability Value for Stochastic Block Configuration

Figure 24.11 shows the THRESHOLD VALUE and PERCENTAGE value entered for the relevant company codes. For example, CANADA has a THRESHOLD VALUE of $6000 Canadian dollars and a PERCENTAGE of 50.00.

24.5.4 Block Due to Amount of an Invoice Item

Sometimes companies decide to block all invoices that have line items with larger values. This is a safety feature to ensure that vendors are not paid on invoices that have incorrectly been sent by the vendor or incorrectly entered by the finance clerks.

The first step in configuring this particular block is to activate the block due to item amount in the IMG, as shown in Figure 24.12. The configuration can be found using the navigation path, IMG • MATERIALS MANAGEMENT • LOGISTICS INVOICE VERIFICATION • INVOICE BLOCK • ITEM AMOUNT CHECK • ACTIVATE ITEM AMOUNT CHECK.

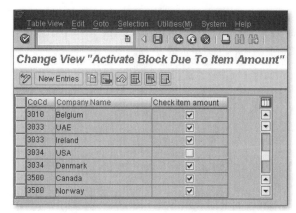

Figure 24.12 Configuration of Activation Flag for Each Company Code

After the CHECK ITEM AMOUNT indicator has been activated for a company code, the detailed configuration of the item amount can commence. The first part of the configuration can be found using the navigation path, IMG • MATERIALS MANAGEMENT • LOGISTICS INVOICE VERIFICATION • INVOICE BLOCK • ITEM AMOUNT CHECK • SET ITEM AMOUNT CHECK.

This configuration, shown in Figure 24.13, allows the user to determine which invoice line items are checked by the system. The item amounts for invoice items are checked on the basis of the item category and the GOODS RECEIPT indicator, depending on the configuration.

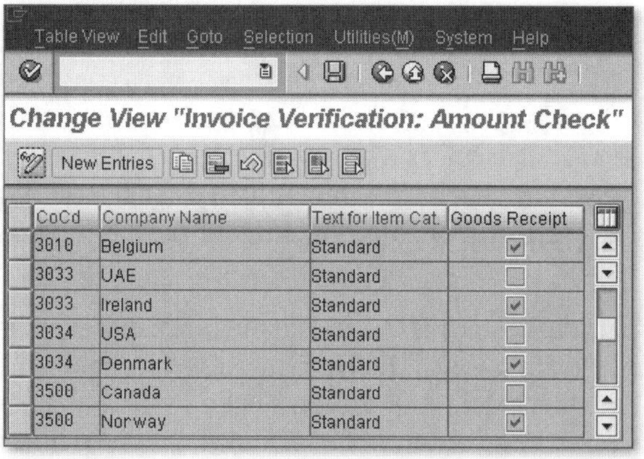

Figure 24.13 Configuration for Checking the Item Amount for the Item Category and Goods Receipt Indicator

The final step of the configuration is to set the amount at which the invoice is blocked, as shown in Figure 24.14. Using Transaction OMR6, the amount depends on the company code and the tolerance key. In Figure 24.14, we can see that for COMPANY CODE 6000, the ABSOLUTE upper value has been configured as 10,000.00 pesos.

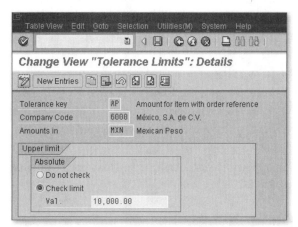

Figure 24.14 Upper-Limit Configuration for the Block Due to the Amount of an Invoice Item

24.5.5 Block Due to Variance of an Invoice Item

A number of blocks can be set due to the variance in an invoice item:

- **Quantity variance (Q):** The block is due to a variance between PO quantity, delivered quantity, and invoiced quantity.
- **Price variance (P):** The price of the item in the PO does not match the price of the item in the invoice.
- **Schedule variance (D):** The delivery of the items has occurred before the scheduled date.
- **Quality inspection (I):** The block is due to an issue with the quality of the items at or after goods receipt.

For blocking due to a variance, the invoice may still be blocked even though the blocking reason is no longer valid. The block must be released either automatically or manually for the invoice to be paid. Let's examine the releasing of invoices next.

24.6   Releasing Invoices

After the invoice has been blocked, a procedure needs to be set up to ensure that the invoices are released when the reason for the block is no longer valid. The whole invoice is blocked despite the fact that only one line item may be causing the block. Therefore, before the invoice can be paid for all of the line items, the invoice must be released. We do this by canceling the blocking indicator that was set when the invoice was originally posted.

24.6.1   Releasing Invoices Automatically

The automatic release of blocked invoices deletes all blocks that no longer apply to the invoices the user has selected for review.

To release the invoices automatically, use Transaction MRBR, which is shown in Figure 24.15. The transaction can be found using the navigation path, SAP MENU • LOGISTICS • MATERIALS MANAGEMENT • LOGISTICS INVOICE VERIFICATION • FURTHER PROCESSING • RELEASE BLOCKED INVOICES.

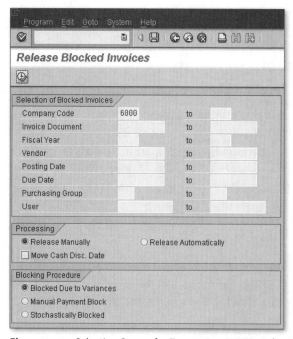

Figure 24.15   Selection Screen for Transaction MRBR: Releasing Invoices Manually

If the AP department decides that it wants to review all invoices before release, then Transaction MRBR allows the user to flag that the release of the invoices will be made manually. In this case, the program will display all of the relevant blocked invoices for the selection criteria entered.

The detailed display for the invoices shows the reasons for the blocked invoices and highlights those where the block is still in place but no longer valid. The user can then choose to release manually any invoices, as shown in Figure 24.16. In this case, there are two invoice lines that can be released from the same invoice, 5105607372.

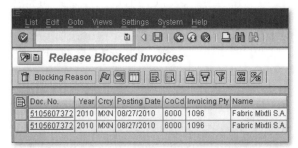

Figure 24.16 Releasing Blocked Invoices Identified by Transaction MRBR

24.7 Business Examples – Invoice Verification

Invoice Verification is an important part of the AP process. Vendors send their customers an invoice for materials or services that they have provided. The verification of the invoice ensures that the quantities and the pricing are correct and that neither party has made an error.

24.7.1 Evaluated Receipt Settlement

ERS is the process whereby the goods receipt and the PO are matched and posted without any invoice. The evaluated receipt process requires a high level of cooperation and trust between customer and vendor.

Example

A specialty chemicals company in Puerto Rico used a small number of local vendors for the majority of its bulk chemicals. Most of the vendors were small and operated on very lean budgets. Since this specialty chemicals company had migrated to SAP ERP, the AP process had become more formalized. Payments to vendors were taking longer because staff had to perform more data entry and get used to the system. Although payments were within the allotted payment terms that the companies had agreed upon, the vendors were used to a more informal process where they received payment soon after each delivery.

The company's vendors voiced their concern that delays in payments would put some of them in danger of having to reduce staff or even close. Without the local vendors, the company would have to import bulk chemicals from the U.S. mainland, which would cause added delay and cost.

The consulting company helping with the implementation offered the company a solution. The consultants suggested that the company pay these vendors on receipt of the product, allowing vendors to forego the invoice process. The company and its vendors discussed this evaluated receipt option, and the company offered each vendor the option of being paid on receipt for a 4% discount on pricing and monthly quality checks at the vendor facilities. The local vendors agreed and received a check for the goods at time of delivery.

24.7.2 Variances

AP departments want invoices to match with no variances, but they do occur. When there is a variance among the PO, goods receipt, and invoice, the SAP ERP system can allow a variance tolerance to be configured so the invoice can post.

Example

A U.S. chemical company purchased its bulk raw materials for tanker delivery. When the PO is created, it is for a standard amount based on the tanker capacity. The tanker arrives at the manufacturing facility and is pumped out into holding tanks. The old method of dipping the tank to show the quantity delivered had been replaced by a flow meter on the pumping station, which gave a more accurate indication of the delivery amount.

When the tanker was empty, the flow meter reading showed the amount pumped. A printout was given to the driver and a copy sent with the delivery note to the AP department.

The chemicals were tested for quality, and after the batch had been approved for use, the AP department reviewed the invoice against the other documents. Based on the amount received, the invoice quantity fluctuated based on the amount the vendor says they pumped into the tank. There was always some minor variance, and the AP department entered the invoice. The SAP ERP system determined if the invoice could be posted based on the configuration of variances, both quantity and value. The configuration entered was usually based on experience with the vendor and the material involved. If the invoice variance was within the tolerances configured, then the invoice was posted and the vendor paid.

24.7.3 Blocking Invoices

A company can decide to block an invoice. When this occurs, the invoice cannot be paid to the vendor. There are a number of ways in which an invoice can be blocked: manual, random, block due to amount of an invoice item, and block due to variance of an invoice item.

Example

A U.S. based automotive parts distributor had begun sourcing some items for Korean and Japanese cars through new vendors in Cambodia. The distributor visited the factories in Cambodia, and quality checks found that the items were within specifications.

The parts were significantly cheaper than parts manufacturing in Korea, China, and Thailand. As standard procedure, when the distributor signed a contract with a new vendor, each delivery was thoroughly checked for quality, damage, and quantity. The first PO was placed, and a delivery promised in six weeks. The distributor received an ASN, and the delivery appeared to be on time. The invoice arrived before the shipment, and the AP department noticed that the invoice showed an amount greater than on the invoice and a price that was almost 20% higher than the contract price. The distributor called the vendor to query the invoice, and another invoice was faxed over for the correct quantity and pricing.

The delivery did not arrive on the specified date and instead another ASN arrived, specifying a date in an additional three weeks. After waiting five more weeks, the parts arrived. The shipment appeared to be packaged well, but inside the shrink-wrapped pallets, the items were not as described. The invoice indicated 300 Toyota exhaust manifolds when in fact there were 100 exhaust manifolds for a Toyota and 150 for a variety of Nissan and Suzuki vehicles that were not part of the contract agreement.

The invoice was placed on hold until discussions with the Cambodian vendor sorted out the issue. In addition to the issue with the parts that were sent, the Toyota parts that were on the invoice failed quality inspection and could not be sold. The quality department did not have specifications for the other parts, so their usage could not be decided.

The distributor decided to use the vendor for small shipments on an as-is basis, but based on this experience, the company required the AP department to automatically block all invoices from the vendor until thorough checks were made.

24.8 Summary

This chapter described the processes involved in Invoice Verification. The entry of the invoice is a simple process. However, after the invoice is entered, the AP department must decide if the invoice is correct and how to proceed if the invoice does not match the information from the PO or the goods receipt. Blocking invoices is a very common occurrence, so it is important to understand how these different types of blocks work and why they are in place.

The next chapter discusses balance sheet valuation. The balance sheet is a financial statement that a company often refers to because it shows a financial snapshot of the company.

Balance sheet valuation is the calculation of the material value for use in balance sheets. The method employed may depend on country-specific tax regulations, state and federal legal requirements, corporate financial practices, and internal accounting policy procedures.

25   Balance Sheet Valuation

A balance sheet is a financial statement of a business at a specific point in time. The balance sheet reports on the source of funds to a business and how those funds have been used or invested. Within the Use of Funds section of the balance sheet, there are two areas, Fixed Assets, and Working Capital. Fixed assets are those that can be depreciated, such as machines and buildings. Working capital refers to the funds used to provide the flow of material and services to achieve sales and satisfy the customer. Working capital can be two areas: current assets and current liabilities. Current assets are cash, payables, receivables, and the material in the warehouse. The material includes raw material, work in process, and finished goods. The stock value is the lowest cost or the net realizable, or saleable, value.

25.1   LIFO Valuation

Last in, first out (LIFO) valuation is based on the principle that the last deliveries of a material to be received are the first to be used. If this is true, then no value change occurs for older material when new materials are received. Because of the LIFO method, the older material is not affected by the higher prices of the new deliveries of material. If the older material is not affected, that means it is not valuated at the new material price. If the older material value is not increased, this stops any false valuation of current inventory.

LIFO valuation enables the increased amount of material stock per fiscal year to be valuated separately from the rest of the material stock. This is important because it ensures that the new material is valuated at the correct amount, while old stock remains valuated without being affected by the new material price. A positive variance between the opening and closing material balances of a fiscal year is known as a layer for LIFO valuation. The layer is valuated as a separate item. The total of a material is the sum of all layers.

A layer is dissolved if there is a negative difference between the opening and closing stock balances at the end of a fiscal year. This would happen, for example, if all of the new stock was consumed plus some of the existing stock.

25.1.1 Configuration for LIFO

The first step in configuration is to ensure that LIFO is active by using Transaction OMWE, which can be found in the navigation path, IMG • MATERIALS MANAGEMENT • VALUATION AND ACCOUNT ASSIGNMENT • BALANCE SHEET VALUATION PROCEDURES • CONFIGURE LIFO/FIFO METHODS • GENERAL INFORMATION • ACTIVATE/ DEACTIVATE LIFO/FIFO VALUATION.

After the LIFO valuation has been activated, as shown in Figure 25.1, the LIFO valuation can be configured for each company code or valuation area by using Transaction MRLH as shown in Figure 25.2.

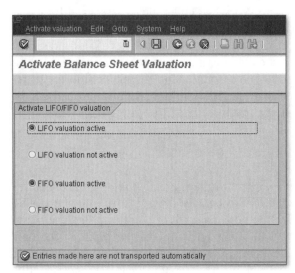

Figure 25.1 Activate LIFO Valuation Screen

The LIFO method also depends on the movement types being set up as relevant for LIFO. The configuration is shown in Figure 25.3.

In Figure 25.3, for example, there are two records that have been flagged as LIFO (the LIFO indicator has been checked). Both records flagged as LIFO are for movement type (MvT) 101 and movement indicator (MvtInd.) B. This transaction can be accessed using Transaction OMW4 or via the navigation path, IMG • MATERIALS MANAGEMENT • VALUATION AND ACCOUNT ASSIGNMENT • BALANCE SHEET VALUATION

PROCEDURES • CONFIGURE LIFO/FIFO METHODS • GENERAL INFORMATION • DEFINE
LIFO/FIFO RELEVANT MOVEMENT TYPES.

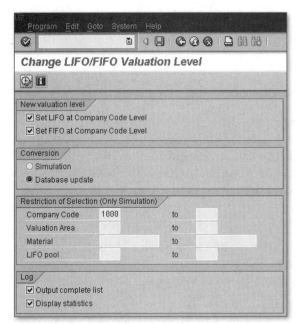

Figure 25.2   Configuration for LIFO and FIFO at Plant or Valuation Area Level

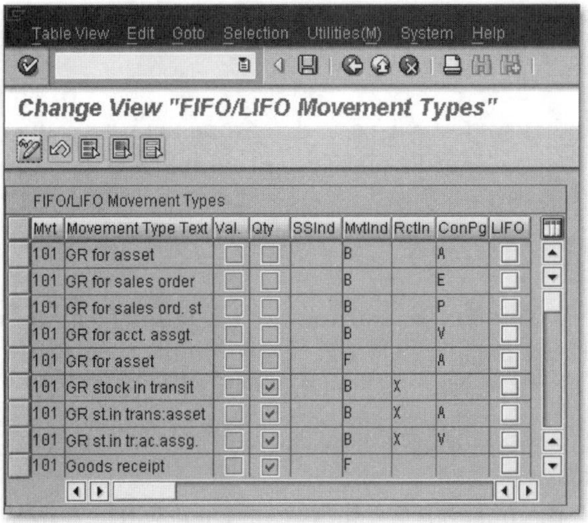

Figure 25.3   Movement Types Configured as Relevant for LIFO Valuation

25.1.2 Preparation for LIFO

To instigate LIFO valuation, a number of preparation steps must be completed. These steps include ensuring the materials are defined for LIFO, setting up the base layers for valuation, and setting up the basis for comparison.

Material Master Records

To prepare for LIFO valuation, you must make sure that the materials you want to value are flagged for LIFO. The flag is located within the Material Master on the accounting screen.

You can use Transaction MRL6 to update the LIFO flag for a selection of materials, material types, plants, and so on. This transaction can be found using the navigation path, SAP MENU • LOGISTICS • MATERIALS MANAGEMENT • VALUATION • BALANCE SHEET VALUATION • LIFO VALUATION • PREPARE • SELECT MATERIALS.

Base Layers

As discussed previously, the measurement of material value changes is based on comparing different layers. Before LIFO can be started, the base layer should be created from information on the older existing material.

The base layer is shown in Figure 25.4. The base layer can be created using Transaction MRL8 or using the navigation path, SAP MENU • LOGISTICS • MATERIALS MANAGEMENT • VALUATION • BALANCE SHEET VALUATION • LIFO VALUATION • PREPARE • CREATE BASE LAYER.

In Transaction MRL8, the user needs to enter the materials to create the base layer for and enter the LIFO method that is to be used.

The user should select the values that are to be used to determine the layer value. The choices include PREVIOUS MONTH, MNTHBEFORELAST, PREVIOUS YEAR, and YR BEFORE LAST.

Determination of Basis for Comparison

Before running a LIFO valuation, a basis for comparison needs to be determined. During LIFO valuation, the stocks are compared at a particular point in time with the total of the layer quantities. These are periods that are defined in SAP ERP:

- **GJE:** The stock at the end of the previous fiscal year is compared with the total quantities in the existing layers.
- **VOM:** The stock at the end of the previous period is compared with the total quantities in the existing layers.

▶ **VVM**: The stock at the end of the period before last is compared with the total quantities in the existing layers.

▶ **CUR**: The current stock is compared with the total quantities in the existing layers.

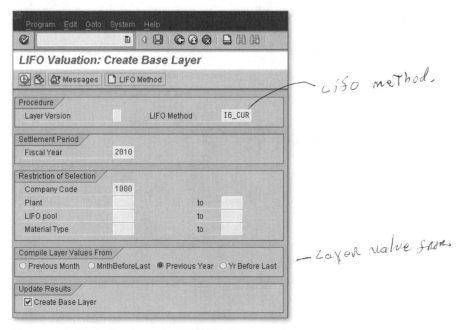

Figure 25.4 Create Base Layer for LIFO Valuation

25.1.3 Running a LIFO Valuation

After all of the configuration and preparation has been completed for the LIFO valuation, the transaction can be executed to run the valuation. The transactions that can be run are the following:

▶ MRL1 for single material level

▶ MRL2 for the pool level

▶ MRL3 for comparison of lowest values

The navigation path to find these transactions is SAP Menu • Logistics • Materials Management • Valuation • Balance Sheet Valuation • LIFO Valuation • Perform Check.

In Transaction MRL1, shown in Figure 25.5, the user can choose the LIFO method, the selection criteria, and the value determination for the new layer. In Figure 25.5, the LIFO METHOD M2_CUR has been chosen. In the RESTRICTION OF SELECTION criteria fields, the COMPANY CODE 1000 has been entered. The value determination for the new layer has been selected as TOTAL ACCOUNTING PERIOD. After these have been entered, the transaction can be executed, and the result for LIFO method M2_CUR can be seen in Figure 25.6. Different LIFO methods will produce different reports. In Figure 25.6, a number of materials can be seen on the report that now has LIFO valuations based on the M2_CUR method. The first material on the report, 500-130, has a total stock quantity of 11,020 with a LIFO valuation of $17,754.98 USD.

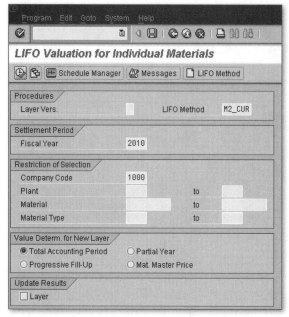

Figure 25.5 Selection Screen for LIFO Valuation Transaction MRL1

This section has shown how materials can be flagged as LIFO. We have examined the LIFO valuation method in which the material that is purchased or produced last is sold, consumed, or disposed of first. The next section reviews the reverse of this method, that is, the FIFO (first in, first out) method.

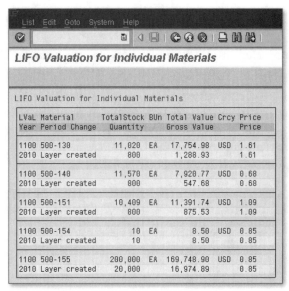

Figure 25.6 Result of LIFO Valuation Transaction MRL1

25.2 FIFO Valuation

First in, first out (FIFO) is a valuation method in which the material that is purchased or produced first is also sold, consumed, or disposed of first. Companies
whose material are batch-managed, have an expiry date, or degrade in quality with
time will often use this method. Use of this method presupposes that the next item
to be shipped will be the oldest of that material in the warehouse. In practice, this
usually reflects the underlying commercial method of companies rotating their
inventory.

Newer companies commonly use FIFO for reporting the value of merchandise to
bolster their balance sheets. As the older and cheaper materials are sold, the newer
and more expensive materials remain as assets on the balance sheet. However, as
the company grows, it may switch to LIFO to reduce the amount of taxes it pays
to the government.

25.2.1 Configuration for FIFO

The configuration steps for FIFO are very similar to those of configuring the LIFO
valuation. The first step in configuration is to ensure that FIFO is active by using
Transaction OMWE, which can be found in the navigation path, IMG • MATERIALS
MANAGEMENT • VALUATION AND ACCOUNT ASSIGNMENT • BALANCE SHEET VALUATION

PROCEDURES • CONFIGURE LIFO/FIFO METHODS • GENERAL INFORMATION • ACTIVATE/ DEACTIVATE LIFO/FIFO VALUATION.

After FIFO valuation has been activated, it can be configured for each company code or valuation area using Transaction MRLH.

Last, configure the movement types being set up to be relevant for FIFO. The configuration can be found using Transaction OMW4 or via the navigation path, IMG • MATERIALS MANAGEMENT • VALUATION AND ACCOUNT ASSIGNMENT • BALANCE SHEET VALUATION PROCEDURES • CONFIGURE LIFO/FIFO METHODS • GENERAL INFORMATION • DEFINE LIFO/FIFO RELEVANT MOVEMENT TYPES.

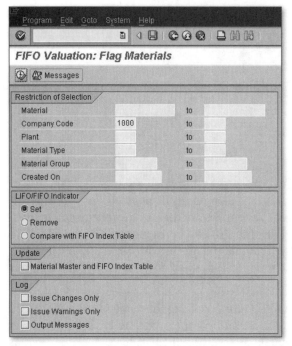

Figure 25.7 Material Selection for FIFO Valuation Method

25.2.2 Preparation for FIFO

After configuration for FIFO is complete, the materials relevant for FIFO need to be selected using Transaction MRF4, as shown in Figure 25.7. The screen shows that the FIFO valuation flag can be set for a number of selections, for a single MATERIAL or a range of materials, a PLANT, a MATERIAL TYPE, or a MATERIAL GROUP. In this example, all of the materials of COMPANY CODE 1000 are going to be flagged as FIFO. This transaction can be found using the navigation path, SAP MENU •

Logistics • Materials Management • Valuation • Balance Sheet Valuation • FIFO Valuation • Prepare • Select Materials.

25.2.3 Running a FIFO Valuation

After all of the configuration and preparation has been completed for the FIFO valuation, Transaction MRF1 can be executed to run the valuation as shown in Figure 25.8. The transaction can be found using the navigation path, SAP Menu • Logistics • Materials Management • Valuation • Balance Sheet Valuation • FIFO Valuation • Perform Check.

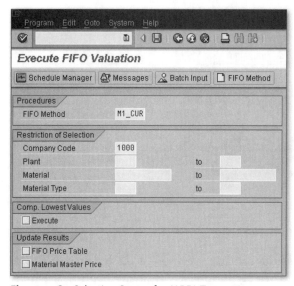

Figure 25.8 Selection Screen for MRF1 Transaction

After the transaction has been executed, the FIFO valuation is formed for the selected materials, plant, and so on, and a report is displayed as shown in Figure 25.9.

This section has shown how materials can be flagged as FIFO. We have seen that FIFO is a valuation method in which the material that is purchased or produced first is sold, consumed, or disposed of first. The next section reviews the lowest value determination, which uses the valuation method of the lowest value principle.

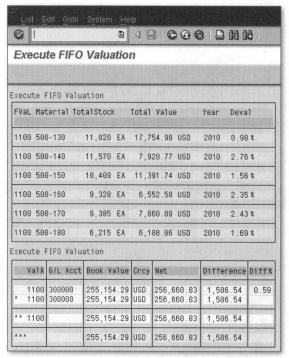

Figure 25.9 Result of FIFO Valuation Transaction MRF1

25.3 Lowest Value Determination

Lowest value determination uses the valuation method of the lowest value principle (LVP). This method is used widely in industry in many countries. Simply put, LVP indicates where the material is valued at the lowest value held on the system.

Three types of value determination can be used to calculate the material value:

- Based on market prices
- Based on range of coverage
- Based on movement rate

25.3.1 Lowest Value Determination Based on Market Prices

To determine the lowest value based on market prices, the SAP ERP system searches for the lowest price from the different prices stored for each material. The procedure looks at the material price from the following:

- POs
- Scheduling agreements
- Goods receipts for POs
- Invoices for POs
- Purchasing information records

Transaction MRNO is used to run the lowest value based on market price and can be found in the navigation path, SAP MENU • LOGISTICS • MATERIALS MAN-AGEMENT • VALUATION • BALANCE SHEET VALUATION • DETERMINATION OF LOWEST VALUE • MARKET PRICES.

The selection screen, shown in Figure 25.10, allows the user to enter a range of MATERIAL, PLANT, MATERIAL TYPE, or VALUATION CLASS.

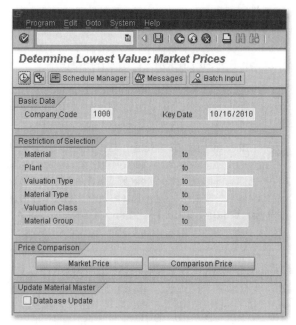

Figure 25.10 Selection Screen to Determine the Lowest Value Based on Market Prices

After the selection criteria have been entered, the transaction can be executed. The resulting display, shown in Figure 25.11, shows the new price and the percentage change.

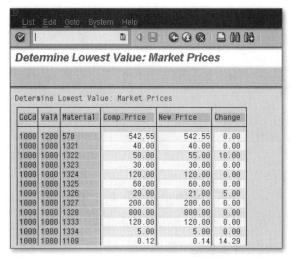

Figure 25.11 Determination of Lowest Price Report

25.3.2 Lowest Value Determination Based on Range of Coverage

With this method, the SAP ERP system checks whether the price for a material should be devaluated because it has a high range of coverage. The system defines the range of coverage as the average stock divided by the average consumption.

The user can configure the percentage discount for devaluating materials by company code. The configuration to define the devaluation is found in Transaction OMW5, shown in Figure 25.12, or via the navigation path, IMG • MATERIALS MANAGEMENT • VALUATION AND ACCOUNT ASSIGNMENT • BALANCE SHEET VALUATION PROCEDURES • CONFIGURE LOWEST VALUE METHODS • PRICE DEDUCTIONS BY RANGE OF COVERAGE • MAINTAIN DEVALUATION BY RANGE OF COVERAGE BY COMPANY CODE.

The configuration allows the user to enter a range of coverage value (RNGE/CVRG.), which is the average stock divided by the average consumption; and a devaluation percentage (DEVAL. %) for each company code (COCD).

Transaction MRN1 is used to run the lowest value based on range of coverage and can found in the navigation path, SAP MENU • LOGISTICS • MATERIALS MANAGEMENT • VALUATION • BALANCE SHEET VALUATION • DETERMINATION OF LOWEST VALUE • RANGE OF COVERAGE.

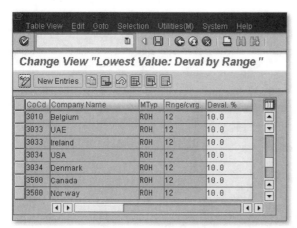

Figure 25.12 Configuration for Devaluation by Range of Coverage

The selection screen, shown in Figure 25.13, allows the user to enter a range of coverage. The values in the coverage for the lowest value determination can include Material, Plant, Valuation Type, Material Type, Valuation Class, and Material Group. In this example, the coverage has been limited to Plant 3000.

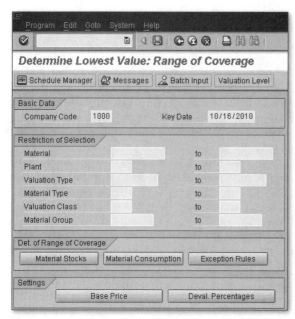

Figure 25.13 Selection Screen for Transaction MRN1

After the selection criteria have been entered in Figure 25.13, the transaction can be executed. The resulting display, as shown in Figure 25.14, shows the range of coverage, which determines the devaluation percentage and the calculated new value.

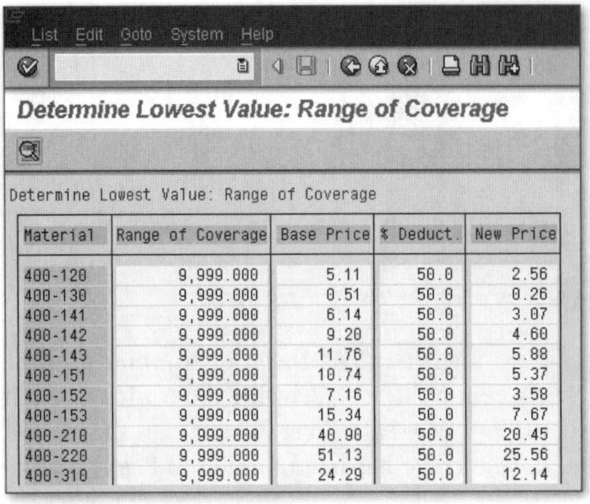
List Edit Goto System Help
Determine Lowest Value: Range of Coverage
Determine Lowest Value: Range of Coverage
Material Range of Coverage Base Price % Deduct. New Price
400-120 9,999.000 5.11 50.0 2.56
400-130 9,999.000 0.51 50.0 0.26
400-141 9,999.000 6.14 50.0 3.07
400-142 9,999.000 9.20 50.0 4.60
400-143 9,999.000 11.76 50.0 5.88
400-151 9,999.000 10.74 50.0 5.37
400-152 9,999.000 7.16 50.0 3.58
400-153 9,999.000 15.34 50.0 7.67
400-210 9,999.000 40.90 50.0 20.45
400-220 9,999.000 51.13 50.0 25.56
400-310 9,999.000 24.29 50.0 12.14

Figure 25.14 Results from Transaction MRN1

25.3.3 Lowest Value Determination Based on Movement Rate

In using the lowest value based on movement rate, we determine the value of the material based on the slow movement or non-movement of a material. The system defines the movement rate as a percentage, where the total quantity of receipts is divided by the material in stock and then multiplied by 100 to give the figure as a percentage.

For example, if a company has stock of 400 units of material ABC in a valuation area, and the number of movements has been only 40 in the period, then the movement rate is movements divided by the stock, that is, 40/400, multiplied by 100 to calculate the percentage, which in this case is 10%.

The devaluation percentage is configured in Transaction OMW6, in a similar manner as Transaction OMW5 for range of coverage, where a percentage is configured per company code. Using the previous example, if a decision was made that a slow-moving material is anything with a movement rate of below 15%, then the material ABC would be a slow-moving stock. This means the stock is devalued.

Transaction MRN2 is used to run the lowest value based on movement rate as shown in Figure 25.15. The selection criteria is the same as shown earlier in Figure 25.13, which includes MATERIAL, PLANT, VALUATION TYPE, MATERIAL TYPE, VALUATION CLASS, and MATERIAL GROUP. This transaction can be found in the navigation path, SAP MENU • LOGISTICS • MATERIALS MANAGEMENT • VALUATION • BALANCE SHEET VALUATION • DETERMINATION OF LOWEST VALUE • MOVEMENT RATE.

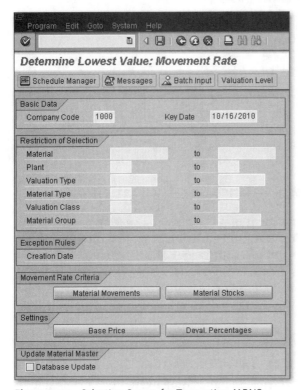

Figure 25.15 Selection Screen for Transaction MRN2

After the selection criteria have been entered, the transaction can be executed. The resulting display in Figure 25.16 shows the indicator with the corresponding percentage discount. This discount is then applied to the base price to calculate the new lowest price.

This section has examined the lowest value determination, which uses the valuation method of the LVP.

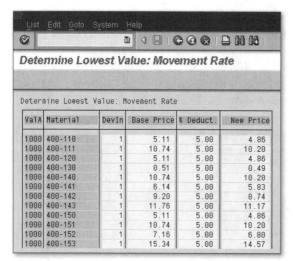

Figure 25.16 Calculate New Lowest Price Based on Movement Rate

25.4 Business Examples – Balance Sheet Valuation

A balance sheet is a financial statement of a business at a specific point in time. There are three types of valuation that can be used. Last in, first out (LIFO) valuation is based on the principle that the last deliveries of a material to be received are the first to be used. First in, first out (FIFO) is a valuation method in which the material that is purchased or produced first is sold, consumed, or disposed of first. Lowest value determination uses the valuation method of the lowest value principle (LVP).

25.4.1 LIFO Valuation

LIFO valuation is based on the principle that the last deliveries of a material to be received are the first to be used. LIFO valuation enables the increased amount of material stock per fiscal year to be valuated separately from the rest of the material stock.

Example

The purchasing department of a U.S. based hand tools manufacturer informed the accounting department that the cost of its products would probably increase as the raw materials prices had raised more than 15% in one year. The accounting department had been reviewing the valuation of the company's products, and they were discussing LIFO or FIFO valuation with the company's auditors.

The auditors informed the company that using LIFO valuation for the materials in the SAP ERP system would result in a better situation for the company. Initially, the use of LIFO results in less taxable income and less tax owed than if the company had FIFO valuation. Over a long period of time, or when costs increase dramatically, the lower income tax payments under LIFO will be significant.

The second reason concerned matching costs with sales when raw material costs are increasing. Using LIFO, the cost of replacing raw materials is always higher, and the cost of goods sold reflects the new higher price under LIFO valuation, rather than FIFO.

25.4.2 FIFO Valuation

FIFO is a valuation method in which the material that is purchased or produced first is sold, consumed, or disposed of first. Newer companies commonly use FIFO for reporting the value of merchandise to bolster their balance sheets.

Example

A small U.S. based high-tech manufacturer of specialty routers was reviewing its financial results with its accountants. The company had been using FIFO valuation for its stock because it felt it was important to sell the routers made in the previous year before the latest batch. The company felt that its routers only had a life of nine months before a new version had to be launched.

The cost of raw materials, labor, and components had remained steady, so the cost of goods sold had not increased. The accounting firm concurred that based on the lack of inflation and the stable costs, the choice of FIFO valuation was currently appropriate.

25.4.3 Lowest Value Determination

Lowest value determination uses the valuation method of the lowest value principle (LVP). The LVP indicates where the material is valued at the lowest value held on the system. Three types of value determination can be used to calculate the material value: based on market prices, based on range of coverage, or based on movement rate.

Example

The small U.S. based high-tech manufacturer of specialty routers used to manufacture DSL modems for some telephone companies. The market for these modems had suffered and as such the company had a significant inventory of increasingly obsolete DSL modems. The company realized that the modem inventory needed to be valuated correctly because the value was estimated to be far lower than currently stated.

The company's accountants recommended that the modems be valuated after the quantity of the sales or movement rate had fallen to less than 5 per month. At that point, the items could be devalued.

25.5 Summary

This chapter discussed how material is valued using the LIFO and FIFO methods and lowest value determination. Companies refer to the method of their material valuation in annual reports, and all of these methods are used. There is no one correct method, and companies choose whichever method is best suited to them at the time. As described in the chapter, newer companies often use FIFO to inflate their stock value, whereas mature companies can use LIFO to reduce their tax payments. Although not a core MM subject, the MM consultant should have a good understanding of how material is valuated in SAP ERP. The majority of the material that is stored in the plant or warehouse has a value assigned to it. Valuations such as LIFO and FIFO drive how material is moved out of the plant, so the MM consultant needs to be aware on what valuation methods are used at the client and how these valuation methods work.

Chapter 26 examines the material ledger. This may be an unfamiliar topic, but it is a part of the MM suite that should be understood to get a total picture of material valuation and costing at a company.

The benefits of the material ledger include keeping inventory records in up to three currencies, thus facilitating consolidation for companies belonging to multi-national groups. It also includes calculating the actual costs for procured material or material from production.

26 Material Ledger

Companies use the material ledger when material is required to be available in a number of currencies. The material ledger allows a material to have an actual cost calculated, which takes into account all of the costs of materials that have been moved, not just the price on the Material Master.

26.1 Material Ledger Overview

The material ledger serves two purposes. First, it records actual costs of materials and at the same time considers and records all of the factors behind price fluctuation. This functionality of the material ledger enables faster and more effective decision making regarding MM, controlling, and production. Second, the material ledger can hold values in three currencies simultaneously, which is a major benefit for companies that need to report valuation in different currencies. In addition, the material ledger makes it possible to revaluate stock on the basis of real calculation, which is legally required in some countries.

Using actual costing, all goods movements within a period are valuated at the standard price. In parallel, all price and exchange rate differences for the material are collected in the material ledger.

Within the material ledger at the end of the period, an actual price is calculated for each material based on the actual costs for that particular period. The actual calculated price is called the periodic unit price and can be used to revaluate the inventory for the period to be closed. This calculated actual price is the standard price for the next period.

26.1.1 Activating the Material Ledger and Actual Costing

To use the material ledger, the functionality must be activated. The transaction in configuration is shown in Figure 26.1. This example shows the VALUATION AREA, the CO CODE, and a material ledger active (ML ACT.) indicator. In Figure 26.1, the VALUATION AREA 0006 and company code 0006 has the material ledger active indicator set to indicate that this valuation area/company code combination has an active material ledger. The configuration to activate it is Transaction OMX1, which can be found in the navigation path, IMG • CONTROLLING • PRODUCT COST CONTROLLING • ACTUAL COSTING/MATERIAL LEDGER • ACTIVATE VALUATION AREAS FOR MATERIAL LEDGER.

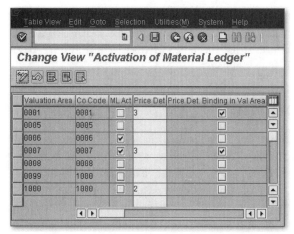

Figure 26.1 Configuration for Activation of the Material Ledger for Certain Valuation Areas

In addition, the configuration to activate actual costing can be found via the navigation path, IMG • CONTROLLING • PRODUCT COST CONTROLLING • ACTUAL COSTING/ MATERIAL LEDGER • ACTUAL COSTING • ACTIVATE ACTUAL COSTING.

26.1.2 Benefits of Using the Material Ledger

Many multi-national companies appreciate that the SAP ERP system allows them to operate inventory in up to three currencies. However, there are a number of other benefits to using the material ledger:

- Users can find the real costs for purchasing material across currencies over a period of time.
- The different currencies in the material ledger remove any price variances so vendor selection can be made without the concern of currencies.
- Accurate material valuation can be made with regards to production costs and vendor pricing across currencies.
- Accurate cost of goods sold calculations, independent of currency, allows management to see the true profitability of finished goods.
- Keeping inventory records in up to three parallel currencies can result in advantages in consolidation within the businesses that are part of the multi-national company.
- The material ledger provides information that can be used to decide on the most advantageous currency for the purchase of materials.

This section has given an overview of the material ledger and the configuration to activate it for a company code and valuation area. The next section examines the material ledger data and how it used.

26.2 Material Ledger Data

Material ledger data is found in the Material Master record and in the valuation and control data for a material in a plant for a particular posting period. The valuation and control data is collected in the material ledger as it is entered in the system.

26.2.1 Material Master Record

Several items must be checked before a material can be used in the material ledger:

- The material ledger indicator must be set in the material.
- The material must be assigned to a valuation class.
- The material type must allow the material's valuation to be updated.

The material type can be checked to see if the material valuation can be updated by viewing the configuration transaction shown in Figure 26.2, which can be found via the navigation path, IMG • LOGISTICS - GENERAL • MATERIAL MASTER • BASIC SETTINGS • MATERIAL TYPES • DEFINE ATTRIBUTES OF MATERIAL TYPES.

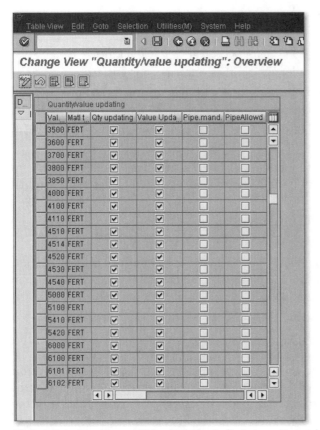

Figure 26.2 Quantity and Value Updating Indicators on Material Type Configuration

Transaction MM01 is used to add the accounting details for each material. The Material Master record contains the flag that determines whether a material is relevant for the material ledger. The ML ACT. flag is on the accounting screen and should be set for the material ledger, as shown in Figure 26.3. After this is set, data is collected about this material for the material ledger.

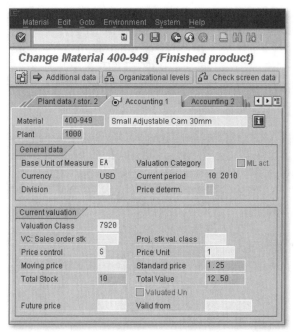

Figure 26.3 Material Ledger Indicator and Valuation Class in the Accounting Screen of the Material Master Record

26.2.2 Data for the Material Ledger

For materials that have been activated for the material ledger, the system automatically collects information on valuation-relevant transactions. Information is also collected on account postings from Inventory Management, Invoice Verification, and order settlement. This collected data is used during material price determination.

The transaction variances or differences are posted to the material ledger. Three types of differences are collected:

▸ Price differences

▸ Exchange rate differences

▸ Differences caused by revaluation

Transactions that cause an inward flow of data to the material ledger include Inventory Management, Invoice Verification, and production order settlement. The outward flow of data from the material ledger includes data for the Financial Accounting component and the Controlling information system.

This section examined the material ledger data from the Material Master record and the valuation-relevant transactions collected in the material ledger. The next section reviews the different types of material price determination, including single-level, multi-level, and transaction-based material price determination.

26.3 Material Price Determination

There are three methods to determine the price of material in SAP ERP: single-level, multi-level, and transaction based. Single-level and multi-level price determination calculates the periodic unit price for a material. Transaction-based material price determination allows the calculation of the moving average price after every goods movement. This section begins with a review of material price analysis.

26.3.1 Material Price Analysis

The material price analysis shows the valuated transactions. It also displays the results of material price determination, with price and exchange rate differences for a given material in a plant in a specific period.

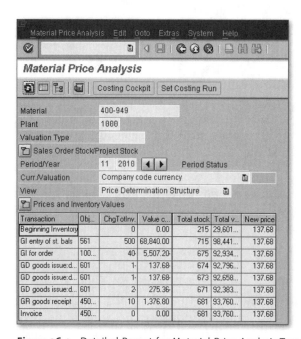

Figure 26.4 Detailed Report for Material Price Analysis Transaction CKM3

Transaction CKM3 is used to run the material price analysis and can be found via the navigation path, SAP MENU • LOGISTICS • MATERIALS MANAGEMENT • VALUATION • ACTUAL COSTING/MATERIAL LEDGER • MATERIAL LEDGER • MATERIAL PRICE ANALYSIS.

After the transaction is run, a report is displayed showing the BEGINNING INVENTORY, GOODS RECEIPTS, GOODS ISSUED, INVOICE, and so on as shown in Figure 26.4.

26.3.2 Single-Level Material Price Determination

Single-level material price determination takes into account the differences that arise directly when a material is purchased. The differences can be price differences, exchange rate differences, and differences that are created by revaluations.

Single-level material price determination calculates a unit price for a material for a specific previous period. The actual costing for single-level price determination calculations are made for the previous period and do not affect the current period. The single-level calculation is valid only for materials that are flagged for standard price control and for which the price determination field is set to 3 for single-level and multi-level price determination. Both of these indicators are found on the ACCOUNTING screen of the Material Master record.

The single-level determination refers to the fact that the price differences are only for one level, and no other material price differences are examined. Other price differences occur for materials used in making this material. Where these price differences are taken into account, we refer to multi-level price determination. Figure 26.5 shows the ACCOUNTING screen of the Material Master Transaction MM02.

The price that is determined by the single-level calculation, shown in Figure 26.5, is the standard price of the material, plus or minus any price differences and exchange rate differences.

Price differences can occur for the following reasons:

- ▶ Goods receipts for a PO
- ▶ Invoice receipts
- ▶ Settlement of production orders
- ▶ Transfer postings
- ▶ Initial entry of stock balances (movement type 561)

- ▸ Free delivery of goods for a PO
- ▸ Inward movements from consignment

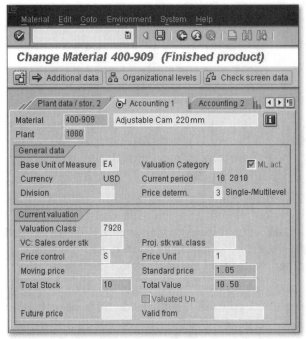

Figure 26.5 Material Valid for Single-Level Price Determination, with Standard Price Control and Price Determination Flag of 3

The differences between the standard price of the material and the price determined by this calculation are updated in the material ledger.

The single-level price determination, as shown in Figure 26.6, can be accessed through Transaction CKMH or through the navigation path, SAP MENU • LOGISTICS • MATERIALS MANAGEMENT • VALUATION • ACTUAL COSTING/MATERIAL LEDGER • PERIODIC MATERIAL VALUATION • DETERMINE MATERIAL PRICES (SINGLE LEVEL).

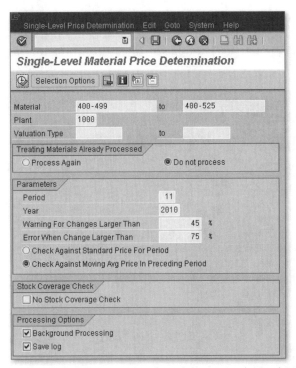

Figure 26.6 Selection Screen for Calculating Single-Level Price Determination

26.3.3 Multi-Level Material Price Determination

Whereas a single-level price determination looks at the material in isolation, the multi-level price determination looks at all price determinations of the materials that go into making the final material. All of these price determinations roll up to produce a single price determination. For a multi-level price determination to be calculated, a single-level calculation has to be complete for all of the component materials.

26.3.4 Transaction-Based Material Price Determination

This price determination permits the moving average price to be calculated after every goods movement that is relevant to the material. This type of price determination does not require the material ledger to be active. If the material ledger is not active, then the moving average price is calculated in one currency, as determined on the Material Master. If the material ledger is active, then the price is calculated in up to three currencies on the material ledger.

To have the material activated for transaction-based material price determination, the material should be flagged for moving-average price control, and the PRICE DETERM. field should be set to 2 for transaction-based price determination, as shown in Figure 26.7.

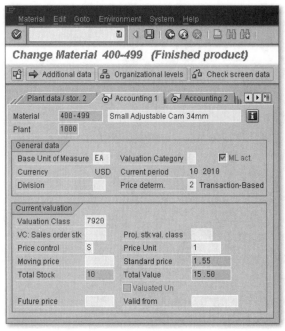

Figure 26.7 Material Valid for Transaction-Based Price Determination with Moving-Average Price Control and Price Determination Flag of 2

26.4 Business Examples – Material Ledger

Companies use the material ledger when material is required to be held in more than one currency. The material ledger permits a material to have an actual cost calculated, which takes into account all of the costs of materials that have been moved, not just the price on the Material Master.

26.4.1 Material Ledger Overview

The material ledger can serve two purposes. First it records actual costs of materials and at the same time considers and records all of the factors behind price fluctuation. Second, the material ledger can hold values in three currencies simultaneously, which is a major benefit to multi-national firms.

Example

An Austrian beverage company had operations in Austria, Germany, and France. Using its SAP ERP system, the company was able to value its finished goods in one currency, that is, the Euro. However, the company planned to move into new markets, such as Latvia and Poland, where the national currencies still remain, the lats in Latvia and the zloty in Poland.

The company purchased a manufacturing facility in Poland and realized that a decision had to be made about how to value the materials in Poland. The company could value materials in Euros because Poland would eventually drop the zloty and adopt the Euro, or the company could use the material ledger and keep the valuation of the materials in Poland in zloty.

Based on consultation from the company's accountants, the company decided to use the material ledger and keep two currencies. To adopt the Euro would require a change in the Polish constitution and that may be a number of years away.

26.4.2 Material Price Determination

There are three methods to determine the price of material in SAP ERP: single-level, multi-level, and transaction based. Single-level and multi-level price determination calculates the periodic unit price for a material. Transaction-based material price determination allows the calculation of the moving average price after every goods movement.

Example

A South African electronic components distributor found that its purchases of items from China, Korea, and India had increased in price significantly each month. The rise in costs was mainly due to increased freight charges. The company configured its SAP ERP system for single-level price determination so that changes for purchased materials would be reflected in the system. In some instances, the standard price on the Material Master records was less than 50% of the price now reflected in recent purchases.

26.5 Summary

This chapter dealt with the material ledger, which retains the actual costs of materials and at the same time considers and records all of the factors behind price fluctuation. It can also hold values in three currencies at the same time, which is needed by companies frequently using or reporting in different currencies. It is important that decisions are made on the material ledger so that information needed for the Material Master can be decided upon at an early stage of the implementation.

There are a number of benefits for a company to use the material ledger, including the ability to keep inventory records in up to three parallel currencies, which can result in advantages in consolidation within the businesses that are part of the multi-national company. Another benefit is that the material ledger provides information that can be used to decide on the most advantageous currency for the purchase of materials.

Chapter 27 examines classification, which has been touched on in discussions of batch determination. The classification system is not specific to MM, but it is a central function used in a number of MM areas, such as classifying materials and batches. Chapter 27 describes how the characteristics and classes are created and how classification is used as a search tool.

The classification system is a powerful tool that allows objects in SAP ERP to be described by characteristic values. These characteristics are used for the same group of objects, that is, vendors and materials. The classification system uses these values to perform powerful searches.

27   Classification System

Classification systems occur everywhere. The Dewey Decimal system is used in libraries is a classification system, zoologists use the Linnaean system for animal classification, and the U.S. government uses the Standard Occupational Classification (SOC) System for classifying workers into occupational categories. There are many more examples.

27.1   Classification Overview

A definition of a classification system by the Public Work and Government Services Department of Canada states,

> *A classification system is a structured scheme for categorizing entities or objects to improve access, created according to alphabetical, associative, hierarchical, numerical, ideological, spatial, chronological, or other criteria.*

27.1.1   What Is the SAP ERP Classification System?

The classification system in SAP ERP fits the definition just described because it is a structured framework primarily used for searching objects based on a series of characteristics that describe the object. The object can be a material, vendor, batch, and so on.

The classification system can be an extremely powerful tool if it is constructed in a strategic manner with a significant amount of planning. Classification systems that are ignored by companies have evolved over time with no planning and are cumbersome and difficult to maintain. The more planning that is put into creating a classification system, the more likely it is to become a worthwhile tool.

Some companies employ outside consultants to review the materials they have and develop a structured naming and classification framework based on the description and use of the material. Although this can be an expensive and time-consuming project, it enables the company to start implementing the classification system with rules and procedures already in place.

27.1.2 Describing an Object

In developing the classification system, there are three areas that need to be addressed:

► Object
► Characteristics
► Class

You need to examine the object to be described and define a set of standard descriptions or characteristics. For instance, for an object such as a vendor, characteristics that may be used to describe it include how many employees does the vendor have, is the vendor a minority-owned company, how many products does the vendor sell, is the vendor a registered small business, and so on.

These descriptions are called characteristics, and each characteristic has values or a range of values For example, if we again consider the vendor as an object and look at the characteristic "how many employees the vendor has," a valid value could be 20,000. The value can be an exact figure, or the value can be configured to be a range, if required.

The characteristics are grouped together in a class. The class contains a number of characteristics that are of similar values. The class is the entity that is assigned to the material in the Material Master.

A class is associated with a class type. The class type is the key to which object the class can be assigned. For example, if a class is assigned to class type 010, then the class can only be assigned to those objects relevant for class type 010, that is, vendors.

This section provided an overview of the classification function in SAP ERP. The next section reviews the creation of the characteristic and how it can be used in classification.

27.2   Characteristics

As already described, the characteristic describes an object, and the characteristic can have values or a range of values that are valid for each characteristic.

27.2.1   Create Characteristics

After the company has decided upon a set of descriptive characteristics for an object, the next step is to create the characteristic. Transaction CT04 is used to create the characteristic and can be found via the navigation path, SAP Menu • Cross-Application Components • Classification System • Master Data • Characteristics.

On the basic data screen shown in Figure 27.1, the following can be included:

- ▶ Description for the characteristic
- ▶ Data Type, which can be numeric, date, currency, time, or character
- ▶ Format of the Data Type, Number of Characters, and so on
- ▶ Template, if necessary
- ▶ Single Value or Multiple Values
- ▶ Entry Required flag

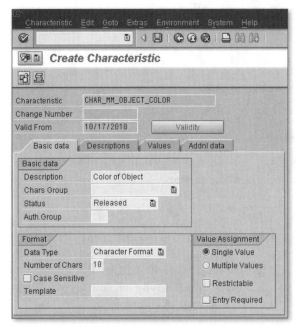

Figure 27.1   Basic Data Screen for Transaction CT04

After the data has been entered for the basic screen, allowed values for the characteristics can be entered.

In the value screen, shown in Figure 27.2, the values that have been determined for the characteristic can be entered. One of these values can be made a default value by setting the D flag on the value line. If no defined values are entered, then any value will be allowed.

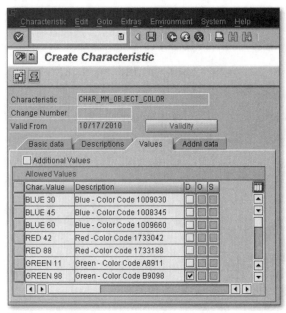

Figure 27.2 Values Screen for Transaction CT04

27.2.2 Configuring Characteristics

A number of elements need to be examined when configuring a characteristic. These elements are described in the following sections.

Characteristic Defaults

A number of configuration steps can be performed to allow characteristics to operate according to the user's requirements. The first of these is to set default settings for the characteristic. If a certain field must be set in one particular manner, this can be configured to default to that requirement each time a characteristic is created. The configuration for the defaults can be seen in Figure 27.3.

To access the transaction and configure the default settings, use the configuration navigation path, IMG • CROSS-APPLICATION COMPONENTS • CLASSIFICATION SYSTEM • CHARACTERISTICS • DEFINE DEFAULT SETTINGS.

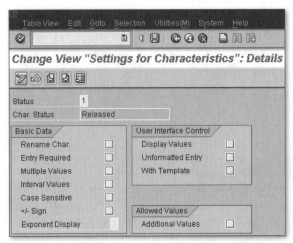

Figure 27.3 Configuration Screen That Allows the User to Set Defaults for Characteristics

Characteristic Status

The characteristic can be set to different statuses, which are predefined in SAP ERP as RELEASED, IN PREPARATION, or LOCKED. There is a configuration transaction, shown in Figure 27.4, which allows the user to create new statuses that may be needed by the client. For example, a status can be configured that allows for review.

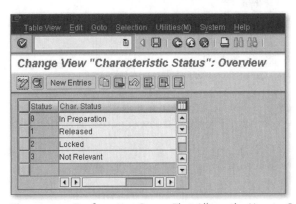

Figure 27.4 Configuration Screen That Allows the User to Create New Characteristic Statuses

To configure the characteristic status, a user can access the transaction by following the configuration navigation path, IMG • Cross-Application Components • Classification System • Characteristics • Define Characteristic Statuses.

Value Templates

SAP ERP includes a number of templates that can be used for the entry of information into the characteristic values. If a new template is required for a specific characteristic value, this can be configured.

Many characters are configured for use in the templates. These can be found using the configuration navigation path, IMG • Cross-Application Components • Classification System • Characteristics • Define Template Characters.

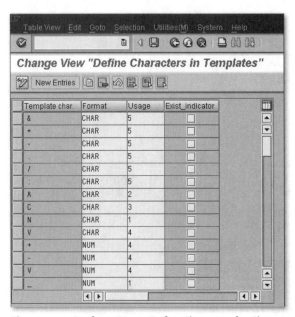

Figure 27.5 Configuration to Define Characters for Characteristic Templates

Figure 27.5 shows the characters that are defined for use in the templates. The Usage field determines how the character is used. Following are the options for the Usage field:

▶ **1**: Numeric character that is valid for numeric and character formats.

▶ **2**: Alphanumeric character that is valid for character formats.

- **3**: Character that is valid for the character format.
- **4**: Preliminary sign that is valid for the character format.
- **5**: Separator that is valid for the character format.

Accessing the transaction using the configuration navigation path, IMG • Cross-Application Components • Classification System • Characteristics • Define Templates, allows the user to configure new characteristic value templates or to modify existing templates.

Figure 27.6 shows the templates that have been configured for use with characteristics.

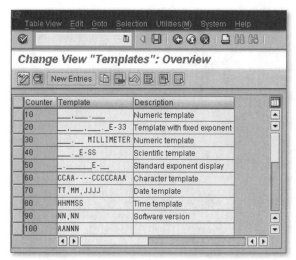

Figure 27.6 Configuration Screen That Allows the Creation and Modification of New Characteristic Value Templates

This section examined the creation of the characteristic and how it is used in classification. The next section reviews the creation and use of the class.

27.3 Classes

As described in the introduction, a class contains a number of characteristics that are grouped together.

27.3.1 Create Classes

After the relevant characteristics have been created, the characteristics can be grouped together by assigning them to a class. The class can be created by using Transaction CL02, shown in Figure 27.7, or by using the navigation path, SAP MENU • CROSS-APPLICATION COMPONENTS • CLASSIFICATION SYSTEM • MASTER DATA • CLASSES.

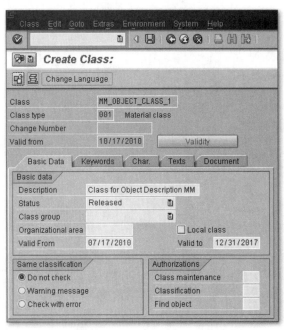

Figure 27.7 Basic Data Screen for Transaction CL02

The basic data screen requires a CLASS TYPE. The class type is discussed later in this chapter. The user can enter KEYWORDS that can be used to search for the specific class. The keywords can be entered on a separate screen within Transaction CL02. After the basic data has been entered, the specific characteristics that should be assigned to this class can be entered as shown in Figure 27.8.

Figure 27.8 Characteristics Assigned to the Class in Transaction CL02

This section reviewed the class and how it can be created. The following section describes the functionality of the class type.

27.4 Class Type

A class type is an indicator to identify which objects are relevant for a class. Each class must belong to a class type.

27.4.1 Class Type Overview

As mentioned in the previous section, when creating a class, the class must belong to a class type. The class type represents the type of objects the class is being created for. In Figure 27.7 shown earlier, the class MM_OBJECT_CLASS_1 has been assigned to class type 001, which is the class type defined for the material object. Consequently, the characteristics in the class will pertain to a material. If the user creating the class had entered class type 002, this would have meant that the characteristics were describing a piece of equipment because equipment is the object defined for class type 002. Figure 27.9 shows some of the class types available when creating a class.

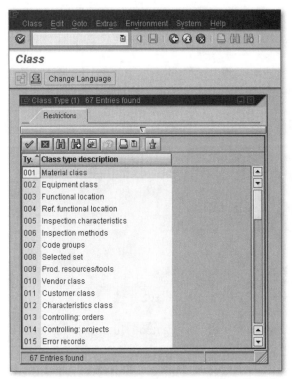

Figure 27.9 Class Types and Objects Assigned to Class Types

27.4.2 Configuring a Class Type

Many class types are already defined within SAP ERP. However, on occasion, the user might need to create a new class type. This may be an instance where the client has a unique combination of objects, that is, a vendor/equipment combination that has no defined class type. If the client needs to describe this combination of objects, then the class requires a new class type so that it accesses the correct tables.

The class type refers to an object. When starting to create a new class type, the correct object must be selected. If the object is not currently listed in configuration, it can be added.

The configuration for object types and class types can be found using the configuration navigation path, IMG • Cross-Application Components • Classification System • Classes • Maintain Object Types and Material Types.

A new object can be added in this transaction, as shown in Figure 27.10, by selecting EDIT • NEW ENTRIES and choosing a new object to include. Most SAP ERP objects are already included in this transaction.

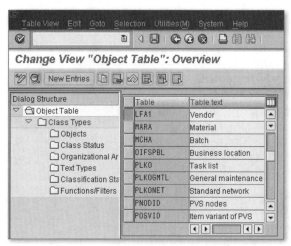

Figure 27.10 Partial Object List for the Class Type

To create a new class type, the user selects the object, which is linked to the class type. The user then clicks on class types in the dialog structure to display current class types for that object, as shown in Figure 27.11.

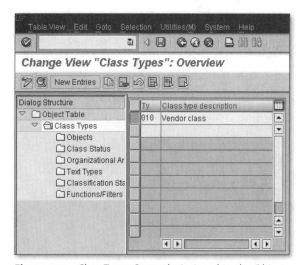

Figure 27.11 Class Types Currently Assigned to the Object

A new class type can be created for this object by selecting EDIT • NEW ENTRIES or by using the [F5] function key. A screen appears, as shown in Figure 27.12, for the new class type information to be entered. The new class type (Ty.) should be a three-character value. The normal protocol is that a new class type begins with the number 9. However, check with your client's data governance group for any policies relevant for classification. A CLASS TYPE DESCRIPTION should be added for the new class type also.

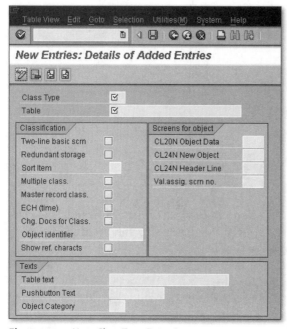

Figure 27.12 New Class-Type Entry Screen

This section described the use and configuration of the class type. The next section examines the class hierarchies that can be created in classification.

27.5 Class Hierarchies

As with other classification systems, the SAP ERP classification system can create a hierarchy within the class structure.

27.5.1 Creating a Class Hierarchy

A class can be assigned to another class to create a class hierarchy by using Transaction CL24N or by the navigation path, SAP MENU • CROSS-APPLICATION COMPONENTS • CLASSIFICATION SYSTEM • ASSIGNMENT • ASSIGN OBJECTS/CLASSES TO CLASS.

In Figure 27.13, the following are assigned classes MM_OBJECT_CLASS_2, MM_OBJECT_CLASS_3, and MM_OBJECT_CLASS_4 to be subordinate classes of MM_OBJECT_CLASS_A.

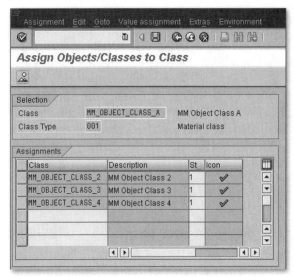

Figure 27.13 Assignment of Classes to a Class Using Transaction CL24N

The class hierarchy can be seen using Transaction CL6C or through the navigation path, SAP MENU • CROSS-APPLICATION COMPONENTS • CLASSIFICATION SYSTEM • ENVIRONMENT • REPORTING • CLASS HIERARCHY.

27.5.2 Inherited Characteristics

A characteristic is inherited when a characteristic and its value are passed from a superior class in the class hierarchy to the subordinate classes. The main advantage of inheritance is that the end user does not need to enter the characteristic in the subordinate classes because it has been entered once in the superior class and then inherited.

This section examined the hierarchies that can be defined for classes that can be used in object searches. The next section describes the object dependencies that can be defined in classification.

27.6 Object Dependencies

The object dependency in classification refers to the limitations that can be placed on objects to ensure that the correct classification occurs.

27.6.1 Object Dependency Overview

Object dependencies can force values for characteristics to be allowed only if a certain value for another characteristic has been selected. For instance, if the characteristic called *Color* has values *Red, Blue,* and *Green,* and another characteristic called *Finish* has values *Matte, Gloss,* or *Semi-Gloss,* then the user can define a dependency that states that only *Gloss* can be selected for characteristic *Finish* if the value *Green* is selected for *Color.* This prevents incorrect characteristic values from being chosen.

27.6.2 Dependency Creation

To create a dependency, follow these steps:

1. Within the class Transaction CL02, display the characteristics.
2. To create a dependency between characteristics, select the characteristic required, and then choose ENVIRONMENT • CHANGE CHARACTERISTIC.
3. The display shows the change characteristic transaction. Choose EXTRAS • OBJECT DEPENDENCIES • EDITOR.
4. A dialog box appears that allows you to choose a PRECONDITION, SELECTION CONDITION, ACTION, or PROCEDURE. After you select the appropriate object dependency, the dependency editor appears.
5. In this editor, create the dependency based on normal syntax.

This section described the use and creation of object dependencies in classification. The next section examines how the classification system can be used as a search tool to find objects that have been classified.

27.7 Finding Objects Using Classification

The standard feature of the classification system is that it can make the selection of objects easier because they can be found by using values that have been entered for that specific object.

27.7.1 Classifying Materials

In MM, the most common function through which classification is seen is in the creation of the Material Master. When a material is created, one of the creation screens is for assigning classes to the material.

In the Material Master creation Transaction MM01, the classification screen allows a class or classes to be assigned to the material, as shown in Figure 27.14.

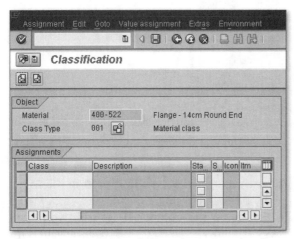

Figure 27.14 Assignment of Classes for a Material in the Material Master Creation Transaction MM01

A class can be selected and then assigned the values for the characteristics as shown in Figure 27.15. The material can be assigned to any number of classes.

In Figure 27.15, the material 400-522 has been assigned to class MM_OBJECT_ CLASS_1. This class has three characteristics assigned to it. When the class is assigned to the object, in this case, material 400-522, values can be assigned to the characteristics. Of the three available characteristics that can have values assigned, only two have been entered. The characteristic named COLOR OF OBJECT has been assigned the value GREEN – COLOR CODE B9098, and the characteristic TEMPERA-TURE OF OBJECT has been assigned the value of 7.

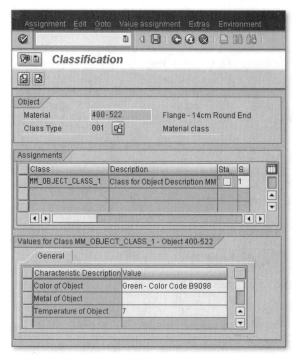

Figure 27.15 Selection of Characteristic Values Associated with the Class Assigned to the Material

27.7.2 Classifying Objects

An object can be assigned to a class or classes. This method is used in the Material Master creation or to assign many objects to a single class as shown in Figure 27.16. The VENDOR, in Figure 27.16, is shown as number 1011, and two classes have been assigned, VENDOR_CLASS_01 and VENDOR_CLASS_02. The values for the characteristics in VENDOR_CLASS_01 have been entered. The CHARACTERISTIC DESCRIPTION is shown, and a VALUE has been entered for each. In this example, the characteristic ISO CERTIFIED has been given the value Y, the characteristic SMALL BUSINESS VERIFIED has been given the value Y, and the characteristic STATE APPROVED has been assigned the value N.

Transaction CL20N allows the many classes to be assigned to an object. This transaction can be found through the navigation path, SAP MENU • CROSS-APPLICATION COMPONENTS • CLASSIFICATION SYSTEM • ASSIGNMENT • ASSIGN OBJECT TO A CLASS.

Transaction CL24N allows many objects to be assigned to a single class. This saves time if a new class has been created and needs to be assigned to many objects, which is shown in Figure 27.17. This transaction can be found through the navigation path,

SAP MENU • CROSS-APPLICATION COMPONENTS • CLASSIFICATION SYSTEM • ASSIGNMENT •
ASSIGN OBJECTS/CLASSES TO A CLASS.

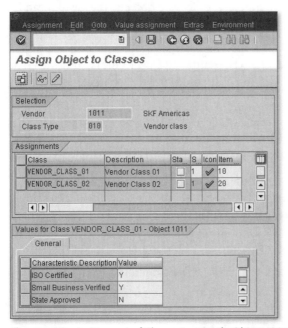

Figure 27.16 Assignment of Classes to a Single Object Using Transaction CL20N

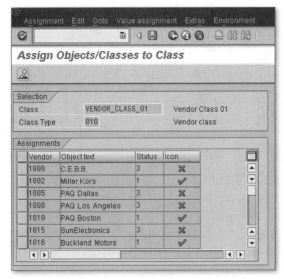

Figure 27.17 Assignment of Objects to a Single Class Using Transaction CL24N

27.7.3   Finding Objects

After implementing the classification system by creating characteristics and classes, assigning classes to objects and assigning values for the objects, the system can be used to find objects.

The key to finding an object is to use the characteristic values to find the object or objects that fit the value. The search criteria the end user enters, and the characteristics and the values assigned, are compared with the characteristic values assigned to the objects.

Transaction CL30N can be used to find objects using characteristic values. This transaction can be found using the navigation path, SAP MENU • CROSS-APPLICATION COMPONENTS • CLASSIFICATION SYSTEM • FIND • FIND OBJECTS IN CLASSES.

The initial screen asks the end user to enter a specific class and class type. There is a matchcode selection if the end user is unclear about the class name. The detail screen shows the characteristics for the class that was chosen, and values can be entered against those characteristics. The transaction is then executed by selecting FIND • FIND IN INITIAL CLASS or by using the [F8] function key.

The transaction returns all objects that have the characteristic value that was entered as shown in Figure 27.18.

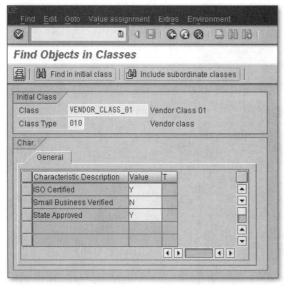

Figure 27.18   Objects Found Using the Characteristic Value Entered in Transaction CL30N

27.8 Business Examples – Classification

The SAP ERP classification is a structured framework primarily used for the searching of objects based on a series of characteristics that describe the object. It is possible to classify a wide range of objects including materials, vendors, batches, and so on.

27.8.1 Characteristics and Classes

Characteristics describe an object, and the characteristic can have values or a range of values that are valid for each characteristic. Classes are groupings of characteristics that are used to describe a particular type of object such as a material or batch.

Example

A German chemical company produced a number of finished products that were very similar in chemical composition, but each had a specific range of properties that were important to their customers. Although each product did have a unique specification, the individual batches that were manufactured were slightly different. Despite this, each batch available to the customer was within the product tolerances.

The sales staff sold items to the customers based on the finished product specifications, and this was a problem for a number of customers. The requirements by some customers were more specific than the general information accessible to the sales staff. Some customers preferred to purchase batches of finished product that had a certain chemical property, but the sales staff could only call the quality department and ask them to review the chemical properties of each batch to see if any satisfied the customer. Not only was this frustrating for the customer but also a waste of resources for the sales and quality departments.

The company decided to use the classification system to create the characteristics required by the customers. Each test carried out by the quality department was created as a characteristic in SAP ERP and a class was created that contained these tests. The class was assigned to the relevant batches of the finished product and values assigned to the characteristics based on the quality tests.

The sales staff then had the ability to review with the customer the chemical properties of each batch. This gave the customer the ability to make a better-informed choice of which batches to purchase.

27.8.2 Finding Objects Using Classification

The key of the classification system is that it can make the selection of objects easier because they can be selected using values that have been entered for that specific object.

Example

A U.S. manufacturer of custom-built conveyor systems manufactured equipment for companies such as food manufacturers and distribution firms. Each system would take months to manufacture and have tens of thousands of parts. Each element of the system was custom built and required the company to manufacture its own tools because off-the-shelf items were not suitable. Each of the tools had unique properties and was used infrequently. The maintenance team stored the tools and maintained the characteristics for each tool.

When the design team developed the conveyor system for a new client, they not only created the design of each part of the system, but they also created the specifications of the tools needed to manufacture each part. When the client approved the design, the maintenance team was asked to take each of the specifications for the tools required in the manufacture and identify if a suitable tool existed or whether it needed to be manufactured.

The maintenance team used the specifications given to them and entered them into the classification system. Each required value was entered into the relevant characteristic and a search was performed on the tools that had a value assigned for that characteristic. If tools were found that had the same characteristic, the maintenance team would review other necessary characteristics or defer to the design team for a final decision.

27.9 Summary

This chapter described the classification system in SAP ERP in detail. The classification system is a great tool for finding material that may appear to be similar to other materials but can be found easily using the characteristic value that has been assigned to it via the classification of the object. Classification is a long-term process that requires a significant level of commitment from the client and then ongoing maintenance to ensure that new materials, vendors, equipment, or whatever objects are classified when they are entered into SAP ERP. If the classification system is correctly defined and implemented, it offers a powerful and comprehensive search tool.

Chapter 28 describes the functionality that can be found in document management. Document management is a part of the central functions and not part of MM. It is a powerful tool that enables a company to link documents to objects, such as a material inside the Material Master record.

Document management is a powerful tool within SAP ERP that enables a company to link important documents to objects within the SAP system. Not having to duplicate or move the original document saves both time and effort.

28 Document Management

The Document Management System (DMS) allows the user to link external documents to objects within the SAP system. Company documents such as CAD drawings, technical specifications, MSDS (material safety data sheet) files, and photographs are often found on different computer systems, in different locations, and in different applications. DMS allows a company to link these documents to the appropriate object within SAP ERP. This functionality is very useful for companies that have their documentation scanned and on a central server. These documents can be quickly linked to the correct objects and be available through access to SAP ERP instead of having to access a separate system.

28.1 Document Management Overview

Document management is important for companies that are precertified or certified ISO 9000. Also, the strict requirements of the HIPAA (Health Insurance Portability and Accountability Act of 1996) and Sarbanes-Oxley Act of 2002 require businesses to manage documents more carefully. DMS gives auditors and administrators documented evidence of internal controls that communicate, store, and protect documents. DMS allows unalterable logs or databases showing who has accessed which pieces of information, where, and when.

DMS in the SAP system uses a document information record to link the document to the object in SAP ERP.

28.2 Document Information Record

The document information record is the master record in SAP ERP that describes the information pertaining to the external document. The document information record contains the external file name and location of the file on the network.

28.2.1 Document Number

The document number can be defined in an identifier with up to 25 alphanumeric characters. The identifier can be internally or externally defined, and the number assignment can be configured in IMG.

28.2.2 Document Type

The document type is used to categorize the type of document. The document type is defined as a three-character field, as shown in Figure 28.1. For example, DRW is defined as the document type for an engineering drawing, EBR is the document type for a batch record, and SB is the document type for a service bulletin.

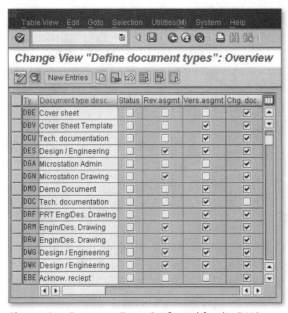

Figure 28.1 Document Types Configured for the DMS

The document type can be configured in IMG. The navigation path to reach the transaction is IMG • CROSS-APPLICATION COMPONENTS • DOCUMENT MANAGEMENT • CONTROL DATA • DEFINE DOCUMENT TYPES.

The other indicators in Figure 28.1 are described here:

▸ **Status switch**: The STATUS indicator shows that the status must change when you change a field in the document information record after this indicator is set.

▸ **Revision level assignment**: If the REV. ASGMT indicator is set, then a revision level is automatically assigned to a document with reference to a change number, if used.

▸ **Version assigned automatically**: If the VERS. ASGMT indicator is set, a new version number is assigned automatically when the DMS user creates a new version of a document.

▸ **Change document**: If the CHG. DOC indicator is set, then a change document is created when the document is changed.

28.2.3 Document Part

A document part is defined as part of a document that is maintained as a separate document. This may be needed if the original document is large and can be divided into relevant sections. For example, if a large specification document has relevant information for many materials, the specification can be divided into parts for the relevant materials.

28.2.4 Document Version

The document version describes the version number of the document. This is particularly important in keeping the document current in situations where modifications may have been made to specifications, engineering drawings, and so on.

28.2.5 Document Status

The document can be given a status depending on where it resides within the process. A status may be RELEASED, IN APPROVAL, REJECTED, LOCKED, and so on. The status can be defined in configuration and is shown in Figure 28.2.

The status can be configured using the navigation path, IMG • CROSS-APPLICATION COMPONENTS • DOCUMENT MANAGEMENT • CONTROL DATA • DEFINE DOCUMENT TYPES.

This section described the document information record that contains all of the relevant information needed to link a document. The next section examines how to create a document.

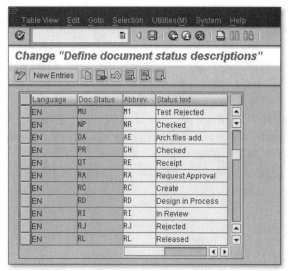

Figure 28.2 Document Statuses Configured in the DMS

28.3 Creating a Document

Before an external document can be linked to an object, a document record must be created in DMS. This section describes how a document record is created.

28.3.1 Create a Document

To create a document record, Transaction CV01N is used as shown in Figure 28.3. The transaction can be found using the navigation path, SAP MENU • LOGISTICS • CENTRAL FUNCTIONS • DOCUMENT MANAGEMENT SYSTEM • DOCUMENT • CREATE.

The initial screen allows a DOCUMENT number to be entered if it is externally assigned or left blank for an internal number assignment. The document type can be added as well as the document PART and VERSION if applicable.

Description

Once in the detail screen for creating a document, a long DESCRIPTION should be added that can be the title of the external document.

Figure 28.3 Detail Screen for Creating a Document Using Transaction CV01N

Document Status

The DOCUMENT STATUS field describes whether the document is in its primary stage, initial stage, locked, or temporary.

Change Number

The document can be linked to a CHANGE NUMBER that links documents for the change.

The next section describes how the document record that has been created can be linked to an object.

28.4 Linking an Object to a Document

After the document record has been created, it is available to be linked to an object. This section describes the process of linking a material and a document record.

28.4.1 Configuration for Linking Documents

After the document record has been created, it can be linked to the object that it relates to. For instance, a MSDS can be assigned to the material it was produced for.

The document type has to be configured to allow links between the document type and the object, as shown in Figure 28.4. If a drawing is involved, document type DRW needs to be assigned to the WBS element. The link then must be created between DRW and the object PRPS. This configuration can be found using the navigation path, IMG • CROSS-APPLICATION COMPONENTS • DOCUMENT MANAGE- MENT • CONTROL DATA • DEFINE DOCUMENT TYPES.

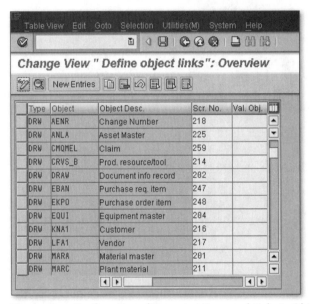

Figure 28.4 Configuration of Document Types and Links to Objects Within SAP ERP

28.4.2 Linking a Document to a Material Master Record

The most common link is between documents and the Material Master record. The Material Master has a built-in link process, so documents can be linked quickly.

Using Transaction MM01 for Material Master record creation, the DMS user can access the links to document management from the BASIC DATA TEXT screen. The DMS user can select the ADDITIONAL DATA icon from the header menu to display the additional data tabs for DESCRIPTIONS, UNIT OF MEASURE, EUROPEAN ARTI-CLE NUMBERS (EAN), INSPECTION TEXT, and DOCUMENT DATA.

When the DOCUMENT DATA tab is selected, a screen appears in which linked documents can be entered, as shown in Figure 28.5.

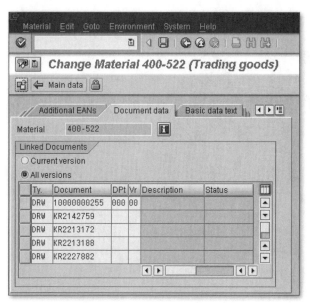

Figure 28.5 Entry Screen for Linked Documents for a Material Master Record Using Transaction MM01

28.4.3 Linking a Document to a Vendor Master Record

Another common object to have linked documents is the Vendor Master. The vendor can have documents linked to it via the Vendor Master creation Transaction XK01 or change Transaction XK02, as shown in Figure 28.6.

The document links can be added to the Vendor Master record when the DMS user selects EXTRAS • DOCUMENTS.

This section described how objects and document records are linked. The next section examines the use of the classification functionality with documents.

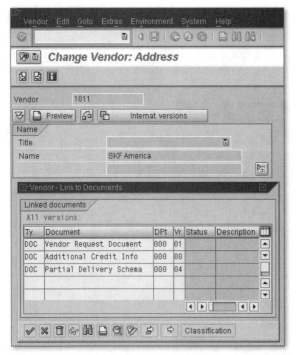

Figure 28.6 Linked Documents to the Vendor Created Using Transaction XK02

28.5 Documents and Classification

Using the classification system, characteristics can be used to describe a document. This becomes increasingly more important as more and more document records are loaded into DMS and finding the correct document becomes more difficult.

28.5.1 Using Classification for Documents

In standard SAP ERP, class type 017 has been predefined for documents. Therefore, to create a classification of documents, a set of characteristics can be created to combine into a class that can be assigned to a document, in the same way classification is set up for any other object. This is shown in Figure 28.7.

Using Transaction CL24N, the class can have any number of objects — in this case, documents — assigned to it. The values for the characteristics can then be added. This helps the end user find specific documents.

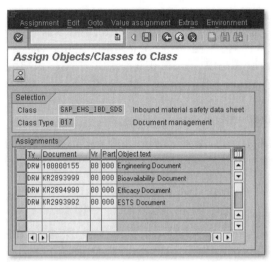

Figure 28.7   Assignment of Documents to a Specific Class in Transaction CL24N

28.6   Business Examples – Document Management

DMS allows the link between external documents and objects within the SAP ERP system. Each object can be linked to documents such as CAD drawings, technical specifications, MSDS files, and photographs, which can be found on disparate computer systems.

28.6.1   Document Information Record

The document information record in SAP ERP describes the information of the external document. The document information record contains the external file name and location of the file on the network.

Example

A German chemical company produced a number of finished products that were very similar in chemical composition. The sales staff was able to review the chemical quality of each batch but was unable to give the customer information on the MSDS. This information was held on a paper record and on the MSDS database system, which was the PC application that printed the MSDS for each delivery.

On occasion, a customer requested information from the MSDS of a finished item or from one of the raw materials that was a component in the manufacturer. To help the sales staff, the company decided to link the MSDS documents to the Material Master records by using DMS. For each of the MSDS records, a document information record was created and linked to the appropriate document on the MSDS PC application that was on the company's network. After this was done, the document information record was assigned to the relevant Material Master record, so that if they were asked, the sales staff could access the MSDS via the Material Master.

28.6.2 Linking an Object to a Document

A document can be linked to an object after a document information record is created. Many documents can be linked to an object, and documents can also be used in the classification system.

Example

The purchasing department of an Austrian beverage company found that in the past some vendors failed to adopt the terms and prices from the signed purchasing agreement. The AP department did not always have immediate access to the current purchase agreements, so they were unaware that the vendor was not using the agreed terms.

To ensure that the AP team members were able to quickly pull up any relevant purchasing agreements, the purchasing department decided to scan each of the current agreements and load them on to the company server. The purchasing team asked the SAP ERP support team how the documents could be accessed from SAP ERP. They were informed that by creating document information records and linking them to the vendors, SAP ERP users could quickly see the purchasing agreements.

After each agreement was linked to the appropriate vendor, the purchasing department reviewed its other documents and identified other documents such as warning letters and agreement updates that could be linked to the vendor in future projects.

28.7 Summary

This chapter described the processes included in the Document Management System (DMS). Most companies have developed or are developing strategies regarding their documents. Having hard copy documents moving around an organization can cause delays, errors, and miscommunications. Scanning documents on receipt, for example, invoices from vendors, is one way in which companies can reduce the time between approvals and payments to vendors. Knowledge of the DMS in SAP ERP is paramount when advising clients on best practices for Purchasing and other areas where document management can be an issue.

The preceding chapters examined the functionality that is fundamental to the Materials Management functionality in SAP ERP and some central functions that, although not part of MM, are used significantly in MM functions. This chapter examines the lessons learned from this book and makes suggestions for further skill development.

29 Conclusion

In this book, we have examined the Materials Management (MM) functionality within the SAP ERP product. In this chapter, we will go over the lessons learned from this book and look at the future direction of the MM functionality.

29.1 Lessons Learned

The preface indicated that this book would not only be of interest to MM consultants but also to others who work in some of the related functional areas such as Warehouse Management (WM) and Production Planning (PP). This book has shown you that there are many integration points among MM, WM, and PP. In addition, those of you working in more supply chain management roles have seen how the MM function is vital to many processes in the supply chain.

Chapter 2, Materials Management Organizational Structure, described the organizational structure of MM. It is important to understand how the client, company, plant, storage location, and warehouse fit together.

Chapter 3, Master Data in Materials Management, examined the master data, such as the Material Master, Vendor Master, Batch Management, serial records, and purchasing information records. Chapters 4, Material Master Data – Part 1, and 5, Material Master Data – Part 2, expanded on the information reviewed in Chapter 3 and explained the structure of the Material Master file. The Material Master file contains all of the information for a material that is required by any department, and accurate data is an important factor to any implementation.

Chapter 6, Vendor Master Data, reviewed the Vendor Master file, whereas Chapter 7, Purchasing Information Data, examined the purchasing information. To the purchasing department, the Vendor Master file and the purchasing information record are the basis for successful procurement. The purchasing department performs negotiations with vendors, and without that correct information in the purchasing data, any savings made with the vendors will not be realized.

Chapter 8, Batch Management Data, reviewed the Batch Master record. The information entered into a batch is valuable to many parts of the organization. Batch determination is found in PP, SD, and WM, so this is an area that is key for integration with these components.

Chapter 9, Material Master Record, explained how material records are created, changed, and deleted. The process is reasonably simple in SAP ERP, but each company has its own policies and protocols that should be followed. The key lesson here is to understand how the functionality works but be more aware of the way your client wants to implement the function. Chapter 10, Vendor Master Record, discussed the same function for the Vendor Master file. Again, the process is reasonably simple, but each company will have its own method of how to create and change vendors.

Chapter 11, Purchasing Overview, started a discussion on the purchasing functionality in MM. Chapters 12 through 15 discussed the elements of the purchasing suite: Chapter 12, Purchase Requisition; Chapter 13, Request for Quotation; Chapter 14, Quotation; and Chapter 15, Purchase Order. These elements are not always implemented at a company. Some companies only use the very basic purchase order and very little else, whereas others implement the whole suite. Each company will have different requirements regarding purchasing. It is important to understand how the elements work individually and also as a purchasing flow.

Chapter 16, External Service Management (ESM), reviewed the ESM functionality. Many companies now use Purchasing in SAP ERP for service purchases. This functionality requires knowledge of the Service Master and how the service is recorded. As more companies use SAP ERP for the procurement of services, it will be important to be familiar with how this functionality works.

Chapter 17, Consumption-Based Planning, began a discussion on consumption-based planning (CBP), material requirements planning (MRP) (Chapter 18), and forecasting (Chapter 19). Although CBP is an MM function based on material consumption, the planning of material is considered more of a PP function. However, it is important for the MM consultant to be aware of the functionality behind CBP, MRP, and forecasting. Many clients will expect the MM consultant to have as much knowledge of these areas as a PP consultant, so review these chapters to increase your understanding.

Chapter 20, Inventory Management Overview, started a review of the Inventory Management functionality. Chapters 21 through 23 examined goods issue, goods receipt, and physical inventory, respectively. Both of the chapters on goods issue and goods receipt touched on other components, such as the goods issue to a sales order and goods receipt from a production order. Many Inventory Management transactions post to objects, such as a cost center or production order, which are not part of the MM function. A key lesson is to understand the requirements of such inventory movements. Chapter 23 on physical inventory reviewed integration with WM because counting material can also be performed in cycle counting, which is commonly used in WM.

Chapter 24, Invoice Verification, examined this functionality that has key integration with Financial Accounting (FI). The invoice that is received from a vendor is traditionally matched with the purchase order and the goods receipt note. Although the match is defined as part of MM, the AP component in FI is used to pay the vendor. One important takeaway from this chapter is to understand the other ways in which invoices are paid in SAP ERP, especially the Evaluated Receipt Settlement (ERS). As companies try to make small savings, the decision to implement ERS can reduce costs but requires additional configuration, and as a consultant, it is important for you to understand the principles behind the subject.

Chapters 25, Balance Sheet Valuation, and 26, Material Ledger, also reviewed subjects that are more familiar to financial consultants than to MM folks. Balance sheet valuation and material ledger are not traditional MM subjects but are part of the MM function and should be investigated to give you a more rounded education of the MM functionality as a whole.

Chapters 27, Classification System, and 28, Document Management, described functionality that is found in the SAP ERP central functions but is used in MM to a large extent. The classification system is used extensively in MM in such areas as purchasing release strategy, batch determination, and in the Material Master record. The Document Management System (DMS) allows the linking of documents to objects in SAP ERP, such as the Material Master. In many industries, it is important to have material drawings or CAD/CAM files available, and it is possible to link these with the material on the Material Master file.

29.2 Future Direction

Whether you are a consultant or a MM expert for your company, this book provides valuable information for use in your job function by examining the functionality of the MM software as it exists today in SAP ERP.

Although at this time we cannot predict what will be new or updated in ECC 7, we can consider some of the functionality that you can see today in the SAP Supply Chain Management suite (SAP SCM 7.0). The two key areas in SAP SCM that relate most closely to MM are the SAP Supply Network Collaboration (SAP SNC) and the SAP Forecasting and Replenishment function.

The SAP Supply Network Collaboration is an Internet-based software that allows vendors easy access to a customer's inventory and demand information. Master data on plants, vendors, Material Masters, or data records can be transferred from SAP ERP to SAP SCM. A key element of SAP SNC is supplier-managed inventory (SMI), which is a procurement process where the supplier assumes responsibility for replenishment planning.

The SAP Forecasting and Replenishment function includes functions that you will recognize from MM, such as Safety Stock Planning. One of the key elements of the SAP Forecast and Replenishment function is the Collaborative Planning, Forecasting, and Replenishment (CPFR). CPFR works by having cooperative management of inventory through visibility between vendor and supplier and replenishment of products throughout the supply chain. CPFR has been a concept since 1995, and SAP is one of the companies working to develop this concept along with IBM and Wal-Mart.

Although some of you may not have access to SAP SCM 7.0, you should educate yourself on some of the relevant functionality in the business suite, such as SAP SNC and SAP Forecasting and Replenishment. Read any white papers from SAP or view online demos to get a feel of the functions that are available.

In conclusion, use this book as a valuable guide to the Materials Management functionality in SAP ERP at work and throughout your career.

Appendices

A   Bibliography

Bruce R. Parker and J. Gregory Lahr. *Pharmaceutical Recalls: Strategies for Minimizing the Damage*, Drug Information Journal, April – June 1999.

Douglas M. Lambert. *Supply Chain Management: What Does It Involve?* Supply Chain & Logistics Journal, Fall 2001.

Ellen Fussell. *The Yoga of Batch.* Instrument Society of America, April 2003.

European Agency for the Evaluation of Medical Products (EMEA), Inspection Sector. *Mutual Recognition Agreement between Australia and the EU*, July 6, 2001.

European Committee on Banking Standards. *Annual Report of the ECBS, 2004.* April 2005.

Glenn Restivo. *Standard Goes Live for Life Sciences: A New Approach to Navigating Regulatory Requirements*, Instrument Society of America, November 2004.

James A. Brimson. *Activity Accounting: An Activity-Based Costing Approach*, John Wiley and Sons, February 1991.

Michael K. Evans. *Practical Business Forecasting*, Blackwell Publishers, March 2002.

Michael L. George. *Lean Six Sigma: Combining Six Sigma Quality with Lean Production Speed*, McGraw-Hill, First Edition, April 2002.

National Motor Freight Traffic Association. *Directory of Standard Carrier Alpha Codes*, February 2005.

Nicholas Sheble and D. A. Coggan. *A Batch of Rules and Regulations.* Instrument Society of America, December 2004.

Oracle Corporation, Cap Gemini Ernst & Young U.S. LLC and APICS. *The Adaptive Supply Chain: Postponement for Profitability.* APICS International Conference and Exposition, October 2003.

Pennsylvania Department of Environmental Protection. *The Beneficial Use of Municipal and Residual Waste*, 2005.

Stephen N. Chapman. *The Fundamentals of Production Planning and Control*, Prentice Hall, March 2005.

Virginia Polytechnic Institute and State University. *Program for Participation by Small Businesses and Businesses Owned by Women and Minorities.* September 2004.

Warren H. Hausman. *Financial Flows and Supply Chain Efficiency.* Visa Commercial Solutions, March 8, 2005.

B   Glossary

Account Assignment   When creating an SAP requisition, charging the goods and/or services to a specific cost object and general-ledger account on the Account Assignment screen.

Account Assignment Category
Determines which account assignment details are required for the purchase order item (e.g., cost center or account number).

Account Determination   A system function that determines automatically the accounts in Financial Accounting to which the amount(s) in question should be posted for the user during any posting transaction.

Alpha Factor   Smoothing function in forecasting.

ASAP   Standardized methodology for R/3 implementations.

Assembly   Products that are combined. An assembly can be used as a component in another assembly.

Authorization Check   Check performed to determine whether a user is authorized to execute a particular function.

Authorizations   Access to a transaction in the SAP system is based on a set of authorized values for each of the fields in the system. Users are given access to the appropriate fields, screens, and data using the authorization or security programs.

Automatic Reorder Point Planning
In consumption-based planning, if a material falls below its reorder point, a purchase requisition is created during the MRP run.

Availability Check   Check that is run as part of a goods movement to ensure the material stock balance does not go negative.

Backflushing   Automatic issue of materials after they have been used in a production order or physically moved.

Base Unit of Measure   The unit of measure for a material from which all other units of measure for the material are converted.

Batch   An amount of material that is unique and managed separately from others.

Batch Determination   Function that allows a program (e.g., a sales order) to select a batch based on selection criteria.

Bill of Materials (BOM)   List of all of the items, including quantity and unit of measure, that make up a finished product or assembly.

Blanket Order   Standing purchase order (contract) with fixed start and end dates for repetitive purchases from a single vendor. Requisitioners can purchase against the order until the amount of the blanket order is depleted or the blanket order expires.

Blocked Stock   Valuated stock of a material that cannot be used. In the availability check, blocked stock is "not available."

Change and Transport System (CTS)
A tool for managing and transporting configuration changes from the development and quality systems to the production system.

Change Management   The change involved in implementing an SAP system with new processes and procedures requires a level of change management to assist employees and management with the effects of change.

Characteristic   Description of a material that is defined by the user, such as color, viscosity, and so on.

Characteristic Value   The value that is assigned to a characteristic when it is used to describe a material, for example, for the characteristic Color, the value may be entered as Blue.

Chart of Accounts   Consists of a group of GL accounts. For each GL account, the chart of accounts contains the account number, name, and any technical information.

Class   Grouping of characteristics that in total describe an object.

Client   A self-contained unit in the SAP system with its own separate master records and set of tables.

Company Code   Used to represent an organizational unit with its own complete, self-contained set of cost objects for reporting purposes.

Condition   Used to calculate prices, discounts, taxes, and more, according to the selection of vendor, customer, material, and so on.

Configuration   The formal process of establishing the SAP settings to support a company's specific business rules, validations, and default values.

Consumption-Based Planning (CBP)
A generic term for the procedure in material requirements planning (MRP) for which stock requirements and past consumption values are critical.

Contract   Long-term outline purchase agreement against which materials or services are released according to user requirements over a specified period of time.

Cost Center   Organizational unit within a controlling area that represents a separate location of cost incurred. Cost centers can be set up based on functional requirements, allocation criteria, activities or services provided, location, or area of responsibility.

Customer   A business partner with whom a relationship exists that involves the issue of goods or services.

Customizing   The process of configuring the SAP system to meet the business needs of the company.

Cycle Counting   The physical inventory that is performed on materials several times during the year, unlike a yearly physical inventory.

Document   The electronic record of a transaction, entered in SAP. Examples include a material document or an accounting document.

Document Management System (DMS)
The system that captures and manages documents within an organization.

Dunning   Notifying vendors to ensure the resubmission of vendor declarations that are about to reach their expiration dates.

Electronic Data Interchange (EDI)
Electronic communication of business transactions, such as orders, confirmations, and invoices, between organizations.

Factory Calendar   Defined on the basis of a public holiday calendar. Shows the workdays for the client.

FIFO — First In, First Out   Materials and products are withdrawn from stock for sale or use in the order of their acquisition.

Financial Accounting (FI)   The SAP functionality that monitors real-time values from financially relevant transactions and maintains a consistent, reconciled, and auditable set of books for statutory reporting and management support.

Forecast   Estimation of the future values in a time series.

Gamma Factor   A smoothing factor for the seasonal index.

GL Account — General Ledger Account
A six-digit code that records value movements in a company code and represents the GL account items in a chart of accounts.

Goods Issue   A reduction in warehouse stock due to a withdrawal for consumption in-house or the delivery of goods to a customer.

Handling Unit (HU)   A physical item consisting of a material and packaging material. A handling unit has an identification number that can be used to recall the data on the HU.

IDoc (Intermediate Document)
Data container for data exchange between SAP systems or between an SAP system and an external system.

Implementation Guide (IMG)
Explains the steps in the implementation process. The structure of the IMG is based on the application-component hierarchy and lists all the documentation that is relevant to implementing the SAP system.

Inventory Adjustment   Correction to the material stock level due to physical inventory or goods movements.

Inventory Valuation   Process of calculating the value of the material in the plant.

Invoice   Bill sent to the client from a vendor for goods and/or services delivered.

Item Category   Indicator that identifies whether certain fields are allowed for a material.

KANBAN   A procedure for controlling production and material flow based on a chain of operations in production.

LIFO — Last In, First Out   Materials and products are withdrawn from stock for sale or use in the order of the most recent purchase.

Lot Size   A defined quantity to purchase or produce.

Manufacturer Part Number (MPN)
A material number that the vendor uses to identify a material.

Material Group   A group that classifies materials by commodity or service type and is used by the purchasing department for reporting purposes.

Material Requirements Planning (MRP)
A term for procedures in Production Planning that take into account and plan future requirement during the creation of order proposals.

Material Type   A grouping of materials with the same basic attributes such as raw materials, semi-finished products, or finished products.

Material Valuation   The determination of the value of the material in stock.

Movement Type   Indicates the type of goods movement. It enables the system to use predefined posting rules determining how the accounts are to be posted and how the material master record is to be updated.

MRP Controller   The person responsible for a group of materials in MRP at a plant.

MRP List   A document in SAP that shows an overview of the result of the MRP run.

MRP Type   A key that controls the MRP process for a material.

Navigation Path   Transactions are organized into folders in a directory structure in the navigation area. A navigation path is the series of folders you access to find and launch an SAP transaction.

Negative Inventory   A logical situation where the inventory is below zero due to a goods issue being performed before the goods receipt has been entered.

One-Step Stock Transfer   Issue of material in one step where the material is issued and received simultaneously.

One-Time Vendor   A term for a Vendor Master record used for processing transactions with vendors who are normally not used or have never been used.

Operation   A manufacturing activity step in a routing. Used in Production Planning.

Output Device   The name of the printer to which your SAP printouts will be sent, for example, LPT1 or US99. Many SAP printers are labeled with the output device name.

Park   Saving a document, such as invoice, so that changes can be made at a later time.

Physical Inventory   The recording of actual stock levels of materials by counting, weighing, or measuring at a given location at a specific time.

Pipeline Material   A material that flows directly into the production process such as electricity from power lines, water from a pipe, and so on.

Plant   An organizational unit within the company code where material is produced, purchased, and planned.

Procurement Card   An item issued by a company to employees who purchase material from selected vendors.

Purchase Order (PO)   Document generated by the purchasing department. A purchase order is an official order sent from the client to a vendor requesting goods and services.

Purchase Requisition   A request by a user or a process to the purchasing department to purchase certain material at a specific time.

Purchasing Group   A person or group of people in the purchasing department responsible for purchasing a type of good or service.

Purchasing Information Record
An information record that defines the specific details for a vendor/material combination.

Purchasing Organization   An organizational unit that procures materials or services and negotiates the conditions of purchase with vendors.

Putaway   Used in warehouse management to describe the physical movement of the material into the bin locations.

Quota Arrangement   A purchasing concept that allows the source of supply for a material to be determined via quotas decided upon with a number of vendors: Vendor A supplies 40%, vendor B supplies 35%, and Vendor C supplies 25%.

Quotation   A reply to a request for quotation from a vendor specifying its terms and conditions for the materials or servers required by the purchasing department.

Release   To approve a purchase requisition or a purchasing document.

Release Strategy   A set of business rules used to evaluate a purchase document or line item to determine the type of approvals needed before it can be released.

Request for Quotation (RFQ)
A request to a vendor or number of vendors for a quotation to supply materials or services.

Reservation   A request to the warehouse to ensure that certain materials are available on a certain date.

Routing   Defines one or more sequences of operations for the production of a material

Safety Stock   The level of material in stock below which a material shortage may occur.

Scheduling Agreement   A purchasing agreement with a vendor where the vendor supplies material to the customer at agreed upon days and times.

Serial Number   A unique number assigned to a single item. Each item will have a unique number. For example, each vacuum cleaner produced at a plant has its own serial number.

Subcontracting   A form of outsourcing, where an external vendor produces material for the customer.

Tolerance   The dollar amount or percentage by which a document may exceed specification. For example, a tolerance for a purchase order could be no more than 10% per line item and no more than $500 for the total of the purchase order.

Transaction Code   A unique command that is a shortcut to run an SAP transaction. A transaction code can contain letters or a combination of letters and numbers, for example, ME21 for creating a purchase order, or MMBE for stock overview report.

Transfer Order   A warehouse management term that describes the request to move material to or from a storage bin.

Transport Request   A method of organizing changes to an R/3 system. The transport request records changes made to the system and controls what is transported to other systems in the landscape, for example, development to quality then to production.

Two-Step Stock Transfer   A procedure whereby the stock is issued from one plant and then received at the receiving plant. This is the same for transfers between storage locations.

Unit of Measure   Defines the amount or size of the material or service such as bottle (BT), each (EA), hour (Hr), and so on.

Universal Product Code (UPC)
Standardized number used in the United States to uniquely identify a material. The EAN is used in Europe.

Valuation   The process of estimating the value of the company's stock.

Vendor   A business partner from whom materials and services are purchased.

Vendor Evaluation   The functionality that allows the vendors to be evaluated based on price, quality, service, and delivery reliability. The evaluation can determine how a material is sourced.

Warehouse   An organizational structure that resides within the Warehouse Management functionality. It can be linked to Materials Management via the storage location.

Work Center   A location used in Production Planning where a manufacturing operation is performed.

Workflow   A routing tool in SAP that forwards documents for review or approval. For instance, a requisition that needs to be approved is sent to the appropriate approver's inbox.

C   List of Materials Management Transaction Codes

ME01	Maintain Source List
ME03	Display Source List
ME04	Changes to Source List
ME05	Generate Source List
ME06	Analyze Source List
ME07	Reorganize Source List
ME08	Send Source List
ME0M	Source List for Material
ME11	Create Purchasing Information Record
ME12	Change Purchasing Information Record
ME13	Display Purchasing Information Record
ME14	Changes to Purchasing Information Record
ME15	Flag Purchasing Information Record for Deletion
ME16	Purchasing Information Records for Deletion
ME17	Archive Information Records
ME18	Send Purchasing Information Record
ME1A	Archived Purchasing Information Records
ME1B	Re-determine Information Record Price
ME1E	Quotation Price History
ME1L	Info Records per Vendor
ME1M	Info Records per Material
ME1P	Purchase Order Price History
ME1W	Info Records per Material Group
ME1X	Buyer's Negotiation Sheet for Vendor
ME1Y	Buyer's Negotiation Sheet for Material
ME21	Create Purchase Order (Traditional)
ME21N	Create Purchase Order

ME22	Change Purchase Order (Traditional)
ME22N	Change Purchase Order
ME23	Display Purchase Order (Traditional)
ME23N	Display Purchase Order
ME24	Maintain Purchase Order Supplement
ME25	Create Purchase Order with Source Determination
ME26	Display Purchase Order Supplement (IR)
ME27	Create Stock Transport Order
ME28	Release Purchase Order (Traditional)
ME29N	Release Purchase Order
ME2A	Monitor Confirmations
ME2B	POs by Requirement Tracking Number
ME2C	Purchase Orders by Material Group
ME2J	Purchase Orders for Project
ME2K	Purchase Orders by Account Assignment
ME2L	Purchase Orders by Vendor
ME2M	Purchase Orders by Material
ME2N	Purchase Orders by Purchase Order Number
ME2O	SC Stock Monitoring (Vendor)
ME2S	Services per Purchase Order
ME2V	Goods Receipt Forecast
ME2W	Purchase Orders for Supplying Plant
ME308	Send Contracts with Conditions
ME31	Create Outline Agreement
ME31K	Create Contract
ME31L	Create Scheduling Agreement
ME32	Change Outline Agreement
ME32K	Change Contract
ME32L	Change Scheduling Agreement
ME33	Display Outline Agreement
ME33K	Display Contract

ME33L	Display Scheduling Agreement
ME34	Maintain Outline Agreement Supplement
ME34K	Maintain Contract Supplement
ME34L	Maintain Scheduling Agreement Supplement
ME35	Release Outline Agreement
ME35K	Release Contract
ME35L	Release Scheduling Agreement
ME36	Display Outline Agreement Supplement
ME37	Create Scheduling Agreement
ME38	Maintain Scheduling Agreement Schedule
ME39	Display Scheduling Agreement Schedule
ME3A	Transmit Release Documentation Record
ME3B	Outline Agreements per Requirement Number
ME3C	Outline Agreements by Material Group
ME3J	Outline Agreements per Project
ME3K	Outline Agreements by Accounting Assignment
ME3L	Outline Agreements per Vendor
ME3M	Outline Agreements by Material
ME3N	Outline Agreements by Agreement Number
ME3P	Recalculate Contract Price
ME3R	Recalculate Scheduling Agreement Price
ME3S	Service List for Contract
ME41	Create Request for Quotation
ME42	Change Request for Quotation
ME43	Display Request for Quotation
ME44	Maintain RFQ Supplement
ME45	Release RFQ
ME47	Create Quotation
ME48	Display Quotation
ME49	Price Comparison List
ME4B	RFQs by Requirement Tracking Number

ME4C	RFQs by Material Group
ME4L	RFQs by Vendor
ME4M	RFQs by Material
ME4N	RFQs by RFQ Number
ME4S	RFQs by Collective Number
ME51	Create Purchase Requisition (Traditional)
ME51N	Create Purchase Requisition
ME52	Change Purchase Requisition (Traditional)
ME52N	Change Purchase Requisition
ME52NB	Buyer Approval: Purchase Requisition
ME53	Display Purchase Requisition (Traditional)
ME53N	Display Purchase Requisition
ME54	Release Purchase Requisition (Traditional)
ME54N	Release Purchase Requisition
ME55	Collective Release of Purchase Requisitions
ME56	Assign Source to Purchase Requisition
ME57	Assign and Process Requisitions
ME58	Ordering: Assigned Requisitions
ME59	Automatic Generation of Purchase Orders (Traditional)
ME59N	Automatic Generation of Purchase Orders
ME5A	Purchase Requisitions: List Display
ME5F	Release Reminder: Purchase Requisition
ME5J	Purchase Requisitions for Project
ME5K	Requisitions by Account Assignment
ME5R	Archived Purchase Requisitions
ME5W	Resubmission of Purchase Requisitions
ME61	Maintain Vendor Evaluation
ME62	Display Vendor Evaluation
ME63	Evaluation of Automatic Sub-Criteria
ME64	Evaluation Comparison
ME65	Ranking List of Vendors

ME6A	Display Changes to Vendor Evaluation
ME6B	Ranking List of Vendor Evaluations Based on Material
ME6C	Vendors Without Evaluation
ME6D	Vendors Not Evaluated Since
ME6E	Evaluation Records Without Weighting Key
ME6F	Print Vendor Evaluation Sheet
ME6G	Vendor Evaluation in the Background
ME6H	Vendor Evaluation Analysis: Selection
ME80	Purchasing Documents (General Analysis)
ME80A	Purchasing Reporting: RFQs
ME80AN	General Evaluations (RFQs)
ME80F	Purchasing Reporting: Purchase Orders
ME80FN	General Evaluations (Purchase Orders)
ME80R	Purchasing Reporting: Outline Agreements
ME80RN	General Evaluations (Outline Agreements)
ME81	Analysis of Order Values
ME81N	Analysis of Order Values
ME82	Archived Purchasing Documents
ME84	Generation of Scheduling Agreement Releases
ME84A	Individual Display of Scheduling Agreement Release
ME85	Renumber Scheduling Agreement Schedule Lines
ME86	Aggregate Schedule Lines
ME87	Aggregate Purchase Order History
ME88	Set Agreement Cumulative Quantity/Reconciliation Date
ME91	Purchase Orders: Reminders/Expediters
ME91A	Purchase Orders: Reminders/Expediters
ME91E	Purchase Orders: Reminders/Expediters
ME91F	Purchase Orders: Reminders/Expediters
ME92	Monitor Order Acknowledgment
ME92F	Monitor Order Acknowledgment
ME92K	Monitor Order Acknowledgment

ME92L	Monitor Order Acknowledgment
ME97	Archive Purchase Requisitions
ME98	Archive Purchasing Documents
ME99	Messages from Purchase Orders
ME9A	Message Output: RFQs
ME9E	Message Output: Scheduling Agreement Schedules
ME9F	Message Output: Purchase Orders
ME9K	Message Output: Contracts
ME9L	Message Output: Scheduling Agreements
MEAN	Address Maintenance
MEB0	Cancel Settlement Runs
MEB1	Create Rebate Arrangements (Subsequent Settlement)
MEB2	Change Rebate Arrangements (Subsequent Settlement)
MEB3	Display Rebate Arrangements (Subsequent Settlement)
MEB4	Settlement: Vendor Rebate Arrangements, Purchasing
MEB5	Listing of Vendor Rebate Arrangements, Purchasing
MEB6	Listing of Vendor Business Volume Data, Rebate Arrangements
MEB7	Extension of Vendor Rebate Arrangements: Purchasing
MEB8	Detailed Statement: Vendor Business Volumes, Rebate Agreements
MEB9	Statement: Statistical Data, Vendor Rebate Arrangements
MEDL	Price Change Involving Vendor's Contracts
MEI1	Changes to Purchasing Documents Due to Changes in Conditions
MEI2	Mass Adjustment of Documents Due to Changes in Documents
MEI3	Recompilation of Document Index
MEI4	Automatic Document Adjustment: Create Worklist
MEI5	Automatic Document Adjustment: Delete Worklist
MEI6	Delete Purchasing Document Index
MEI7	Make Price Change in Open Purchase Orders
MEI8	Recompilation of Document Index for Payment Documents
MEI9	Recompilation of Document Index for Vendor Billing Documents
MEK1	Create Conditions (Purchasing)

MEK2	Change Conditions (Purchasing)
MEK3	Display Conditions (Purchasing)
MEK31	Condition Maintenance: Change
MEK32	Condition Maintenance: Change
MEK33	Condition Maintenance: Change
MEK4	Create Conditions with Reference
MEKA	Conditions: General Overview
MEKB	Conditions by Contract
MEKC	Conditions by Info Record
MEKD	Conditions for Material Group
MEKE	Conditions for Vendor
MEKF	Conditions for Material Type
MEKG	Conditions for Condition Group
MEKH	Market Price
MEKI	Conditions for Incoterms
MEKJ	Conditions for Invoicing Party
MEKK	Conditions for Vendor Sub-Range
MEKL	Price Change Involving Vendor's Scheduling Agreements
MEKLE	Currency Change for Scheduling Agreement Conditions of Vendor
MEKP	Price Change Involving Vendor's Info Records
MEKPE	Currency Change for Info Record Conditions of Vendor
MEKR	Price Change Involving Vendor's Contracts
MEKRE	Currency Change for Contract Conditions of Vendor
MELB	Purchasing Transactions per Requirement Tracking Number
MEPA	Order Price Simulation/Price Information
MEPB	Price Information/Vendor Negotiation Sheet
MEPO	Display Purchase Order
MEQ1	Maintain Quota Arrangement
MEQ3	Display Quota Arrangement
MEQ4	Changes to Quota Arrangement
MEQ6	Analyze Quota Arrangement

MEQ7	Reorganize Quota Arrangement
MEQ8	Monitor Quota Arrangements
MEQB	Revise Quota Arrangement
MEQM	Quota Arrangement for Material
MEU2	Perform Comparison of Business Volumes
MEU3	Display Business Volume Comp.: Rebate
MEU4	Display Business Volume Comp.: Rebate
MEU5	Display Business Volume Comp.: Rebate
MEW1	Create Requirement Request
MEW2	Status Display: Requirement Requests
MEW3	Collective Release of Purchase Requisitions
MEW5	Collective Release of Purchase Order
MEW6	Assign Purchase Orders WEB
MEW7	Release of Service Entry Sheets
MEW8	Release of Service Entry Sheet

D   The Author

A native of London, England, **Martin Murray** joined the computer industry upon his graduation from Middlesex University in 1986. In 1991, he began working with SAP R/2 in the Materials Management area for a London-based multinational beverage company, and, in 1994, he moved to the United States to work as an SAP R/3 consultant. Since then, he has been implementing the Materials Management (MM) and Warehouse Management (WM) functionality in projects throughout the world. He is employed by IBM Global Business Services.

Martin is the author of the best-selling first and second editions of this book, as well as *SAP Warehouse Management, Discover Logistics with SAP ERP, Maximize Your Warehouse Operations with SAP ERP,* and *Understanding the SAP Logistics Information System.* He lives with his wife in Orange County, California.

Acknowledgments

The author would like to specially thank Meg Dunkerley of SAP PRESS for her faith in the author and her tireless efforts in getting this book completed.

Index

Q

U

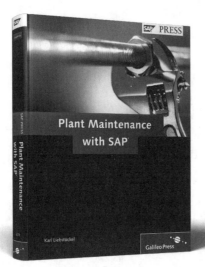

Master real-life business processes and the structuring of plant maintenance technical systems

Discover tips and tricks for implementing daily operations

Explore interfaces, reporting, and technologies – MAM, RFID, SOA, NetWeaver Portal, and much more

Karl Liebstückel

Plant Maintenance with SAP

This is a must-have guide for anyone interested in learning about the implementation and customization of SAP EAM. Consultants, managers, and administrators will learn learn the basics of the plant maintenance process, how to evaluate which processes work best for them, and the actual configuration steps of these processes using SAP EAM. This new edition includes practical tips and best practices for implementation projects, including extended coverage on pool asset management, subcontracting, and SAP Easy Document Management.

approx. 600 pp., 2. edition, 69,95 Euro / US$ 69.95
ISBN 978-1-59229-372-8, Dec 2010

>> www.sap-press.com

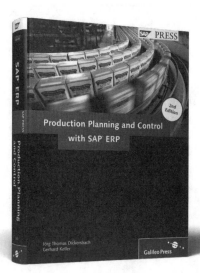

Provides an up-to-date, comprehensive guide to discrete manufacturing with Production Planning in SAP

Explains the business processes and customization steps for customizing SAP ERP

Includes a new chapter on special forms of procurement

Jörg Thomas Dickersbach, Gerhard Keller

Production Planning and Control with SAP ERP

This new, extended edition provides readers with a detailed introduction to the tasks associated with industrial operations and detailed descriptions of the core processes of Production Planning in SAP ERP. With step-by-step instruction and detailed, expert guidance, this book enables you to successfully implement and apply Production Planning in SAP ERP in your own company. This book also includes valuable information on exploring the potential of SAP SCM integration, and includes a new chapter on special forms of procurement.

approx. 515 pp., 2. edition, 69,95 Euro / US$ 69.95
ISBN 978-1-59229-360-5, Nov 2010

>> www.sap-press.com

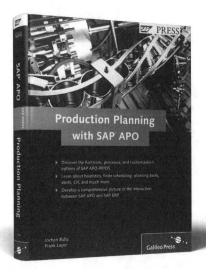

Provides a comprehensive and practical look at the functions, applications, and customization of Production Planning and Detailed Scheduling in SAP APO

Includes complete coverage on the APO Core Interface

Covers materials requirements planning with SAP ERP-MRP

Jochen Balla, Frank Layer

Production Planning with SAP APO

Whether you are a consultant, managers, or a key user, this book will provide you with the information you need to learn how to implement, customize, and use SAP APO-PP/DS. You will be able to familiarize yourself with the complex world of Production Planning/Detailed Scheduling, and use this comprehensive reference for implementing and customizing PP/DS. It's the one-stop resource you need to learn what PP/DS is, how you can use it with your company's needs in mind.

402 pp., 2. edition 2010, 69,95 Euro / US$ 69.95
ISBN 978-1-59229-354-4

>> www.sap-press.com

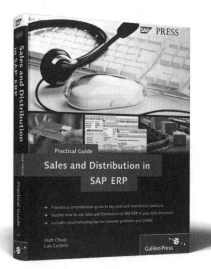

Provides a comprehensive guide to key sales and distribution functions

Teaches how to use Sales and Distribution in SAP ERP in daily processes, including sales, pricing, delivery, transportation, and billing

Includes support and troubleshooting information for common problems and pitfalls

Matt Chudy, Luis Castedo

Sales and Distribution in SAP ERP - Practical Guide

If you use SAP ERP for sales and distribution, this book is a must-have resource that uses a process-driven approach to teach you how to use key sales and distribution functions effectively in your day-to-day processes. You'll learn how to perform transactions with fewer steps and less effort, and you'll discover how to troubleshoot minor problems and system issues. In addition to the core areas of sales and distribution, you'll also find coverage of more advanced topics such as billing and reporting. And there are several appendices dedicated to quick-reference materials, such as lists of transaction codes and menu paths.If you work with sales and distribution on a daily basis, this guide can help you master the system and work more efficiently.

406 pp., 2010, 69,95 Euro / US$ 69.95
ISBN 978-1-59229-347-6

>> www.sap-press.com

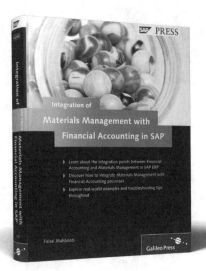

Gives a detailed overview of the finance integration points in materials management

Teaches how to integrate MM with the Financial Accounting and Controlling components of SAP ERP Financials

Provides best practices and real-world examples of various logistics business transactions

Faisal Mahboob

Integration of Materials Management with Financial Accounting in SAP

If you work with Materials Management and SAP ERP Financials, this book teaches you about the intersection points between them. It explains how to configure the system effectively to streamline your business processes and continually improve your procurement processes. You'll learn about account and controlling postings, and their impact on MM functional design and configuration. With the practical examples, troubleshooting techniques, and step-by-step instructions, this is the must-have guide you need to master MM and FI integration.

429 pp., 2010, 79,95 Euro / US$ 79.95
ISBN 978-1-59229-337-7

>> www.sap-press.com